CITY WOMEN

City Women

Money, Sex, and the Social Order in Early Modern London

ELEANOR HUBBARD

OXFORD
UNIVERSITY PRESS

Great Clarendon Street, Oxford OX2 6DP

Oxford University Press is a department of the University of Oxford.
It furthers the University's objective of excellence in research, scholarship,
and education by publishing worldwide in

Oxford New York

Auckland Cape Town Dar es Salaam Hong Kong Karachi
Kuala Lumpur Madrid Melbourne Mexico City Nairobi
New Delhi Shanghai Taipei Toronto

With offices in

Argentina Austria Brazil Chile Czech Republic France Greece
Guatemala Hungary Italy Japan Poland Portugal Singapore
South Korea Switzerland Thailand Turkey Ukraine Vietnam

Oxford is a registered trade mark of Oxford University Press
in the UK and in certain other countries

Published in the United States
by Oxford University Press Inc., New York

© Eleanor Hubbard 2012

The moral rights of the author have been asserted
Database right Oxford University Press (maker)

First published 2012

All rights reserved. No part of this publication may be reproduced,
stored in a retrieval system, or transmitted, in any form or by any means,
without the prior permission in writing of Oxford University Press,
or as expressly permitted by law, or under terms agreed with the appropriate
reprographics rights organization. Enquiries concerning reproduction
outside the scope of the above should be sent to the Rights Department,
Oxford University Press, at the address above

You must not circulate this book in any other binding or cover
and you must impose the same condition on any acquirer

British Library Cataloguing in Publication Data
Data available

Library of Congress Cataloging in Publication Data
Library of Congress Control Number: 2012930314

Typeset by SPI Publisher Services, Pondicherry, India
Printed in Great Britain
on acid-free paper by
MPG Books Group, Bodmin and King's Lynn

ISBN 978–0–19–960934–5

1 3 5 7 9 10 8 6 4 2

For Leo

Contents

Acknowledgments viii
List of Figures ix
List of Tables x
List of Abbreviations xi
Note to the Reader xii

Introduction 1

1. In Search of Preferment 16
2. Making a Match 48
3. Maidservants Adrift 79
4. Household Mistresses 111
5. Public Lives 148
6. Her Honest Labor 189
7. Dealing with Death 235

Conclusion 273

Bibliography 277
Index 289

Acknowledgments

In researching and writing this book I have incurred many debts. I am very grateful for the advice, comments, and criticism of Mark Kishlansky, who supervised the project from its beginning as my doctoral dissertation, giving me the benefits of his keen eye and insight. Indeed, without his ingenious help and that of Ann Hughes, I would never have been able to live in London for more than six months, much less conduct research there for nearly two years. I am also particularly indebted to David Armitage, Laurel Ulrich, Noah McCormack, and Theodore Rabb among others for their thoughtful comments on different drafts.

Staff members at the London Metropolitan Archives, the Guildhall Manuscript Library, and the Harvard and Princeton libraries all provided me with cheerful and efficient help in locating and gaining access to materials. In graduate school, my research was funded by the Clive Fellowship, the John Thornton Kirkland Fellowship, the Frank Knox Memorial Traveling Fellowship, and the Jens Aubry Westengard Scholarship, while a Mellon/ACLS Dissertation Completion Fellowship enabled me to spend a final year writing. I would also like to thank my colleagues in the history department at Princeton University for providing me with time, helpful criticism, and a congenial setting in which to complete my work. At Oxford University Press, Christopher Wheeler, Stephanie Ireland, Emma Barber, and others have patiently and efficiently supervised its publication.

I must also thank my family, especially my grandmother, Vee Burke, and my mother, Barbara Burke, for their comments and editorial assistance. Most of all, I am indebted to my husband, Leo Nguyen, for his unfailing support. Over the last few years he traveled to Cambridge innumerable times, moved to London for the two years I spent in the archives there, listened patiently to my daily discoveries and dilemmas, taught me how to deal with quantitative data, and read hundreds of pages of drafts. Without his aid and encouragement, this would all have been much more difficult, and infinitely less fun.

List of Figures

0.1	Age and marital status of female witnesses	13
1.1	Age at arrival in London	21
1.2	London and the surrounding areas *c.*1600	31
2.1	Percentage of maiden witnesses by age	54
2.2	Age differences between spouses for migrant and native wives under 36	62
7.1	The percentage of widows in the ever-married population	239
7.2	Spousal age differences for younger and older wives	249

List of Tables

1.1	Origins of London immigrant women in comparative context	18
1.2	Origins of migrant Englishwomen relative to population distribution in England	19
1.3	London women's origins over time	20
1.4	Region of residence according to migration and marital status	26
1.5	Migrant women: residence and marital status	27
1.6	Duration of services	30
2.1	Age and marital status	53
2.2	Age at marriage for migrant and London-born women	56
2.3	Husbands' status for migrant and London-born women	57
2.4	Maidservants' self-reported worth	59
6.1	Wives' and widows' work, 1570–1640	196
7.1	Rates of widowhood by age	238
7.2	Estimated percentages of wives previously widowed, by age	240
7.3	Remarrying widows' preference for bachelor bridegrooms	248

List of Abbreviations

BRHA   Bethlem Royal Hospital Archive
GL   Guildhall Library Manuscripts Section
LMA   London Metropolitan Archives
sl.   slide (used to identify microfilm slides for long unpaginated volumes)

Note to the Reader

All dates have been given old style, with the year understood to begin on January first. For the sake of readability, I have consistently modernized spelling, added punctuation, and expanded abbreviations in quotations from early modern texts. The clerks who took down depositions tended to use extremely variable spellings, but these provide little insight into the words of the witnesses who were speaking, and the cost in terms of clarity of retaining the original forms would have been considerable. Quotations from printed texts have also been modernized for the sake of consistency. I have also standardized names, and use English rather than Latin spellings: Hellen appears as Helen, Johanna as Joan, and Margret as Margaret, for example. The common early modern English terms 'maid' and 'maiden' are used to refer to never-married girls and young women in preference to the legalistic and almost equally archaic term 'spinster' and the awkward alternative of 'life-cycle single woman.' Where manuscript or printed volumes of parish registers are not given for the dates of baptisms, marriages, and deaths, I have relied on FamilySearch.

Introduction

The narrow streets and lanes of early modern London were filled with women's voices. Chatting, quarreling, and advertising their wares, London women notoriously took every opportunity to defy conventions of feminine silence, adding their irrepressible noise to the raucous clatter of urban life. In the historical record, however, this cacophony of female voices is largely silenced. Instead, the weighty deliberations of aldermen, the wit and pathos of poets, the rhetorical flourishes of Members of Parliament, and the interminable sermons of popular preachers dominate what remains of early modern London speech. When women's writing and speech survive, those in question were often exceptional, members of the gentry or radical religious sects. Ordinary women and their ordinary lives have largely faded away.

In recent years, historians of early modern England have striven to recapture the experiences and voices of ordinary women. In the absence of diaries and letters, they have concentrated on women's encounters—voluntary or not—with the structures of discipline and administration that preserved glimpses of the people whose lives they ordered. Reading carefully and often against the grain, these scholars have explored courtship, sex and marriage, work, neighborhood life, crime, reputation, and more.[1] The results have been enlightening. It is becoming increasingly clear that histories of gender that distinguish baldly between male privilege and female disability fail to capture the subtleties of early modern English social interaction. Some women exercised authority that was denied many men,

---

[1] See e.g. Martin Ingram, *Church Courts, Sex and Marriage in England, 1570–1640* (Cambridge, 1987); Susan Dwyer Amussen, *An Ordered Society: Gender and Class in Early Modern England* (New York, 1988); Peter Earle, 'The Female Labour Market in London in the Late Seventeenth and Early Eighteenth Centuries', *Economic History Review* 42.3 (1989), 328–53; Amy Louise Erickson, *Women and Property in Early Modern England* (New York, 1993); Jenny Kermode and Garthine Walker (eds), *Women, Crime and the Courts in Early Modern England* (London, 1994); Laura Gowing, *Domestic Dangers: Women, Words and Sex in Early Modern London* (Oxford, 1996); Tim Hitchcock, 'Unlawfully Begotten on Her Body': Illegitimacy and the Parish Poor in St Luke's Chelsea', in Tim Hitchcock, Peter King, and Pamela Sharpe (eds), *Chronicling Poverty: The Voices and Strategies of the London Poor, 1640–1840* (New York, 1997); Tim Stretton, *Women Waging Law in Elizabethan England* (Cambridge, 1998); Diana O'Hara, *Courtship and Constraint: Rethinking the Making of Marriage in Tudor England* (Manchester, 2000); Tim Meldrum, *Domestic Service and Gender 1660–1750: Life and Work in the London Household* (New York, 2000); Bernard Capp, *When Gossips Meet: Women, the Family and Neighbourhood in Early Modern England* (Oxford, 2003); Laura Gowing, *Common Bodies: Women, Touch and Power in Seventeenth-Century England* (New Haven, Conn., 2003); Garthine Walker, *Crime, Gender and Social Order in Early Modern England* (Cambridge, 2003); Amanda Flather, *Gender and Space in Early Modern England* (Rochester, NY, 2007).

and if men were constrained as well as empowered by the dictates of patriarchy, so women led lives that were not solely defined by gender.[2] This book takes these conclusions as a starting point: rather than identifying women as victims, rebels, or collaborators in a patriarchal social order, it investigates what they themselves saw as their struggles, aspirations, and preoccupations. Its focus is the burgeoning capital city between 1570 and 1640, a period of tremendous change. London women were, by and large, not natives of the capital but migrants drawn by the promise of employment and opportunity. Some climbed the social ladder while others struggled to keep afloat, but all pursued visions of success, whether as grand as a rich marriage or as humble as a sober spouse, a new petticoat, or food for their children. This study explores what London women hoped to achieve, how they went about turning their ambitions into reality, where and why they were free to act, and where and why they were constrained. The picture that emerges is a complicated one. The limits and extents of London women's agency were determined in many ways by gender, but charting those margins is not a matter of gender alone. Although notions of sexual order played an important role in delimiting the sphere of female agency, concerns about economic order often conflicted with sexual anxieties. An examination of those sites of conflict makes it clear that both magistrates and communities were inclined to privilege worries about money over those about sex, creating unexpected opportunities for women. For their part, London women were quick to take advantage of these openings.

To address the lifelong careers of urban women, this study presents a composite biography, following the stages of London women's lives from adolescence to old age. This structure brings out women's lifelong strategies for self-preservation and advancement rather than typecasting them as subordinate daughters, servants, or wives. London women moved rapidly from family to family: as maidservants they frequently changed services, and as adults they were likely to be widowed and to remarry, sometimes several times. Although they always belonged to some household or other—even if it were simply the tiny household of a solitary widow—their long-term strategies were necessarily those of individuals. Their preferment depended on making the right choices when they moved from one role to another.

For women—even more than for men—marriage strategies were an essential component of personal advancement, and these receive particular attention. As one

---

[2] See Martin Ingram, '"Scolding Women Cucked or Washed": A Crisis in Gender Relations in Early Modern England?' in Kermode and Walker (eds), *Women, Crime and the Courts in Early Modern England*; Garthine Walker, 'Expanding the Boundaries of Female Honour in Early Modern England', *Transactions of the Royal Historical Society*, 6th series, 6 (1996), 235–45; Bernard Capp, 'Separate Domains? Women and Authority in Early Modern England', in Paul Griffiths, Adam Fox, and Steve Hindle (eds), *The Experience of Authority in Early Modern England* (New York, 1996); Bernard Capp, 'The Double Standard Revisited: Plebeian Women and Male Sexual Reputation in Early Modern England', *Past and Present* 162 (1999), 70–100; Martin Ingram, 'Law, Litigants and the Construction of "Honour": Slander Suits in Early Modern England', in Peter Coss (ed.), *The Moral World of the Law* (Cambridge, 2000); Alexandra Shepard, *Meanings of Manhood in Early Modern England* (Oxford, 2003) and 'Honesty, Worth and Gender in Early Modern England, 1560–1640', in H. R. French and Jonathan Barry (eds), *Identity and Agency in England, 1500–1800* (New York, 2004).

might expect, women's marriage strategies and opportunities in London—a large city with high mortality rates, populated predominantly by immigrants—were different from those found in the rural parishes that have often formed the basis of studies of courtship and marriage formation.[3] The unusually high proportion of men in London's population and the relatively advantageous legal treatment of widows' inheritance there provided opportunities for ambitious women across the life cycle. Poor maidservants from the countryside routinely married, and the remarriage of widows was both common and rapid. Migrating to London, as a large majority of city women had done in their youth, was a risky but potentially rewarding strategy.

In addition to pursuing their preferment in marriage, London women sought to protect and promote their own and their families' material welfare and social status. To do so, however, they had to negotiate ambiguities in their own dual roles as wives and household mistresses. Husbands and wives were usually allies, keeping servants and children in awe, combining their efforts to make a living, and supporting one another in neighborhood disputes. However, disagreement over how best to spend household money was a common source of conflict. Wives were enjoined to avoid extravagance and to save household wealth: they were endowed with responsibility but not with power. This task was difficult for women whose husbands' expenditures in alehouses and taverns threatened their family economies. When their complaints are taken seriously, it becomes clear that most 'shrewish' wives in popular literature were not, in fact, rebels against male authority but the embattled defenders of household budgets. Conversely, a common male complaint was that London wives, burning with desire to exceed their neighbors in dress and domestic display, drove their unhappy spouses to the brink of bankruptcy. Both husbands and wives, it seems, found it easy to privilege frugality over each other's same-sex sociability, but found it more difficult to resist the temptations of social competition on their own behalf. Whereas husbands were legally able to enforce their will, however, the wives of improvident and destructive men were forced to rely on dissimulation, their own strength of character, and neighborly interventions.

Like men, women strove to lift themselves up, away from the fears and miseries of poverty and towards the warmth of their neighbors' admiration and esteem. However, being excluded from full participation in most formal institutions, women pursued advancement through different means than men. The livery companies, with their formal regulations, often structured the male life cycle: many young men migrated to London to enter apprenticeships, earned their citizenship, and took part in the government of the City, serving, if they were prosperous, as churchwardens and aldermen. In comparison, young women who migrated to London sought informal employment as maidservants. They achieved adult status by marrying, not by becoming citizens. London women lived their social lives overwhelmingly in the geographical constraints of the neighborhood

---

[3] See e.g. Diana O'Hara's close study of five parishes in Kent, *Courtship and Constraint*.

rather than the occupational communities of the livery companies. In their own streets and lanes, they paid their respects to the 'better sort' of local matrons, and combined to cast judgment on suspicious interlopers. They joined together to support women in childbed as well as to shame those men and women whose actions threatened to cast themselves or their families on the parish poor rates. Toiling in the largely unregulated and over-crowded labor sector that existed beyond the protected confines of the guilds, even poor women claimed credit for helping to maintain their families. Within the limits imposed by their gender and their station, women did what they could to enhance their status.

Women were constrained by legal and cultural understandings of their roles, but these constraints were by no means uniformly imposed. The powerful sexual double standard that has been explored by historians of gender often came into conflict with the demands of economic order.[4] While it is true that scolds, whores, and witches—traditional incarnations of disorderly femininity—haunted the imaginations of anxious men, they were far from being the only bugbears of the early modern English psyche. Just as threatening were the miscreants whose actions threatened to throw the fragile edifice of neighborhood and household stability into disarray. Vagrants, thieves, and sturdy beggars were obvious threats, but some of the worst damage could be done from within, by men who fathered bastards, drunks who consumed their families' goods in alehouses and brothels, and raging husbands who cast their wives out on the streets. While adulterous women struck a largely symbolic blow against the patriarchal social order, men who failed to fulfill their responsibilities did material damage to local economies. If they did not support their wives and children, charity and parish rates would be called upon to make up the difference, or desperate women and children might slip into prostitution, beggary, or crime.

These two sets of anxieties—sexual and economic—did not necessarily run hand in hand, and individuals and governors were often forced to choose between competing priorities. These tense moments provide a valuable point of entry for understanding the driving forces of early modern English society. The way men and women spoke and wrote about the sexual and economic fears that troubled them enables us to elucidate those anxieties and enriches our understanding of their mental worlds. However, to gain a more precise idea of the relative importance of these different concerns and to determine their impact on the lives of early modern men and women, it is necessary to go beyond discourse and to examine material outcomes. How did communities deal with illegitimate children and their mothers? Was it easier for men to defy their elders in courtship than for women? How did neighbors react when husbands accused their wives of adultery, and strove to cast them out? Or when wives complained of brutality and neglect? When were women barred from working for wages and when were they applauded? What opportunities

---

[4] For male anxieties about controlling female sexuality, see Elizabeth Foyster, *Manhood in Early Modern England: Honour, Sex and Marriage* (New York, 1999) and Anthony Fletcher, *Gender, Sex and Subordination in England 1500–1800* (New Haven, Conn., 1995), 51, 71–3. Gowing shows that popular gender ideologies were similarly stark: *Domestic Dangers*, 275–6.

were open to widows and what uses did they make of them? An investigation into these and other questions suggests that when economic concerns conflicted with rigid notions of gender, women were quick to exploit the resulting moments of opportunity—but that they had little recourse when material anxieties reinforced a strict sexual order.

By exploring the importance that ordinary London men and women attributed to social order, this study provides a new perspective on the stability of early modern England in general, and of London in particular. Historians have long been struck by the relatively calm and cohesive nature of the English capital, even in the terrible decade of the 1590s, when harvest failure and plague joined long-term inflation to afflict the common people. Apprentices' riots in June of 1595 seriously worried City authorities, who responded with harsh measures, but the urban disorders notably failed to spiral into broader unrest. To explain this, historians have debated the extent of social strain in London as well as the ways in which authorities kept the city quiet.[5]

This study investigates the problem from the perspective of a population that has largely eluded prior research. Ordinary Londoners were not simply a voracious mass, only kept in check by the harsh threats and calculated benevolence of magistrates. Rather, households and neighborhoods struggled to remain afloat, and they did so by promoting and upholding conservative hierarchies and values. Women went out nurse-keeping, washing, and scouring 'to get a penny', neighbors routinely arbitrated between quarrelsome residents, and respectable parishioners looked askance at men whose drinking and violent tempers threatened precarious household economies. Poor rates did much to establish a common interest in stability: those who paid them resented supporting paupers who, they felt, had fallen on the parish by reason of other men's irresponsibility, while those who received alms had a clear interest in sharing their meager allowances with as few poor residents as possible. One of the reasons London's rulers were able to govern the city so successfully was that much of the city's population was amenable to being governed; they too valued social and economic stability, and worked to uphold it.

SOURCES

The main archival sources for this study are the deposition books of the London consistory court between 1570, when record survival for the court became fairly reliable, and 1640, when the court ceased operations in the confusion of political breakdown. The consistory court was one of a set of ecclesiastical courts with

---

[5] See A. L. Beier, *Masterless Men: The Vagrancy Problem in England 1560–1640* (New York, 1985); Michael J. Power, 'A "Crisis" Reconsidered: Social and Demographic Dislocation in London in the 1590s', *London Journal* 12 (1986), 134–46; Steve Rappaport, *Worlds within Worlds: Structures of Life in Sixteenth-Century London* (Cambridge, 1989); Ian Archer, *The Pursuit of Stability: Social Relations in Elizabethan London* (Cambridge, 1991); Joseph P. Ward, *Metropolitan Communities: Trade Guilds, Identity, and Change in Early Modern London* (Stanford, Calif., 1997); Paul Griffiths, *Lost Londons: Change, Crime and Control in the Capital City 1550–1660* (Cambridge, 2008).

overlapping jurisdiction over a set of moral offenses.[6] Its records constitute a source of unparalleled richness for the study of early modern London women. Due to the jurisdiction of the consistory court, and the nature of the canon law that governed it, the court drew high numbers of ordinary women both as litigants and, even more importantly, as witnesses. Although this population was largely illiterate, depositions were recorded in writing, producing a trove of circumstantial information touching on many areas of women's lives.

The ecclesiastical courts were long dismissed as fossilized relics of pre-Reformation England, despised for their old-fashioned interests, cumbersome and inefficient process, and lack of means of enforcement. However, since Martin Ingram's ground-breaking work on the courts in Wiltshire, the value of ecclesiastical court records has been increasingly recognized, particularly with regard to women's history, as they provide a rare view into the lives of poor and middling women. Although the pre-1640 London records have been comparatively neglected,[7] English church court records have been used in studies of gender,[8] labor,[9] courtship and sexual mores,[10] honor and reputation,[11] and literacy.[12]

This study is based on a combination of quantitative and qualitative evidence drawn from the deposition books of the consistory court for the diocese of London. To focus on the urban capital, witnesses and cases from the rural parishes in the diocese of London have generally been excluded, while the built-up suburbs beyond the City's boundaries have been included. The geographical definition of London used here includes the parishes of St Leonard Shoreditch, Stepney, Whitechapel, St Katherine by the Tower, St James Clerkenwell, St Martin in the Fields, St Giles in the Fields, St Margaret Westminster, St Mary le Strand alias le Savoy, and St Clement Danes from Middlesex, and St Thomas, St Olave, St George, and St Saviour in Southwark.[13]

Each deposition follows a set pattern. The first section is an autobiographical summary, mostly in Latin, that includes the name and status of the deponent, as

---

[6] For the church courts' jurisdiction and procedures, see R. B. Outhwaite, *The Rise and Fall of the English Ecclesiastical Courts, 1500–1860* (Cambridge, 2006).

[7] Laura Gowing is the only historian to have made a systematic study of them. See *Domestic Dangers*; *Common Bodies*.

[8] See Flather, *Gender and Space*; Gowing, *Common Bodies*; *Domestic Dangers*.

[9] See Earle, 'The Female Labour Market' and *A City Full of People: Men and Women of London, 1650–1750* (London, 1994); Meldrum, *Domestic Service and Gender*.

[10] See O'Hara, *Courtship and Constraint*; P. Rushton, 'Property, Power and Family Networks: The Problem of Disputed Marriages in Early Modern England', *Journal of Family History* 11 (1986), 205–19; Ingram, *Church Courts, Sex and Marriage*; Shannon McSheffrey, *Marriage, Sex and Civic Culture in Late Medieval London* (Philadelphia, 2006).

[11] See Ingram, 'Law, Litigants and the Construction of "Honour"'; Shepard, 'Honesty, Worth and Gender' and 'Poverty, Labour and the Language of Social Description in Early Modern England', *Past and Present* 201 (2008), 51–95.

[12] David Cressy, *Literacy and the Social Order: Reading and Writing in Tudor and Stuart England* (Cambridge, 1980).

[13] While witnesses living in Southwark have been included, the area south of the Thames fell within the diocese of Winchester, so cases from there would ordinarily not have reached the London consistory court. So few witnesses were resident in other parts of urban Surrey (Bermondsey, St Mary Newington, Lambeth, and Rotherhithe) that these areas have been excluded.

well as a residence history and summary of age and origins. While independent men provided information only about themselves, servants and apprentices stated their employers' names and occupations, and wives provided the same for their husbands. Wives often stated how long they had been married in addition to how long they had resided in their current parish, while servants usually only said how long they had been in their current service. Taken together, this large body of demographic data constitutes a major source of quantitative data about migration, residence patterns, and marriage.[14]

Following the introduction is the main body of the deposition. Most of this section is in English, and it is much less formulaic. Often these two parts (including the deponent's mark or signature at the bottom) make up the whole of the deposition. Sometimes, however, there is also a cross-examination, or interrogatory, which could follow the deposition directly or appear scores of pages away. This was used to clarify important points or to cast doubt on the witness's credit. Witnesses who were cross-examined were often asked how much they were worth, or how they were maintained.

The subject and level of detail of an individual deposition depend largely on the nature of the specific case. Consistory court cases could be fought between individuals ('instance' cases), or they could be directed against a suspected person by the court itself ('office' or *ex officio* cases). In practice, the vast majority of the cases used in this study were instance cases: the court functioned more as a resource for the resolution of neighborhood and personal disputes than as an Anglican inquisition.[15] The types of cases over which the church courts held jurisdiction attracted high numbers of female litigants and witnesses. While the church courts also dealt with tithe disputes, clerical discipline, and testamentary cases, most depositions addressed defamation and matrimonial disputes.

By far the most important of these, in terms of the sheer quantity of cases, was defamation: injured men and women could sue their tormenters for accusing them of misbehavior subject to ecclesiastical jurisdiction, usually sexual immorality or (much less often) drunkenness. While defamatory language could be remarkably inventive, the most common kind of case in the consistory court was one in which a woman sued someone for calling her 'whore', 'queane', 'bawd', or some similar epithet.[16] In typical cases, the injured party presented witnesses who documented three things: that the offending words had been spoken, that they had been spoken

---

[14] While there are often long stretches of detailed depositions, it is not uncommon to find periods of months or years in which certain elements are omitted, most often the residence history and the length of marriage for married women. As a result, not all depositions are included in all analyses.

[15] Ralph Houlbrooke, *Church Courts and the People During the English Reformation* (Oxford, 1979), 263.

[16] Shepard notes that the narrow range of sexual issues that appear in ecclesiastical court records cannot be taken as a complete picture of what constituted female honor. Rather, it reflects the jurisdiction of the court: calling a woman a 'drunken whore' was actionable; calling her a 'murdering thief' was not. Shepard draws attention to the questions that witnesses were asked in cross-examinations as a means of gaining a fuller view of female reputation. There, to determine their social credit, women as well as men were questioned more about their economic status than about their behavior. Shepard, 'Honesty, Worth and Gender', 88–9, 91.

maliciously, and that the injured party had suffered a social blow as a result. It was not necessary to present evidence of specific social injury. At no point did the court generally address the truth of the defamatory words: defamed women went to court to prove that they had been called whores, not to prove that they were chaste. In fact, for the defendant, proving the veracity of the defamatory words was not a defense unless he or she could also show that the words had not been spoken maliciously. A private, well-intentioned rebuke was not defamation, but a public and vindictive one was, even if the allegations were perfectly true.

The great number of defamation cases probably has more to teach us about the intensity of social competition between London women than about the fragility of female reputation. Gowing's analysis of the theatrical nature of defamatory speech leads her to conclude that 'insult was often related only opaquely to real sexual events' and that 'slander was constructed not as a project of normative moral regeneration, but as one of creative malice'.[17] London neighborhoods were more fluid than those of rural villages: people moved frequently in or out of the city, and between parishes. Death rates were higher than in the countryside, and population losses were quickly replenished with the arrival of new immigrants from elsewhere in England and beyond. With new faces constantly appearing on the streets, local social hierarchies were in flux. Just as the opening days of school are characterized by uncertainty as new students attempt to find their places in the social order, so London women jostled for status. Loud insults were one kind of display of dominance, and going to court was a response that aggressively escalated the dispute; it demonstrated that the plaintiff had money to spend (always a crucial element of social status), as well as the support of her husband and neighbors.

The consistory court also played a role in affirming and dissolving marriages. In this period, the question of what constituted a binding marriage was far from settled, leaving ample room for confusion and disagreement. Ideally, marriages were performed in the church, before witnesses, after the publication of banns or the obtaining of a valid license. Most marriages were, in fact, performed this way. However, according to canon law, far less was necessary to make a marriage binding in the eyes of God. All that was needed to make a firm contract was for the couple to make a clear verbal commitment to marriage, for example by saying: 'I take thee to be my wedded wife' and 'I take thee to be my wedded husband.' If, as in the preceding example, they spoke in words of the present tense (*per verba de praesenti*), then they were married. If they spoke in words of the future tense (*per verba de futuro*), the contract became a binding marriage when it was consummated. If the contract was made in the future tense upon conditions (for example, 'if my friends consent' or 'if your portion is of twenty pounds'), then it became binding when the conditions were fulfilled. A binding contract could be broken if both parties agreed, but a binding marriage could not. The pre-existence of a binding contract invalidated any subsequent marriages to other parties.

---

[17] Gowing, *Domestic Dangers*, 124, 125.

In practice, it was not easy to prove the existence of a marriage contract if one party later denied it. Authorities fully recognized the danger of entrapment and the exploitation of young heirs and heiresses. If unwitnessed contracts were upheld, what was to prevent men and women from making spurious claims? In addition, when the courts enforced contracts that had taken place without parental consent, they seriously undermined parental authority. To prove a contract, the forsaken party needed to provide witnesses of sufficient credit and neutrality, and usually circumstantial evidence of courtship as well, such as the breaking of a gold coin (each partner kept half) or the gift of a ring.

Even with additional evidence, the court became less and less willing to affirm disputed contracts, and the number of courtship cases fell accordingly. While these had been fairly common in the fourteenth century, their number had already fallen substantially by the beginning of Elizabeth's reign, and was further reduced between 1570 and 1640, nearly disappearing by the end of the period.[18]

The court could not declare divorce in the modern sense, with the possibility of remarriage; rather, litigants sued for separation from bed and board, the right to live apart. However, the term 'divorce' was routinely used to refer to marital separation in early modern London, and there was some confusion over whether remarriage was possible or not.[19] According to canon law, the ecclesiastical courts could grant the aggrieved spouse separation on the grounds of cruelty or adultery on either side.[20] In practice, only women were likely to allege cruelty, and men were more likely to complain of adultery alone.[21] If the wife was the innocent party, her right to maintenance was not revoked by her husband's misbehavior and she could sue

---

[18] See Ingram, *Church Courts, Sex and Marriage*, 192; Gowing, *Domestic Dangers*, 33.

[19] For example, in 1574 a maidservant reported to the Bridewell governors that one John Barber propositioned her, saying 'that he should now be divorced from his wife and that if she would grant him to have the use of her body he would marry her.' BRHA, BCB 2, fo. 51v. One Robert Parker testified to the consistory court in 1572 that 'he hath been married to his wife that he now liveth withal by the space of seven years or thereabouts whose name is Joan who had been before married unto one Spence of Much Waltham in Essex, and saith that she was divorced from him for adultery committed by him the said Spence about a year before her marriage.' Robert Parker, 1572, LMA, DL/C/211/1, fo. 58v. The question of remarriage was not definitely resolved in law until the case of *Rye c. Fuljambe* in Star Chamber in 1602. See *The English Reports*, 91 vols. (Edinburgh, 1900–1932), vol. lxxii, 838; and Edmund Gibson, *Codex juris ecclesiastici Anglicani*, 2 vols. (London, 1713), vol. i, 536. When new canons were drawn up in 1603, it was felt necessary to specify that sentences of divorce should state the prohibition on remarriage and that they not be finalized until both parties gave securities to the court that they would not remarry. See Canon 97 in *Constitutions and canons ecclesiasticall* (London, 1604), sig. M3r.

[20] See Henry Consett, *The practice of the spiritual or ecclesiastical courts* (London, 1685), 256; and John Godolphin, *Repertorium canonicum, or, An abridgment of the ecclesiastical laws of this realm* (London, 1678), 61.

[21] There were exceptions. Roger Noble from Chipping Barnett tried to divorce his wife, Agnes, 'a very furious woman in her anger', around 1602 on the grounds of cruelty. She had already left him, and when some neighbors went 'to talk with her about her living from her husband and to persuade her to live with him as with her husband as she ought to do,' she apparently answered that 'if she should be constrained to live with him she would stab him with a knife.' Witnesses said Roger Noble 'dareth not well dwell and live with his said wife Agnes for fear of some desperate cruelty he thinketh she would do to him.' Hugh and Anne Pawling, *Roger Noble c. Agnes Noble*, 1602, LMA, DL/C/216, sl. 1098–101.

for alimony, although enforcing payment was by no means straightforward. However, if she was divorced for adultery, she was left without maintenance and forfeited her dower rights.[22] In practice, a minority of divorce cases sued by both men and women proceeded to sentence, although men's suits were more likely to reach a final conclusion. When a sentence was given, it was almost invariably in the plaintiff's favor.[23]

The sample of women who made use of the London consistory court as litigants and who appeared as witnesses is strikingly large. Laura Gowing has shown that female participation in the London consistory court was unequalled in England, and indeed increased remarkably over the period from 1572 to 1640, as defamation cases became more and more numerous. Excluding the rural parishes in the diocese of London heightens the heavily female nature of the court's business: 40.5 per cent of cases were fought entirely between women in urban London. In the mariners' neighborhoods of Stepney and Wapping, where men were often away at sea, fully half of all cases were fought between women. Overall, in cases originating in the City and the suburbs, including the eastern parishes along the Thames, nearly 66 per cent of all 2,765 litigants were female.[24] The high number of female litigants meant that very large numbers of women testified as witnesses for the court. Defamation cases involving women, like cases dealing with marriage, usually centered on incidents that had taken place in the presence of other women, and about which they could speak with knowledge and conviction. An incident of defamation would be noticed by everyone around: apprentices, servants, men and women in their shops, and old people sitting out in the sun might be called in to testify. In contrast, the cases in which only men usually testified, dealing with tithes, churchwardens' accounts, and inheritance disputes, drew from a more homogenous population of solid middle-aged citizens. About 2,500 women and as many men living in urban London testified for the consistory court between 1570 and 1640; their depositions form the foundation of this study.

Litigants and witnesses were usually members of London's craft and trade communities. People who came to the court as litigants in defamation cases were drawn primarily from the humbler middling ranks of society: they were not too dignified to wash their dirty laundry in public, but could afford at least to pay the fees to begin a case, if not necessarily to carry one through to final sentence. They might keep small establishments such as victualling houses, like Joan Harper, who sued a woman for calling her 'pocky-faced jade' in 1615. Mary Wharton, a butcher's wife, met and bargained with her husband's customers, sometimes

---

[22] See Erickson, *Women and Property in Early Modern England*, 112–13, 124–7.

[23] 42% of men's suits reached a sentence, compared to 26% of those sued by women. Gowing, *Domestic Dangers*, 181.

[24] Ibid. 37. This trend continued. By the mid-eighteenth century, 96% of cases involved at least one female litigant, and 61% were fought between women exclusively. See Tim Meldrum, 'A Women's Court in London: Defamation at the Bishop of London's Consistory Court, 1700–1745,' *The London Journal* 19.1 (1994), 1–20.

'men of mean condition', in alehouses and taverns, an activity that left her open to Elizabeth Barwicke's insinuating remarks.[25]

The litigants in marriage cases were richer than those in defamation cases, but still included men and women of humble station. Proving the existence of a marital contract or obtaining a marital separation was relatively expensive, requiring the attendance of many witnesses and the payment of many fees. Such high-stakes cases were often heatedly disputed; they could stretch on for months, and were more likely to be followed through to a full, expensive conclusion than defamation cases, which were often dropped or resolved out of court. Because contract and separation cases often hinged on disputes over portions or alimony, the sums of money at stake generally had to be greater than the court fees for prolonged litigation to be a reasonable option. However, poorer men and women did go to court when they thought they could prove the existence of a marriage contract with a richer party who had since forsaken them—and perhaps when they hoped for an advantageous settlement out of court. In separation cases, poor women were probably more likely to sue for separation from intolerable spouses than the reverse, as unhappily married men found it easier to abandon their unwanted wives. Since married women could not usually legally own property, a wife who fled an unbearable husband was always at risk of being stripped of her goods when he found her again; indeed, the failure of such informal separations was sometimes the catalyst for consistory court cases.

Witnesses could be of much lower status: their ranks included portionless maidservants and impoverished widows, elderly porters and pauper tailors.[26] The overwhelming majority of men asked whether or not they were assessed for the subsidy answered in the negative, and many witnesses described themselves humbly as being 'poor but honest', laying emphasis, for lack of a better option, on their self-reliance and honest labor. However, even the witness population excludes the very lowest level of society: even if beggars and vagrants could be located to testify on events that had taken place several months before, their words could hardly carry weight in a society in which social and financial credit were largely synonymous.[27] The records of Bridewell Hospital, where an active court of governors questioned and punished men, women, and children for vagrancy, prostitution, petty crime, and domestic disorders, have been used to compensate for this lack.

---

[25] John Swift, *Joan Harper c. Anne Coleman*, 1615 (LMA, DL/C/224, fo. 12r); and Anne Usher, *Mary Wharton c. Elizabeth Barwicke*, 1617 (LMA, DL/C/230, fo. 426r).

[26] See Table 2.3 in Ch. 2 for the occupations of female witnesses' husbands.

[27] There were some exceptions. For example, Joan Goddin, a widow who testified in 1633 was said to get her living 'by begging in the highway and in the streets' and at 'great men's houses' to supplement her parish pension of twelvepence a week. When she worked gathering peascods in Fulham, her employer suspected her of stealing a peascod sack, and found it 'under a bundle or wad of straw which she had made for her bed'. Agnes Harling, a poor candlemaker's wife, said that she and her husband had 'no other habitation than by sufferance of one Mr Hyde who being their friend hath permitted them for one quarter of a year last past to dwell in a part of the windmill in Shoe Lane'. When a controversy over the mill prevented them from sleeping there, they took refuge in the hayloft of another man's stable. See Joan Goddin, Edmund Lawrence, and William Weaver, 1633 (LMA, DL/C/630, fos. 125v, 208, 177); and Agnes Harling, 1588 (LMA, DL/C/213, p. 419).

While poverty and dependence did not necessarily disqualify witnesses, extreme youth was a bar. Although a smattering of girls and boys in their mid-teens testified for the court, none was younger than 13, and young witnesses were often questioned dubiously about their education and understanding of the gravity of testifying under oath. Neighbors also testified that children were malleable and unreliable. When questioned about Anne Colburne, a 16-year-old maidservant, a tailor reported that she had admitted to him that she had been promised a piece of lace in exchange for testimony. She and another young maid were 'very young girls and such as are not fitting to be received as witnesses . . . beggarly wenches of no worth', he said, and what was more, Anne had 'without her said master's or mistress's privity or consent . . . run away from them leaving them destitute without a servant'.[28] Thomasine Hall, also 16, was described as an unfit witness 'in respect of her young years and her childishness in behavior'. Her former mistress said she was 'a child in comparison of a woman', and recounted how, two years before, Thomasine had filched a sixpence left on the floor of a house of office by a stranger. When her mistress asked her about the sixpence, Thomasine 'stood very stiffly in denial thereof, saying that she had it not and with great protestations wished and desired that her eyes might be burned out of her head if she had the same sixpence', but later confessed that she had spent the money.[29]

Fig. 0.1 provides a visual summary of the demography of the women resident in London (including parts of Middlesex and Surrey) who deposed for the consistory court between 1570 and 1640, about 2,500 individuals. This population sample is the basis of all the statistical calculations made in this study. It is made up of many women from their late teens to old age and includes unmarried women, wives, and widows. The data is not flawless; as the spikes that occur at every decade in Fig. 0.1 indicate, older witnesses often rounded their ages to the nearest ten, and the ages of the very oldest witnesses are probably very approximate. However, there is little reason to believe that witnesses were intentionally untruthful in reporting their age and marital status, since these were recorded as a matter of course and had no bearing on the outcome of the cases in question.

While court records have increasingly been recognized as a valuable historical source, the trustworthiness of testimonies has been debated. Some previous work on court records presents testimonies as heavily constructed narratives that are more useful for understanding ideologies than for reconstructing events that had taken place.[30] Indeed, testimonies were shaped by legal expectations and genres as well as individual witnesses' desires to represent themselves in a good light and to attain a

---

[28] Anne Colburne, 1619 (LMA, DL/C/225, fo. 389r) and William Edwards, 1619 (LMA, DL/C/226, 8th series, fos. 11v–12r).
[29] Thomasine Hall, 1619 (LMA, DL/C/225, fo. 390r), Richard Okeley, clothworker, 1619 (LMA, DL/C/226, 1st series, fo. 35v), and Jane Chambers, 1619 (LMA, DL/C/226, 8th series, fo. 15v). It is just possible that this 'Thomasine Hall' was the same 'Thomas Hall' whose ambiguous gender identity came to the attention of the Virginian authorities in 1629. Both were born in Newcastle upon Tyne, and 'Thomas Hall' reported living in London as a girl in his teens. See H. R. McIlwaine (ed.), *Minutes of the Council and General Court of Colonial Virginia*, 2nd edn (Richmond, Va., 1974), 194–5.
[30] See Natalie Zemon Davis, *Fiction in the Archives: Pardon Tales and their Tellers in Sixteenth-Century France* (Stanford, Calif., 1987); Gowing, *Domestic Dangers*.

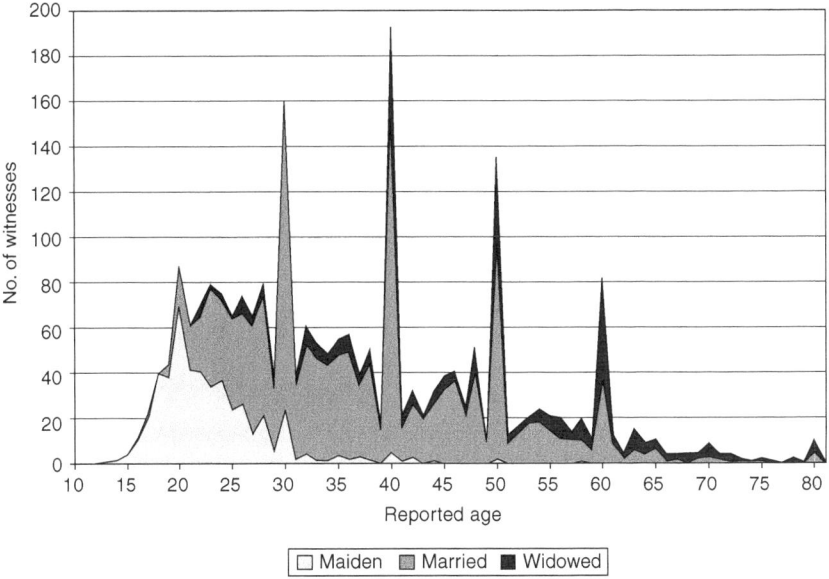

Figure 0.1 Age and marital status of female witnesses

particular legal result.[31] However, while it is impossible to guarantee the truthfulness of testimony, in order to be convincing, testimony needed to be plausible and could not contradict contemporary expectations of what might reasonably be expected to occur. A maidservant might lie, for example, that her suitor met her in a tavern and contracted himself with her in marriage in a private room over a pint of wine—but there would be little point in such a fabrication if that sort of behavior did not frequently take place.

In addition, though only defendants accused of serious misbehavior were sworn under the notorious *ex officio* oath,[32] all witnesses were regularly examined under oath, and the moral gravity of perjury ought not to be dismissed altogether. Even Elizabeth Lane, a young girl of scanty religious education, knew that lying under oath was a serious sin.

> When she dwelt at Ratcliffe her aunt's daughter did teach her some of the catechism but since she hath not been instructed by any book neither can she nor her aunt read and she hath learned to say 'Our father which art in heaven etc.' and 'I believe in God the Father Almighty etc.' but hath not been taught other points of religion that she can now remember neither hath been taught what the danger of an oath is, otherwise than this, that she ought not to forswear herself which she expoundeth to be swearing or

---

[31] Joanne Bailey has pointed out that a straightforward distinction between legal fiction and historical reality is itself problematic, as events are perceived differently by different individuals, and even by the same individuals at different times. 'Voices in Court: Lawyers' or Litigants'?', *Historical Research* 186 (2001), 392–408.

[32] See Ingram, *Church Courts, Sex and Marriage*, 329–31.

speaking upon her oath that which is false, and she thinketh if she should swear that which is false she should never enter into heaven.

Elizabeth Griffin more confidently told the court: 'she is above the age of sixteen years and hath not as yet received the Holy Communion yet sayeth she is of that capacity and understanding that she knoweth right well the danger of an oath and the punishment due unto those that shall forswear themselves.' Divine punishment for bearing false witness could come before death as well as after: after taking five shillings for deposing that a woman was a whore in an adultery case, Anne Moore confessed to an acquaintance that for 'her said unjust oath she did fear that God would inflict a punishment upon her or the child she then went withal'.[33]

In fact, it is rare to find cases in which there was any substantial disagreement over what had happened. In defamation cases there were usually no witnesses for the defense, and when they appeared, they usually testified that provocation had taken place, or that they could not hear the allegedly defamatory words, or that they had not been present, but knew the witnesses for the prosecution to be of little credit. The speaking of the defamatory words was not usually directly denied. Disputes over facts were much more common in high-stakes matrimonial cases, where opposing witnesses routinely provided blatantly contradictory accounts. It seems that while some early modern Londoners were willing to forswear themselves in matters of great import for themselves or their kin and friends, they were much less willing to lie under oath about minor neighborhood disputes.

In addition to mining consistory court testimony and the minutes of the Bridewell court of governors, this study delves into the wealth of material that flowed from London's printing presses, particularly prescriptive and satirical texts and popular broadside ballads. The conduct books written by such godly moralists as William Gouge and William Whately provide detailed descriptions of how husbands and wives, parents and children, and employers and servants were supposed to behave, as well as the many ways that they were often seen to transgress against the patriarchal ideal. Satirists like Thomas Dekker and Francis Lenton offered different and usually highly critical views of London manners, catering to the popular taste for witty denunciation.

Broadside ballads are a particularly valuable source for understanding the spectrum of popular social knowledge and belief. Couched in bouncing verse and set to well-worn tunes, ballads straddled the divide between print and oral culture. Anyone with a few coins to spend could afford to buy one, and even an illiterate charwoman could memorize the ones she overheard. Ballads reflected popular attitudes in ways that more expensive printed books might not: cheap and popular, they were written to appeal to ordinary people.[34] This is not to say that ballads provide an unvarnished window into social reality, or even into one unified social outlook. Rather, they illustrate the wide range of ways in which Londoners—always

---

[33] Elizabeth Lane, 1610 (LMA, DL/C/219, fo. 87v); Elizabeth Griffin, 1620 (LMA, DL/C/227, fo. 94v); and Martha Booth, 1623 (GL MS 9189/1, fos. 91v–92r).
[34] See Sandra Clark, 'The Broadside Ballad and the Woman's Voice', in Cristina Malcolmson and Mihoko Suzuki (eds), *Debating Gender in Early Modern England 1500–1700* (New York, 2002).

the first though not the only intended audience—could think about important issues. One ballad might condemn a coy maiden for denying herself to her lover, for example, while another lambasted a cruel seducer for abandoning his fallen sweetheart. Similarly, some ballads denounced nagging, drunken wives, while others attacked violent husbands. Balladeers like the prolific Martin Parker wrote for the market: the lack of consistency within their own work mirrored the heterogeneous concerns of their audience. All of these seemingly opposing perspectives coexisted within London society, and sometimes even within individual Londoners, who could draw on a range of cultural scripts according to circumstance.

No sources are perfect or even unproblematic, but with careful combination and attentive reading one can strive to remedy the weaknesses of one kind of text with the strengths of another. Quantitative analyses of marriage patterns, for example, provide pleasingly solid evidence of behavior but only hint at the motives of the people involved, while ballads and narrative testimonies, vivid but dangerously unrepresentative, are more explicit about the range of peoples' fears and hopes. The broad base of sources used in this study—manuscript and print, quantitative and qualitative, legal and literary—is intended to provide the fullest possible picture of women's challenges and aspirations in early modern London. It is not complete: the intimate lives of happily married couples remain shadowy, for example, as does religious experience. However, it should allow the reader once more to hear the voices of London women and to follow their dogged pursuit of survival, preferment, and satisfaction: forgotten struggles that lie at the heart of the early modern city.

1

In Search of Preferment

London's population exploded between 1580 and 1650 as the capital expanded to rival the greatest cities of Europe, Paris and Naples.[1] The green fields surrounding the metropolis rapidly gave way to construction as lanes and alleys sprouted in a tangled mass outside the City walls. London grew in all directions: to the east, shipyards and the humble homes of sailors' wives straggled along the Thames, while to the north, the city stretched out towards Islington. The beginnings of the stylish West End filled the fields between London and Westminster, and the southern bank enticed Londoners with amusement and vice. The city's tremendous growth, due almost entirely to immigration, was viewed with disfavor by civic authorities, who suspected the newcomers of idleness and vagrancy, dirt and disease, and missed the solid, respectable stability of an imagined past.[2] Yet the migrants who arrived daily on weary foot or huddled, bleary-eyed, on carriers' carts and laden ships were the lifeblood of the city. Without this replenishing stream of energetic youth, the plague-scarred city would have wasted away.

For these hopeful girls and boys, their arrival in London was not the end of a better, more orderly age, but the beginning of something new. Leaving behind peaceful villages and quiet towns, they exchanged fields and forests for streets and innumerable buildings, the cackling of hens for the cries of hucksters, streams and rivers for the turbid highway called the Thames. Though the city's close quarters may have initially struck the newcomers with the same awe that stupefied the herds of cattle and sheep driven from grassy pastures to the butchers of Newgate, most youthful immigrants soon found places to call home in the urban labyrinth. Working as apprentices and servants, they were assimilated into new families and grew to know the lanes and customs of their adopted neighborhoods. The same conservative society that relegated the young to subordinate status also put roofs over their heads and food in their bellies, and seemingly frail safety nets of far-flung kin and 'friends' could prove surprisingly strong. The unluckiest migrants, devoid of money and acquaintance in London, fell into vagrancy, were scooped up where they slept under stalls by wary watchmen and marched to Bridewell, or found unwholesome berths in London brothels. Many died of plague, the sweating

---

[1] See Roger Finlay, *Population and Metropolis: The Demography of London 1580–1650* (Cambridge, 1981), 6; and Finlay and Beatrice Shearer, 'Population Growth and Suburban Expansion', in A. L. Beier and Roger Finlay (eds), *London 1500–1700: The Making of the Metropolis* (London, 1986).

[2] See Paul Griffiths, *Lost Londons: Change, Crime and Control in the Capital City 1550–1660* (Cambridge, 2008), 36–66.

sickness, smallpox, or consumption; others, dismayed by city life, surely returned home. But most of the new arrivals entered years of service from which they would eventually emerge as true Londoners—no richer, perhaps, but more skilled and infinitely more familiar with the city and its ways.

Although migrant maids rarely entered formal apprenticeships like their brothers, male and female experiences of migration and service were similar in many ways.[3] Both sexes traveled from all over England, typically arriving in their late teens, and apprentices and maidservants had similar status. In most cases, they became members of small households where the social distance between them and their masters and mistresses was not great. They had similar duties—industry and respectful obedience were expected—and both could hope to learn new skills. However, while apprentices usually remained under one master for their seven-year terms, receiving no wages, maidservants moved between services frequently, and were paid, though meagerly. Young women were both more independent and more vulnerable than their male peers, and marriage, not citizenship, was to be their reward for years of service.

MIGRANT MAIDS

Most inhabitants of early modern London arrived there as migrants from elsewhere in England or further afield. Without this steady influx, London's population would have contracted: like other large early modern cities, it was ravaged by disease, and deaths outnumbered births. In addition to high infant mortality and the litany of usual childhood diseases and accidents, London was periodically swept by vicious epidemics; these were responsible for about 15 per cent of all deaths between 1580 and 1650, and struck the young especially hard. As a result, life expectancy in the poorer parishes was low, and only about half of London-born children survived to the age of 15.[4] Despite these harsh conditions, London's population grew from about 120,000 in 1550 to 375,000 in 1650. This rapid expansion depended largely on the immigration of several thousand people every year.[5] Although historians studying immigration to London have tended to focus on the well-documented stream of prospective apprentices who made the journey to London each year to try their luck in the city, thousands of migrants were female. Fully 77.2 per cent of the London women who testified for the consistory court had been born outside the city.[6] To have been a child in London was a rare experience for the women who minded the city's shops and washed its

---

[3] Not all male migrants entered apprenticeships, of course: many became servants, laborers, or sailors.
[4] Finlay, *Population and Metropolis*, 16–17.
[5] Population estimates from Finlay and Shearer, 'Population Growth and Suburban Expansion', 39.
[6] This figure is based on a sample of 2,406 women. The geographical definition of London used here includes Southwark in Surrey, and, in Middlesex, the parishes of St Leonard Shoreditch, Stepney, Whitechapel, St Katherine by the Tower, St James Clerkenwell, St Martin in the Fields, St Giles in the Fields, St Margaret Westminster, St Mary le Strand alias le Savoy, and St Clement Danes in Middlesex.

clothes. Instead, they had by and large come to London as teenagers or young women, in search of work and husbands.

Many young women traveled for days and even weeks to reach the capital, leaving family and friends far behind. As Table 1.1 shows, migrant women and migrant London apprentices had similar origins, with the largest groups originating in the home counties, and high numbers also migrating from the Midlands and the western counties. While women were slightly more likely than apprentices to come from the home counties, some distant counties were more strongly represented by women than by apprentices, in particular those of the west and the northwest.[7] Few witnesses originated from outside of England and Wales, but in the case of continental Europe, the percentage is surely misleadingly low.[8] Relative to

Table 1.1 Origins of London immigrant women in comparative context

Birthplace	Migrant female consistory court deponents 1570–1640 n = 1,815 (%)	Apprentices, 15 companies 1570–1640 n = 7,676 (%)	Commissary court deponents (both sexes) 1565–1644 n = 1,315 (%)
1. Home counties	20.4	19.0	17.8
2. South Midlands	16.2	17.5	13.4
3. North Midlands	11.0	14.1	11.4
4. Eastern counties	8.0	8.8	12.4
5. Western counties	18.1	16.2	14.6
6. Northeast	6.6	7.5	9.3
7. Northwest	9.9	8.8	11.4
8. Southern counties	5.0	4.3	2.6
9. Wales	2.8	3.4	3.3
10. Scotland and Ireland	0.6	0.4	1.4
11. Abroad	1.4	–	2.4
Total	100	100	100

1. Essex, Hertfordshire, Kent, Middlesex, Surrey.
2. Bedfordshire, Berkshire, Buckinghamshire, Northamptonshire, Oxfordshire.
3. Derbyshire, Leicestershire, Nottinghamshire, Staffordshire, Warwickshire, Coventry.
4. Cambridgeshire, Huntingdonshire, Lincolnshire, Norfolk, Rutland, Suffolk.
5. Cornwall, Devon, Dorset, Gloucestershire, Herefordshire, Somerset, Wiltshire, Worcestershire, Bristol.
6. Durham, Northumberland, Yorkshire.
7. Cheshire, Cumberland, Lancashire, Shropshire, Westmorland.
8. Hampshire, Sussex, Isle of Wight.

Source: Figures for apprentices and commissary court deponents from Vivien Brodsky, 'Mobility and Marriage in Pre-industrial England: A Demographic and Social Structural Analysis of Geographic and Social Mobility and Aspects of Marriage, 1570–1690, with Particular Reference to London and General Reference to Middlesex, Kent, Essex and Hertfordshire', Ph.D thesis, Cambridge (1978), 158–67.

[7] Some of the difference may result from the exclusion of sailors from apprenticeship rolls: since sailors often came from ports like Bristol and Newcastle, the apprenticeship data for those regions is not representative of the male migrant population of London. See Peter Earle, *A City Full of People: Men and Women of London, 1650–1750* (London, 1994), 75–6.

[8] Members of the French and Dutch Churches in London solved their neighborhood disputes internally rather than go to the Anglican consistory court. 'Stranger' witnesses were most likely to

Table 1.2 Origins of migrant Englishwomen relative to population distribution in England

Region	Migrant origins (%)	Population distribution (%)	Population estimates
1. Home counties	21.4	20.4	1,062,463
2. South Midlands	17.0	7.3	381,326
3. North Midlands	11.6	8.1	419,481
4. Eastern counties	8.4	14.2	738,928
5. Western counties	19.0	22.7	1,176,842
6. Northeast	7.0	12.0	624,462
7. Northwest	10.4	10.2	533,934
8. Southern counties	5.3	5.0	258,313

Source: Population distribution and estimates from Roger Finlay, *Population and Metropolis: The Demography of London 1580–1650* (Cambridge, 1981), 65.

population, the areas closer to London were best represented, as can be seen in Table 1.2. The Midlands in particular produced crowds of migrants, male and female, in striking disproportion to their population. In contrast, relatively few women migrated to London from the east and the northeast. However, the existence of substantial long-range migration is undeniable, especially from the poor and hungry northwest.[9] High levels of female migration were to continue into the eighteenth century, albeit less dramatically. As Table 1.3 shows, in the late seventeenth and early eighteenth centuries somewhat fewer female London residents were migrants, though a considerably larger cohort originated in Ireland and Scotland. Overall, large-scale female migration drawing from an extensive geographic field persisted, even as male migration to London contracted.

Residence histories provided by witnesses suggest that most migrant women arrived in London as prospective maidservants in their teens or early 20s. Young witnesses for whom migration was a recent event were most likely to include their age at migration in their depositions. For example, Magdalen Lasley reported that she had worked for her mistress in St Sepulchre for one year, and had previously lived in St Clement Danes for one year and in Westminster for three years; before that, she had lived in Enfield, Middlesex, since her birth. Since Magdalen said she was 17, she had moved to London around the age of 12. Similarly, Joan Buck, 21, had lived in Stepney for five years, in Franten, Gloucestershire, for five years before that, and originally in Aylburton, where she had been born. Her age at migration to London was thus around 16.[10]

---

testify in marriage cases over which the 'alien' churches lacked jurisdiction, and they sometimes made reference to failed reconciliation efforts by French or Dutch elders. See e.g. *Jane Foye c. Peter Foye*, 1578 (LMA, DL/C/629, fos. 24–7, 99).

[9] The northwest of England suffered disproportionately from want and even starvation in the worst years. See Andrew B. Appleby, 'Disease or Famine? Mortality in Cumberland and Westmorland 1580–1640', *Economic History Review*, new series, 26.3 (1973), 403–32. London was better fed. See Paul Slack, 'Mortality Crises and Epidemic Disease in England 1485–1610', in Charles Webster (ed.), *Health, Medicine and Mortality in the Sixteenth Century* (Cambridge, 1979), 36–8.

[10] Magdalen Lasley, 1636 (LMA, DL/C/234, fo. 167v) and Joan Buck, 1614 (LMA, DL/C/222, fo. 24r).

Table 1.3 London women's origins over time

Birthplace	1570–1640 n = 2,357 (%)	1665–1725 n = 2,121 (%)
1. Home counties	15.7	13.1
2. South Midlands	12.5	10.0
3. North Midlands	8.5	7.4
4. Eastern counties	6.2	4.2
5. Western counties	13.9	11.7
6. Northeast	5.1	4.9
7. Northwest	7.6	6.9
8. Southern counties	3.9	2.6
9. Wales	2.2	2.3
10. Scotland and Ireland	0.5	4.0
11. Abroad	1.1	2.4
12. London	23.0[a]	30.6
Total	100	100

[a] The figure 23.0 for the percentage of women born in London represents 541 London natives, of whom 95 were born in the Middlesex parishes of St Leonard Shoreditch, Stepney, Whitechapel, St James Clerkenwell, St Martin in the Fields, St Giles in the Fields, St Margaret Westminster, St Mary le Strand, and St Clement Danes, and 31 were born in Southwark.

Source: The 1665–1725 data is taken from the analysis of post-Restoration consistory court records in Peter Earle, 'The Female Labour Market in London in the Late Seventeenth and Early Eighteenth Centuries', *Economic History Review* 42.3 (1989), 328–53.

Fig. 1.1 shows the age at migration for the 203 witnesses who recounted when they first came to London. The late teens appear to have been the likeliest age for migration, but significant numbers of younger adolescents and women in their early 20s also moved to London, in addition to a handful of children and older women. In general, migrant women were unmarried and entered service in London at roughly the same age that their male counterparts were apprenticed. Fictional accounts of female migration to London, such as that of Long Meg from Lancashire, tell a similar story:

> This Meg growing to the age of eighteen, would needs come up to London to serve, and to learn City fashions: and although her friends persuaded her to the contrary, yet forsooth she had determined, and up she would. Wherefore she resolved to come up with a Carrier a neighbour of hers, called Father Willis, and so she did, accompanied with three or four Lasses more, who likewise came to London to seek service.[11]

---

[11] *The life of Long Meg of Westminster* (London, 1635), sig. B1–B3. Once they came to Islington, the carrier demanded that Meg and her companions pay him ten shillings apiece, but being soundly beaten, agreed to pay them an angel each instead. Meg was hired by the hostess of a Westminster victualling house who decided that her husky build—and the ease with which she persuaded unwilling customers to pay their scores—compensated for her lack of fine needle skills.

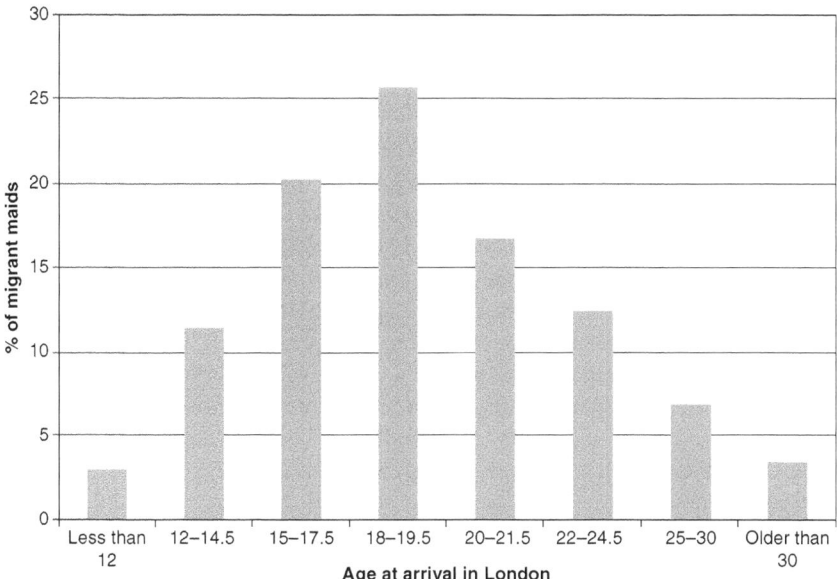

Figure 1.1 Age at arrival in London

While some women surely left the city again, most seem to have stayed there. If young women had usually spent several years in London before moving back to the country, one would expect to see a disproportionate percentage of youthful migrants, but the reverse is true: the percentage of female witnesses born outside of London increased with age. In a sample of 2,353 deponents, only 70.5 per cent of those between the ages of 13 and 19 were migrants, and 74.1 per cent of those aged 20–29. In comparison, the percentage of migrants among older witnesses reached a plateau between 78.9 and 79.9 per cent for women aged 30–59, and climbed still higher to 84.2 per cent for those aged 60 and older.

While little attention has yet been paid to the motivations of these women, they have generally been cast as subsistence migrants, in search of little more than bare survival.[12] While some migrant maids were indeed very poor, others had more ambitious plans. Young women, like young men, sought their 'preferment' in London, as popular stories suggest:

> When country Nan the milkmaid-lasses left,
> She came to London very neat and deft,
> To seek preferment, and her fortunes raise,

---

[12] Vivien Brodsky Elliott's study of migrant women's marriage allegations, has been most widely cited. Finding that 64% of these women had lost their fathers by the time they married at 25 or 26, she suggests that paternal mortality commonly triggered subsistence migration. However, losing one's father by the mid-20s was no rare occurrence in early modern England, and the small sample size calls for caution. 'Single Women in the London Marriage Market: Age, Status and Mobility, 1598–1619', in R. B. Outhwaite (ed.), *Marriage and Society: Studies in the Social History of Marriage* (London, 1981), 90.

> Being indeed (as all the parish says)
> A handsome wench and likely to do well,
> If with a London Mistress she might dwell.[13]

Migrant maids like Samuel Rowlands' fictional Nan were attracted by the opportunities London offered. Although the ultimate prize for a 'handsome wench' was a rich marriage, wages were much higher in London than they were in the country. The typical wage for a maidservant in artisans' and tradesmen's houses in late sixteenth- and early seventeenth-century London was forty shillings a year. This meager stipend contrasted favorably with the thirty shillings per annum declared the lawful wage for female servants over the age of 20 in Norfolk in 1613, and even more with the official yearly wage of thirteen shillings in Yorkshire in the 1590s.[14] Even in the 1640s, Henry Best was annoyed to have to spend twenty-eight shillings for 'a good lusty maid' in Yorkshire.[15] London wages were known to be part of the city's appeal. In a 1567 manifesto, the 'maidens of London' threatened to go back to the country despite the lower wages they would receive there if their mistresses believed scurrilous rumors about them and abridged their 'lawful liberties': '[S]uch as are born in the country should choose rather to tarry at home, and remain there to take pains for a small stipend or wages with liberty, and such as are Citizens born, should repair also to the country, or to other Cities where they might be free, than to abide as slaves and bondwomen in London.'[16]

For all its charms, London was dangerous, and like Long Meg, ambitious maids sometimes moved there against their parents' advice. A maidservant from Barnet mentioned in 1616 that she had 'come from her father against his mind to dwell in London'.[17] The most detailed example we have of a migrant maid's motivations comes from the clergyman Adam Martindale's description of his sister Jane's decision to go to London from Lancashire in 1625:

> There had lately been a great plague in London, causing many that had friends in the country to come down, who having employments to return unto, were full as hasty to go up as consisted with safety; and my sister Jane having conversed with some of them, was as forward as they. Our parents and other prudent friends were against her going for many substantial reasons:
>
> 1. She wanted nothing at home, nor was likely to lack anything; and if she had a mind to be married, my father was then in a good ordinary capacity to prefer her.

---

[13] Samuel Rowlands, *Good newes and bad newes* (London, 1622), sig. C3v.
[14] Norfolk RO, AYL I/I, wage assessments 1613 and J. Harland (ed.), *The House and Farm Accounts of the Shuttleworths*, Chetham Society, 4 vols. (1856–8), vol. ii., 351, cited in Sara Mendelson and Patricia Crawford, *Women in Early Modern England, 1550–1720* (New York, 1998), 266.
[15] Donald Woodward (ed.), *The farming and memorandum books of Henry Best of Elmswell, 1642* (1984), 138–9.
[16] *A Letter sent by the maydens of London, to the vertuous matrones & mistresses of the same in the defense of their lawfull libertie* (London, 1567), sig. A3v. While its authorship remains unclear, this response to a lost pamphlet seems to be a serious statement of maidservants' concerns. Unlike many satires purporting to express female opinions, it appeals to traditional ideas of justice and order rather than dwelling on prurient fantasies.
[17] Elizabeth Tarver, 1616 (LMA, DL/C/223, fo. 372r).

2. She had no friends in London to go to.
3. It was feared the City was not clear of the plague, as it proved to her cost.
4. She had been bred in a most pure air, and being of a fresh complexion and not very hardly,'twas much to be questioned whether the city air would agree with her in the most healthful times.

If Jane Martindale had no need to leave home, why did she choose to brave London's dangers? Her brother surmised that she had social aspirations she could not hope to fulfill at home:

> Freeholders' daughters were then confined to their felts, petticoats and waistcoats, cross handkerchiefs around their necks, and white cross-clothes upon their heads, with coifs under them wrought with black silk or worsted. 'Tis true the finest sort of them wore gold or silver lace upon their waistcoats, good silk laces (and store of them) about their petticoats, and bone laces or works about their linens. But the proudest of them (below the gentry) durst not have offered to wear a hood, or a scarf... no, nor so much as a gown till her wedding day. And if any of them had transgressed these bounds, she would have been accounted an ambitious fool. These limitations I suppose she did not very well approve, but having her father's spirit and her mother's beauty, no persuasion would serve, but up she would to serve a lady as she hoped to do, being ingenious at her needle.[18]

We should not discount Jane Martindale's alleged interest in clothing as a frivolous fancy. Clothing stood for status: the hood, scarf, and gown denied her at home held precious social meaning. In addition to speaking with visiting Londoners, Jane may have heard one of the ballads contrasting ambitious 'City Dames' with humble 'Country Lasses':

> Your City Wives lead wanton lives,
> and if they come i'th Country,
> They are so proud, that each one strives
> for to outbrave our Gentry.
> We country lasses homely be
> for seat nor wall we strive not,
> We are content with our degree,
> our debtors we deprive not.[19]

Jane Martindale was not content with her degree. In London, she could hope to shine as she could not in the country, and so she chose to oppose her parents and risk her life to seek her fortune. Entering service in London would be her first step.

SERVING-MAIDS

In a society where the household was the basic unit of social order, young unmarried people posed a challenge. Because marriage was delayed to the late 20s

---

[18] Adam Martindale, *The Life of Adam Martindale*, ed. Richard Parkinson (Chetham, 1845), 6–7.
[19] M. P., *The countrey lasse* (London, 1628).

for men and the mid-20s for women, bachelors and maids could not be classified indefinitely as children: only in the most fortunate families could parents be expected to survive and support their offspring for so long. However, contemporaries feared that the worst outrages could be expected when volatile, irresponsible young men and women set up their own disorderly households without the steadying foundations of experience and capital. While young men were thought to be most prone to riot if not safely secured in a domestic hierarchy, young women on their own were seen to pose a less violent but equally pernicious danger to the moral and economic body of the community. Prostitution paid better than needlework, and the unwanted progeny of unmarried women might burden the parish.

Service and apprenticeship were England's answer to the problem of youth. Young people were to live in established households while they accumulated the skills and capital they would need to set up their own families. They would subject themselves to the authority of their masters and mistresses, and in return they would receive a certain level of material security. Many young people became servants or apprentices, about three-quarters of the population between the ages of 15 and 24.[20] In the country, they were servants in husbandry, serving annual terms with different families until they married. In towns, youths and some girls entered formal apprenticeships, exchanging labor for instruction and their keep. However, domestic service was the most common occupation for young London women in early modern England, and almost the only one open to them.

Maids could be legally forced into service: the 1563 Statute of Artificers empowered any two justices of the peace or other officers to

> appoint any such woman, as is of the age of twelve years, and under the age of forty years and unmarried and forth of service, to be retained or serve by the year, or by the week, or day, for such wages and in such reasonable sort and manner as they shall think meet. And if any such woman shall refuse so to serve, then it shall be lawful for the said Justices of the Peace, mayor, or head officers to commit such woman to ward until she shall be bounden to serve, as is aforesaid.[21]

While this law was not always enforced, maids faced official disapproval if they attempted to live by themselves or with other single women: they could be ordered to enter service or leave town.[22] While maids were likely to be maidservants, female servants were also almost always maids. Marriage usually marked the end of service, even in the case of a legal contract. The clergyman William Gouge noted that 'our laws do free a maid that is married from her service to master and mistress', and

---

[20] Ann Kussmaul, *Servants in Husbandry in Early Modern England* (Cambridge, 1981), 3.
[21] Masterless men between 12 and 16 years of age without property or prospects could also be 'compelled to be retained to serve in husbandry by the year with any person that keepeth husbandry, and will require any such person so to serve.' 5 Eliz., c. 4 (1563), *The Statutes of the Realm*, 11 vols (London, 1810–1828), vol. iv, 415, 419.
[22] For town officials taking action against charmaids, see Amy Froide, *Never Married: Singlewomen in Early Modern England* (Oxford, 2005), 20.

suspected that some covenanted maids did 'purposely marry to free themselves'.[23] Only about 0.6 per cent of the London wives who testified for the consistory court lived in other households as servants, and no more than 2.7 per cent of the widows. Except for the desperate few, adult status and service were considered to be incompatible.

Service was a crucial stabilizing institution in London. The rapid and unplanned expansion of the city, fed primarily by the immigration of poor young people, could have resulted in the creation of shanty towns inhabited by rootless migrants in the poorest suburban parishes. Indeed, one standard description of migrants' arrival in London depicts rural immigrants settling first in slums ringing the city.[24] However, a more common pattern was for maidservants and apprentices to serve within the City walls first, then to move to poorer outer suburbs when they married and set up their own households, like modern urbanites who rent central apartments in their single years, but find themselves unable to raise families without moving to cheaper, more distant locales. Instead of moving to the poor eastern fringes of the city, female migrants tended to find services in the City itself or in the relatively respectable western parishes: St Martin in the Fields, St Clement Danes, St Margaret Westminster, and others.[25]

The analysis shown in Table 1.4 demonstrates that whatever their marital status, migrants were more likely to live on the outskirts of London and less likely to live in the center than their London-born peers. However, all regions had substantial numbers of both native and migrant inhabitants, and migrant maids were significantly more likely to live within the City than wives or widows who had been born outside London.[26] The proportion of maids in the migrant population was the lowest in the outskirts, as Table 1.5 shows. While country girls found services all over London, they were most likely to serve within the City, then to move further out when they married. The poor eastern suburbs of Stepney and Whitechapel were not attractive destinations for new arrivals. Over 16 per cent of the London women testifying for the court overall were migrant maids, as compared to only 10.4 per cent of the 355 witnesses resident in Stepney and Whitechapel.[27]

---

[23] William Gouge, *Of domesticall duties* (London, 1622), 607.
[24] Finlay, *Population and Metropolis*, 153. See also Peter Clark, 'Migrants in the City: The Process of Social Adaptation in English Towns, 1500–1800', in Peter Clark and David Souden (eds), *Migration and Society in Early Modern England* (Totowa, NJ, 1987), 278.
[25] For domestic servants in the West End, see Jeremy Boulton, 'The Poor among the Rich: Paupers and the Parish in the West End, 1600–1724', in Paul Griffiths and Mark Jenner (eds), *Londinopolis: Essays in the Cultural and Social History of Early Modern London* (2000), 205.
[26] For cheap housing in London, see William Baer, 'Housing for the Lesser Sort in Stuart London: Findings from Certificates, and Returns of Divided Houses', *London Journal* 33.1 (2008), 61–88.
[27] An analysis of the 1695 returns for the marriage duty tax also shows that single people were more likely to live in the center than in the poor suburbs. Mark Merry and Philip Baker, '"For the house her self and one servant": Family and Household in Late Seventeenth-Century London', *London Journal* 34.3 (2009), 205–32.

Table 1.4 Region of residence according to migration and marital status

	City Within (%)	City Without (%)	Suburbs (%)	Sample size
Maids				
Migrant	37.0	37.3	25.8	400
Native	44.7	34.0	21.4	103
Wives				
Migrant	30.0	38.8	31.2	1,140
Native	33.6	40.0	26.4	425
Widows				
Migrant	27.6	38.6	33.8	272
Native	38.9	32.6	28.4	95
All female witnesses	32.5	38.3	29.2	2,435

Note: Parishes straddling the boundary between the City and Middlesex have been included under 'City Without'. These include St Botolph Aldgate, St Andrew Holborn, St Giles Cripplegate, St Dunstan in the West, and St Sepulchre.

Finding a service

While migrant girls were unlikely to arrive in London before the age of 12 or so, London-born girls could enter service even earlier, around the age of 10. Because of the consistory court's bias against 'silly' young deponents, few adolescent girls testified there. Nonetheless, many London maidservants were extremely youthful, as can be seen from the parish register for St Botolph Aldgate from January 1582 to September 1593, when the parish clerk provided not only the names of the dead but also their age, status, and cause of death. In a sample of 167 girls between the ages of 8 and 15 who were buried during the decade (many of whom succumbed to the plague of 1593), 6 per cent of the girls aged 8–9 were described as servants, 31 per cent of those aged 10–11, and 47 per cent of those between the ages of 12 and 16.[28] By the age of 15 or 16, the customary age of first communion, few London girls remained at home: in the Boroughside in Southwark in 1622, Jeremy Boulton finds that fewer than 5 per cent of households contained children of communicable age.[29]

For migrant girls, the first few days in London were thought to be particularly perilous, especially if they fell into the hands of an unscrupulous 'woman broker'. The iconic image of a provincial maidservant's arrival in London appears in the first engraving in Hogarth's *Harlot's Progress*. The 1732 image shows a country girl arriving on a carrier's cart, met by one of the old brokers who allegedly haunted the carriers' inns for that purpose. A similar picture is provided in a 1607 satire that describes how a broker waited by inns 'To see what country wenches come to town/

---

[28] GL MS 9221.
[29] Jeremy Boulton, *Neighbourhood and Society: A London Suburb in the Seventeenth Century* (Cambridge, 1987), 126.

Table 1.5 Migrant women: residence and marital status

Region of residence	Maidens (%)	Wives (%)	Widows (%)	Total (%)
City Within the Walls (n = 565)	26.2	60.5	13.3	100
City Without the Walls (n = 696)	21.4	63.5	15.1	100
Suburbs (n = 551)	18.7	64.6	16.7	100
All of London (n = 1,812)	22.1	62.9	15.0	100

To seek for service'. Having spotted suitable prey, the old woman began 'To speak them fair':

> I pray sweetheart sit down,
> Y'are weary I wosse, what, do you want a service?
> I'll help you to a very gallant mistress.
> She'll give great wages if so be she like you,
> Pray go with me, I'll bring you to her...

However, the 'gallant mistress' in question was 'Meg [who] was carted at Alhallowstide'—that is, a bawd, since they were traditionally punished by being forced to ride in a cart while onlookers jeered derisively. A month's service with her would transform the country lass into 'a shameless strumpet and an arrant whore'.[30] Hogarth's engraving and the earlier satire present a compelling juxtaposition of rustic innocence with urban sophistication and moral decay. While this was a caricature of the 'woman brokers', some of the women who allegedly lived by placing maidservants were probably involved, at least casually, in bawdry. One of the articles for the wardmote inquest, a local court held in each London ward, suggested as much:

> Ye shall also inquire if there be dwelling within your ward any woman broker, such as resort unto men's houses, demanding of their maidservants if they do like of their services; if not, then they will tell them they will help them to a better service, and so allure them to come from their masters to their houses, where they abide as boarders until provided for. In which time, it falleth out that by lewd young men that resort to those houses, they be oftentimes made harlots to their utter undoing and the great hurt of the commonwealth.[31]

The 'common brokers of maidens' were presented by the Cornhill wardmote in 1579, which claimed that their actions tended 'not only to the hurt of such good householders for want of honest servants but also to the destruction of many of the said poor maiden servants'.[32] These brokers were usually older women, often widows, like Jane Long, 40, of St Bride's parish, who claimed that she lived by

---

[30] Richard West, *The court of conscience or Dick Whippers sessions* (London, 1607), sig. E4v.
[31] *An acte for the reformation of divers abuses used in the wardmote inquest Together with the articles of the change of the sayd inquest* (London, 1617), 56.
[32] GL MS 4069/1, fo. 27r. The presentment was repeated in 1580, 1583, 1588, and 1598.

her own labor, but admitted to occasionally placing maidservants in 'great houses'. They had little neighborhood credit. When Magdalen Morton cursed Mary Paine as they were leaving church, accusing her of having caused Magdalen's husband's death, the neighbors 'willed [Mary Paine] not to be dismayed', explaining that no one would believe Magdalen's accusation because she 'was an evil liver and kept many wenches in her house under the pretence of getting them services, and suffered them to be incontinent in her house and was for gain consenting to their incontinence and that she kept a bawdy house'. Indeed, Magdalen Morton lived with 'divers and sundry young women' in Barber Alley, right off Turnbull Street in early modern London's Red Light district.[33]

Even if a woman broker wished to place maidservants 'honestly', it is not clear whether she would have been able to do so. In fact, the *Letter sent by the maydens of London* argued that old women's ability to entice servants away and find them better services was a myth: 'For their broking and helping of servants to services is but a tale of a tub, such poor people's credit is not half so great, that they can shew any so great a pleasure.'

> Yet surely were it not amiss, if any such brokers were, then servants suddenly without warning put out of service, should not by any necessity be constrained to true unhonesty. As what would not one do pinched with penury: hunger breaketh stone walls (as the proverb is) and why should we be afraid in honest wise to complain to our Masters and Mistresses when we find any thing amiss, and desire their good leave to depart, when they will not redress it?[34]

The 'maydens' held that constraining maidservants' opportunities to find new services only made them more likely to resort to prostitution. The restrictions on women brokers were actually driven by householders' desire to control their servants, they suggested, not by the vaunted concern for maidservants' chastity.

In the absence of reliable brokers, maids in search of respectable services usually depended on personal connections and references who would vouch for them. A widow from St Botolph Aldgate reported that a friend of hers had placed Elizabeth Clypson with one Mistress Samborne, and because she 'knew the said Clypson to be an honest servant both true and trusty... [she] did pass her word to the said Samborne for her truth and honesty.' She had been willing to recommend Elizabeth, the widow said, because the young woman had 'lived very well and with good commendations both of her master and mistress, and in particular at one Mr Haynes his house, a gentleman dwelling in Hackney... as also at Mistress Coxe, a widow dwelling in Houndsditch, a woman of great wealth with whom she... might have stayed longer with her if she would'.[35] A good reputation could enable a maidservant to find a service among the friends and acquaintances of her social circle, and a bad one was correspondingly harmful. Rebecca Warner,

---

[33] Jane Long, 1626 (LMA, DL/C/230, fo. 108r); Mary Manfield and Joan Warricke, *Mary Paine c. Magdalen Morton*, 1617 (LMA, DL/C/225, fos. 13r, 16v).
[34] *A Letter sent by the maydens of London*, sig. B4v.
[35] Audrey Wetwood, 1622 (LMA, DL/C/228, fos. 350–351r).

defamed as a 'private whore', was said to be 'much disgraced by the said defamatory words for that she is a maidservant and upon such report except she be guiltless few will admit her into their service'.[36]

Some young women became servants to their own kin: brothers and sisters appear most frequently as masters and mistresses, although uncles and aunts can also be found. Elizabeth Bingham from Rutland and Anne Alchurch from Warwickshire both reported to the court that they served their brothers, who happened to be cooks. Both maids had had prior services in London: Elizabeth, 24, had lived four years with her brother and six years before that in a different parish, while Anne, 20, had only recently moved in with her brother after two different services. Neither had served with kin when they originally migrated to London, although their brothers' presence in the city may have served to smooth the transition.[37]

Broader social networks could also be activated in order to place migrant maidens in service. Anne Hughes from Leicestershire helped a younger countrywoman of hers, Margaret Howe, to find a place. Anne was close to Margaret's parents, 'one of their special friends which they made account of', so she 'bearing some affection to [Margaret], then a pretty girl... sent for her down to Leicestershire, and placed her here in London'. Anne reported that Margaret frequently came to her house and followed 'her advice and direction in all her doings', relying on her for new positions when her terms of service expired.[38]

One country maid found a London service through a tangled web of family and neighborhood networks. A kinswoman of hers was married to John Rogers, a waterman. Rogers told Christopher Mortimer, a friend of his, that he was looking to place the girl, and Mortimer's wife found the maid a service with their neighbor, Elizabeth Aldeworth. Even after the girl was settled in Elizabeth's household, Rogers and Mortimer kept track of her situation. One day, when the two men and one Thomas Clatterbuck were drinking in an alehouse in the Old Bailey, Elizabeth Aldeworth sat down with them. Then, 'understanding that the said Rogers was a kinsman of a wench's whom the said Mr Mortimer had put to the said Mistress Aldeworth to dwell, she did fall in talk with him about the said wench'. She told Rogers 'that the said maid as yet knew not well the fashions of London because she was brought up in the country', but went on to say:

> I have another maid dwelling with me, who is my covenanted servant yet for three quarters of a year to come... who shall teach her the fashions of my house, and by that time she go away your kinswoman shall know my fashions and be able to do better. In the meantime she shall do but little else but to look to my children.[39]

When Elizabeth Aldeworth and Christopher Mortimer later fell out, the maid became an object of contention. Mortimer came to Elizabeth, who was sitting by her door, and charged her with mistreatment of the girl:

---

[36] William Webb, *Rebecca Warner c. Mary Symons*, 1629 (LMA, DL/C/231, fo. 470r).
[37] Elizabeth Bingham, 1628, and Anne Alchurch, 1630 (LMA, DL/C/231, fos. 328v, 649r).
[38] Anne Hughes, *Margaret Howe c. Ellis*, 1587 (LMA, DL/C/213, p. 149).
[39] Thomas Clatterbuck and John Rogers, *Elizabeth Aldeworth c. Christopher Mortimer*, 1573 (LMA, DL/C/211/1, fos. 136v, 137v).

Mistress Aldeworth, it is not unknown to you that my wife did put a wench unto you to dwell which is a friend's daughter of mine whose parents hath put me in trust to look to that wench, and to see that she be well used. And I do understand you do not well use her, but beat her and not so content to use her yourself but you do will her fellow servant in the house to beat her also, and if she will not so do, you do threaten to beat her, which is not well done of you, for it is too much for the wench to have four masters.

Elizabeth Aldeworth denied the charge, and sarcastically called the girl 'to show what wounds she had given her, with her so sore beating'. The ensuing conversation suggests that the maid had not, in fact, been abused.[40] Nonetheless, the incident illustrates how dense networks of kin and other 'friends' could take on quasi-parental responsibility for young migrants, cushioning their arrival into the city, and exerting a protective influence thereafter.

Despite constraints on moving from service to service, maidservants were extremely mobile, usually remaining in a household for only one or two years. Table 1.6 displays the amounts of time that maidservants reported spending in different past services, according to the residence histories they provided. The 195

Table 1.6 Duration of services

Years of service		No. of reported services	% of total services
At least	Less than		
0	1	65	21
1	2	102	33
2	3	53	17
3	4	32	10
4	6	41	13
6	9	16	5
9	17	5	2
Total		314	100

[40] Elizabeth said: '"This is not the cause of your grudge towards me, for you did never bear me good will, since your wife's cousin (meaning one Mistress Keyser, who was Mr Mortimer's wife's sister's daughter) did come to my house to lie." "You say even true," quoth Mr Mortimer, "for it was no neighbourly part for you to take her into your house until first you had known my wife's mind and mine therein, and whether we were willing she should go from us or no." "What would you have had me to have done?" quoth Mistress Aldeworth. "You do know well enough that all the while she ... did lie in your house, your wife and she could never agree together, but fell still forth and (if you do remember) the last time your wife and she fell forth together, your wife did call her whore, arrant whore, and privy whore, yea, and told then with whom she did play the whore, naming even with you yourself, Mr Mortimer, if you do remember, and could you abide that rule, and talk in your house, it had been good for you to have taken your cousin's part in so much your wife did name you to be naught with her." "Well," quoth Mr Mortimer, "even so I did, and did beat my wife for her words, which I wish I had not done, but, Mistress Aldeworth," quoth he, "God forbid all reports should be true, for you do know that even you yourself was called whore, arrant whore and privy whore, yet I do judge you an honest woman."' John Brown (LMA, DL/C/211/1, fo. 105v).

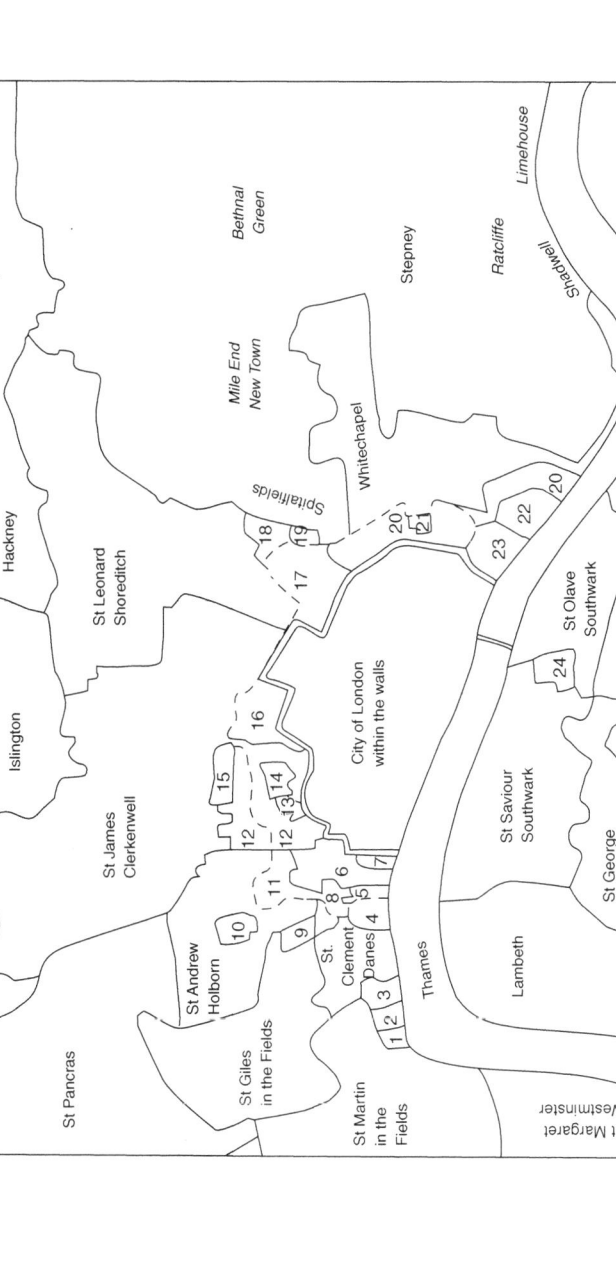

Figure 1.2 London and the surrounding areas c.1600

Notes: 1. Some parishes straddle the boundary between the City and Middlesex.
2. Limehouse, Shadwell, Ratcliffe, Spitalfields, Mile End, and Bethnal Green were all hamlets within the parish of Stepney.
3. The 97 tiny parishes within the City walls are not shown.

maidservants who provided useful information reported a total of 314 separate services, with considerable variations in length. Some maidservants stayed with one family for several years, while others moved around frequently. For example, Susan More came to London from Cambridge when she was about 20, and proceeded to serve in St Peter Cornhill for two years, St Margaret New Fish Street for one year, St Lawrence Pountney for one year, Holy Trinity Minories for three months, and St Giles Cripplegate for one year. She spent ten weeks in Westminster around her delivery of an illegitimate child, then went back to service in St Bride's parish. Agnes Wincheley, a 30-year-old bride from Huntingdonshire, reported that

> before her marriage she ... dwelt in the parish of St Andrew Hubbard with her brother half a year, and before with Mr Gawthorne half a year and more, and before that with Mr Jay in Budge Row two years and a quarter, and before that in the Strand with Mr Belmay two years, and before that with Dr Pattison almost a year, and before that with Mr Jackson at Spalding in Lincolnshire two years, and before that with her father.[41]

In contrast to these mobile young women, Jane Bailey from Essex came to London when she was about 12 years old, and worked for one mistress for twelve years. Agnes Driver, a Stepney girl, had been not quite 10 when she entered the service of the widow Frances Boothe, and was still her servant twelve years later.[42] Girls who came to London very young were more likely to stay in one service than their elders: they may have been orphans whose masters and mistresses took on a parental role.

Some maidservants left their services or were dismissed because of disagreements with their mistresses. Mary Griffith, a Shropshire native, was turned out by Anne Stamford after two or three weeks for her 'ill misdemeanors'; she promptly found a new service with a tailor. Joan Clay stayed with Magdalen Peckham for only two or three months and left her before finding a new service. Living on her savings, she reported that she 'went away from her service in regard her said mistress used her unkindly as well by blows as not giving her sufficient meat and drink as a servant ought to have'. Sixteen-year-old Joyce Greene went back to her previous master (perhaps a relative) after three months with Jane Halliday, finding that 'Halliday's work was too much for [her] to do'.[43]

When discord curtailed services, mistresses and maids blamed one another. Elizabeth Clypson, 30, from Oxfordshire, left the house of Margaret Samborne amid bitter controversy. Her ex-mistress deposed in 1622 that she 'put away the foresaid Elizabeth Clypson out of her service for that she was somewhat cross unto [Margaret's] children and very slow in doing business about her house'. However, the neighbors said that Margaret Samborne had complained that Elizabeth 'was a wench given much to drink and would be drunk sometimes', and 'a runnagate rogue that she was afraid to trust her alone in her house ... she durst not go abroad

---

[41] Susan More, 1608 (LMA, DL/C/218, p. 138); Agnes Wincheley, 1617 (LMA, DL/C/225, fo. 86v).
[42] Jane Bailey, 1606 (LMA, DL/C/217, p. 104); Agnes Driver, 1588 (LMA, DL/C/213, p. 433).
[43] Mary Griffith and John Parfey, 1623 (GL MS 9189/1, fos. 34r, 95v); Joan Clay and Joyce Green, 1624 (LMA, DL/C/229, fos. 28r, 29r).

but until she had locked her the said Clypson into the house for fear she should steal something and run away'. On the other hand, Margaret herself was known for strife, drinking, and blasphemy, and Elizabeth Clypson had told others that she wished 'she had never dwelt with her the said Samborne for that she had used her very badly'.[44]

In some cases employers faced pressure to retain unsatisfactory servants who otherwise might fall on the parish rates. Margaret Barrett, 22, was by all accounts 'a swearing blaspheming wench and drunken wench' and 'a very poor maiden and much given to drunkenness and ... railing or scolding at the neighbors'. However, although she had been 'often turned out of Elizabeth Hollinshed's house', she was equally often 'upon intreaty ... of the neighbours ... received and taken in again'. The neighbors in question had probably been worried that they would have to assume responsibility for Margaret, as they had done one winter when 'she the same Margaret Barrett lay in the street in Pudding Lane in such poor estate as the constable and churchwardens were constrained to take order for her keeping and they gathered money for her'. It is noteworthy that parish officials felt obliged to provide for Margaret even though she was not a native of the parish, St George in Botolph Lane: she had lived there for a total of about five years, having arrived there from Cheshire when she was about 18.[45]

Maidservants who moved around may have been anxious to free themselves from bad employers: lecherous men and husbands who beat their wives were unpopular, as were harsh, stingy mistresses and households with a reputation for lewdness.[46] Although social pressures discouraged abuse, prudence was the best policy. When Richard Rochester offered to hire Dorcas Bemfield, she wisely said 'that she cared not to dwell in a place where there was neither dame nor mistress'. To persuade Dorcas to enter his service, Rochester explained that he was to be married soon, and introduced her to Katherine Aylett, his intended bride.[47]

Leaving an unpleasant or dangerous service might not be easy. Maidservants who wished to depart without their employers' consent were hindered by the difficulty of recovering not only their wages but also their clothing, usually kept in heavy chests that could be held hostage by spiteful masters and mistresses. When maids had good reason to break their contracts, the authorities might order their employers to deliver them their clothes. For example, John and Elizabeth Ball were ordered in 1615 to discharge their maid Joan Akerley and to give her her clothes, because 'the said John Ball hath oftentimes beaten and misused Joan Akerley his servant with undue correction and hath likewise violently thrown a naked knife at her with

---

[44] *Anne Levans c. Constance Waller*, 1621–1622 (LMA, DL/C/228): Margaret Samborne (fo. 150r), Joan Wood (fo. 228v), and Mary Turke (fo. 230r).

[45] Margaret Barrett, Frances Price, and Ellen Steed, 1608 (LMA, DL/C/218, pp. 408, 586, 589).

[46] During the period 1660–1750, marital breakdown was the most common reason servants gave for leaving a service. Tim Meldrum, *Domestic Service and Gender 1660–1750: Life and Work in the London Household* (New York, 2000), 121.

[47] Dorcas, struck by Katherine's slight stature, exclaimed: 'I shall have but a little mistress then!' Henry Fuller, *Richard Rochester c. Katherine Aylett*, 1607 (LMA, DL/C/217, p. 170).

intent to do her harm'.[48] A different tactic was employed by Joan Hartley, who spirited her chest away and fled when her mistress accused her of stealing from one of her lodgers.[49] However, a maidservant who left her service without permission could find herself imprisoned in Bridewell, like Elizabeth Holden, servant to a gentleman and his wife in Gracechurch Street, who was kept there in December 1598 'for that she departed her mistress's service and refused to serve them being their hired servant for one year and for that she used very bad speeches to her mistress'.[50]

In addition to fleeing bad employers, maids sought out good ones. The clergyman William Gouge criticized servants for seeking generous masters and mistress instead of godly ones: 'they never inquire after the religious disposition of their master, nor care though he be popish, or profane, so they may have good wages, diet and lodging.'[51] Wages probably varied less than the standard of food and lodging, and the amount of work that was expected. Forty shillings a year was typical. The lowest wage reported in London was eighteen shillings a year in the poor parish of St Botolph Aldgate in the dearth year of 1597, but this was exceptional; no one else reported earning less than thirty shillings.[52] A handful of maids reported making more than forty shillings: one of them served in a Whitechapel tavern and made fifty shillings a year, and another received the same wage working for 'a merchant or a factor for the Greenland Company' and his wife. The highest single wage, £4 per annum, was reported by Joyce Mowlso; she served Sir Henry Montague and had previously been employed by one Lady Bowyers.[53]

Serving a wealthy master or mistress was advantageous for other reasons as well. If they were lucky, maidservants might find their wages supplemented by gifts or legacies.[54] In poor and middling households, the tips from visitors that padded the

---

[48] *Middlesex County Records*, ed. John Cordy Jeaffreson, 3 vols, old series (London, 1974), vol. ii, 100–101.
[49] Joan told her mistress 'that she should never then search her chest except she brought an officer with her'. A warrant was procured and the chest searched, confirming Joan's mistress's suspicions. William Mullins, 1607 (LMA, DL/C/217, pp. 186–8).
[50] BRHA, BCB 6, fo. 53v.
[51] Gouge, *Of domesticall duties*, 640.
[52] Joan Young, 1597, LMA, DL/C/215, sl. 223. The poorest of all the maidservant witnesses was Anne Fulham, who served a small farmer and his wife in Woodford, Essex. She reported in 1591 that she had been paid 22s. the year before but only 12s. that year 'because it is hard year'. She said 'she never knew who was her father, but ... she was brought up by one Edward Fulham who dwelt at Walthamstowe and by reason thereof she came to be called Anne Fulham'. Another witness called her 'a poor simple wench ... of little credit or account' who 'had a bastard thereabouts in Woodford and did penance for the same'. Anne Fulham and John Beckham, 1591 (LMA, DL/C/214, pp. 27–9, 78–9).
[53] Margaret Barker, 1629 (LMA, DL/C/231, fo. 115r); Bridget Gibson, 1633 (LMA, DL/C/630, fo. 160); Joyce Mowlso, 1615 (LMA, DL/C/223, fo. 143r).
[54] Ben-Amos finds that Bristol merchants often left legacies to servants, and Capp agrees that 'employers often gave generous presents when their servants married, or left them bequests'. However, the transient nature of service in London probably precluded very close relationships between employers and servants, and in many households, every groat and scrap of household stuff was likely to be coveted by kin. Ilana Krausman Ben-Amos, *Adolescence and Youth in Early Modern England* (New Haven, Conn., 1994), 172–4; Bernard Capp, *When Gossips Meet: Women, the Family and Neighbourhood in Early Modern England* (Oxford, 2003), 141.

wages of the gentry's servants were unlikely to provide a substantial boost to a maidservant's earnings. However, they were not unknown. Elizabeth Chatfield, the wife of a tailor who got his living 'by buying and selling of wares of all kinds', claimed in 1613 that she paid her servant Anne Clare forty shillings a year 'besides her vails which are ordinarily worth twenty shillings per annum... which amounteth in all to the sum of three pounds'.[55] Thomas Chatfield, who was said to be in possession of forty pounds, was financially secure but by no means wealthy. In addition to vails, a maidservant in a wealthy household would have more opportunities for the casual pilfering that so irked employers.[56]

In contrast to relatively stable householders, maidservants were highly mobile: when they switched services, they usually switched parishes as well, sometimes moving across London.[57] For example, Joan Clay from Essex left her service in Aldersgate Street to serve an apothecary in nearby Cheapside. Then she moved to St Mary Bermondsey across the Thames, where she stayed for two or three years, before moving north again to St Sepulchre. Margaret Newe migrated to London from Oxford, settling first in St Magnus the Martyr just north of London Bridge, then after two years moved northwest to St Sepulchre. Mary Kys came to London from Warwickshire when she was about 15, and lived first in Islington, north of London, moved in to St Margaret Pattens, and then moved to the periphery again to take a service with a clothworker and his wife in St Andrew Holborn in the northwestern part of the city. In contrast, Margaret Griffin from Denbighshire lived first in St Botolph Bishopsgate on the eastern edge of the City, then moved inward, first to St Bartholomew by the Exchange and finally to St Margaret Lothbury in the heart of London.[58]

The mobility of London maidservants stemmed from several causes. Social pressures discouraged Londoners from hiring their neighbors' maids: hiring away a good maidservant was unneighborly and hiring an unsatisfactory one could also cause local strife. Margaret Durrant, practicing 'the trade of a cook and selling meat and drink', hired a maidservant to serve beer, who 'trusted out her mistress's beer' to some customers who failed to pay their scores. Margaret put the woman out of her service, and when Roger Pepper hired her himself, the neighbors 'blamed the said Pepper that he would receive any other's servant who had dealt so lewdly with her mistress'. They suspected that he had hired the girl to probe for information about Margaret Durrant's private life.[59]

---

[55] Elizabeth Chatfield, 1613 (LMA, DL/C/221, fo. 1230v), and 1611 (LMA, DL/C/220, fo. 466v).
[56] See Capp, *When Gossips Meet*, 166–9.
[57] On householders, see Jeremy Boulton, 'Neighbourhood Migration in Early Modern London', in Peter Clark and David Souden (eds), *Migration and Society in Early Modern England* (Totowa, NJ, 1987).
[58] Joan Clay, 1624 (LMA, DL/C/229, fo. 27); Margaret Newe, 1613 (LMA, DL/C/221, fo. 1434r); Mary Kys, 1610 (LMA, DL/C/219, fo. 60v); and Margaret Griffon, 1594 (LMA, DL/C/214, p. 569).
[59] Robert Greenapp, 1593 (LMA, DL/C/214, pp. 402–3).

Maidservants' tendency to switch parishes when they moved from service to service also suggests that they sought out greener marital pastures.[60] They were always alert to possible marriage opportunities. For example, Elizabeth Doughty, 30, a covenanted servant with the Aldeworths, broke her contract to serve William Brown instead in 1572. Brown, a middle-aged tailor, was single: his family consisted of 'a wench of about sixteen years of age (who was then very sick) and two apprentices, but no wife nor children, and [he] therefore then had much need of another maidservant to look to his house and family'.[61] For Elizabeth, it proved to be a smart move: after a few months she married her new master.[62]

The status of the maidservant

At the heart of service was a mutual exchange: maidservants worked and in return they were lodged, fed, and paid by their masters and mistresses. The 'maydens of London' reminded their dames:

> For as ye are they that care and provide for our meat, drink and wages, so we are they that labour and take pains for you: so that your care for us, and our labour for you is so requisite, that they cannot be separated: so needful that they may not be severed.[63]

However, early modern writers insisted that service was not merely the exchange of labor for wages: instead, masters were to care for servants' physical, moral, and spiritual health, and for their future preferment. Masters and mistresses were instructed to treat their servants like children, and not like donkeys, made only for labor. This meant that they had to provide their servants with sufficient wholesome food and adequate sleep (not less than five hours a night, with seven hours being counted sufficient for anyone). Where meals were concerned, quantity did not make up for defects in quality, 'as when it is kept too long, and grown musty, moldy, or otherwise unsavory: or when the worst kind of food, for cheapness' sake, is bought, even such as is scarce fit for man's meat: the more abundance that there is of such stuff, the more loathsome it is.' When employers were responsible for their servants' apparel, that too was to be decent, warm and not ragged.[64] If a servant fell sick, he or she was to be cared for and 'cherished and nourished with more choice and dainty meat', not to be put out into the street.[65] Some masters, Gouge wrote, endangered their sick servants by telling them 'that they took them for their work, and not to keep them in their bed, to get some thing

---

[60] This would help explain why Brodsky Elliott finds an average length of service within one household of four years in her sample of 88 servants marrying by license in 1598–1619. Maids who were close to matrimony and had been involved in serious courtship for some time had little reason to crisscross the city. Brodsky Elliott, 'Single Women in the London Marriage Market', 92.

[61] William Brown, *Elizabeth Aldeworth c. Christopher Mortimer*, 1572 (LMA, DL/C/211/1, fo. 134v).

[62] Elizabeth Aldeworth, 1572 (LMA, DL/C/211/1, fos. 130v–131r).

[63] *A Letter sent by the maydens of London*, sig. A5.

[64] Gouge, *Of domesticall duties*, 668–70, 674.

[65] Robert Cleaver and John Dod, *A godly forme of houshold government for the ordering of private families* (London, 1612), 376.

by them, not to be at such cost with them: or that they make themselves more sick than needs'. Such 'discontented speeches' could force the 'poor sick servants . . . to rise, even when death is seizing upon them'.[66] Godly writers' condemnations of masters who discharged their sickly servants suggest that employers were all too prompt to rid themselves of burdensome dependents. Thus in 1572 Grace Thirkell, 16, 'chancing to be sick of an ague' after two years of service with her London master, was sent down to her uncle's house in Ware, Hertfordshire. Only when she was mostly recovered did her master send for her again.[67]

Servants were even supposed to have some free time: 'Questionless it is very meet that servants should have some times to refresh themselves this way: for recreation rightly used is a great means to put life, and add spirit, to youth especially.'[68] Maidservants' recreation was disputed in 1567, when a scurrilous pamphlet condemned maids' Sunday feasting and jaunting off to plays. Their reply defended the customary free afternoon on the Sabbath:

> it were too much against reason, to entreat evil, when they have done their duties, to use as slaves or bondwomen, being freeborn, and not rather to cherish them, and make much of them when they take intolerable pains for a trifle. How much against all reason were it, so straitly to deal with us, and so straitly to use us, that after the toil we take in the whole week, we might not enjoy a piece of the holiday, to refresh our spirits, and to rest our wearied bones?

In any case, the maidservants noted, they had little free time even on Sundays, 'the forenoon of we spend at Church or about necessary business at home'. In the afternoons, 'commonly they ring the first peal to Evensong before that we have washed up half our dishes. Then must we either to Church again, or tarry at home to dress your suppers.' A servant, they argued, would be lucky to have two hours to herself, and if she chose to spend half a penny on a drink with a friend, or to go see 'a godly play or interlude' where 'much learning' could be had, no one ought to complain.[69]

Masters and mistresses had the right—and indeed, according to godly writers, a moral obligation—to punish their servants when they misbehaved, though beatings were not supposed to threaten health or life. When correcting servants, employers were supposed to 'give it them with such discretion, pity, and desire of their amendment, as loving parents use to deal with their dear children'.[70] In practice, punishment could be brutal. Very young maids may have been particularly vulnerable to physical abuse, especially when they were orphans without nearby kin. In 1592, three women were imprisoned by the Court of Aldermen for severely beating their child servants. In one case, the age of the child was mentioned:

---

[66] Gouge, *Of domesticall duties*, 677.
[67] John Thirkell, 1572 (LMA, DL/C/211/1, fos. 59–60).
[68] Gouge, *Of domesticall duties*, 644, 670, 675.
[69] *A Letter sent by the maydens of London*, sig. A5v, B2v–B3r.
[70] Cleaver and Dod, *A godly forme of houshold government*, 365.

It is ordered that Susan Belfield who did of late very shamefully and unchristianlike beat and abuse Bridget Holland (a girl of the age of eight years) being her servant shall be . . . forthwith committed to one of the compters of this City there to remain during the pleasure of this court.

Cecily Salwey, a haberdasher's wife, was sent to Bridewell 'there to receive such punishment as this court shall think meet' because she 'did of late very cruelly beat and abuse Frances Drewe a girl being her servant'. More seriously, one abusive mistress was committed to Newgate and her husband later bound over to produce her at the Sessions, 'for that she in most vile manner and monstrous hath at sundry times beaten and wounded Elizabeth Burlington'. The aldermen took the additional step of committing Elizabeth to a different man's custody.[71] Although magistrates did intervene to remove servants from abusive households, in general they were more interested in order than in justice. There was little will to convict masters and mistresses after the fact when violent beatings and deprivation proved fatal.[72]

Less brutal beatings could also occasion neighborhood disapproval. In 1572, 'Mr Mortimer having put a wench of a friend of his to [Elizabeth Aldeworth] to dwell, and understanding she did use the said wench very evil and did beat her about the shoulders with a ladle till she was both black and blue . . . did come unto her to check her.' Sometimes public rebukes over beatings developed into wider quarrels. When Helen Bruett 'took occasion to beat a little girl being her prentice for neglecting her work', a local woman 'heard the girl cry' and 'being grieved thereat' reviled Mistress Bruett, calling her, 'whore, common whore, pocky whore!' Similarly, when Anne North's husband 'fell out with his maidservant and beat her', Katherine Bowes ran up to Anne's chamber, 'fell at variance with her about the beating of the said maidservant', and called her a 'barbarous whore', adding for good measure: 'I will maintain thee to be a whore by cutlers' boys before thou wert married.' Although Anne North had not beaten the girl herself, as her mistress she bore responsibility for her well-being.[73]

The godly moralists agreed that in most cases only the mistress should correct the maids; for the master to do so was 'not comely or meet'. 'Yet if a maid should wax stout, and mannish, and turn against her mistress, she being weak, sickly, with child, or otherwise unable to master her maid, the master may and must beat down her stoutness and rebellion.'[74] Masters and mistresses could also bring troublesome servants to Bridewell for punishment if they were unwilling or unable to beat them themselves. Elizabeth Jackson, the maidservant of one Mistress Sly, was sent in for pilfering in 1576. Mistress Sly further complained that Elizabeth was 'acquainted with many of my Lord of Arundel's servingmen, and that she could not send her for

---

[71] Repertories of the Court of Aldermen, Repertory 23 (LMA, COL/CA/1/1/25). Entries for 30 January, 8 March, 12 February 1593.
[72] See the nuanced account in Capp, *When Gossips Meet*, 135–8.
[73] Edward Wood, *Elizabeth Aldeworth c. Christopher Mortimer*, 1572 (LMA, DL/C/211/1, fo. 114r); Ursula March and Edith Merrie, *Helen Bruett c. Dorothy Smith*, 1614 (LMA, DL/C/222, fo. 27); Anne Glover, *Anne North c. Katherine Bowes*, 1630 (LMA, DL/C/233, fo. 156r).
[74] Cleaver and Dod, *A godly forme of houshold government*, 378; Gouge, *Of domesticall duties*, 662.

a tub of water but she would be amongst them'. The maidservant was 'corrected', and at the request of the Bridewell governors, Mistress Sly was 'contented... to take her again and to try her further'. But Elizabeth was 'not willing to dwell with her mistress any longer, and therefore went with her mother'.[75]

Service was supposed to be educational, and part of a mistress's duties was to teach the servant skills that would be useful to her later in life. This was not always honored:

> such mistresses offend as keep their maids many years together to drudgery work, and never teach them, nor afford them means or leisure to learn points of huswifery, things whereby they may get better maintenance for themselves. Such masters and mistresses use their servants as beasts, only for their own turn, without any respect to the servants' good: whereby they pervert the main end of that relation betwixt master and servant, which is a mutual and reciprocal good to pass from the one to the other.

Servants were a responsibility, not an excuse for idleness, and Gouge harshly condemned 'such mistresses as spend all the morning in lying a-bed and dressing themselves (a custom clean contrary to that which is noted of the good mistress), and at noon when they come out of their chamber, chide and brawl, because things are not more forward'.[76]

Servants, for their part, were bound by ties of obedience enhanced by filial reverence and faithfulness. Like childhood, service was a stage in the lifecycle; as children grew up and became parents, so maidservants expected to marry and often to become mistresses. Gouge used this assumption to encourage good behavior, telling servants that God would, 'when they come to keep servants, provide such servants for them, as they were to their masters.'[77] Servants were supposed to serve their masters and mistresses sincerely and faithfully. This meant that they were to do their work carefully and with good will, to carry themselves humbly and obediently, and to look after their masters' interests as their own. In contrast, bad servants wasted their employers' goods, worked unwillingly, laggardly, and carelessly, seized all opportunities to sneak away to riotous amusements, talked back to their masters and mistresses, and spread household secrets abroad. Apprentices and serving-men were most likely to be 'corrected' in Bridewell for major faults like embezzling their masters' goods, running away, and even striking their masters, while maidservants seem to have been more frequently condemned for pilfering and their saucy tongues.

> The conditions of a good maidservant are that she be careful, faithful, patient, neat, and pleasing, that she be quick, and handsome, and of few words, honest in her word, deed, and attire: diligent in a household, and have skill in washing, brewing, sewing, and spinning, but chiefly in holding her peace.[78]

---

[75] BRHA, BCB 3, fo. 213r.
[76] Gouge, *Of domesticall duties*, 681, 683.
[77] Ibid. 644.
[78] Cleaver and Dod, *A godly forme of houshold government*, 381.

William Gouge instructed servants to refrain from speaking except for good cause, and noted that 'scolding maids that will have the last words of their mistress much offend herein'. Both men and maids were condemned for gossiping: 'Contrary to keeping close the secrets of masters, is blabbing abroad all such things as servants know concerning their masters: which is too common a fault: for when servants of divers houses men or maids meet together, all their talk for the most part is of their masters and mistresses, whereby it cometh to pass that all the secrets of a house are soon known about the whole town or city.' Servants were also overly inclined, Gouge thought, to 'excess in apparel': rather than dressing humbly, they tried to ape their masters and mistresses' fashions on the cheap, 'if not so costly, yet in show as specious and brave'. This was a quiet form of rebellion; it demonstrated servants' inward refusal to accept their subordination. 'If the Queen of Sheba were now living, she would as much wonder at the disorder of servants in these days, as then she wondered at the comely order of Solomon's servants,' the clergyman acidly noted.[79]

Deviation from the godly ideal did not always entail cruelty or exploitation. In middling London households, where little social distance separated mistress and maid (and indeed little physical distance, since maidservants often slept on trundle beds in their employers' rooms), the prescribed formality was softened by the intimacy of everyday life. Maids might maintain friendships with their former mistresses long after leaving service, like Elizabeth Osborne, a young porter's wife, who reported in 1637 that she often visited her old employer Mistress Kinder.[80] Anne Smith, 23, played a practical joke on her employer. One Sunday, 'she came into the Fleet in man's apparel in a merry mind to make herself merry and to try conclusions whether her master would know her by that disguise'.[81]

'About her business'

Maidservants were vague about the precise nature of their work. In the body politic of the household, the maidservants of London told their mistresses, they were adaptable members, ready for any task: 'we are to you very eyes, hands, feet and altogether. If ye bid us go, we run, [and] are as loath in anything to offend you, as ye are to be grieved.'[82] However, a basic set of household chores would have fallen to the lot of almost any maidservant: minding children, serving food and drink, fetching water, running errands, making up beds, emptying chamber pots, washing, scouring, sweeping, cooking, laundering, and starching. When they had a respite from these chores, maidservants took part in household production. Margaret Stockwood 'sate at work knitting at her master's door' when she heard a neighborhood matron call

---

[79] Gouge, *Of domesticall duties*, 599, 603, 628.
[80] Elizabeth Osborne, 1637 (LMA, DL/C/235, fo. 5r).
[81] Anne's escapade came to a soggy conclusion when some boys dunked her into a stone cistern, and she 'was wetted thereby'. However, authority was on her side: when she made complaint to the Warden of the Fleet about the boys, she said, 'he was exceeding angry with them for it'. John Chessus and Anne Smith, 1623 (GL MS 9189/1, fos. 151r, 146v).
[82] *A Letter sent by the maydens of London*, sig. A3v.

Humphrey Richardson a 'lousy rogue, nitty britch knave, and scurvy nitty britch knave' for throwing his pregnant maidservant out into the streets. Margaret Newes was also sitting at work when her fellow servant Thomasine Lambert—confirming Gouge's fears about servant gossip—asked a woman who had come to be paid for some work, 'Wottest thou what my master . . . hath a bastard at keeping?' Another maid overheard a quarrel while 'sitting sewing at her mistress's door'. Some maidservants specialized in particular kinds of needlework, and were paid by the piece rather than receiving yearly wages, like Susan More, who worked for 'one Randall Berk a bookseller without Cripplegate whose wife [used] the trade of point making', and reported that 'she had no wages but wrought her points by the gross and was paid by the gross for them, viz., five shillings and fourpence a gross.'[83]

Maidservants often sold wares or helped out in household shops, especially when the shops were primarily kept by their mistresses. Magdalen Hewes was 'serving of wares' in her mistress Mary Ticer's chandler's shop when Jane Overbury came in and began railing. Mary Barton, 18, worked as a sempster 'buying and selling' in her mistress's sempster's shop.[84] One of the reasons Thomas Bedle's neighbors thought he was courting Margaret Ilman, who lived with her uncle, a chandler, was that he spent so much time at her uncle's shop, where the neighbors had seen him 'assist and help her . . . in the sorting and selling of wares'.[85] Elizabeth Godfrey, a tailor's servant, was delivering 'a starched ruff' to Anne Millichoppe when she interrupted an illicit tryst, prompting Anne's lover to swear 'a great oath that [Elizabeth] had hindered him . . . of a good turn at that time'.[86]

Maidservants also worked in alehouses, victualling houses, taverns, and inns. Margaret Hatrell testified that a group of chapmen called her mistress an 'old whore' when she asked them to drink more peacefully. Sara Springall, maidservant in the Swan with Two Necks, was 'attending at the table' when some friendly chaffing about courtship turned into a food fight, culminating in the hurling of a trencher and a bloody nose. The Welshwoman Rose Morris worked as a tapster; she drew beer for the widow Margaret Battle and later served another widow who ran an alehouse. Margaret Millam from Cumberland was working in John Hall's victualling house in Houndsditch when she heard one woman abuse the other for following her husband.[87] Working in an alehouse, tavern, or inn

---

[83] Margaret Stockwood, 1610 (LMA, DL/C/219, fo. 122v); Margaret Newes, 1613 (LMA, DL/C/221, fo. 1434r); Isabel More, 1599 (LMA, DL/C/215, sl. 312); Susan More, 1608 (LMA, DL/C/218, pp. 138, 144). Another maid reported that she 'wrought with [a woman named Mary Luckin] and received of her money for her work so much as it came to'. Susan Goose, 1611 (LMA, DL/C/220, fo. 533v).

[84] Magdalen Hewes, 1599 (LMA, DL/C/215, sl. 385) and Mary Barton, 1611 (LMA, DL/C/220, fo. 816r).

[85] Bedle had also been seen to 'take the said Margaret Ilman in his arms and lay her on the counter in the same shop, and kiss her'. Elizabeth Parkhurst, 1633 (LMA, DL/C/232, fo. 4v).

[86] Elizabeth Godfrey, 1618 (LMA, DL/C/225, fo. 247r).

[87] Margaret Hatrell, 1633 (LMA, DL/C/630, fo. 68v); Sara Springall, 1610 (LMA, DL/C/219, fos. 211v–212r); Rose Morris and Margaret Battle, 1616–1617 (LMA, DL/C/224, fos. 128v–130 and 348v–349); and Margaret Millam, 1617 (LMA, DL/C/224, fos. 322v–323r).

was a good way to meet prospective suitors. Agnes Newman deposed that 'by reason she was servant in an alehouse in Holborn (common for all men to resort unto)', one Robert Chapman, a local ostler, 'sitting alone drinking and eating would call [her] to him and drink to her ... after a kind of love sort ... and had [her] sit by him by reason of which kind of courtesy he so showed every time at his coming to the said alehouse'.[88] However, this very public work had drawbacks as well. Joan Newick, a Yorkshire maid whose mistress ran a cook's shop, found herself the object of unwanted attention while she was shutting the shop windows: a man across the street first asked a local man 'where the cook's shop was that had the pretty wenches in it', then suggested: 'Let us go take one of them and hang her up for the sign.' This implied that the shop was in fact a brothel: its wares were young women. When Joan indignantly asked the man whether he was referring to her, his companion insulted her: 'Go to, huswife, you may hold your tongue. Thy mistress is a bawd and keepeth a bawdy house and thou art a whore.'[89]

Maidservants were expected to do anything they were told to do, as long as it was honest.[90] Their employers might lend them to a neighbor: a merchant tailor reported about Elizabeth Doughty that 'sometimes they did borrow her of Mr Browne to help them when they had occasion, as one neighbour would do another neighbour's servants ... she receiving of them no penny for her labour'.[91] They might also be commanded to perform unpleasant personal services. Jane Johnson, whose master was so often dangerously drunk that a friend of his made him agree to forfeit twenty shillings every time, reported often having to put the senseless man to bed. She testified disgustedly to the court that he was no fit husband for a rich orphan he claimed was contracted to marry him.[92] Anne Rumsey, in 1616, still remembered that 'about nine years sithence' she was told to care for her mistress's grown son, Richard Wade, 'then lying sick of the disease called the French pox in his said mother's house'. Under the direction of 'Mr Clowes and one Mr James, chirurgeons', it came to her lot to 'anoint the said Richard Wade and do other offices for him at that time for the said Richard Wade did smell in such intolerable manner that the said chirurgeons refused to handle him and were unwilling to come near him'.[93]

---

[88] Agnes Newman, *Robert Chapman c. Agnes Newman*, 1588 (LMA, DL/C/213, pp. 416, 418–20, 437).
[89] Joan Newick, *Joan Matthews c. Richard Kimble*, 1614 (LMA, DL/C/222, fo. 269). Of course, prostitution itself could be classified as a variant of maidservants' work, as we shall see in Ch. 3.
[90] Indeed, as Laura Gowing has shown, some masters considered that even sexual services fell within the expected purview of maidservants' work. *Common Bodies: Women, Touch and Power in Seventeenth-Century England* (New Haven, Conn., 2003), 61.
[91] Gabriel Coste, 1572 (LMA, DL/C/211/1, fo. 135v).
[92] The suit was dropped when the drunkard went bankrupt and disappeared from London to avoid his debtors. Jane Johnson, *Francis Browne c. Anne Parstowe*, 1616 (LMA, DL/C/224, fo. 343v).
[93] Anne Rumsey, 1616 (LMA, DL/C/224, fo. 281r).

RARE ALTERNATIVES: INDEPENDENT WORK AND APPRENTICESHIP

In London, young unmarried women had few licit alternatives to service: almost no women were apprenticed in London's companies after 1450, the small businesses run by wives and widows required capital, and maids were specifically prohibited from hucksetering and charring. Civic authorities often assumed that maids out of service were loose or idle, and treated them with hostility.[94] Although a few independent spinsters can be found among the consistory court witnesses, they were rare exceptions. Elizabeth Hart from Gloucestershire, 37, told the court that she had formerly worked as a maidservant but had just recently moved to Southwark, where she got her living 'by winding of silk'. She was 'a very poor woman and little worth', and had recently given birth to an illegitimate child, living for the five months surrounding her delivery with her aunt and uncle in Shoreditch.[95] She had probably been obliged to leave service during her pregnancy. Katherine Welsh, a 19-year-old immigrant from Salisbury, sold oysters on the street in defiance of the rule that only sober matrons could be fishwives, and 30-year-old Dorothy Calverley from Herefordshire worked as a live-in sick-nurse and also sold 'oaten cakes'. There was even one shopkeeper, Mary Jones, 21, from Cheshire, who reported: 'she keepeth a shop to mend stockings and by that profession she getteth her living and is worth in her goods her debts paid forty shillings and hath not been taxed.' Mary rented a shop from a widow and lodged in her house; the fact that she was living with a responsible adult may have sheltered her from official disapproval.[96]

Although women were not able to enter the London companies through apprenticeship like men, they could still be trained in particular crafts. Elizabeth Barton, 27, from Shropshire, learned 'to make gold and silver bone lace of several sorts and fashions' from a woman who also employed 21-year-old Elizabeth Dover, a London native, in lace-making.[97] There were also formal apprenticeships, like that of Mary Griffin, a 16-year-old Welsh girl, apprenticed for seven years to Anne Hawes, a musician's wife who kept a sempster's shop.[98] While Mary Griffin probably hoped to become a sempster in her own right, most formal female apprenticeships offered little in the way of specialized training: apprentice girls were essentially unpaid servants.

---

[94] See Marjorie Keniston McIntosh, *Working Women in English Society, 1300–1620* (Cambridge, 2005), 135, 38; Griffiths, *Lost Londons*, 128; Froide, *Never Married*, 25–34.
[95] Elizabeth Hart, *Edward Snowden c. William Roberts*, 1618 (LMA, DL/C/225, fos. 371–372r).
[96] Katherine Welsh, 1634 (LMA, DL/C/630, fo. 228v); Dorothy Calverley, 1621 (LMA, DL/C/228, fos. 128r, 129v); Mary Jones, 1617 (LMA, DL/C/225, fos. 21–22r).
[97] Elizabeth Barton and Elizabeth Dover, *Helen Wigmore c. Sara Webb*, 1631 (LMA, DL/C/232, fos. 27r, 26v). Ellen Jordan (Elizabeth Barton's countrywoman and perhaps her sister) had originally negotiated Elizabeth Barton's 'apprenticeship' with Sara Webb. When Helen Wigmore, Sara's neighbor, informed Ellen Jordan that the agreement was not being honored, Sara called Helen 'a base queane and a jade'. See Ellen Jordan, 1631 (LMA, DL/C/232, fos. 25v–26r).
[98] Mary Griffin, 1610 (LMA, DL/C/219, fos. 145–146r).

44   City Women

Pauper apprentices in huswifery were in practice the least fortunate of maidservants, and the most vulnerable to exploitation by employers like Alice Fulham, a woman living in Miter Alley, who seems to have specialized in taking in apprentice girls. In a 1611 defamation case, no fewer than five of Alice Fulham's current or former apprentices testified. Isabel Scillicorne, a Welsh girl of about 18, had been there for one and a half years. Ursula Roberts, 24, reported that she had 'been apprentice to [Alice Fulham] these four years last past and hath no wages of her or her husband'. Elizabeth Broome, also 24, of Bristol, had served six years, and Elizabeth Bourne, 21, had served eight. This last apprentice reported that her mistress had once beaten her 'with a holly wand for giving her cross speeches and so much as she saith she felt the same strokes a good while after'. They all agreed that 'none of them receive any wages ... but have only meat, drink, lodging and apparel allowed them'. However, according to Jane Borer, a former apprentice, the apparel in question was hardly adequate. She had left her mistress on bitter terms, only fully escaping when her husband redeemed her. After five years of apprenticeship, she reported, she had intended to leave Alice Fulham, but her mistress 'earnestly entreated [Jane] to continue with her still and promised to give [her] forty shillings a year', changing her status from apprentice to ordinary servant. Jane Borer said that she 'not having clothes sufficient for her necessary wearing was contented to stay with her if the said Alice would then provide her of sufficient clothes, which ... the said Alice did accordingly'. After two years of service and a further six weeks spent lodging with Alice, Jane proposed to leave, presumably to marry her future husband, the point-maker Richard Borer. Then 'the said Alice brought in a reckoning of fifty-two shillings which she said [Jane] did owe her for a part of the money which she laid out to furnish [her] with clothes and for some other charges besides, which money [Jane] thought hardly of ... for that she did verily think the said Alice had not disbursed so much money for clothes and other necessaries for her'. However, to free his bride, Richard Borer ultimately paid Alice Fulham the full sum.[99]

While apprenticeship had the merit of stability, it offered little else. Most apprentice girls did not choose their lot: they were orphans, foundlings, or the children of overburdened parents who agreed to give up their children in exchange for poor relief. These pauper apprentices began their terms at a much younger age than craft apprentices, in extreme cases directly after leaving their nurses, and parishes paid masters and mistresses a small premium for their keep. London officials complained that they were burdened with the poor children of surrounding rural districts as well as their own, as some parishes dumped their unwanted children in the city, sending them with carriers to London where theoretically they were to be apprenticed but in fact they were simply left on the streets.[100] These

---

[99] *Alice Fulham c. Ellen Alsop*, 1611 (LMA, DL/C/220): Isabel Scillicorne (fos. 597–8), Ursula Roberts (fos. 592–3), Elizabeth Broome (fos. 594–5), Elizabeth Bourne (fos. 595v, 597r), and Jane Borer (fo. 546).

[100] Griffiths, *Lost Londons*, 105–6; A. L. Beier, *Masterless Men: The Vagrancy Problem in England 1560–1640* (New York, 1985), 45–6, 217.

frightened children were the humblest migrants of all; for them, even a harsh apprenticeship may have been a welcome refuge.

MIGRATION AND MORTALITY

Migrant maids moved to London in hopes of high wages, fine apparel, and good marriages, but many found their deaths in the city instead. Jane Martindale's parents, who worried that their daughter would succumb to the city's foul air, had reason to fear for her health:

> After her arrival in the city she was quickly infected with the pestilence. Yet it dealt pretty favorably with her (perhaps too favorably for she after had it again), but though the pest was over the plague was not, for she was still kept shut up, and her money grew very low. Then with the prodigal, she thought oft upon the plenty of her father's house, yet knowing upon what terms she had left it, she concealed her straits from us ... [H]er money grew so near an end, that she had thoughts to sell her hair, which was very lovely both for length and colour.[101]

Ultimately, city air seems to have agreed with Jane. She survived the pestilence, married a gentleman, and set up an inn, only to succumb to smallpox seven years later on her way home, having decided to move closer to her father after her mother's death.[102] Many others met their ends sooner. In addition to smallpox and consumption, London was periodically visited by devastating outbreaks of plague, with the crisis years of 1593, 1603, and 1625 accounting for nearly 15 per cent of all London deaths between 1580 and 1650.[103] The young, untested by previous epidemics, were particularly likely to die. Court records provide little evidence of plague other than an eloquent silence,[104] but parish records tell a fuller story. Among those buried in the parish of St Botolph Aldgate in late spring of the fatal year 1593 were a number of maidservants:

> Dorothy Merrick, servant unto Robert Jones, a glover, was buried the twentieth day of May.   15 years old
> Alice Fletcher, servant unto Thomas Perker, a gunmaker, was buried the twenty-third day of May.   22 years old
> Elizabeth Bricket, servant to the late deceased John Edge, buttonmaker, was buried the fifth day of June.   18 years old
> Elizabeth French, servant to John Edge, a buttonmaker, was buried the eleventh day of June.   20 years old
> Anne Anderson, servant unto John Arnold, a basketmaker, was buried the twenty-fourth day of June.   12 years old[105]

---

[101] Martindale, *The Life of Adam Martindale*, 7–8.
[102] Her brother thought this showed 'that God doth what, when, and by what means he pleaseth'. Ibid. 18.
[103] Finlay, *Population and Metropolis*, 17.
[104] For example, 58 women testified in 1624, but only 6 in 1625. By 1626 the court had recovered, with 88 female witnesses.
[105] GL MS 9221, Burial register of St Botolph Aldgate, May–June 1593.

By August, the burial rate had quickened; the first week alone saw the deaths of ten maidservants in the parish. Their burials were recorded amid a sea of others, including what must have been most of the parish's young children. In poor parishes like St Botolph Aldgate, masters and servants perished together; in wealthier parishes, where householding families might leave for the countryside, servants left to mind the house were particularly at risk.[106]

Serious illness cannot have been pleasant for any early modern Londoners, but maidservants were worse off than married people and young children, who could expect to be cared for in their homes, and perhaps even than apprentices, whose ties to their masters were stronger. In many cases the hardships of illness were compounded by unemployment and even homelessness, especially for maids who suffered from lingering bad health. These young women relied on kin and friends to help them, like Alice Chitham, who deposed in 1629 that she 'being sickly and not able to undergo service is now maintained by her brother'.[107]

Alice was fortunate to have such a refuge. Ellen Stone, who died around 1615, probably of consumption, was tended in the last two weeks of her life in King's Hospital in Highgate, but her experience before reaching that doubtful haven was aggravated by callous treatment from parish authorities. Ellen's closest friends in London were Mary and Thomas Wolley: her parents and Mary's had been neighbors in the country, and before her illness Ellen worked making collars with Thomas Wolley.[108] When Ellen fell 'very sick... by reason of which sickness she was brought into so weak and low estate of body that she was not fit nor able to do any service for her living', she lived with the Wolleys in Plow Yard, Fetter Lane, for a few weeks, then was moved to the house of another acquaintance, Roger Arney, a poor gentleman who lived 'by writing of reports at the common law'. It seems likely that she moved to Arney's house to avoid the attentions of parish officials, but in any case, they found her there the next day. Arney reported that after Ellen had been there one night, 'the constables of St Andrew's... fearing that the said parish should be charged with the keeping of her in her sickness caused the said Ellen Stone to be carried away'.[109]

The dying woman was given 'an order or warrant... for the conveyance of her from constable to constable until she should be brought into that parish where she was born'. Unable to walk, she was carried by porters: Arney said she was taken away from his house in one of his chairs. However, in her feeble state she could not endure travel: Mary Wolley, perceiving that Ellen could not 'be carried any further without danger of present death', had her taken to the hospital in Highgate, a former lazar house, instead.[110] There, Mary Wolley negotiated with the matron, Elizabeth Stockwell, for her care. While hospitals filled the wealthy with terror and

---

[106] Finlay, *Population and Metropolis*, 129.
[107] Alice Chitham, 1629 (LMA, DL/C/231, fo. 423r).
[108] However, she had also spent a spell in Newgate on suspicion of having stolen 'a beaker and five spoons'. See Agnes Baseley, *Elizabeth Stockwell c. Mary Wolley*, 1615 (LMA, DL/C/223, fo. 129v).
[109] Roger Arney, 1615 (LMA, DL/C/223, fos. 124v, 125r).
[110] See John H. Lloyd, *The history, topography, and antiquities of Highgate, in the county of Middlesex* (Highgate, Middlesex, 1888), 179–80.

disgust, having a quiet bed to die in was an improvement over being hustled about by porters. Stockwell's niece at the hospital said that Elizabeth Stockwell 'was very careful and watchful over her and provided for all her convenient necessaries fitting her quality.'[111] Such care that Ellen received may have been motivated in part by interest in her goods, for even she had a trunk of clothes in the Wolleys' house: this account of her death reached the courts when Mary Wolley and Elizabeth Stockwell both laid claim to it. Indeed, it is possible that Ellen made promises to both parties, using her possessions as a bargaining chip to procure some kindness in her final days.

It could not have comforted dying maidservants to know that their deaths would leave no lasting void. The most vulnerable sectors of the population were also the most replaceable. High birth rates quickly refilled streets that must have seemed bare of children after plague years, and the deaths of maidservants and apprentices were rapidly obscured by the streams of hopeful migrant youths who flocked to take their places.

[111] Roger Arney and Elizabeth Aldersey (LMA, DL/C/223, fos. 125r, 130).

2

Making a Match

Popular ballads described London as a paradise for poor maidens. There, a country maid boasted, even a friendless girl could find herself rich in eager suitors:

> This London is a gallant place
> to raise a Lass's fortune;
> For I that came of simple race
> brave Roarers do importune:
> I little thought in Worcestershire
> to find such high preferment here,
> For I have but a Mark a year,
> and that my mother gave me.

Men of every sort vied for her favor, she claimed: 'Though I am but a silly Wench/ of country education,/Yet I am woo'd by Dutch and French,/and almost every nation.' They showered her with expensive gifts and she lived like a lady, with the newest fashions and lackeys at her command. She urged her fellow maids to hasten to London to share in her good fortune:

> I would my sister Sue at home,
> knew how I live in fashion,
> That she might up to London come
> to learn this occupation . . .
> Now blessed be that happy day
> that I came to the City:
> And for the Carrier will I pray,
> before I end my Ditty.[1]

This was a fantasy of courtship endlessly prolonged. In reality, a migrant maid's life in London was one of toil, not 'perfumed gloves' and horse-drawn coaches. However, it contained a kernel of truth: poor girls could marry better in London than at home. Geographical mobility was one of the few advantages of going into service, and by journeying to London and its favorable marriage market, maids pursued their 'preferment' through the restricted means open to them. Moving to the capital was a risky strategy, but likely to pay off for young women of strong

---

[1] M. P., *A fayre portion for a fayre mayd: or, The thriftie mayd of Worstersheere* (London, 1633). Along the same lines, Thomas Powell advised a gentleman in straitened circumstances to place two of his daughters in service in London where they could capture the affections of lonely, upwardly mobile young men. *The art of thriving. Or, The plaine path-way to preferment* (London, 1636), 118–19.

health and nerves, who chose to leave familiar certainties behind to seek their fortunes in the city. Word of London's marital opportunities spread far: a 'Lancashire lass' in a different ballad recounted how she heard:

> ... that London is a place,
> Where Lasses may to preferment come,
> within a little space: ...
> These words did my desire inflame,
> at home I could not bide
> But up to London in haste I came.

However, as she soon found, preferment was by no means inevitable in London.[2] Maidservants seeking matrimony would need to keep their wits about them as they negotiated the hazardous and emotionally fraught terrain of courtship, striving to avoid unwanted entanglements while shoring up desirable attachments with all the means at their disposal.

'A HAPPY HUSBAND'

Finding a good husband was crucial for a London maid. A good match brought wealth, security, companionship, and status; a bad one could be disastrous. Young women could not afford to blindly accept the first suitor at hand: their future welfare and happiness were at stake. Joan Hartley, accused of thieving from her mistress's lodger, bitterly confessed that one Mistress Gill had persuaded her to steal the goods, promising to find her a husband as a reward, '"which," quoth she, "a husband indeed she help me with but he was nothing worth for which I am as much bound to curse her as for bringing me into these troubles."' When a more prudent London maidservant discovered in 1613 that her suitor had been treated in St Thomas's Hospital, worrying that he was infected with the pox, she sent her aunt to make inquiries. Although he protested that he had acquired the disease innocently and that it probably was not the pox anyway, she called off the match.[3]

Fortunately for early modern maids, there was plenty of advice to be had: in addition to the counsel of friends and family, conduct books and ballads had much to say about the making of marriage. Early modern writers generally agreed that virtue and equality in age, rank, and wealth marked a good spouse, whether male or female. The clergyman Daniel Rogers wrote that 'such equality as possibly can be attained, should be in this condition, as of years, education, disposition, breed,

---

[2] The girl found a suitor soon enough, but he was slain just before their marriage, leaving her pregnant. She hoped to die rather than to go home and shame her kin, but was persuaded instead to tell them that her husband had died in the Swedish wars. Following this wise advice, she married a yeoman and lived happily ever after. M. P., *The bonny bryer, or A Lancashire lass her sore lamentation, for the death of her love, and her owne reputation* (London, 1630).

[3] William Mullins, 1607 (LMA, DL/C/217, pp.186–8); Phyllis Gay, Katherine Currier, and Edward Barwicke, *Robert Ibotson c. Elizabeth Tarver*, 1613 (LMA, DL/C/224, fos. 118v, 119v, 94).

estate, and the like', and noted disapprovingly that 'young are married to old, rich to poor, untaught to well trained, harsh to amiable'. Patrick Hannay, author of *A Happy Husband; or, Directions for a Maide to Choose her Mate*, agreed that equality of birth was desirable, and told his readers that the ideal husband was a paragon of moderation, comely but manly, neither too short nor too tall. Riches should be esteemed less than virtue, and a good man must be free of the three great vices: drinking was the root of all troubles, a gamester was likely to end his days in shameful poverty, and past unchastity in a husband presaged a philandering future. What was more, a lewd husband was likely to be jealous as well, 'For vice is ever conversant in ill,/And guilty as itself thinks others still.' In addition to avoiding these major vices, a good husband possessed the virtues of honesty, wisdom, and piety. He feared God, but out of love, not superstition. He was of few words but spoke graciously, was moderately learned but no scholar; he was prudent, just, valiant, and temperate.[4]

Popular ballads provided a different perspective for maids in search of mates. These also denounced the masculine vices of drinking, whoremongering, gambling, and jealousy, but praised good looks, good temper, and generous provision more than sober moralists might have thought seemly. One 'young lass' announced:

> Some wed for money,
>   and some wed for Land;
> But I'll choose a honey,
> Shall be a handsome young man.

She would prefer a man 'of good size,' she said, but as long as he was wise and good-looking, she would not be picky. She refused to marry a fool, no matter how rich, and equally scorned an ill-tempered 'clown'.

> ... with anger he'll frown;
> Then must I beware,
>   perchance with his hand
> He'll strike me o'th ear:
> But I'll have no such man.

Nor would she marry a man 'somewhat jealous': 'oh hang up such a man!' she scoffed. These particulars aside, she was open to suggestions:

> Let him be a Tailor,
>   or a neat Shoemaker,
> A Weaver or a Baker:
> If he be neat and comely,
>   my love is soon won ...
> Then shall he be welcome
>   unto pretty Nan,

---

[4] Daniel Rogers, *Matrimoniall honour: or, The mutuall crowne and comfort of godly, loyall, and chaste marriage* (London, 1642), 27; Patrick Hannay, *A happy husband or, Directions for a maide to choose her mate* (London, 1619), sig. B1v–C1r.

Making a Match 51

> For I am delightsome
> To a handsome young man.[5]

A 'merry conceited lass' in a different ballad was eager to find a husband who could buy her fancy clothing so she could impress her friends:

> I am a young woman and fain I would have,
> *tera la tal da rat de ra do,*
> A husband that will maintain me brave,
> 'Tis that which my heart doth wish and crave.

She wanted a 'new hat and gown', she said, so she could 'flaunt it up and down/ With some of the bravest in the town', a sure route to neighborhood glory. If he was good to her, the lass promised, 'a courteous wife he shall me find'. If not, she would repay him in kind. She, too, feared marrying a drunkard who would go out boozing, only to come home penniless, sick, and in a foul temper.[6] In *The married-woman's case*, a wife advised maids to choose their husbands cautiously. '[A]quarreling Coxcomb', she warned, would inevitably raise his hand against his wife: 'She seldom shall go without her face black.' Whoremongers were to be utterly shunned, as they might be 'bitten with . . . the Pox' or some other infectious disease. A drunkard would love drink better than his family:

> A Woman that married a drunken sot,
>   must look for no competent living;
> For he all the day will sit at the Pot,
>   and never takes thought for thriving:
> From alehouse to alehouse all day he will roam,
> While she sits with bread and fair water at home,
> Whatever he gets, he giveth her none . . .
> And if she have children, her grief is the more,
>   to hear them complain for vittle,
> While their wretched father ith'Alehouse doth roar,
>   and thinketh of their want but little.

A gambling or jealous husband was also bound to poison married life. She concluded that maidens must try their suitors before they married them, 'for time will bring every action to view'.[7] With the benefit of all this advice, a London maid who attended religious services, listened to ballads, and paid attention to the lives of those around her could conclude that the ideal husband was young, cheerful, and comely, an industrious, virtuous workman who would spend his free time making merry with his wife (not with whores or his boon companions),

---

[5] *A pretty new ditty: or, A young lasses resolution, as her mind I truly scan, who shews in conclusion, she loves a handsome young man* (London, 1633).
[6] L. P., *The merry conceited lasse, whose hearts desire was set on fire, a husband for to have; in hope that he would certainly, maintaine her fine and brave* (London, 1640).
[7] Martin Parker, *The married-womans case, or, Good counsell to mayds, to be carefull of hastie marriage by the example of other married-women* (London, 1627).

and a good provider who would make much of her, granting her leisure and money for her own concerns.

THE LONDON MARRIAGE MARKET

The ideal husband was an elusive creature, but he and his imperfect fellows were easier to find in London than elsewhere: the guilds, the port, and the court attracted thousands of youths looking for work or advancement. The city swarmed with young men, with 113 men dying for every 100 women for the period from 1629 to 1642. Finlay suggests a sex ratio among the living population of perhaps 110 men for every 100 women, but other estimates are even higher: in 1622 Boulton finds a ratio of 123 male servants and apprentices to 100 maidservants in the Boroughside, Southwark. Pointing to the large numbers of apprentices who left London and were not buried there, Leonard Schwarz proposes a sex ratio for the population aged 15 and over as high as 124:100 in 1550 and fully 139:100 in 1600.[8] London's high mortality rates also increased marital opportunities for migrant maids: the frequent deaths of spouses and children meant that rather than progressing decorously down lineages, family capital might be shuffled between new marriage partners with alarming—or alluring—rapidity. Given a favorable marriage market, even impecunious migrant servants appear to have been able to find husbands.[9]

London women married early: their age at first marriage was substantially lower than that of Englishwomen generally. Table 2.1 shows the percentage of women at each age who were or had been married, and Fig. 2.1 illustrates the age distribution of maiden witnesses. These data, based on 2,416 responses, suggest that London women married for the first time around the age of 23, with hardly any remaining single into their 40s. In contrast, marriage in rural England was comparatively late: Schofield and Wrigley find a mean age at first marriage of 26 for women and 28 for men for the period 1600–1649.[10]

Although London maids married relatively young, very youthful marriages were rare. Both cultural and economic reasons dictated that marriage be delayed at least until the late teens. Adolescent girls were not considered physically fit for marriage and its accompanying sexual and maternal duties. When James Billingsley and his two brothers abducted the heiress Susan Wittey and forced her to marry him, a number of witnesses in the ensuing case mentioned Susan's age as well as her tears in the church, vehement objections, attempts to escape, and refusal to eat or

---

[8] Roger Finlay, *Population and Metropolis: The Demography of London 1580–1650* (Cambridge, 1981), 140–1; Jeremy Boulton, *Neighbourhood and Society: A London Suburb in the Seventeenth Century* (Cambridge, 1987), 135; Leonard Schwarz, 'London Apprentices in the Seventeenth Century: Some Problems', *Local Population Studies* 38 (1987), 21.

[9] By the time Rogers published his text on marriage in 1642, the tide had already begun to turn. He thought that 'the multitude of the female sex, and the contempt thereof, hath brought it to pass, that every boy new out of his prenticeship, values himself by the scores and hundreds, although scarce worth a groat besides his occupations'. *Matrimoniall honour*, 51.

[10] E. A. Wrigley and R. S. Schofield, *The Population History of England 1541–1871: A Reconstruction* (London, 1981), 255, 260.

Table 2.1 Age and marital status

Age of witnesses	% married or widowed	Total witnesses
13–15	0	6.5
16–18	4	74.0
19–21	23	193.0
22–24	50	223.0
25–26	70	140.0
27–28	76	144.0
29–31	87	236.0
32–33	95	113.5
34–35	95	103.0
36–38	96	145.5
39–42	97	262.5
43–47	99	155.5
48–52	99	222.5
53–57	100	99.0
58–65	99	162.5
66 and older	100	55.5

Note: The uneven age categories are designed to smooth over flaws in the data resulting from witnesses rounding their ages to the nearest full decade, and to provide meaningful sample sizes. The startling presence of fractional witnesses reflects the practice of some women of reporting their age imprecisely, e.g. '31 or 32'. A handful of women were counted twice because they appeared in court at substantial time intervals. For example, Cicely Noone from Dorset testified in 1615 when she was 26 and married to a tailor, and again in 1620 when she reported that she was a widow and 32 years old (see LMA, DL/C/223, fo. 209r and DL/C/227, fo. 215v). However, most women who testified multiple times did so in the context of a single set of disputes within the same year or two, and were counted only once.

undress. One man deposed that she was no older than 13 or 14, and 'also for that she is of a very small stature of body she is very unfit to be married and to live with a man as his wife'. Another mentioned 'her tender years' and 'the small stature of her body'.[11] Even girls in their late teens could be considered too young for marriage. When the chandler John Swinsted asked Elizabeth Broad, 17, to marry him, she said she would if her mother would consent. However, when asked, Elizabeth's mother said that it would be good to delay the marriage for two or three years. Indeed, a teenage bride could hardly exercise proper household authority: as a pamphleteer noted, she 'knows not how to chide her man without laughing, having been so childishly familiar with servants before her marriage'.[12]

A large majority of London women in the consistory court sample married by the age of 30. Only about 5 per cent were left unmarried in their early 30s, and only 2 per cent remained single in their 40s. Lifelong female spinsterhood was almost

[11] John Highby and Peter Holt, *James Billingsley c. Susan Wittey*, 1614 (LMA, DL/C/222, fos. 91v, 162r).
[12] John Swinsted, 1597 (LMA, DL/C/215 sl. 204–5); 'A Young Novice's New Younger Wife', in Henry Parrot, *Cures for the itch* (London, 1626), sig. A7v.

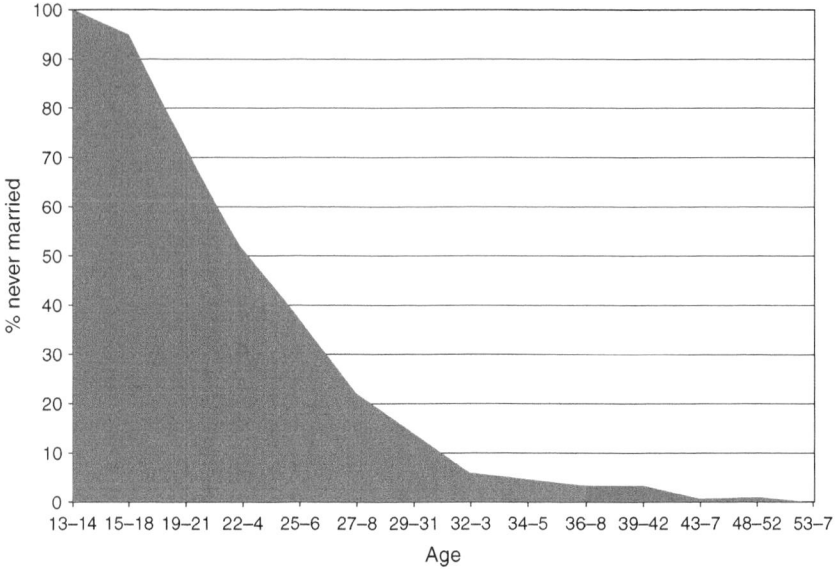

Figure 2.1 Percentage of maiden witnesses by age

completely absent: all but two of the women over 50 described themselves as wives or widows. This universality of marriage presents a stark contrast with the high rates of lifelong singlehood found in most English parishes in the early seventeenth century: estimates suggest that while only 4.2 per cent of women born around 1566 did not marry, the comparable figure for those born around 1586 had climbed to 17.4 per cent, and over a fifth of women born around 1606 never wed.[13] Moreover, a number of the older London spinsters who appeared as witnesses were recent arrivals in the city, like Magdalen ap Richard, 50, who had arrived from Wales at the age of 48, and Luce Golson, 42, who had immigrated from Bury St Edmunds only a year before she testified in 1636.[14] Out of 967 London witnesses who were 40 or older, only fourteen had never been married, and of these, at least six had migrated to the city in their late 30s or 40s.

Given the choice, nearly all London women preferred to marry and to escape the drudgery and subordination of service. Aside from the often dubious security of a

---

[13] Keith Wrightson, *Earthly Necessities: Economic Lives in Early Modern Britain* (New Haven, Conn., 2000), 223. See also Wrigley and Schofield, *Population History of England*, 260; Judith M. Bennett and Amy Froide, 'A Singular Past', in Bennett and Froide (eds), *Singlewomen in the European Past 1250–1800* (Philadelphia, 1999). While Finlay argues from burial registers that in London 'marriage was by no means universal', his figures are based on a small sample of 283 women, and he tends to classify ambiguous cases as maids. A larger sample of 478 women from the burial register of St Botolph Aldgate between 1582 and 1593 corroborates the consistory court data: 57% of 22–24-year-olds were married, and 96% of the 214 women who died between the ages of 32 and 50 were either wives or widows. See Finlay, *Population and Metropolis*, 139; GL MS 9221.

[14] Magdalen ap Richard, 1617 (LMA, DL/C/225, fo. 81r); Luce Golson, 1635 (LMA, DL/C/234, fo. [2]51r).

husband's provision, marriage was an essential rite of passage for full participation in neighborhood life, and most maids surely saw marriage as a step towards status and power rather than a retreat from independence. One ballad heroine declared to her prospective husband:

> ... I am minded
> to lead a merry life:
> And be as well maintained,
> as any City wife:
> And live a gallant Mistress
> of Maidens that shall be
> More fairer than the blossoms,
> that bloom upon the Tree.[15]

Under the circumstances, women who never married or married very late tended to be unlucky or unusual, like Margery Noble, the oldest single witness, who testified in 1622, when she said she was 34 and maidservant to one Sir Anthony Twyne, and again in 1633, when she claimed to be 58.[16] Her carelessness in reporting her age was characteristic: other witnesses thought her very unreliable indeed. In 1622, a witness reported that no Sir Anthony Twyne lived in Margery's parish, St Martin in the Fields, and that she was a 'wandering person'. A Westminster victualer's wife who had known her for six years reported her to

> have lived idly and carelessly up and down the court in the nature of a laundress and while she lived in and about Westminster where she could get her a lodging, not staying long in any one place, her behaviour and course of life was such that she did set men and their wives at deadly hatred and dissension together insomuch as her said ill course of life in that kind being made known to men of authority there, they did expel her out of that place as this deponent was told thereof by a barber's wife living there whose husband and she the said Margery did set at strife together.

Another woman said Margery had 'no other means of living but only by preferring of young maids to services'—not, as we have seen, a respectable mode of life.[17] In 1633, the deputy keeper of a prison in Clerkenwell said that she had been committed there in 1632 'for detaining divers clothes and other goods from Elizabeth the wife of Richard Rochester'. He remembered her well:

> the said Margery Noble did behave herself in an ill fashion whilst she was in the prison and did abuse and revile [him] and his wife and made complaint to Justice Long that [he] or his wife did detain from her a chain of five pounds value which [his] child had

---

[15] *A country new Jigge betweene Simon and Susan* (London, 1620). Elsewhere, lifelong singlehood was more common, and singlewomen developed their own strategies for living outside conventional family roles. See Amy M. Froide, *Never Married: Singlewomen in Early Modern England* (Oxford, 2005).

[16] Margery Noble (GL MS 9189/1, fo. 3r; LMA, DL/C/630, fo. 214). If the second age estimate was correct, then the Margery Noble brought to Bridewell in 1607 for 'being found drunk in a tavern' may also be the same woman. BRHA, BCB 5, fo. 251r.

[17] Philip Davies, Martha Booth, and Katherine Davies, 1622 (GL MS 9189/1, fos. 86v, 92r, 88v).

Table 2.2 Age at marriage for migrant and London-born women

Age	% migrants married or widowed (n = 1,180)	% natives married or widowed (n = 370)
13–15	0	0
16–18	2	10
19–21	19	32
22–4	41	71
25–6	57	79
27–8	73	93
29–31	83	88
32–3	93	97
34–5	93	100
36–8	96	100
39–42	96	98

lost with playing with it and afterward being found appeared to be worth not five shillings.[18]

She had done another stint in prison in 1633 for defamation. Whether Margery was forced into a disorderly lifestyle by the absence of other opportunities for poor middle-aged spinsters, or whether she preferred the freedom of living 'idly and carelessly up and down' cannot be determined, but her continual brushes with the law underline the irregularity of her position.

While nearly all London women married, migrant women did so at somewhat older ages than native Londoners. Breaking down the consistory court witnesses into migrants and London-born women, we find that the native women married, on average, by the age of 21 or 22, while the migrants only did so by the age of 24 or 25 (see Table 2.2). This pattern echoes the conclusions of Vivien Brodsky Elliott, who finds that London-born maids who married by license wed at an average age of 20, while migrant women did so later, around 24.[19]

Migrant women also married men of somewhat lower social status than London-born maids, but not overwhelmingly so. As can be seen in Table 2.3, a comparison of the occupations of the husbands of migrant and London-born women suggests that the two groups married men of roughly similar rank.[20] Only for the very highest and very lowest classifications of male status do significant differences appear: migrants were significantly less likely to be married to gentlemen and

---

[18] Thomas Ayre, 1633 (LMA, DL/C/630, fo. 248v).

[19] The Londoners who testified for the consistory court married a year or so later than those who wed by license, perhaps because they were drawn from a poorer, more representative population. Brodsky Elliott, 'Single Women in the London Marriage Market', 84–6. For the growing popularity of marriage by license in London, see Jeremy Boulton, 'Itching After Private Marryings? Marriage Customs in Seventeenth-Century London', *London Journal* 16.1 (1991), 15–34.

[20] Reflecting the importance of immigration in the London population, 76.7% of all the women in this sample were migrants, so percentages above and below that figure imply that migrants were over- and under-represented, respectively.

Table 2.3 Husbands' status for migrant and London-born women

Status	Husband's occupation	Migrants	London natives	Migrants
Group 1	Gentleman	38	18	
	Esquire	3	0	
	Total	41	18	69.5%
Group 2	Draper	8	2	
	Goldsmith	14	5	
	Merchant tailor	32	12	
	Merchant	2	0	
	Grocer	12	2	
	Yeoman	34	9	
	Haberdasher	18	6	
	Mercer	0	2	
	Ironmonger	0	1	
	Scrivener	10	0	
	Clergyman	3	2	
	Vintner	12	1	
	Stationer	5	1	
	Total	150	43	77.7%
Group 3	Innholder	4	2	
	Brewer	11	4	
	Sailor	66	19	
	Clothworker	23	6	
	Chandler	4	2	
	Barber-surgeon	18	8	
	Cooper	14	2	
	Pewterer	7	2	
	Total	147	45	76.6%
Group 4	Tanner, leatherdresser	3	0	
	Tailor	94	23	
	Blacksmith, nailsmith, locksmith	13	3	
	Carpenter, joiner, turner, shipwright	57	13	
	Shoemaker, cordwainer	44	18	
	Baker	12	4	
	Butcher	21	11	
	Glover	8	2	
	Bricklayer	13	4	
	Weaver	24	12	
	Wheelwright	1	0	
	Cutler	20	4	
	Total	310	94	76.7%
Group 5	Waterbearer	5	0	
	Laborer	26	4	
	Porter	19	6	
	Total	50	10	83.3%

Note: For occupation rankings see Vivien Brodsky, 'Mobility and Marriage in Pre-industrial England', 81.

more likely to be married to menial laborers. However, for the bulk of the sample of 908 London wives—the 789 who fell in the middle three groups—the proportion of migrants holds remarkably steady.[21]

Not only did London maids marry surprisingly well, they often did so despite lacking good portions. Few maidservants saved more than a few shillings or at most a few pounds in money through their own labors, as can be seen in Table 2.4, which is based on the responses of 122 maids to questions about their financial worth.[22] Maidservants' statements suggest two conclusions about service in early modern London. First, most London maidservants appear to have had very small portions, or, in many cases, no portions whatsoever.[23] Second, there is little evidence that service enabled poor girls to amass a dowry.[24] Most maidservants did not think they had saved anything worth mentioning, or indeed that they could be expected to do so, despite the relatively good wages they received.

The largest category, maidservants who possessed little besides their clothing, produced a range of responses. Twenty-nine of them said they had little or nothing beyond their clothes. These include Frances Tillie, 'a poor servant worth nothing but her apparel', and Dorothy Craven, a cook's servant in St Peter Cornhill, 'a poor maidservant... little or nothing worth'. Rose Burgess was 'worth nothing save the clothes on her back', and Philippa Griffin was 'nothing worth save the clothes which she weareth'.[25] These clothes were not, of course, valueless. Anne Tristram said she was 'worth her wearing clothes which she values to be worth £4 or £5', and Margaret Marsh, a brewer's servant, estimated the value of her clothes at £4–£6.

---

[21] In contrast, Brodsky Elliott holds that migrant servants were likely to marry men of lower status than their fathers, while London-born women made upwardly mobile marriages. She suggests that migrant maids were driven to the city by orphanhood, not attracted by marital opportunity. However, the migrants in her sample had high-status fathers: 11.1% were the daughters of gentry, 10.4% were descended from high-status tradesmen and clergymen, and another 40.2% came from yeoman families: more than 60% had fathers classified in the top two ranks according to Table 2.3. It is difficult to reconcile subsistence migration with these backgrounds, nor is it clear whether maids could ordinarily expect to wed men of their fathers' standing. The downward mobility of daughters and younger sons was a natural consequence of primogeniture. Brodsky Elliott, 'Single Women in the London Marriage Market', 94, 99.

[22] The sample is made up of maidservants and maids who had recently been in service, but excludes eleven apprentices who said they had little or nothing. There is no way to verify these responses, but the maidservants are unlikely to have exaggerated their poverty. Witnesses usually presented themselves in the most favorable terms they could muster. For example, one pauper apprentice stressed that she was no longer a burden on parish rates: she was, she said, 'a poor girl but hath been and was put to be an apprentice to her said mistress or dame by the parish of St Clement aforesaid and at their charge, but for these five years last past she hath not been any way chargeable to the parish or parishioners here'. Sara Clarke, 1626 (LMA, DL/C/230, fo. 318v).

[23] It is possible that some of the maidservants who said they were little or nothing worth were not counting their anticipated portions, although it is unclear why they would neglect to mention something so strongly to their credit.

[24] See also Jane Whittle, 'Servants in Rural England c.1450–1650: Hired Work as a Means of Accumulating Wealth and Skills Before Marriage', in Maria Agren and Amy Erickson (eds), *The Marital Economy in Scandinavia and Britain 1400–1900* (Burlington, Vt., 2005).

[25] Frances Tillie, 1608 (LMA, DL/C/218, p. 273); Dorothy Craven, 1621 (LMA, DL/C/228, fo. 26r); Rose Burgess, 1618 (LMA, DL/C/225, fo. 390v); Philippa or Philip Griffin, 1619 (LMA, DL/C/226, 2nd series, fo. 16r).

Table 2.4 Maidservants' self-reported worth

	No.	%
Little or nothing beyond her clothing	72	58.7
At least 40 shillings, less than £4	17	14.0
£4 to £6	8	6.6
£10 and more	3	2.5
£15	3	2.5
£20	2	1.7
£20 or £30	1	0.8
£40 to £50	2	1.7
Some money, won't specify	2	1.7
£10 yearly after her mother's death	1	0.8
Expects a portion, does not know how much	14	11.3

These women were neither very poor nor very rich: Anne served a merchant tailor and could write her initial A, suggesting a respectable middling background, and Margaret expected a portion from her father. While the ornate clothes of the wealthy could be worth much, much more, Anne and Margaret's clothes may have been more expensive than those of the average maidservant. Anne Paine, a gentleman's servant, estimated her clothing to be 'better worth than forty shillings', while Mabel Robinson from Yorkshire only claimed to have 'the clothes on her back which are worth twenty shillings and not much more'.[26]

Twenty-six others in this category said they were poor, little worth, nothing worth, or something similar, like Mary Cacott, who said: 'she is a servant having nothing but her wages to live on and therefore is not neither can (as she sayeth) be much worth'. Twelve answered that they had nothing but their wages. A few of the maids made reference to small amounts of money, such as Dionise Gray of Stepney, who claimed to be worth seven shillings, Elizabeth Evans, a plasterer's servant, worth ten shillings, and Elizabeth Humberden, who estimated that she was not worth above twenty shillings.[27]

A conflict over a dead maidservant's goods provides an example of the sorts of things a poor but not destitute maidservant might have. Ellen Stone, who died in King's Hospital around 1615, was described by a hospital servant as wearing 'an old petticoat, an old smock, a pair of shoes and stockings and a coif on her head', all worth the measly sum of twelvepence. However, Ellen told the same servant that she had left her goods at the house of her countrywoman; these included 'a trunk, two boxes, a gown, a petticoat, a new pair of bodies, a pair of hose and shoes, a green apron, and bands and ruffs and other apparel'. Another acquaintance said

---

[26] Anne Tristram, 1633 (LMA, DL/C/630, fo. 110v); Margaret Marsh, 1629 (LMA, DL/C/231, fo. 422v); Anne Paine, 1592 (LMA, DL/C/214, pp. 317–19); Mabel Robinson, 1600 (LMA, DL/C/216, sl. 255, 257).

[27] Mary Cacott, 1608 (LMA, DL/C/218, p. 330); Dionise or Dennis Gray, 1609 (LMA, DL/C/220, fo. 447r); Elizabeth Evans, 1616 (DL/C/224, fo. 210v); Elizabeth Humberden, 1599 (LMA, DL/C/216, sl. 254).

that Ellen's possessions were worth £6 6s. 8d. Like most maidservants, Ellen Stone's wealth amounted to a few pounds, entirely or largely invested in clothing. She was richer than the poorest maidservants, who owned nothing but what they wore on their backs: she had old clothes to die in, and a good suit of apparel for better occasions.[28] Investing their savings in finery may have been a strategic move for marriage-minded servants, who were thus able to display their prosperity to all potentially interested eyes. After marriage, fine clothing could be sold and the proceeds converted to more practical uses.

The next two groups in Table 2.4, those who had at least forty shillings but no more than six pounds, made up of a total of twenty-five maids. Their little capital probably did represent savings from service, perhaps including small legacies as well. As a marriage strategy, saving money in service was ineffective: six pounds, a paltry marriage portion, represented three years' worth of wages without any expenses for clothing or maintenance between services.[29] After subtracting costs, saving even a small portion required long years of toil. Agnes Driver, 21, had served her mistress for twelve years, and reported proudly: 'she is worth her apparel and somewhat else which is sufficient for her calling, and she hath some money which she hath gotten by her long service, and wheresoever she shall become she is able as she sayeth to get a sufficient living for herself.' However, she refused to say exactly how much she was worth: 'she thinketh she is not bound to answer.'[30] Her reticence suggests that her savings were meager.

It seems likely that any capital beyond a few pounds was an inheritance rather than saved income. Blanche Howell, a bookseller's servant, reported pathetically: 'she is a poor servant little worth, although she sayeth she had £40 left in the chamber of London by her father but she... knoweth not how to come by it.' Elizabeth Lane had a similar problem: 'her said aunt hath kept her... since her father died which is almost eleven years as she thinketh and hath [her] legacy or portion in her hands which was £50 and so much [she] is worth if she may have it paid.' Anne Chapple was 'a poor servant but her own father hath left for her preferment in marriage £15'. Christian Stavely did not explicitly call her £20 a legacy, but said: '[she] liveth by her service and some means that she hath of her own.' The maidservants who referred to expected portions distinguished between their current poverty and future prospects, implicitly emphasizing the impossibility of saving a decent portion in service. Cicely Crocket reported: 'she is a servant and liveth of her wages, and little worth but what her father will bestow on her and not fit for subsidy.' Elizabeth Bletchford was 'as yet but a poor servant, and nothing worth but the clothes of her back, yet her parents she sayeth are living from whom

---

[28] Agnes Baseley and Roger Arney, *Elizabeth Stockwell c. Mary Wolley*, 1615 (LMA, DL/C/223, fos. 129v, 126v).

[29] Amy Louise Erickson gives portion sizes as following: 'the aristocracy, upwards of £5000; the gentry, £1000–£5000; the county gentry, £500–£1000; clerks, wealthy yeomen and tradesmen, £100–£500; prosperous yeomen, tradesmen and craftsmen, £50–£100; the great bulk of yeomen, husbandmen, tradesmen, craftsmen and labourers, up to £50 but generally under £30.' *Women and Property in Early Modern England* (New York, 1993), 88–9.

[30] Agnes Driver, 1588 (LMA, DL/C/213, fo. 434).

she expecteth her portion such as pleaseth them to bestow on her', while Isabella More replied: 'she is worth six shillings but how much she is worth she sayeth she cannot tell, but twenty shillings at the best she is worth, besides the hope she hath of her mother and of her friends' gift.' Mary Cull was more specific: 'she is a poor servant and little worth besides her wearing clothes, but after her mother's decease she is to have £10 a year during her life.'[31]

A poor maidservant could hope to overcome her lack of a portion by marrying a widower in greater need of the labor and comfort of a wife than of start-up capital.[32] Such unequal matches attracted the ire of moralists like Daniel Rogers, who warned that they were doomed to disintegrate into resentment and distrust. Poor brides, he suggested, were vulnerable to jealousy: 'because they are privy to themselves of unequality, therefore they are jealous of their husbands' respect and love, think themselves despised, as not worthy to hold quarter with them, and when there is of all other least cause, yet then come they in with their irksome suspicions, and they imagine their husbands to show more affection to strangers than themselves.'[33] While marrying an older widower with children was not ideal, for a poor maid it could be a crucial means of getting a foot in the door of the London marriage market. The maidservant poet Isabella Whitney suggested as much in her mock-testament:

> For Maidens poor I Widowers rich,
>   do leave, that oft shall dote:
> And by that means shall marry them,
>   to set the Girls afloat.[34]

Brodsky Elliott finds that 16.5 per cent of 1,302 single women marrying by license between 1598 and 1619 wed widowers.[35] Similarly, Fig. 2.2 shows that a large minority of both migrant and London-born women married substantially older men who were probably widowers. In this sample of 116 married couples in which the wives were younger than 36—and likely to be still married to their first husbands—age gaps of twenty years appear infrequently but regularly, and one migrant even married a man thirty-nine years her senior.[36] While migrant maids generally

---

[31] Blanche Howell, 1608 (LMA, DL/C/218, p. 171); Elizabeth Lane, 1610 (DL/C/219, fo. 87r); Anne Chapple, 1618 (LMA, DL/C/225, fo. 263r); Christian Stavely, 1615 (LMA, DL/C/223, fo. 340r); Cicely Crocket, 1610 (LMA, DL/C/219, fo. 105r); Elizabeth Bletchford, 1620 (LMA, DL/C/226, 7th series, fo. 34r); Isabella More, 1599 (LMA, DL/C/215, sl. 314); Mary Cull, 1633 (LMA, DL/C/233, fo. 14r).
[32] It was rare for men to keep house without the help of a wife: widowers remarried rapidly. See Boulton, *Neighbourhood and Society*, 128–131.
[33] Rogers, *Matrimoniall honour*, 68.
[34] Isabella Whitney, 'Wyll and Testament', in *A sweet nosgay, or pleasant posye contayning a hundred and ten phylosophicall flowers* (London, 1573), sig. C6v.
[35] Vivien Brodsky, 'Widows in Late Elizabethan London: Remarriage, Economic Opportunity and Family Orientations', in Lloyd Bonfield, Richard Smith, and Keith Wrightson (eds), *The World We Have Gained: Histories of Population and Social Structure* (New York, 1986), 131.
[36] Mary Clayton, a 30-year-old immigrant from Cambridge, was married to a scrivener who said he was 69. Mary and William Clayton, *Margaret Bridge c. John Bridge*, 1616 (LMA, DL/C/224, fo. 103). In this sample, married people both testified, stating their ages for the court.

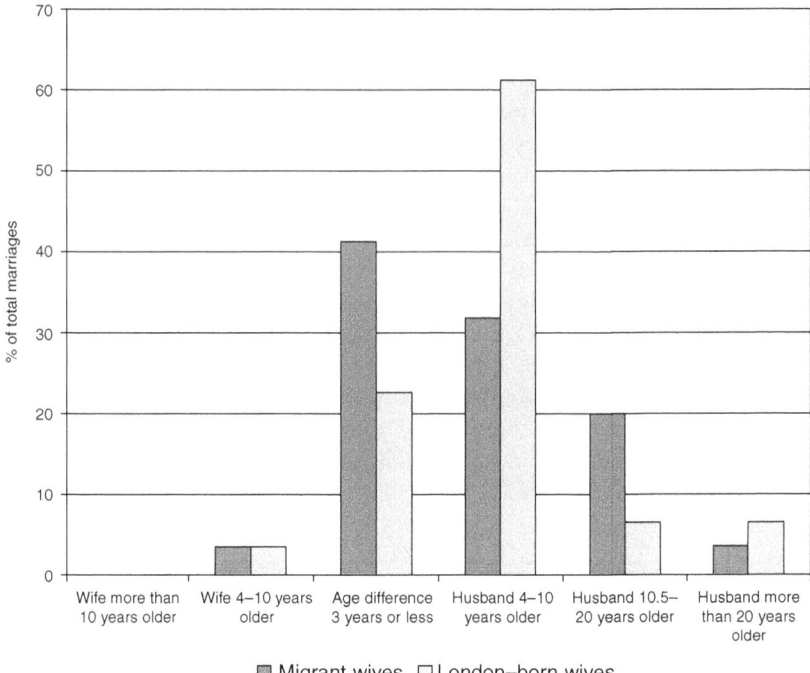

Figure 2.2 Age differences between spouses for migrant and native wives under 36

married bachelors close in age to themselves, 24 per cent of the migrants in this sample married men who were more than ten years their seniors—and who were probably widowers. In contrast, only 13 per cent of London-born maids married much older men, although given their youthful ages at first marriage, even bachelor husbands were usually several years older than they were.[37]

Maids marrying widowers sometimes literally stepped into their predecessors' shoes. At a courting breakfast, Robert Eastfield showed Jane Griggs 'his other wife's linen and apparel', and 'bade her see what would serve her turn if that day came because then he would save money'. Jane tried on Robert's first wife's wedding kirtle, and 'did take certain head clothes and ruffs of his said wife's' along with 'a silk pair of hose of his wife's', but when the widower thriftily suggested that he 'had a ring of his wife's for to make a wedding ring . . . she said that she had one that was her grandmother's that might be made fit'.[38]

While such unions were certainly practical, they were hardly ideal. A poor maid who entered a widower's household as his new wife gained security, but she might find it difficult to assert proper authority, like Elizabeth With, a disenchanted bride

---

[37] This corroborates Brodsky Elliott's description of the marriage patterns of migrant and London-born maids: since the male age at first marriage varied little, the age gap for migrant women was slimmer than that for early-marrying natives. 'Single Women in the London Marriage Market', 84–6.

[38] Robert Eastfield, *Jane Griggs c. Robert Eastfield*, 1578 (LMA, DL/C/629, fo. 53v).

who recounted her wretched marriage to an elderly widower in equally wretched verse:

> I had not been married one month unto him
> But in the Seas of sorrow I daily did swim;
> That better have lived I might in a Jail,
> He and his children did at me so rail.

Her husband allowed his sister to usurp her position as mistress of the household, she complained; moreover, he gave her finest clothing to his married daughter. Neither was Elizabeth permitted to embrace the honorable status of motherhood, as her husband desired no more children, and mourned when she bore him a son. 'All you young women ... Marry not with old men,' she warned.[39] Young women with strong marital prospects seem to have taken her advice: Brodsky Elliott finds that migrant maids who married widowers were on average 28.5 years old, substantially older than most migrant brides. Their late marriages to relatively undesirable bridegrooms may have reflected a strategy of compromise after previous disappointments.[40]

COURTSHIP

While it was easier for some London maids to find a good husband than for others, migrating to the heavily male capital and moving around within it was, by and large, a promising marital strategy. Still, migration was not enough: a maid in search of a spouse would also need to attract a desirable suitor, promote his courtship, and make sure that he followed through with marriage, all while avoiding mishaps and undesirable entanglements. London maids were likely to meet their suitors in the households where they lived and worked, in their neighborhood, or through kin and friends. Once a mutual interest was established, a sometimes prolonged courtship could begin. Though men were expected to take the initiative, young women took more discreet action, for example by finding occasions to meet with their suitors, away from disapproving eyes and preferably in the presence of friendly witnesses. Migrant maids could call on their masters and mistresses for guidance and supervision, or might seek the aid of kin, former employers, fellow servants, and other 'friends'. Amorous couples walked abroad in the fields together, drank wine in taverns, and stole moments here and there for whispered conferences. If all went well, the young man would bestow gifts—knives, gloves, a purse—on his sweetheart, who might respond with a homemade offering. Finally, most couples preferred to seek parental consent if possible, and their elders negotiated the young woman's portion and investigated the young man's prospects.

---

[39] Elizabeth With, *Elizabeth Fools warning being a true and most perfect relation of all that has happened to her since her marriage* (London, 1659), 3, 4.
[40] Brodsky Elliott, 'Single Women in the London Marriage Market', 88–9.

A binding contract, symbolized by the exchange of a ring or the breaking of a piece of gold, might precede the wedding ceremony.[41]

The following case studies provide detailed examples of how young Londoners themselves took on the challenge of making a match. As they are drawn from legal battles, these courtships ended badly, and offer an unrealistically bleak picture of marriage-making in the city. In addition, marriage contract cases were the most hotly disputed of all consistory court suits; the narratives told in the court cases were aimed at proving a point and facts were often disputed. Nonetheless, the stories told by litigants and witnesses were meant to be credible, and thus necessarily reflected common practice. Despite their shortcomings, these case studies vividly illustrate some of the most salient patterns of youthful London courtship. The exact value of a maid's portion was often not decided until late in courtship when emotions were deeply engaged, which could result in heartbreak when negotiations failed. The fact that apprentices were forbidden to marry meant that courtships involving them were often kept secret and could be drawn out over long years, often straining the loyalty of one or both partners. Financially lopsided attachments were likely to develop when young men and women lived in the same household, and when they did, the wealthier party—male or female—was likely to be pressured or coerced into breaking off relations by prudent 'friends' or kin. Even in the absence of external pressure, young people could be genuinely torn between affection and practical considerations.

Rich maid and poor apprentice

Rebecca Bowling and Thomas Savage worked in the same household, that of the skinner John Gawthorne in the parish of St Stephen Walbroke. Privacy was hard to come by, so when the two developed an understanding, Rebecca took advantage of errands to speak with Thomas alone. When she and another maidservant, Susan Wheeler, were to go together to Gawthorne's other house at Peckham, Rebecca made sure that Thomas escorted them rather than the servant initially assigned to do so. Susan reported: 'they went all three together early in the morning before it was light and the said Rebecca suffered [Susan] to go alone before them and all the way... kept company with the said Thomas Savage.' On the way home, Rebecca 'required' Susan to 'go before and stay for her' at a sadler's house, because 'she intended to have some speeches with the said Thomas Savage and would not have [her] to hear what they said'. When Rebecca and Thomas finished their secret talk, they picked her up and all three went to drink a pint of wine in a tavern before returning home to their master's house.[42]

---

[41] Sexual relations, too, could precede matrimony: over 16% of London brides were pregnant when they married, though this was less than the national average of 21% (Finlay, *Population and Metropolis*, 150). As we shall see in the following chapter, prudent couples would be wary of consummating a relationship unless marriage was imminent.

[42] Susan Wheeler, *Thomas Savage c. Rebecca Bowling alias King*, 1617 (LMA, DL/C/225, fo. 25).

Rebecca and Thomas wished to keep their courtship secret from their master, and for good reason: Thomas was Gawthorne's apprentice, and had three years to go before he could contemplate marriage. What was more, he was worth no more than fifty pounds. Rebecca, on the other hand, was no penniless migrant: her parents, who lived in Bishopsgate Street, were wealthy people. Rebecca's father was purportedly worth two or three thousand pounds, and her brothers were well provided for: one was an apprentice scrivener while the other was bound to the master of a ship. Rebecca's portion was to be a few hundred pounds, far exceeding Thomas's modest capital.[43]

However, the young people of the house were not fooled. Thomas Tiggin, Gawthorne's journeyman, reported that the couple 'did make much show of love and affection the one to the other as well in private as in public'. Once when Rebecca asked him 'to help her to carry a flasket of clothes into the churchyard' to lay them out to dry, he asked her whether she planned to marry Savage, and she answered that she would rather marry him than any one else, 'in regard he was so like to one that married her sister'. However, she 'much desired to be made sure to the said Thomas Savage for she much doubted that if she were not made sure to him her father would cross her in her love'. Spurred by Rebecca's anxiety, Savage asked Tiggin to accompany the couple to the Exchange, where the journeyman served as their witness as they contracted themselves and kissed. Then, 'it being dark and cold weather', they took refuge in a tavern where they drank a pint of hot, sweet "burnt" wine and broke a piece of gold as a token of their engagement.[44]

Later, Rebecca confided to Susan Wheeler that she and Thomas Savage were betrothed, and showed her the broken piece of gold, saying she 'would keep it as long as she lived'. But that ritual gift was far from being Thomas's only offering. Rebecca also told Susan that Thomas had paid a debt for her, and showed her other gifts: a pair of garters, a pair of gloves with red tops, a white waistcoat, and a silver bodkin.[45] He also arranged for a gown cloth to be dyed for Rebecca, paying for it himself, and gave her a chain of pearls worth four pounds, a Bible, and a muff of black velvet worth about nine shillings.[46]

Rebecca's parents, ignorant at first of her love, encouraged the suit of one Mr Walker: Gawthorne thought they 'were very desirous that the said Mr Walker should have had the said Rebecca to his wife'. Walker visited Rebecca at Gawthorne's house, but met with a chilly welcome. Rebecca's former fellow-servant Agnes, who had her confidence, testified that when Walker visited, 'Rebecca was much discontented thereat, and told [her] that she would not consent to take Mr Walker to her husband for that she was contracted to the said Thomas Savage whom she could not forsake.'[47] At this point, Gawthorne found out his

---

[43] John Gawthorne and William Richardson, 1617 (LMA, DL/C/225, fos. 85r and 125v).
[44] Thomas Tiggin, 1617 (LMA, DL/C/225, fos. 8v–10).
[45] Susan Wheeler, 1617 (LMA, DL/C/225, fos. 25v–26).
[46] Agnes Winchely, Thomas Tiggin, and William Buckley, 1617 (LMA, DL/C/225, fos. 85v–86r, 8v–11v).
[47] John Gawthorne and Agnes Wincheley (LMA, DL/C/225, fos. 84v, 85v–86r).

maidservant's secret too: one night, he and his wife 'having been abroad at supper', they returned home to find Mr Walker and Rebecca at the door of the house. Rebecca was attired with aggressive modesty: Gawthorne was surprised to see her 'dressed with her forehead cloth down to her eyes otherwise than formerly she used', and asked 'what was the cause Mr Walker went not up into the house, and that she was dressed in her forehead cloth?' The man angrily replied that 'he had the coldest entertainment that ever he had'. Later that evening, the men spoke privately, and Walker told Gawthorne 'he feared that she affected some other man better than himself'. Indeed, when Gawthorne questioned Rebecca, she confessed 'that she loved the said Thomas Savage and that they were contracted in matrimony together, and therefore she could not show any further affection to Mr Walker, and said that Mr Walker had pressed her to have a promise of her to marry him, and therefore she was fain to deal plainly and to refuse him, being sure to the said Thomas Savage'. She further requested her master 'to deal kindly with the said Thomas, else she said he would undo himself'. Gawthorne thought Rebecca was 'very far in love with him'.

The young couple encountered opposition from every angle. Gawthorne found the lovesick Thomas a bad servant; he 'had so ill service of him while he was in love with the said Rebecca that he would willingly have broken the match, and could not so long as she was in [his] house.' Rebecca was sent or summoned home, and went 'against her mind being loath to go home to her parents'.[48] She told another fellow servant that she wanted Thomas to marry her 'out of hand' because she feared her parents would marry her against her will to Walker.[49] She was nervous about confronting her parents. Gawthorne 'met the said Rebecca in Houndsditch going from her uncle's house to her father, and the said Rebecca looked as though she were not well and shivered as though she had an ague, whereupon [he] asked her what she ailed, and she said she was going to her father to make an end of the matter about Mr Walker, and said she had no heart to go about it'. Once home, Rebecca 'fell dangerously sick and told [her former fellow-servant Agnes Wincheley] that the cause of her sickness was the grief that she had taken that her parents had urged her to forsake Thomas Savage and sought to marry her to Mr Walker'.[50] Savage loyally procured 'marmalade and conserve of barberries and such other things' for his ailing sweetheart, but was rebuffed by her father, who told Gawthorne that 'Thomas Savage was lingering about his house, but he would have broken his pate if he could have met him.'[51]

Rebecca impressed her mother with her attachment to Savage. John Gawthorne recounted the following conversation at Rebecca's parents' house:

> Mistress Bowling said to [him]: 'You think that your man,' meaning Thomas Savage, 'and my daughter stand free, but it is not so, you shall hear what she will say,' and then Rebecca Bowling being called down [he] upon her mother's motion asked her whether

---

[48] John Gawthorne (LMA, DL/C/225, fos. 84–85v).
[49] William Buckley (LMA, DL/C/225, fo. 10v).
[50] John Gawthorne and Agnes Wincheley (LMA, DL/C/225, fos. 84v, 86r).
[51] Agnes Wincheley and John Gawthorne (LMA, DL/C/225, fos. 86r, 85v).

Thomas and she stood free or not, and she said 'no,' and said she loved him, and would have him, and so departed, to the which her mother answered: 'Did not I tell you? She thinks she shall not be saved if she forsake your man, somebody hath so told her.'[52]

Mistress Bowling visited Gawthorne's house and made inquiries about Savage's estate, which his fellow-apprentice Buckley said would be good when he finished his apprenticeship. Savage's uncle also met with Mr Bowling, and assured him that he would 'do something' for his kinsman. When Savage went himself to discuss the match with Mistress Bowling, she said 'she would not dislike it, but . . . she doubted her daughter would not stay so long'.[53] Savage had three years to go before he would be able to marry, a long time for Rebecca to withstand parental pressure and alternative suitors.

In January 1616, for reasons that are not entirely clear, Rebecca married an entirely different man, William King, by license in St James Clerkenwell, and moved to Hertfordshire with him. There are some indications that Thomas and Rebecca had been kept apart: when asked what he thought about the match between Rebecca and William King, Thomas told an intermediary that 'unless he might speak with the said Mr Bowling and his said daughter he had nothing to say to either of them'. He also reportedly said 'that if she should be married to another, he would not trouble her therefore', but did in fact sue her for breaking their contract.[54] Marrying King may have represented a workable compromise for Rebecca, who was so adamantly opposed to Mr Walker, but her decision to do so was a bitter blow to her first lover, who lost on all counts. Forsaken and disgraced, Thomas ended up leaving his apprenticeship before getting his freedom.

Rich apprentice and poor maid

The case of *Joan Carew c. Ralph Yardley* is in many ways analogous to that of Rebecca Bowling and Thomas Savage, except that the sexes are reversed: Ralph Yardley, a grocer's apprentice, succumbed to family pressure to abandon his impoverished sweetheart. The young man's convoluted explanations illustrate the vulnerability of apprentices to outside influence: their preferment was dependent on their masters and their friends. Ralph, the long-time apprentice of William Hutton in the parish of St Stephen Coleman, fell in love with his master's maidservant Joan Carew, a girl from St Botolph Aldgate whose widowed mother worked as a laundress. Although they lived in the same house, Ralph 'being a fond youth and not well advised what he did, did write and deliver letters of protestation of love and friendship unto the same Joan'. He introduced Joan to a friend of his, the maidservant Bridget Powell, and they all three went walking 'into the fields upon a Sunday in the afternoon'. Ralph and Joan visited the widow Carew together, and the apprentice asked Joan's mother for her goodwill, saying 'that he

---

[52] John Gawthorne (LMA, DL/C/225, fo. 84v).
[53] William Buckley (LMA, DL/C/225, fo. 11v).
[54] William Richardson and George Blundell (LMA, DL/C/225, fos. 103v, 110r).

had been a suitor to her daughter for marriage "but," quoth he, "all this while I have been but an usurper of her, I pray you mother, give her unto me."' Sara Carew accordingly joined their hands, saying 'I pray God bless you.'[55]

When their secret was discovered, Ralph's brother-in-law and his master both visited Sara Carew to learn how far the matter had gone, but the widow, flustered and uncertain how much Ralph had told them, 'made it something strange and would not tell them that she knew anything between them'. They came away with an unfavorable impression of the mismatch between Ralph, with his good prospects in a wealthy company and poor Joan: Edward Erbie, Ralph's sister's husband, said that Sara Carew 'seemed to be so needy and so poor a woman as a little pail of suds being by chance spilt, she cried out saying she was undone, whereupon there was a penny offered to have been given her for that loss, but she seeming to be distracted at it and said that they brought her out of her wits, [they] came away and so left her'. Ralph's friends laid down the law, telling him that if he contracted himself to Joan, 'he would utterly undo himself' and 'none of them would do anything for him'. Cowed, Ralph 'confessed unto them that he loved her' but submitted, telling them 'that his love was no more but he could leave her company when he would'. He promised to break it off, and when they seemed 'to doubt thereof, he... knowing not how better to satisfy them of his intent therein... took a book in his hand that then lay by and did swear by that book that he would never come at her more without their consent'.[56]

The anxious apprentice also took the precaution of trying to buy back his six love letters:

> Considering how that many masters went about to hinder their servants when they came near out of their years, and to hinder their servants of their freedom upon slight occasions, and he... knowing nothing worse in such a case than love letters, greatly feared lest she the same Joan Carew should injuriously give his... master some advantage that way.

Ralph, worried lest 'thereafter there should any jar arise between his... master and him... by any of those letters,' promised Joan 'five pounds within a year after he was free, and five pounds more within a year after that if she would give him... all his letters again.'[57] However, Joan declined the offer, tempting as it must have been for a servant whose wages in her new service were a mere thirty shillings a year, and sued him for marriage. According to her mother, she declined three other offers of marriage, from an Essex widower, a plasterer, and a fishmonger, hoping to wed Ralph. However, aside from the letters, Joan's case was weak because no one but her mother had witnessed the alleged contract: when the Carews asked her to testify, Bridget Powell told them she had nothing to say, 'whereupon they both began to exclaim upon her... saying that she would not say anything because

---

[55] Ralph Yardley, Bridget Powell, and Sara Carew, *Joan Carew c. Ralph Yardley*, 1608 (LMA, DL/C/218, pp. 251, 284, 289).
[56] Sara Carew, Edward Erbie, and Ralph Yardley, 1608 (LMA, DL/C/218, pp. 290, 287–8, 252–3).
[57] Ralph Yardley, 1608 (LMA, DL/C/218, p. 253).

she...would have him...herself'.[58] Ralph went on to marry one Rose Davis about four years later, but nothing is known of what became of Joan Carew.[59]

Uncertain portions: jesting and tears

The courtship of Thomas Saunders and Susan Harrison illustrates how maids lacking kin in London might turn instead to other 'friends'. Susan had known Anne Westfield for twelve years, perhaps having served her during Anne's previous marriage before she wed Nicholas Westfield. This bond was valuable but limited: the Westfield family took on many of the roles of kin for Susan Harrison, except, crucially, that of providing her with a portion. They stored her trunk, supervised her courtship, attended portion negotiations, and finally testified at the consistory court in a last attempt to induce Thomas Saunders to marry her.[60]

Since Thomas and Susan did not work in the same household, they often met at the Westfields' house. The family saw the couple flirt and joke together: Nicholas Westfield reported that once 'in a merry and jesting manner he the said Thomas said... that he would now fool widows, and requested [Nicholas] to go along with him and he should see how they would hang about him'. Susan readily answered: 'If you go to widows, I will see young fellows', prompting Thomas's reply: 'No you must not, I will not allow of that.' The pair kissed 'lovingly' when they met and when they parted, according to Rebecca, who also heard Thomas make 'faithful promises and protestations of his love and affection'. He declared that Susan 'should not go to service anymore, nor go to a place where there was too much work.' The couple did not always court indoors; like Ralph Yardley and Joan Carew they also walked abroad together, once to Islington, where they 'heard part of a sermon'. They ventured across the river to a victualling house in Southwark where 'because there were no cakes there, [they] called for white bread and cheese and... drank and were merry together, and there he kissed her or was kissed by her often'.[61]

With marriage on the horizon, the question of Susan's portion arose. Rebecca Taylor reported that Thomas protested to Susan 'in a loving manner that if he had £500 he should think himself well bestowed on her if she had not so good clothes to her back as she had on at that time'. However, he took a careful interest in Susan's prospects. Susan asked Thomas, the Westfields, and Thomas's friends Nicholas Brown and his wife to meet her at the house of her uncle, apparently her only London kin, to see what he would do for her. Susan's uncle allegedly 'did promise to make a deed of gift of his estate unto him the said Thomas Saunders after his and

---

[58] Sara Carew and Bridget Powell (LMA, DL/C/218, pp. 293, 285).
[59] For Yardley's family, see Lyon G. Tyler (ed.), *Tyler's Quarterly Historical and Genealogical Magazine*, 33 vols (Richmond, Va., 1921), vol. ii, 118–23.
[60] Anne and Nicholas Westfield, *Susan Harrison c. Thomas Saunders*, 1636 (LMA, DL/C/234, fos. [2]49r, [2]46v). This volume has pagination errors: the folios (numbered on the left-hand side) are numbered up to 199, then begin again at 100. These depositions are in the second set.
[61] Nicholas Westfield and Rebecca Taylor, 1636 (LMA, DL/C/234, fos. [2]47r–[2]48v, [2]35v–[2]36r); Thomas Saunders, 1636 (LMA, DL/C/194, fos. 178–9).

his wife's decease in case he married his kinswoman'. He suggested that the young couple marry on his own anniversary, and Susan's aunt offered them a ring.[62] This was not ideal, because there would be no immediate portion, but Thomas reportedly remarked that 'he would now be speedily married unto her lest the old man her uncle should die before the time formerly proposed'. He told the Westfields that they were invited to the wedding, unlike the disapproving Browns: 'Nicholas Brown and his wife... should not be at their marriage because he the said Brown was so forward to set him on to get a great portion which he said he cared not for.' In fact, Thomas even 'requested the said Mr Westfield that he and the said Susan might be married out of his house and then promised [Rebecca] a good pair of gloves and then desired Mr Westfield to be her father to give her and that they might have their wedding dinner there'.[63] He went to the country to Buckinghamshire to acquaint his mother with his intentions.

At this late point, perhaps hearkening to his own friends and family, Saunders began to have second thoughts about Susan and her portion. He had hoped for £200, but began to worry that no such sum would be forthcoming. Another meeting was arranged with Susan's kinsman, but this time 'her uncle not coming there grew some words betwixt' the lovers. One day when Anne Westfield and Thomas Saunders were walking Susan home, Anne asked Thomas about his intentions regarding the marriage, and he asked Susan if she was willing to stay the wedding until Lady Day, to which 'Susan being unwilling made answer, "If I must, I must."'[64] She told him that she 'loved him with all her heart.' But love was not enough. The Westfields soon noticed a change in Susan's mood. At first she 'seemed somewhat discontented', but as her prospects of marriage with Thomas became more and more remote, they thought her desperate and 'ready to run mad because he... had forsaken her.'[65] The Westfields pressed Thomas about his intentions. Rebecca reported that 'Thomas Saunders feigned some dislike of her the said Susan and seemed willing to give over the prosecution or effecting of the marriage with her... which [Nicholas and Anne Westfield] perceiving asked the said Saunders if with safe conscience he could break off.' Thomas reportedly replied: 'I know that I cannot forsake her.' By this point Susan in her misery had moved without informing Thomas or the Westfields where she lived; Anne said that Thomas, with tears in his eyes, 'desired' them 'not to suffer her to have away her trunk till she would tell them where she dwelt'. Even though he no longer meant to marry Susan, he worried about what might happen to her if she lost contact with her best friends in the city.[66]

---

[62] Rebecca Taylor (LMA, DL/C/234, fo. [2]35r) and Thomas Saunders (LMA, DL/C/194, fo. 177v).
[63] Nicholas Westfield and Rebecca Taylor (LMA, DL/C/234, fos. [2]47v, [2]36).
[64] Thomas Saunders (DL/C/194, fo. 177v) and Nicholas and Anne Westfield (DL/C/234, fos. [2]48v, [2]50r).
[65] Thomas Saunders (DL/C/194, fo. 178) and Anne Westfield and Rebecca Taylor (LMA, DL/C/234, fos. [2]49v, [2]37r).
[66] Rebecca Taylor and Anne Westfield (LMA, DL/C/234, fos. [2]36v, [2]50v).

Uncertain portions: a tavern romance

The delay of portion negotiations may have helped some poor maids to make good matches by giving them time to make sure of their suitors' affections, but as Susan Harrison found, when the strategy failed the aftermath could be painful. Elizabeth Wilson also faced the grief of being forsaken after a long commitment. She lived as a servant with her older brother Jeffrey Wilson, an ale-brewer and a Yorkshire native, in his tavern, the Crown in Warwick Lane. Since he was unmarried, she 'had the chief charge and government of [the Crown]'. She and James Harrison were neighbors; he was apprenticed to a chandler in nearby Newgate Market. When their courtship began, Jeffrey Wilson opposed it on the grounds that he did not want an apprentice to frequent his sister; witnesses reported that he occasionally drove James out of his house. Once, when Wilson noticed Elizabeth's absence in the tavern, the servants told him that 'she was gone to James Harrison and had carried him broth being sick', and Wilson went there, 'found it so', and beat her home. On a different occasion, when Elizabeth was sent to 'fetch a quart of wine at the Bell in Newgate Market', she dallied so long with James Harrison that by the time she returned, her brother had angrily locked the door against her, and had to be persuaded by a victualler who was there to let her in.[67] During their long courtship, James gave Elizabeth many gifts: in addition to a 'ring of silver gilt', he bestowed on her 'a pair of gloves, a pair of knives tript with silver, a silk girdle of mixed color, a purse of red velvet, a pair of knives with bare hafts, a brass groat, two pennies of gold and a purse of cloth of silver', sometimes using an ostler at the Crown as his messenger.[68]

James finally won Wilson's consent to court his sister when Elizabeth was dangerously ill around 1595. Elizabeth was so sick that Wilson hired a poor carpenter's wife to look to her for six weeks. The nurse reported that 'James Harrison would continually come to her the same Elizabeth every day and was very sorrowful and careful for her the same Elizabeth's sickness'. He begged the nurse 'to look carefully to her and willed her she should want nothing and if at any time she... did want any money to pay necessaries for [Elizabeth] that she... should take money of the tapster in the house and he the same James Harrison would pay it again'. The anguished youth 'did oftentimes weep for her thereby showing a very great love and affection'.[69] Elizabeth for her part, 'being very likely to die that the bell tolled for her', gave James the keys to her chest 'wherein was all such things as she had and all her wealth'. Matters came to a head when Jeffrey found James weeping by the girl's bedside. Jeffrey told him sternly that he was 'the cause of her sickness', and 'willed him to be gone', but James stood his ground and said, 'Good brother Jeffrey, be contented and not angry with me for coming to her,

---

[67] Jeffrey Wilson and Thomas Stevenson, *Elizabeth Wilson c. James Harrison*, 1599 (LMA, DL/C/215, sl. 352–3, 355).
[68] James Harrison and Thomas Ball (LMA, DL/C/215, sl. 373, 391).
[69] Katherine Foxley, LMA, DL/C/215, sl. 409. Sickness played a large role in this courtship: when James was sick, Elizabeth often visited him 'with her divers things which she bought at the apothecary's for him'. See John Medcalfe (LMA, DL/C/215, sl. 408).

for she is my wife and I her husband, aye, before God, and she shall never lack for anything that I can do for her', adding heroically that he would remain steadfast even if Jeffrey killed him. Elizabeth 'being very sick and weak, scarce able to speak, put her hand out of the bed when he said that she was his wife, and took him by the hand seeming to affirm the same'. Vanquished by their constant affection, Jeffrey relented: 'God give you joy together. I for my part will never go about to hinder you therein again.'[70]

After several years, with James's apprenticeship nearing its end, Wilson organized a dinner at his new tavern, the Cock, to settle the match. According to George Leake, a 50-year-old yeoman and just the sort of solid witness whose presence was desirable on such occasions, Wilson 'desired him . . . to come to his house saying that James Harrison had seemed a long time to carry good will to his sister Elizabeth Wilson in the way of marriage, "and therefore," quoth he the said Jeffrey, "I will have a meeting to make a final end between them one way or other, and to see what is between them."' James's friend Oliver White, a young tallow chandler, was also invited. Once the guests finished eating, Leake asked the couple whether they were contracted. They 'held their peace a great while looking one upon another. At last she referred the report thereof to his conscience and he to her conscience, but neither of them did or would in [his] hearing confess or acknowledge any contract of matrimony between them.' According to White, James finally answered: 'I must confess I have born her goodwill, but yet there hath neither faith nor troth passed between us.' Elizabeth bitterly remarked: 'He that hath denied me once, will deny me again, and as the faith so say I.' The bargaining proved her right: James asked for £60, and Wilson said that was impossible, but he would do what he could, eventually offering twenty marks, or £13 6s. 8d. James 'made a tush' at this, and proposed £40, and Jeffrey 'last yielded he would make her worth £20', but 'they could not agree about the matter,' and 'so brake off'.[71]

It is not clear why Wilson and Harrison were unable to come to an agreement. Wilson's refusal to give Elizabeth more than £20 is surprising in light of his apparent prosperity. Brewers and tavern-holders were no paupers, and Wilson told the court he was assessed at £3 in the subsidy.[72] On the other hand, he also claimed to be worth no more than £20. This suggests that Wilson had overextended himself, his financial difficulties coming as an unpleasant surprise to James Harrison, or that the brewer was, despite his apparent consent, still hostile to the match (perhaps preferring to keep Elizabeth at home to run his tavern) and therefore hoped to force James to accept her with a small portion or to renounce her. A maid whose fortune lay in others' hands would always be vulnerable to such machinations.

---

[70] Katherine Foxley and Jeffrey Wilson (LMA, DL/C/215, sl. 409, 353).
[71] George Leake, Oliver White, and Jeffrey Wilson (LMA, DL/C/215, sl. 392–3, 369, 360, 393).
[72] Assessments of property and landed income for the subsidy tax often far understated actual holdings. Most London householders did not appear in the subsidy book at all.

Long engagements: an inconstant apprentice

Apprentices' prolonged engagements were risky for maids, particularly as youths were often wary of making their matrimonial intentions public. When circumstances changed, and lovers found themselves discarded after years of secret plans, the consequences could be emotionally devastating and a serious blow for those who had rejected other promising proposals along the way. One such victim was Susan Hills, who met Robert Lowther when they both served in the house of one Richard Green. Because Robert was an apprentice, 'in case it should be known that he was about a wife it might be his great hindrance', so the two resorted to the house of Susan's countrywoman Sara Hodgkinson to court. Sara, a weaver's wife and a Berkhamsted native who had lived in London for at least fifteen years, had known Susan since her childhood. She testified that 'Robert Lowther and Susan Hills did bear good will each to other in the way of marriage, and did oftentimes meet together at [her] house situate in Houndsditch ... and there continued in very loving and familiar manner as lovers do, kissing and dallying.' Sara acted as a chaperone and a witness 'present at such meetings and passages'.[73]

Robert Lowther sailed to Italy during his apprenticeship as a factor for his master, and stayed away for a couple of years. Before he left, he and Susan were formally contracted. They broke a half-crown of gold together, and he gave her a Bible, both of which she showed to Sara.[74] Robert wrote to Susan's father, Thomas Hills, who soon thereafter came up to London. At Sara Hodgkinson's house, Robert 'desired the said Thomas Hills to give his good will and consent thereunto who did then there freely accordingly consent and liked well of the intended marriage.' Robert also arranged with Susan's brother John to leave her £100 in case he should not live to return to England. While the apprentice was abroad, he and Susan maintained contact, exchanging letters and gifts. She 'did send a letter and a token thither' to him, and he 'in answer and requital whereof... did return a letter to the said Susan bearing a date the thirtieth day of March 1624'. It began with the words: 'Susan, my love remembered,' and ended with: 'I fear you can hardly read this because you do not practice.'[75] As a token it enclosed a 'ring of gold with a red stone in it'.

When Robert finally returned, Susan left her service in the house of Sir Gilbert Garrett in Harrow on the Hill, and took a lodging at the house of another friend, Susan Perridge, a glazier's wife and former fellow-servant of hers in Surrey during Robert's travels. Mistress Perridge reported that Robert visited Susan several times at her house in Aldermanbury. He brought her 'three pairs of sheets, eight cushions, a little feather bed, with other linen', and 'bargained with [the Perridges] for the diet and lodging of her the said Susan for five years following or some longer

---

[73] Sara Hodgkinson, *Susan Hills c. Robert Lowther*, 1626 (LMA, DL/C/230, fos. 115v–116r).
[74] Robert later claimed that 'Susan Hills wanting a Bible desired [him] being her fellow servant to lend her a Bible whereupon [he] did lend her a Bible, which was his sister's' (LMA, DL/C/193, fo. 207v).
[75] Sara Hodginkson (LMA, DL/C/230, fo. 116); Robert Lowther (LMA, DL/C/193, fo. 207v). Perhaps Lowther had begun teaching Susan how to read.

time at four shillings the week'. Clearly, he envisaged a prolonged engagement. He told them 'that she the said Susan Hills was his wife, and that [they] were man and wife together before God. And further said that he could have greater matches but that his conscience tied him unto her the said Susan.' However, Robert asked the Perridges to keep the matter quiet because 'if his friends should know thereof he would keep his means or portion from him'. Susan remained true to her lover, and refused several other proposals of marriage, including one from the steward of her former employer Sir Gilbert, who visited her at the Perridges' house several times, offering her (according to Mistress Perridge) £30 a year in lands. She 'told him that he came too late'.

Unhappily for Susan, as his fortunes rose, Lowther's ardor cooled, and he began to doubt the wisdom of tying himself to a serving maid. He visited the Perridges with a porter, and after drinking a pint of wine with them, announced that he had decided to move Susan, 'saying he could provide for her the said Susan more reasonably or cheaper in the country', and left, taking the household goods with him. Soon thereafter, it became clear to Susan that Robert intended to delay their marriage indefinitely and she attempted to force his hand by bringing him to court.[76]

Long engagements: an impatient maid

While maidservants were vulnerable to the inconstancy of upwardly mobile apprentices, they might also decide that they could no longer afford to wait, and marry elsewhere before their first lovers' years of service were expired, as Mary Luce did. She and Thomas Baxter met when they served 'in one Mr Edward Altham's house in London'. They kept their affection secret from their master, but declared their wish to wed before their fellow servants William Stede and Alice Swan. However, Thomas had many years of apprenticeship left. After two years, Mary 'departed thence into Essex to a town called North Wokingdon' where she served one Mr Warren. Thomas 'sent divers times to her by one Mr Shepard then dwelling upon London Bridge'.[77]

When Thomas Baxter learned that he was to go beyond the seas, he decided that they should renew their commitment. His travel companion, a young skinner, reported that they 'purposed to travel into Suffolk to see their friends where they were both born [and] rode to Chelmsford and there lodged all night, and the day following in the morning the said Baxter required him to go forth of the way to see a friend of his'. On the way, they met a young gentleman who was hunting squirrels, and Thomas 'required him to go with him ... to be a witness to a contract of matrimony'.[78] At length they came to where Mary lived, who was 'then occupied in dressing up the house', and they all went into a parlor together and spoke for

[76] Susan Perridge and Robert Perridge (LMA, DL/C/230, fos. 118v–121v).
[77] Mary Luce alias Fadsham, *George Fadsham c. Mary Luce and Thomas Baxter*, 1572 (LMA, DL/C/211/1, fo. 78r).
[78] Peter Everett and William Farmer (LMA, DL/C/211/1, fos. 77r, 76r).

about two hours. Thomas told Mary 'that he intended shortly to go overseas and therefore came of purpose to let her understand what she should trust unto touching their marriage'. Hand in hand, they repeated the traditional vows and Thomas kissed her and 'took half an English crown and broke it in two pieces whereof the one part he gave to her, the other he reserved to himself'.[79] He told Mary he 'had three years to service of his prenticehood by reason whereof he could not forthwith marry her'.[80]

Baxter did not come back to England for almost a year, but the lovers were finally reunited in London where Mary was serving her old mistress, Edward Altham's wife. They quarrelled about where Mary should live during the long engagement: 'there chanced to be somewhat breach... betwixt the said Baxter and Mary Luce touching the placing of the said Mary which he liked not of.' However, Mary's brother arbitrated between them, and 'Mary offered herself to be ordered touching her placing as should like best the said Baxter'.[81] Reconciled, the two met 'sundry times together' at Mary's married sister's house. Her brother-in-law, the shoemaker William Pitman, hearing that they were sure together, said 'they were both welcome to [his] house and had such cheer as he could make them'.[82] Eventually, the temptation to consummate their love became too great, and Thomas 'got her with child'.[83] Baxter was back in Antwerp when Mary's condition became known, but his friend Robert Shepard wrote to him of it and was asked 'to lay forth money for the said Mary's necessity as she should need'. Mary testified that 'she was delivered at a place in Essex ten miles distant from London and in a house there not joining to any town... and she was kept there at the charges of the said Baxter almost half a year and the child being a manchild and named John was kept there at his charges ever since that time'. Shepard 'disbursed money for the finding of her and her child' for 'one whole year', to a total of twenty marks.[84] Thomas acknowledged the boy as his son, and the child was still living five years later.[85]

However, about a year after the birth of her child, with her lover still beyond the seas, Mary, 'persuading herself that the said Baxter was dead by reason of his long absence and not hearing from him', gave up on her first courtship and married one George Fadsham. Her brother John Luce testified that he had been 'sorry to understand' of his sister's marriage, and that he had been in Shropshire at the time, or he would have prevented it.[86] When Thomas Baxter finally returned, free to marry, his sweetheart was living with her husband. At first he did nothing, but after Mary and George had been married for four years, he told his friend Shepard that he was 'much troubled in conscience' because he considered Mary to be his

---

[79] Mary Luce (LMA, DL/C/211/1, fo. 78r). Farmer insisted that Baxter broke the coin in three parts, and gave the last one to him as a witness. See fo. 76v.
[80] Thomas Baxter (LMA, DL/C/211/1, fo. 79v).
[81] Richard Shepard (LMA, DL/C/211/1, fos. 80v–81r).
[82] Mary Luce and William Pitman (LMA, DL/C/211/1, fos. 78v, 81v).
[83] Mary Luce (LMA, DL/C/211/1, fo. 78v).
[84] Robert Shepard and Mary Luce (LMA, DL/C/211/1, fos. 81r, 79v).
[85] John Luce (LMA, DL/C/211/1, fo. 80r).
[86] Mary Luce and John Luce (LMA, DL/C/211/1, fos. 78v, 80r).

wife. Shepard advised him 'to leave the matter as it was seeing that it had proceeded thus far', but to no avail.[87] There is no evidence that Mary and George Fadsham had children together and this—together with the existence of his son John—may have convinced Thomas Baxter that, in the eyes of God, Mary was truly his wife. Fadsham sued to annul his bigamous marriage, and Mary's cooperation (she readily admitted being contracted to Thomas, and only insisted that she had thought him dead when she married Fadsham) suggests that she, too, was willing to be reunited with her former lover.

A widower in want of a wife

A more prosaic view of courtship can be seen in the case of Katherine Jones and William Tomlinson, who nearly married in 1600. Tomlinson was a widower whose courtship of Katherine was largely motivated by his need for a wife to help him run the cook's shop he rented at Pye Corner. The absence of high-flown promises in the case testimony suggests that the rushed courtships of widowers—often driven by the pressing need to replace the household mistress—were less likely to exhibit the trappings of romance than the impractical entanglements of lovelorn apprentices.

Tomlinson's wife's death had deprived him of essential aid in his business. His landlord, John Cope, said he had often advised Tomlinson to 'get him either a wife or else some other ancient staid woman to oversee his house'. Little is known about the beginning stages of the courtship, but Tomlinson reported that one summer day, as he and Katherine were going hand in hand together to Smithfield, presumably to buy meat, she 'got off a little jemowe [sic] ring of silver and gilt from [his] finger'. He said: 'Let that ring alone, it is a pawn for eighteen pence unto me and if I give thee a ring I will give thee one of gold which shall be better than that for that is but silver and gilt'. Tomlison ultimately enlisted his friend Francis Wade in his courtship of Katherine Jones, asking him 'to go to her mistress's house in Barbican and speak with her about him in the way of marriage and to learn of her what portion she had'. Katherine apparently told Wade that she had 'six pounds in ready money herself and £14 more she had in a friend's hands'.[88] Just as Tomlinson recruited a friend to act for him, so Katherine asked John Thompson, the husband of a kinswoman of hers, to talk with Tomlinson. However, Thompson did not know anything more about Katherine's situation than she told him. He testified that Tomlinson 'did ask [him] something about her portion; whereunto [he] could say little until he had spoken again with her the same Katherine, and then afterward when he the same Tomlinson spake with [him] again, he could tell and did tell him that he thought she should have some twenty pounds or thereabouts.'[89]

Thompson made a bond to pay Tomlinson the fourteen pounds the day after the marriage. At this point, the match seems to have been taken for granted, and a

---

[87] Robert Shepard (LMA, DL/C/211/1, fos. 80v–81r).
[88] John Cope, William Tomlinson, and Francis Wade, *Katherine Jones c. William Tomlinson*, 1600 (LMA, DL/C/216, SL. 70, 187, 172).
[89] John Thompson (LMA, DL/C/216, SL. 74).

supper was held at Tomlinson's house. The widower's tapster, John Westby, partook in a celebratory pint of wine, and bade God give them joy. Thompson and Tomlinson addressed each other as 'cousin', and Tomlinson 'took her the same Katherine Jones by the hand and kissed her, saying, "Welcome sweetheart."'

> And supper being ended she the same Katherine made some haste to be gone home to her mistress's house where she dwelt, and William Tomlinson said unto her to this effect: 'Take you more care now to serve your mistress? You have now a house of your own shall serve your turn and mine too.'[90]

Indeed, Katherine had already spent several nights at the house when 'her mistress thrust her out of doors and so she knew nowhere to lie or to become'.[91] The next day, Tomlinson proclaimed his desire to marry quickly: 'I will have it dispatched on Monday or Tuesday next for I lose forty shillings a week for want of a wife to look to my business.' However, on the Saturday before the wedding, the match was broken off because Tomlinson lost his confidence in Katherine's ability to produce her portion. She refused to pay him her six pounds in advance, and according to Wade, the cook said: 'You that will break with me for six pounds that you promised me and said you had, I know I shall never have the fourteen pounds and therefore I would have you depart my house for I never mean to marry you while I live.'[92]

While these failed courtships necessarily provide a disproportionately gloomy picture of the making of marriage in London, they tell us about the kinds of things that courting couples did, and the troubles they were likely to encounter. It is clear, for example, that love and money were tangled together in early modern courtship. Some of the stories above depict romance frustrated by parental constraint, but in many of them, the young people themselves appear to have been torn, both sincerely attached to their sweethearts and averse to imprudent marriage. James Harrison made a serious romantic commitment to Elizabeth Wilson, but ultimately abandoned her for a matter of twenty pounds. Thomas Saunders wept at the end of his courtship of Susan Harrison, but forsook her all the same. Perhaps Rebecca Bowling could have persuaded her parents to consent to her marriage with Thomas Savage if she had not ultimately decided that the mismatch between their portions was, after all, too great. The fact that practical considerations played a significant role in courtship did not mean that it was not, in many cases, an intensely emotional experience.[93]

Parents' influence over courtship was closely linked to their control over their children's financial futures. It is often stated that young women were less free in

---

[90] John Westby and John Thompson (LMA, DL/C/216, SL. 73, 75–6).
[91] Tomlinson insisted that they had not slept together. He recounted having gallantly offered her his own room: 'I have never a several chamber in my house but mine own chamber where I usually lie myself and rather than you shall be to seek of a lodging you shall lie there.' He said he had given her the key, and she had locked herself in alone. LMA, DL/C/216, SL. 188.
[92] John Thompson and Francis Wade (LMA, DL/C/216, SL. 76, 173).
[93] See also Diana O'Hara, *Courtship and Constraint: Rethinking the Making of Marriage in Tudor England* (Manchester, 2000), 237.

courtship than young men.[94] However, in the cases above, wealth was a better predictor of parental control than sex. Men and women married fairly freely when their parents were poor or when they already had possession of their portions, but when their capital was still in others' hands, 'friends' wielded extensive influence. Indeed, male freedom from constraint may have been exaggerated. Men's friends were not always 'allies in the initiatives of courtship'.[95] Pressure applied by friends prevented Robert Lowther and Ralph Yardley from proceeding openly with their suits, while Thomas Baxter would surely have married Mary Luce had he been able to do so. These young men were dependent on the favor of masters or relatives who could seriously damage their prospects.

Just as young men were not always free in courtship, so young women were not always passive. The maids in the case studies above took an active role in courtship that went far beyond receiving or rejecting suitors' proposals and gifts. Rebecca Bowling engineered opportunities to speak privately with her suitor, and Elizabeth Wilson defied her brother to meet with James Harrison. Mary Luce, who had already quarreled with Thomas Baxter over where she would live, decided to forsake him and marry another man even though she had already borne a child. Female agency appears in subtler guises as well, as when Susan Harrison and Susan Hills recruited friends—often older women—to help them. Their strategy of compensating for absent parents by involving kin and people they knew from home or through their work serves as a useful reminder that the involvement of friends in courtship did not always obstruct personal freedom.[96] While penniless maidservants far from home could theoretically make any match they pleased, poverty could be as immovable a barrier to matrimony as any irate parent. Under the circumstances, the aid of friends was one of the best weapons in maidservants' admittedly scanty arsenal: these allies could provide safe places to court and supportive witnesses to agreements. While nearly all London maids did eventually marry, success was by no means guaranteed: even in the city, where maids' prospects were exceptionally bright, finding a good husband required both luck and skill.

[94] See Ilana Krausman Ben-Amos, *Adolescence and Youth in Early Modern England* (New Haven, Conn., 1994), 202; Laura Gowing, *Domestic Dangers: Women, Words and Sex in Early Modern London* (Oxford, 1996), 149; Richard Adair, *Courtship, Illegitimacy and Marriage in Early Modern England* (Manchester, 1996), 134–5; Keith Wrightson, *English Society, 1580–1680* (New Brunswick, NJ, 1982), 76.
[95] Gowing, *Domestic Dangers*, 151.
[96] See also Catherine Frances, 'Making marriages in early modern England: rethinking the role of family and friends', in Agren and Erickson (eds), *The Marital Economy in Scandinavia and Britain 1400–1900* (Burlington, VT, 2005).

3

Maidservants Adrift

On a spring day in 1630, one John Lole asked two neighbors to help him resolve a dispute with his former servant Anne Kenfield, who refused to return some goods belonging to him. At a meeting at the Ship Tavern in the Old Bailey, the mediators asked Anne what she wanted in exchange for the goods. First of all, she complained, Lole owed her a quarter year's wages; but that was the least of her grievances. He had 'promised her marriage, and...had had the use of her body, and...she thought she was with child by him,' the maidservant claimed 'in a very impudent and bold manner'. The mediators, distressed, inquired 'whether she was with child or not, and whether the said John Lole had known her carnally'. The young woman repeated her accusation, declaring that 'she was not fitten for any other service besides the said John Lole's.'[1]

Anne Kenfield's assurance in accusing her master of having gotten her with child runs counter to traditional assumptions about pregnant maidservants in early modern England. These women are often described being cast out from service, trudging along muddy highways, expelled by suspicious matrons from parish after parish, and giving birth miserably in streets and fields. According to the classic double standard, they—and only they—were to blame. What then gave Anne the confidence to demand restitution? Simply put, she could expect the neighbors to believe her. For all their sexual prejudices, parishioners recognized that the unwanted fruits of illicit encounters required support and care. They knew that single mothers could not provide for their children themselves, and that in the absence of a plausible father, a bastard baby could only fall upon the parish, burdening the community as a whole. Unwilling to pay increased poor rates, communities and magistrates sought to pin financial responsibility where they felt it belonged: on the father. The paternity of illegitimate children was always doubtful, of course, but for want of a better solution, it rested on the mother's word.

This framework shaped the incentives and risks governing the behavior of men and women. When illegitimate pregnancies came to light, both parents suffered unless they married swiftly. The father was embarrassed and forced to pay for the upkeep of the child as well as the costs of childbirth; if he could not pay, he was

---

[1] We do not hear what followed, but Lole's neighbors may have instructed him to pay Anne some money to end the dispute. When Lole sued Anne for defamation later than year, it had probably become apparent that she had never been pregnant. Thomas Boggest and Robert Harris, *John Lole c. Anne Kenfield*, 1630 (LMA, DL/C/231, fos. 673–4).

likely to be whipped. The mother was more severely humiliated and could be whipped and, after 1609, imprisoned as well. As a result, those responsible for illegitimate pregnancies often preferred to come to private agreements whereby a secret delivery was arranged and the man paid for the costs. The inconvenient child might thereafter be put out to nurse or discreetly abandoned to the tender mercies of some unlucky parish. When this strategy was successful, both the father and the mother escaped notoriety and the whip.

The legal treatment of bastardy and the strategies parents employed to escape the stern eye of the law have much to teach us about sex, money, and society in early modern England. On a practical level, single women who became pregnant could claim some financial support, and maidservants were less likely to be abused when the alleged father could expect to share in the material and social costs of bastardy. On a cultural level, the legal treatment of bastardy illustrates the limits of the double standard: early modern English communities and authorities were well aware that two offenders were responsible for the births of illegitimate children. Because bastardy was seen as a danger to the order and prosperity of the community—the same order and prosperity that traditional hierarchies were supposed to protect—fathering illegitimate children was an offense against early modern patriarchal values. When communities and magistrates had to choose between upholding a rigid sexual double standard and keeping parish rates low, they overwhelmingly chose the latter.[2] However, these laws and practices were designed to defend parishes from having to pay for other men's misdeeds, not to protect maidservants from rape and sexual coercion. Women's ability to make use of them depended on the strength of their social networks and their own legal knowledge and determination, and some men were more liable to pressure than others.

IMMODEST PROPOSALS

The case of one maidservant seduced by her master's business partner illustrates the remarkable extent to which 'bastard-bearers' could call on support both within their households and from the authorities. Susan More lived as a servant with the bookseller Randall Berk and his wife, Anne, close to Cripplegate, where she worked with Anne weaving silk points, or ribbons. She was sitting in her master's shop one day when a printer named Thomas Creede came by on business. Creede 'began to praise the handsomeness of Susan More', saying to Berk: 'Randall, thou hast gotten a pretty wench to thy maid here. I would I could be acquainted with her. I will give

---

[2] This would change. The Poor Law Amendment Act of 1834 reversed the tradition of determining paternity by the mother's word alone, introducing a new and difficult requirement for corroborative evidence. See U. R. Q. Henriques, 'Bastardy and the New Poor Law', *Past and Present* 37 (1967), 103–29. For scrutiny of female testimony in the years before reform, see Thomas Nutt, 'The Paradox and Problems of Illegitimate Paternity in Old Poor Law Essex', in Alysa Levene, Thomas Nutt, and Samantha Williams (eds), *Illegitimacy in Britain, 1700–1920* (New York, 2005).

her a pint of wine for that she is so like my first wife.'[3] He asked Susan her name, and when she told him, exclaimed that he had a sister by that name. The printer invited Susan to drink wine with him, but she declined. He persuaded the Berks to go as well, however, and with these chaperones took Susan to the King's Head in Redcross Street. On the way home, Anne Berk noticed, he lingered behind, speaking with Susan.

The next morning Susan told her mistress that Creede had 'promised her to come again and to give her as good a breakfast as ever she had in all her life'. Mistress Berk 'earnestly persuaded her not to go to him nor with him if he came', but that morning Creede came by the shop and beckoned to Susan when Anne was upstairs; when Anne came back down, she found her maidservant gone, she 'knew not whither'. Picking up her child, Mistress Berk set off to seek her wayward maid: 'going along in Redcross Street', Anne 'espied her the same Susan's head out a casement of a window in the same tavern.' She rebuked the pair in no uncertain terms, finding 'great fault with them both, first with him telling him that it was neither fit nor credit for him nor for any other married man to sit spending his money with a young maid in a tavern, and then with her for neglecting her business in that sort'. She announced that she would fetch her husband and (though Creede protested: 'No no, fetch not him, for he is a blab and will tell it at the end of the town') leaving her child with Susan, she went home to call Berk, who accompanied her back to the tavern.[4] On the way, they chanced to meet a chapman who wanted to confer with Creede about buying books, and they all ended up drinking wine together.

Anne Berk could not always neutralize these trysts, and Susan More became dangerously accustomed to slipping off to drink with Creede. Finally, around midsummer, at the Sun Tavern in Aldersgate Street, he gave her so much wine that, Susan recalled, she 'was drunk and sick withal'. The printer took her 'to one widow Grimes' house by Pickhatch, an alehouse, and had her up into a chamber where she ... lay down on a bed to sleep, and she sayeth that at that time he the same Thomas Creede had the carnal knowledge of her ... body.' Susan testified that Creede coerced her into continuing the liaison, becoming 'very angry' when she held back, and sending 'sometimes tavern boys and sometimes the boys of the forenamed widow Grimes, to come and stand in the way' by the Berks' shop, to 'beckon her ... to come to them'. Inevitably, she found herself pregnant, and told Creede. He bluntly replied:

> If you had gone from your master and left his house, and would have been at my disposition as I told you I would have had you to have done, then I would have provided for you and you should have wanted nothing. But seeing you have continued still there at Berk's, go seek you another father to your child if you will, for I mean not

---

[3] Anne Berk, *Office prom. Scales c. Thomas Creede*, 1608 (LMA, DL/C/218, p. 156). Creede was an important literary printer. See David L. Gants, 'Creede, Thomas (b. in or before 1554, d. 1616)', in H. C. G. Matthew and Brian Harrison (eds), *Oxford Dictionary of National Biography* (Oxford, 2004).

[4] Anne and Randall Berk, 1608 (LMA, DL/C/218, p. 174).

to father it. I will shift it off well enough, and my wife will help to clear me of this matter and to shift it off as she hath shifted me of such matters as this is before now.[5]

Susan hoped to solve her problem without confessing to her mistress. She confided her troubles to the Berks' kitchenmaid, Blanche Howell, and sent her to Creede's house to ask for help again.[6] Blanche testified that Creede denied fathering Susan's child, 'yet willed her to speak softly that his wife might not hear it', and said he would come to speak with Susan. He did not, however, and Susan again sent Blanche 'to desire him but to provide a house for her and she would not further trouble him'. She threatened to tell Berk if he did not, but Creede told Blanche that Susan 'should not gull him neither would he be gulled of her or her master either, and that if she were with child she should go seek some other father for it for him'.[7]

In desperate straits, Susan went to her mistress and 'desired to speak with her alone, and they being in a room alone together, she the same Susan very penitently and sorrowfully told her ... that she was with child by Thomas Creede'. Anne, who had recently defended Susan against a neighbor's aspersions, was 'very much abashed and grieved'. She scolded her:

> Did not you promise me long since that you would never come in his company anymore, and of late when Mistress Worrall and my husband fell out and called you 'whore' and 'Creede's whore' for it, did not you then deny all such matters? Why would you trouble the woman, when you knew yourself guilty?[8]

Susan explained that Creede had told her to deny the accusation to save his credit. Mistress Berk sadly told her husband what had happened, and Randall went to speak with Creede, but the printer continued to deny responsibility, blustering: '"Doth she say so? Well you know, Master Berk, if a whore will swear a child upon a man he must keep it and so must I belike, but sure if it be mine," quoth he, "she is something big."'[9] Finally a meeting was arranged between Susan, the Berks, and the Creedes, to take place at a tavern—the Sun, where Susan had originally been made drunk.

Margery Creede was the last to arrive. When she came in, she asked what the matter was. 'That wench thereby,' Anne said, pointing at Susan More, 'is with child

---

[5] Susan More (LMA, DL/C/218, pp. 139–40).

[6] Blanche had her own entanglement with Creede. Susan said that she once came home 'with some extraordinary behaviors and her face red'. Perceiving that she had been drinking, Susan questioned her closely. Blanche confessed that Creede had asked her to drop off Anne's child, whom she had been tending, at home and to 'meet him at Goodwife Grimes' house', but Susan, understandably, 'would not suffer her to go'. Susan More (LMA, DL/C/218, p. 143).

[7] Blanche Howell (LMA, DL/C/218, pp. 169–70).

[8] According to Randall, 'one Worrall's wife reported that he ... kept a whore in his house, and being asked who that was, she said it was Susan that wrought there, saying she was Creede's whore the printer, and [Berk] had gotten an impression of books and his wife a three or four gross of work and so they had smothered up the matter at an alehouse. And he sayeth, that upon these speeches which came to his ... ear and understanding, and he telling Creede of it, Susan and the same Creede took out a process and sued her the same Worrall's wife in a cause of defamation, and upon the serving of the process the matter was agreed at a tavern ... she the same Susan avouched at the tavern that she knew no hurt by Thomas Creede.' Anne and Randall Berk (LMA, DL/C/218, pp. 158, 175).

[9] Anne Berk (LMA, DL/C/218, p. 158).

and as she sayeth by your husband.' Mistress Creede advanced on Susan 'with a very fierce and angry countenance', asking: 'Are you with child by my husband?' Susan fell on her knees, admitted her fault, and begged for forgiveness. Then, Anne reported, 'Creede's wife threatened her that if she would not find another father for her child she would have her to Bridewell and have her whipped every court day and work all the week, and she [Mistress Creede] would have the benefit of her work and keep her with brown bread and water, and so in such terrible threatening manner terrified the wench as much as she could.' Susan said that she was so frightened she 'could not tell what to do', because Mistress Creede threatened her that if she laid the child to her husband she would make her 'repent it all the days of her life'.[10]

Anne Berk intervened, saying that Susan 'was born at Cambridge where she had some friends'. A solution was devised whereby Mistress Creede 'persuaded the wench to go to her friends in the country'. She herself gave Susan ten shillings, Berk gave her six more on Creede's account, and Anne contributed eighteen pence. The two wives summarily escorted Susan to the Cambridge carrier at the Bull in Bishopsgate, while Susan provided more details about Creede's affairs at the widow Grimes' house: 'he used to have other women besides her there, as namely one from Lambeth, another that had a great belly, and a third that was there in the same widow Grimes' house but she being grown now something old she said that he had told her that he cared not for her now.' They 'saw her set in the wagon to go away to Cambridge and saw her going out at Bishopsgate'.[11]

Mistress Creede and the Berks then went together to Pickhatch for some detective work. The widow Grimes denied knowing Creede, but a servant recognized Susan's description.[12] These revelations left Margery Creede despondent, and when the three went to eat and drink in the more respectable surroundings of the Half Moon in Aldersgate Street, she

> began to bewail her case to [Anne Berk] and her husband, nobody being there but them three, saying that her husband was bare of money and much behindhand or at least nothing aforehand, and oftentimes wanted money for his necessary use, and she was constrained to make shift for it. 'Ay, sometimes,' quoth she, 'to pawn my own clothes to my back, and,' quoth she, 'thus this way doth he waste his money,' she meaning by his unchaste life. And further said thus: 'It is not yet,' quoth she, 'above eight weeks agone since I was fain to shift off a like matter for him as this is.'[13]

When the Berks returned home, thinking Susan More and her big belly safely on the way to Cambridge, little did they know that she would only get as far as Ware before turning back. It was winter—Susan had first told Anne about her pregnancy on the twelfth day of Christmas—and the season was so cold that when Creede had tried to sign a bond for the six shillings Berk lent him to pay Susan, the ink had

---

[10] Anne Berk and Susan More (LMA, DL/C/218, pp. 159, 140–41).
[11] Anne Berk (LMA, DL/C/218, p. 159).
[12] Susan commonly wore 'a colored waistcoat, a stuff kirtle or petticoat, a green apron, and a green silk scarf before one of her eyes' because it was sore. Ibid. p. 160.
[13] Ibid. pp. 160–61.

been frozen. Because of 'the great frost' Susan found that she was 'not able to endure the uneasy going of the wagon'. She did not dare approach her master and mistress again, and although she had some money, accommodation was difficult to find for a lone pregnant woman. She stayed in 'one old Mother Cop's house near unto Brickhouse' for five nights, but then her former mistress heard she was there, so Susan 'got herself secretly away', and 'walked up and down the streets one night'. She said she 'could not get a place to lie in of a great while, but lay abroad in the streets', but eventually took refuge 'in a poor woman's house in Gravel Lane in Houndsditch where she lay two days and two nights without meat or drink'.[14]

Once Anne Berk found out that Susan had returned to London, she informed Margery Creede: 'this wench Susan More is come again.' Mistress Creede 'was something amazed and grieved', and when Thomas Creede found out, 'he began to swear a great oath, saying he would not be gulled'. Anne tried to persuade the Creedes 'that there might be some course taken in the matter, but he ... still swore great oaths saying, "hath she taken my money and is now come again? I will not be gulled!"' Since the Creedes 'seemed to make light of the matter', the long-suffering Mistress Berk took responsibility once again. She assembled two witnesses and tracked Susan down to her lodging in Gravel Lane. There, she 'entreated the two men to take pains to talk with her and examine her as strictly as they could'. Susan stuck to her story, and at last was persuaded, though 'very unwilling to take any such course', to 'have him the same Creede to be called before some Justice and then he would take some order for her'.[15]

In fact, the law was more favorable to Susan than she had feared. When Sir Stephen Soame first heard Creede's story, he was inclined to release him, but after questioning Susan privately he 'was then of another mind', and bound Creede over to the Sessions, instructing him to pay Susan's keep for one month before her delivery and one month after. Mistress Creede spoke graciously to Susan in Soame's presence, seeming 'to make very much of her ... bidding her ... to come home to her, to her house and she should have such as she had to do her good until she were delivered'. When 'by reason of her kind words' Susan went to see the Creedes a week later, Thomas 'began to speak very churlishly to her asking her in a furious manner wherefore she came thither?' She explained: 'if his wife had not bid her, she said she would not.' However, Margery continued to treat Susan gently: she called her by her first name and bade her to 'get her a place to lie in', promising to take care of the baby.[16]

On Anne Berk's advice, Susan went to Westminster to ask one Rebecca Handley if she could stay with her and her husband while she lay in, with the guarantee that Creede 'would pay all charges'. Edward Handley, a poor laborer, was a countryman of Randall Berk, and Rebecca's father was a bookseller, so they knew Susan, the Berks, and Thomas Creede, and agreed to accommodate the young woman. While

---

[14] Susan More, 1608 (LMA, DL/C/218, p. 141).
[15] Anne Berk and Susan More (LMA, DL/C/218, pp. 161–2, 141).
[16] Susan More (LMA, DL/C/218, pp. 146–7, 142).

Susan was there, she continued to weave points for Anne, with the Handleys fetching 'work from Berk for her ... to do when she was able to do it'.[17]

Soame had mandated that the birth be attended by a neutral party: 'it were good there should be a strange midwife,' he 'said expressly, "thus not provided by you, Mistress Creede, nor yet by Berk."' This was necessary because Creede had sought to lay the blame on Randall Berk. Susan reported that 'he would say thus unto her ... : "Do not thy master love thee? His wife is a foul sow and if I had so pretty a wench in my house as thou art I must needs love her."'[18] A neutral midwife would determine the child's paternity by questioning Susan when she would not dare to lie. Accordingly, when Susan went into labor, Rebecca sent for the Westminster midwife Philippa Webb, a female neighbor, Margery Creede, and Anne Berk. Only the local women came in time, but they both affirmed that Susan stuck to her original story and 'in her greatest pain and extremity of childbirth did confess and acknowledge unto the midwife' that 'Thomas Creede was the father of her child', providing for good measure the details of how he had 'enticed and procured her to meet him at one widow Grimes' house'.[19]

After the birth, Thomas Creede and his wife took charge of the baby, putting it out to nurse in the country.[20] Susan More's name is absent from the Bridewell books, so she may have escaped punishment. Nor, her honor lost, did she sink irretrievably into prostitution. Instead, she went back into service with a stationer, Hugh Jackson, in St Bride's, having spent ten weeks with the Handleys. Presumably she would always be vulnerable to accusations of whoredom unless she moved to a neighborhood where no one knew her, but it is unlikely that her chequered past prevented her from marrying and leading a normal life. Creede, whose philandering strained the patience of the community as well as that of his wife, was prosecuted for bastardy.

EVERYDAY ABUSES?

Historians have often emphasized maidservants' vulnerability to sexual abuse, 'an ever-present hazard from masters, masters' sons, and fellow servants'. Maidservants were supposedly a convenient prey, for the 'sexual abuse of female domestics by masters, their sons or servants could occur in closed bedchambers, barns or halls'. Their struggle for personal privacy never ended: 'To maintain the boundaries of

---

[17] Rebecca Handley (LMA, DL/C/218, p. 133).
[18] Creede took a very different line with Anne to her face, using 'many wanton speeches and behaviours to her ..., saying unto her that she ... had a sweet pair of lips, and if she were a good wench she would let him have some part with her husband', attempting her chastity no fewer than three times. Susan More and Anne Berk (LMA, DL/C/218, pp. 147, 149, 163).
[19] Isabel Chaundler and Philippa Webb (LMA, DL/C/218, pp. 134–7).
[20] Randall Berk (LMA, DL/C/218, p. 185). Creede admitted this, but feigned ignorance of the child's origins: 'about two or three months last past there was a young child laid upon the stall of [his] shop in an evening when [he] and his wife were not at home, which child [his] maidservant took into his house without [his] knowledge ... since which time [he] of charity hath and doth keep the child at his charges.' Thomas Creede (LMA, DL/C/218, pp. 185, 177).

chastity against the intrusive touch of masters, their sons and their friends could be a constant battle.'[21] 'Service in a household was supposed to be a refuge for young unmarried women; yet, for some, it was more hazardous than the life of a vagrant.'[22] Some have seen sexual exploitation as a common *abuse* of early modern household hierarchies, while others have argued more radically that the patriarchal household structure itself encouraged masters to take sexual advantage of their servants, because the similarity between 'the ties of obedience and duty that bound servants and masters and those that bound wives and husbands' suggested 'that sexual and economic power would be entwined in relations between masters and servants as it was between husbands and wives'.[23]

Scholars have tended to be equally pessimistic about the fate of the pregnant servant in early modern England, seeing the burden of responsibility to fall heavily on her erring body: 'she was likely to be dismissed instantly, prosecuted in court, subjected to public penance, treated with suspicion and hostility by justices, neighbours and midwives, and was forced to move from place to place in search of assistance and support.' These young women 'were in an especially vulnerable position; often dismissed by their masters, they had to try to return to their homes or find some other place of shelter for their delivery'.[24] Charitable persons unwise enough to take in a big-bellied wanderer might find themselves in court for bawdry. Harborless maids 'might be forced to join the vagrant population on the roads, where they were liable to find the doors of charity closed to them... Pregnant single women... could be forced to turn to prostitution, an illegal form of work, in order to survive.' 'If service for young women was a step on the ladder of opportunity that defined a working life, pregnancy was guaranteed to throw them off it.' Unmarried mothers were 'likely to have trouble making even the most basic arrangements for lying in', and might be driven from parish to parish by local officials.[25] During childbirth, unmarried mothers were virtually tortured: midwives were bound by oath to withhold aid until they confessed who had fathered their children; 'the extremity of pain was meant to force the truth from women's otherwise opaque and recalcitrant bodies.'[26] Once they had recovered from childbirth, they could be whipped. Men, on the other hand, free of the physical stigma of pregnancy, could use their influence to silence accusations, or simply flee and find work elsewhere.

---

[21] Sara Mendelson and Patricia Crawford, *Women in Early Modern England, 1550–1720* (New York, 1998), 106; Ilana Krausman Ben-Amos, *Adolescence and Youth in Early Modern England* (New Haven, Conn., 1994), 202–3; Laura Gowing, *Common Bodies: Women, Touch and Power in Seventeenth-Century England* (New Haven, Conn., 2003), 73.

[22] Mendelson and Crawford, *Women in Early Modern England*, 107.

[23] Amussen, *An Ordered Society*, 159; Gowing, *Common Bodies*, 62.

[24] Ben-Amos, *Adolescence and Youth*, 202–3; Ingram, *Church Courts, Sex and Marriage in England, 1570–1640* (Cambridge, 1987), 286.

[25] Mendelson and Crawford, *Women in Early Modern England*, 268; Gowing, *Common Bodies*, 117–18.

[26] Laura Gowing, 'Ordering the Body: Illegitimacy and Female Authority in Seventeenth-Century England', in Michael J. Braddick and John Walter (eds), *Negotiating Power in Early Modern Society* (Cambridge, 2001), 53. See also Richard Adair, *Courtship, Illegitimacy and Marriage in Early Modern England* (Manchester, 1996), 73.

Abuses did occur, and pregnant maids did face harsh realities. Yet scholars who have engaged closely with the concrete realities of illegitimacy have found them difficult to reconcile with this stark picture. Walter King finds that, rather than godly morality, it was parishes' dislike for supporting pauper bastards that informed every aspect of their response to illegitimacy. Men were not imprisoned, he argues, because they could not support their illegitimate children from behind bars, and in any case the expense of imprisoning unwed mothers for the full statutory year rendered the penalty impractical. In Cheshire, Garthine Walker finds that bastard-bearing women were usually forced to pay for their children's upkeep (like the alleged fathers) rather than being whipped or imprisoned. In addition, Cheshire women used the law to present themselves as the victims of unscrupulous men. Despite the alleged vulnerability of maidservants, recorded rates of illegitimacy were low throughout England, but particularly so in London, where it was rare for more than one per cent of christened babies to be described as base-born. Of these, Adair finds that most resulted from servant courtships which 'though unstable, were serious relationships... A constant trickle of servants—no more than that—bore children fathered on them by their masters.'[27]

The movement of unlawfully pregnant women in and out of the city diminishes the usefulness of illegitimacy rates for assessing the risk to London maids. City women, if they had family within reach, were likely to return home for a safe harbor, while country women might come—or be sent—to the city for a discreet and anonymous delivery. In a popular 1652 text, 'an ounce of London deliverance' was slyly listed as part of 'an excellent recipe for the recovery of Maidenheads'.[28] The metropolis was an ideal place to bury shameful secrets. When one Mr Hall in Acton, Middlesex, got his maidservant Elizabeth Carter with child, he spirited her away to the city to avoid trouble. After Elizabeth's condition was noticed in Acton, a constable came to Hall's house, but to escape the ignominy of having fathered a bastard, Hall told the constable and Elizabeth's anxious parents that the girl had run away. Only some months later, when some local marketwomen spotted Elizabeth in London, did her parents discover her whereabouts. She told her father that Hall had placed her in a shoemaker's house for her delivery, and later put her in service with a linen-draper near Charing Cross. Elizabeth explained that Hall had frightened her into keeping quiet, saying that 'if her mother knew where she was, she would spoil her and slit her nose'.[29] While Hall's subterfuge was discovered by chance, city parishes commonly deployed a range of methods to discourage childbearing tourism. In 1618, for example, a watchful beadle noticed a mysterious infant in the house of the wet-nurse Jane Gurnett. An investigation unearthed the midwife and eventually the guilty parents: Anne Darrell, a gentlewoman from Berkshire who had left her husband, and her

---

[27] Walter J. King, 'Punishment for Bastardy in Early Seventeenth-Century England', *Albion* 10.2 (Summer 1978), 138–140; Garthine Walker, *Crime, Gender and Social Order in Early Modern England* (Cambridge, 2003), 229–37; Adair, *Courtship, Illegitimacy and Marriage*, 218–19.

[28] A. L. Beier, *Masterless Men: The Vagrancy Problem in England 1560–1640* (New York, 1985), 53; D.N., *The Figure of Six* (London, 1652), List 71.

[29] Leonard Carter in *Office c. Hall*, 1623 (GL MS 9189/1, fos. 115–116r).

lover, Thomas Savage. They had concealed her pregnancy and delivery from the household where they lodged, bribing the midwife, hiding the newborn in a cloak, and arranging for a private christening, but in the end Savage was arrested and hauled to Bridewell, while Anne—dispensed from arrest on the grounds of her delicate health—took the opportunity to disappear.[30] This moral policing doubtless diminished London's attractions as an anonymous safe haven—although it may still have compared favorably with small villages and towns, where on occasion thrifty parishioners physically carried vagrant women in labor into neighboring parishes.[31]

The peregrinations of pregnant women aside, the low rates of illegitimacy recorded both for London and for the country as a whole seem inconsistent with the notion that maidservants were easily subjected to sexual exploitation. For one thing, as Bernard Capp suggests, respectable male householders of the middling sort cared very much about maintaining a reputation for sexual honesty. To cast all men indiscriminately as potential sexual predators is to ignore the strong moral views that kept many of them on the straight and narrow path. Cases drawn from the records of Bridewell and the Old Bailey show that women were able to use male concern over sexual reputation to achieve their own ends, leaving respectable men 'vulnerable to wronged or calculating women'.[32] Capp's analysis provides valuable insight into the mentalities of middling men, but while it is surely true that many men embraced the prohibition of fornication for both sexes, morality was not the only force that protected maidservants from unwanted advances and spurred unwilling fathers to make private compositions for the upkeep of their illegitimate progeny.

BASTARDY AND THE LAW

The laws dealing with bastardy were based on the assumption that illegitimate children, the innocent victims of their parents' misdeeds, required and deserved financial support: in the absence of parental contributions, they were to be supported by parish poor rates. This was not intended to facilitate the abandonment of illegitimate children on the parish, however. To the contrary, legal structures were devised to identify, bind, and punish delinquent parents. In *The countrey justice*, a manual for justices of the peace, Michael Dalton instructed magistrates to bind over the suspected father as soon as possible: 'otherwise there

---

[30] See *John Darrell c. Anne Darrell*, 1618 (LMA, DL/C/227, fos. 35–6, 46–9; DL/C/226, 1st series, fos. 4–5v, 13v–17v, 20v–22r, 23v–25v, 29r–32r, 47v–48v and 2nd series, fos. 13r–15r, 36r–37r; DL/C/192, fo. 75).

[31] See Gowing, 'Ordering the Body'.

[32] However, Capp concludes that threats of exposure and false accusations were a 'double-edged' weapon for women: '[w]hile they might have benefited individuals, and perhaps made men think twice before turning away pregnant servants empty-handed, sexual allegations judged to be malicious would have simply confirmed the traditional distrust of female testimony.' 'The Double Standard Revisited: Plebeian Women and Male Sexual Reputation in Early Modern England', *Past and Present* 162 (1999), 72, 74, 100.

will be no Putative father, when the two Justices (after the birth of the child) shall come to take order'. The justices were to 'take order (by their discretion) as well for the relief of the parish, and keeping of the child (by charging the mother or reputed father, with the payment of money, or other relief), as also for the punishment of the mother and reputed father. But such a Bastard child must be one that is left to the charge of the Parish, or one likely to be (or which may be) chargeable to the Parish.' If the justices did not agree on who was responsible, 'it seemeth the mother may be examined upon Oath, concerning the reputed father, and of the time, and other circumstances'. The 1609 revision to the law increased the penalties for unwed motherhood from whipping alone to punishment and imprisonment. The mother was to be sent to a house of correction, 'there to be punished and set on work for one year', but only 'after the child be born, and that it be living; for it must be such a child as may be chargeable to the parish.'[33] Illicit sex may have been equally culpable in the eyes of God whether or not a child was born, but the law was primarily concerned with the creation of an unwanted burden on the public weal.

In London, this legal process underwent certain practical modifications. Although Dalton declared that both parents could be charged for the costs of bastardy, it was extremely rare for the mother to be held financially responsible. In the case of migrant maidservants, who made up the majority of unwed mothers, this was surely due to their complete inability to support or care for their children while in service.[34] The usual course was for infants to be put out to nurse at their fathers' expense, or at the charge of the parish if no solvent father could be located. Only rarely did mothers retain the custody of illegitimate children. Widows or married women who had left their husbands might do so,[35] and an unwed mother who subsequently married might take custody of her illegitimate child. Testimony in a 1617 defamation case describes child support being paid by the father in this circumstance. Speaking with a companion about a base child his wife had borne in her widowhood, John Lear said that Anthony Gibson, the presumed father, 'was behindhand ten or twelve shillings for keeping the said child'.[36]

In practice, then, ordering support for the child was primarily a matter of identifying and binding over the alleged father. As Dalton suggests, the identification of the father was largely contingent on the mother's evidence, but simply asking her for the father's name created a problem. Justices had to balance the interests of the parish against those of individual men who could be wrongly

---

[33] Michael Dalton, *The countrey justice containing the practise of the justices of the peace out of their sessions* (London, 1619), 32–3.

[34] Payments were expected, however, from the families of unwed mothers, if they were available. When two penniless young people, Thomas Powlter and Sara Harman, produced an illegitimate child in 1574, the Bridewell court decreed 'that Thomas Powlter's father shall pay 8d. the week and her father 4d. the week for the keeping of the child.' BRHA, BCB 2, fo. 44r.

[35] Elizabeth Hawkins, who left her husband and spent several years in Ireland, bore a child following a liaison with a serving-man there and nursed it herself. John Hawkins, *William Hawkins c. Elizabeth Hawkins*, 1625 (LMA, DL/C/229, fos. 139v–140r).

[36] Gibson maintained that he was only a go-between for the actual father; he 'received with one hand and paid with the other hand for the nursing' of the child. Walter Hull and John Hall, *Anthony Gibson c. John Lear*, 1617 (LMA, DL/C/225, fos. 237r, 119v).

accused of fathering bastards. In addition to insisting on a certain level of plausibility, magistrates resolved this dilemma by decreeing that the mother be formally questioned during labor by a licensed midwife, in a ritual that relied on her pain and fear to guarantee her sincerity. Although these midwives have been compared to torturers who extracted 'true words from bodies in pain', their dramatic roles as coercive interrogators often masked a more consensual reality. In fact, few pregnant singlewomen had reason to protect the identities of the men involved unless they had made advantageous private agreements in exchange for silence. Often, the childbed confession simply added a legal seal of approval to claims the woman had been making all along. The 'punitive ritual' of interrogating mothers during childbirth functioned as legal theater, designed to add dramatic legitimacy to that most ambiguous of labels, illegitimate paternity.[37] The harshness of the ritual concealed the power it gave to the mother.

Londoners frequently assumed that men had to abide by women's paternity accusations. Prosecuted for bastardy, the apprentice William Parnaby appealed to this assumption to explain why he had acted so guiltily in the case of Anice Floyd's pregnancy. He recounted that two women had visited him at his master's house and told him he must provide for Anice, 'which at first hearing he refused to do but they affirmed that if she lay it to his charges he must keep it although he were not the father of it, and were full of importunity and clamours against [him]'. William 'being then an apprentice and fearing to lose his freedom by their clamours did consent or promise to send her... into the country, which he did not as being guilty of incontinence... but for fear to lose his freedom by their clamours'. He sent Anice with money and an escort to his father's house in Cambridgeshire for her delivery. William's troubles did not end there, however: on the day when he was to receive his freedom, Anice's representative Anne Hedge 'came with two or three with her to him... and threatened him if he would not give her twenty shillings she would go to the hall and hinder him of his freedom'. He promised her twenty shillings, but, as he smugly noted, 'never did give her the same'. Whether or not Parnaby really was the father of Anice Floyd's child cannot be known, but he hoped the court would believe his convoluted story.[38]

Apprentices, who could ill afford to offend their masters or London magistrates, often did not have to be ordered to pay the charges when they fathered illegitimate children: rather, like Parnaby, they might make private arrangements in hopes of concealing the matter. Denial was not seen to be a viable option. The suit between Dionise Halfhead and John Walker in 1614 illustrates how anxious young men were to conceal the evidence of unwise affairs. Dionise and John were fellow-servants in the household of Sir Lionel Cranfield, where John claimed that she seduced him while he was tipsy, 'somewhat too merry by keeping company with friends'. Unfortunately, Dionise soon became pregnant, and told him that he was responsible. He made no attempt to absolve himself at that time, and saw no other solution than to secretly pay for Dionise's expenses,

---

[37] Gowing, *Common Bodies*, 159–60, 165.
[38] William Parnaby, 1632 (LMA, DL/C/195, fos. 64v–65v).

fearing discredit by her clamour and thinking to have the said crime kept secret and not to be brought to the ears of his said master and the lady his wife, [his] mistress, and others his friends, knowing himself to be the reputed father of the said child, [he] was fain to promise the said Dionise to provide for her and her child wherewith she then went.[39]

John Walker found Dionise a lodging in the house of William Shepherd, a tailor who came to Cranfield's house to visit a countryman of his. Bargaining with Shepherd's wife for her room and board, he agreed to pay the extortionate sum of eight shillings weekly. He was still not sure whether he was the father, and doubtingly asked a married friend, Quinborowe Hall, 'if it were possible for a woman within a month after she had lain with a man to know that she was conceived with child', but she affirmed to him that it was. Soon Dionise's condition became unmistakable, and the Shepherds refused to harbor her any longer. Quinborowe's husband, John Hall, found her a new, less respectable lodging in Southwark, where she was delivered. Walker took the baby, put it to nurse, and 'in consideration towards the said Dionise and for the loss of her time and that she was then out of service gave her four pounds to relieve herself withal and therewith to supply her wants'.[40]

He evidently thought that their relationship was over. Dionise, however, was not content, and sued him for marriage. No one had witnessed a contract, but there was some circumstantial evidence that the relationship between Dionise and Walker was not casual. For example, when Quinborowe and her husband, a farthingale-maker, teased Walker by suggesting that he had been to a brothel, he reportedly replied: 'No, what need I do so having a wife of my own? I can go to her when I will. I have had enough of her and can lie with her when I will. I pay for her board.' Dionise, for her part, often told a washerwoman who came to Cranfield's house that Walker had promised her marriage.[41] The apprentice, unwilling and perhaps unable to marry, complained that Dionise had blackmailed him, taking advantage of his need for secrecy. She came to the custom house where he worked as a clerk, and openly 'railed' at him, accusing him of having begotten her with child. Finally, Walker gave twenty pounds to Dionise's uncle to hold for her, and to give to her under the condition that she 'should not at any time after that revile or exclaim upon [him] or in any wise after that divulge or make known to any person that [he] had the use of her body or sue, trouble, or molest him, or cause or procure him to be sued or molested for the same'.[42]

Thomas Elkyns, a grocer's apprentice, was another such nervous bachelor in 1614. His sweetheart, Anne White, was a servant in the house of Alexander Barney, a merchant tailor, and his wife, Judith. When Anne became pregnant, Thomas admitted to the Barneys that he had procured Anne to open their door one evening and they had lain together in the hall. Upon Elkyns's request for help, the Barneys

[39] John Walker, *Dionise Halfhead c. John Walker*, 1614 (DL/C/222, fo. 46r).
[40] Quinborowe Hall, 1615 (LMA, DL/C/223, fo. 182v); John Walker, 1614 (DL/C/222, fo. 46r).
[41] Quinborowe Hall and Thomasine Evans (LMA, DL/C/223, fos. 182v, 185r).
[42] John Walker (LMA, DL/C/222, fos. 46v–47r).

sent for a connection of theirs, John Wilson from Ugley, a village in Essex. Elkyns agreed with Wilson to pay him twenty pounds to keep Anne in childbed and to care for the resulting child 'until it should come to be of seven years of age'. He paid £5 10s. down, with the rest to come later. However, further negotiations had to be made with the officials of Ugley, who might otherwise expel the unwed mother from the parish. Elkyns told the minister of Ugley that he and Anne were secretly married, 'and desired the same might be concealed because he was an apprentice and that it would endanger his freedom' if it became known. In addition, Elkyns and Alexander Barney signed a bond that the parish would not be liable for the costs of the child.[43]

In both these cases, the young women probably benefited from the good prospects of their lovers, an apprentice grocer and the future Lord Treasurer's clerk. To safeguard their futures, Elkyns and Walker were both willing and able to pay for the expenses of childbed and the upkeep of their illegitimate children. If they had been poor, they would have had less to lose through publicity, and less to spend to defend their reputations. In their position, a poor servant might simply have decided to change career plans and marry, rather than elaborately concealing his mishap, or to decamp to avoid being forced to pay for the child. In neither case, however, could a man hope to be exonerated from a woman's accusation by steadfast denial.

The theme of men's inability to deflect paternity accusations made its way into popular print. In a collection of humorous cautionary tales, *Good newes and bad newes*, Samuel Rowlands recounted the adventures of a country maidservant. At first, her migration to London brought her good fortune: she was rapidly promoted from kitchenmaid to chambermaid:

> And therewithal her wages much did mend,
> Now like a Gentlewoman she doth go,
> And country maids admire to see her so,
> Telling their friends, with all the speed they can,
> They will be Londoners like Mistress *Anne*.

However, Anne's pride came to a fall when she was seduced by a 'scurvy servingman' and became 'as big as ever she can go'. The serving-man denied everything, but both Rowlands and his carefree heroine seemed sure that, in the end, the unwanted child would be maintained by its father:

> ... that same wicked fellow that did this,
> Doth vow and swear the Child is none of his,
> But sets it light, and makes thereof a scoff,
> And thinks in Knavery thus to bob her off:
> But he'll be talked withal ere one month ends,
> For the poor wench hath sent for all her friends,
> And then it will be proved plain, at large

---

[43] Judith and Alexander Barney, *Anne White c. Thomas Alkyn alias Elkyns*, 1614 (LMA, DL/C/222, fos. 7r, 166v).

> That he's the man must bear the Nursing charge.
> Since Nan's Virginity past help is lost,
> They'll teach him what a maidenhead will cost,
> What law will do he shall be sure to find,
> Because he bears such baseness in his mind.
> Meanwhile, be it a daughter or a son,
> No remedy, it is so lately done.
> Nan's Master and her Mistress both abhor it,
> But what says she? *They cannot hang her for it.*[44]

While the fictional chambermaid's lowly seducer was unlikely to escape notoriety, in some cases the mother might be persuaded to 'father' the child on someone else. A householder might bribe a subordinate to take the blame, for example. This was suspected when Elizabeth Hart told a justice of the peace that Andrew Blackman, her fellow servant, was contracted to her and the father of her child. A man present at the examination thought that their master was the guilty man, and said 'it was but a trick which Snowden did put upon Andrew Blackman', adding: 'I will warrant you that he the said Snowden was the father thereof himself.'[45]

In other cases, richer men were the targets of strategic untruthfulness. When the servant Anne Field was found to be with child in 1601, a friend advised her sweetheart to deny responsibility: 'if he would keep a child, he might, but if he would but say that it was none of his ... Stephen Page shall be forced to keep the child.' Page apparently 'had to do with her, or would have had to do with her', so Anne could plausibly father the child on him: 'if you would but say so ... you might escape keeping of the child for if she be wise, she will lay it to the richest.'[46] Page had already been 'fathered' with one illegitimate child by a woman named Mary Lawrence, so his tarnished credit, known interest in Anne Field, and financial ability to support bastard children made him an ideal target. Maidservants' masters were particularly vulnerable, as we have seen in Creede's accusations against Randall Berk. William Gouge worried that masters were all too likely to find themselves charged with fathering their maids' bastards even when their menservants were responsible:

> The sin [of fornication] is doubled being betwixt servants: for as it is a beastly sin in itself, so in the forenamed respect it is greatly dishonourable to their master and his house: besides that the maid so defiled is oft disabled to do her service well: nay many times the charge of the child lieth upon the master. Thus shame and dishonour, grief and vexation, loss and damage all meet together, the more to gall and pierce him to the very heart.[47]

When the real father was a penniless servant, parishes had an incentive to persuade the mother to blame her master instead: he, at least, would be able to pay. The

---

[44] Samuel Rowlands, *Good newes and bad newes* (London, 1622), sig. C4.
[45] Joan Helme, *Edward Snowden c. William Roberts*, 1618 (LMA, DL/C/255, fo. 360r).
[46] John Bennet and Richard Newman, *Stephen Page c. Percival Scott*, 1602 (LMA, DL/C/216, sl. 560, 563).
[47] William Gouge, *Of domesticall duties* (London, 1622), 630.

moral satisfaction of punishing the real reprobate paled in comparison to the relief of ridding the parish of responsibility for the child.[48]

A pregnant maidservant's master might also be ordered to pay for the child or its mother when the actual father was unable to do so: masters were responsible for their servants. This was the case for Peter Martin, master to Alice Fawknall and William Hutchins, when both servants confessed that William had got Alice with child. Martin claimed that he had been ignorant of their activities, but was ordered nonetheless to 'see Alice Fawknall kept until she were brought a-bed and churched'. William Hutchins—presumably a poor youth—was whipped but not ordered to put in sureties for the maintenance of the child. In a different case, master and manservant shared responsibility: Mary Bedford admitted having had sex with both her master and his servant Humphrey Bowker, and told the court she thought Bowker was the father of her child. Bowker admitted the liaison as well, but said that since she had slept with 'divers others . . . therefore he will not marry her'. His determination to remain a bachelor yielded to the pressure exerted by the governors, however. A few days later, the Bridewell court clerk triumphantly recorded: 'Humphrey Bowker is now contented to marry Mary Bedford and it is ordered that their master shall take the child from her and see her kept till she be brought a-bed and churched, and he to be at no charge concerning the child.'[49]

As Mary Bedford's case suggests, the authorities often found marriage to be a satisfactory solution. When fornicating servants were of much lower social degree than their masters and mistresses, a hasty marriage could simply be compelled, as was the case for a tutor, Allen Carr, who in 1597 allegedly got his employers' maid Ellen Vaughan with child. Ellen was determined to force Carr to the altar, but she could not have succeeded without the aid of her master and mistress, Richard and Mary Philips. After Ellen discovered that she was with child, she took the precaution of locking Allen Carr up to prevent his flight: her fellow maidservant Agnes Loveday pretended to need the key of his room 'to lock the kitchen door', but gave it to Ellen instead. Then the servant went 'with tears and weeping and crying' to tell her master and mistress that she was with child, and that 'Allen Carr as she did fear did purpose to depart and go away secretly from his house'. Meanwhile, Carr discovered his imprisonment and called to be released, but Ellen told him 'that he should stay awhile there before he were loosed forth'. He remained locked up all that day, and only submitted to be married the following morning.[50]

Ellen greatly impressed her master with her steadfast determination to make Carr marry her. Indeed, he thought 'she had been lunatic or out of her wits'.[51] As Ellen herself sheepishly testified,

---

[48] See Ian Archer, *The Pursuit of Stability: Social Relations in Elizabeth London* (Cambridge, 1991), 216; Adair, *Courtship, Illegitimacy and Marriage*, 83–7.
[49] BRHA, BCB 2, fos. 63–6, 64v, 72v, 73r.
[50] Ellen Vaughan and Mary Philips, *Allen Carr c. Ellen Vaughan*, 1597 (LMA, DL/C/215, sl. 172–5, 194–6).
[51] Richard Philips (LMA, DL/C/215, sl. 191).

she believeth that she with a loud voice weeping and crying aloud said that she would cause the same Carr to be hanged although she were hanged with him unless he would marry her. And [she] believeth that she said that he should remain and be kept in that said chamber till he had married her and made her amends.[52]

Philips 'had some of the maids take her away' because of her 'mad and frantic behaviours', but notably did not make her give up the key. Instead, he had this conversation with Carr—through the window:

> 'Why,' quoth the same Mr Carr, 'what should I do? Should I marry her?'
> 'So she would have you do,' quoth [Philips].
> 'Well,' quoth the same Mr Carr, 'if I be married and forced thus to marry her, I assure you she shall never enjoy good day with me for I hate her!'[53]

The next morning, Mary Philips asked her friend Lady Dixon for advice, and the two gentlewomen sent for Mr Smart, the vicar. With the vicar at hand, Mary and Richard Philips and Lady Dixon told Ellen to open the door. Carr reluctantly went through with the brief ceremony, but 'utterly refused' to consummate the marriage, saying 'he could not abide her of all other women'.[54] By the time he sued for separation on the grounds that the marriage had been forced, Mary and Richard Philips testified in his favor, saying that Carr had only married Ellen out of fear of punishment. This, combined with the absence of any testimony about a child, suggests that the couple had been willing to force the marriage when they thought Ellen was pregnant, but changed their minds when—as it seems—it became clear that no child was forthcoming.

In London, civic authorities could play the same role as powerful employers in forcing servants' marriages. The governors of Bridewell regularly offered people accused of fornication the choice between matrimony and the whip. For example, when John Gillam and Elizabeth Smith were arrested in 1574, they both confessed to having sex but while Elizabeth claimed that they were betrothed, John, a bookbinder's apprentice, pleaded to be released because she had 'been evil of her body'. The governors were not impressed, and at the next meeting of the court, the clerk recorded: 'It is ordered and John Gillam, bookbinder, is contented and agreed to be bound in £40 to marry and take to wife one Elizabeth Smith at or before Midsummer next.'[55] This mercy could be abused, however, as it was when Joan Hilton escaped punishment by promising to wed one James Hoop. Three years before Hoop sued her in 1572 for breach of a matrimonial contract, Joan had given birth to an illegitimate child in the house of a family friend, Goodwife Ward in Coleman Street. As her hostess explained, when Joan was able to sit up she received many visitors: 'divers young men came to [Elizabeth Ward's] house to see her and to be a suitor unto her in the way of matrimony.' One of these was James Hoop, 'unto whom the said Joan Hilton alias Denny did bear good will, and well liked of,

---

[52] Ellen Vaughan (LMA, DL/C/215, sl. 173).
[53] Richard Philips (LMA, DL/C/215, sl. 191–2).
[54] Mary Philips (LMA, DL/C/215, sl. 196).
[55] BRHA, BCB 2, fos. 57v–58r.

so she appointed him a time to come thither again'. At the second meeting, in the presence of Joan's sister and her husband and James' brother, a marriage contract was made. As Joan testified, James 'asked her if she could find in her heart to love him and to take him to her husband, and she answered "yea"'. Joan's brother-in-law asked pointedly whether Hoop was willing to take her 'to his wife with all her faults'; then, when the contract was complete, he notified the aldermen and Christ's Hospital, and Joan 'was not only released from her punishment due for her deserts but... licensed to depart forth of that ward quietly'.[56] The banns were asked at St Stephen's as well as in James's parish.

Joan was 'appointed to be married and churched both of a day, for the avoiding of such punishment as she should have had', but when the day came, she suddenly changed her mind, informing James that she 'would not then be married unto him because she had no new clothes'. She prudently left St Stephen Coleman Street that very day, and married one John Denny in Whitechapel about two years later.[57] Although no mention was made of any financial arrangement between James Hoop and Joan Denny, it seems clear that Joan and her friends had advertised for a willing bridegroom so that Joan could escape punishment for bastardy by showing evidence of an intended marriage, with a portion to sweeten the bargain. Once the danger was past, Joan appears to have decided that she might as well save her money.[58]

One man who attempted to use this strategy to escape punishment found that he had jumped out of the frying pan into the fire. Thomas Perry was brought to court by Elizabeth Newdigate to enforce a marriage contract in 1591. He explained, with evident discomfort, that he was 'in an unfortunate time having had carnal knowledge of the body of the said Elizabeth'. He had been previously called before the ecclesiastical court for fornication, and 'did indeed in hope of avoiding punishment and public penance for his offence, confess (though untruly) then before the judge of this court that he and the said Elizabeth were contracted together'. On that occasion the judge had told him to repeat the contract, 'which he did in hopes of releasing his public penance and for no other cause as he believeth, never intending or meaning to marry her'.[59] Unfortunately for Perry, bad faith was not likely to be held a good excuse for breaking a witnessed contract.

There is little evidence that men found it easy to avoid paternal responsibilities in the face of firm accusations. When Anne Skillikor was brought to Bridewell in 1574, having been apprehended in a suspected bawd's house, she testified that one Mr Christopher Purthowe, merchant tailor, had 'had the use of her body in his wife's time'. Although Purthowe strongly denied this, and a suspicious woman's word would ordinarily be of little weight against that of a citizen, the governors

---

[56] Elizabeth Bradburn (formerly Ward), Joan Denny alias Hilton, and John Malton, *James Hoop c. John Denny and Joan Hilton alias Denny*, 1572 (LMA, DL/C/211/1, fos. 128r, 131, 127).
[57] Elizabeth Bradburn and James Hoop, 1572 (LMA, DL/C/211/1, fos. 128v, 124v).
[58] She was arrested about three years later 'as a common harlot and nightwalker and for alluring men in the street'. BRHA, BCB 3, fo. 74v.
[59] Thomas Perry, 1591 (LMA, DL/C/214, fo. 68v).

ordered Purthowe to be held prisoner until he put in sureties for his appearance.[60] Similarly, when Joan Durrant named Miles Harrison as the father of her child, the Bridewell clerk recorded: 'he denieth that ever he had to do with Joan Durrant but the said Joan doth avouch the same to the face of the said Miles, wherefore it is ordered that the said Miles... shall be bound for the keeping and discharging the City of the child.'[61] The standards of proof for paternity at Bridewell were far lower than those for fornication: those who firmly denied the latter were routinely let off without punishment. The glazier Thomas Brewer and Fortune Lasse both denied sex when they were arrested in 1574, but nonetheless Brewer was ordered to be 'bound that if the said Fortune be found with child to keep the child and her, and also to be of good behaviour'. Although the evidence against Brewer was sufficiently strong to make him responsible for any hypothetical child, it was not strong enough to warrant the whipping of either party, the usual punishment for fornication.[62]

The register of christenings of St Botolph Aldgate corroborates the strength of allegations of paternity: illegitimate children were almost always baptized with their reputed fathers' names. For example, the clerk recorded the christenings of 'Bridget Gymer daughter to one Richard Gymer, sailor, begotten of one Margeret Bedall a singlewoman, and dwelling with her mother widow Bedall' and 'Margery Hatton (a bastard) daughter to one Edward Hatton a brewer's servant, of St Katherine's by the Tower of London, the mother named Anne Badman, lodging in the house of one Rowland Pratchet, labourer'. Widows' illegitimate children were also baptized with their fathers' names, as when the clerk exercised his wit on 'Grace Saunders the reputed daughter of one William Saunders, nailsmith, the mother named Rose Hatton, a Graceless widow of our parish'. Only the children of prostitutes—or, at any rate, women that the clerk did not hesitate to characterize as 'lewd' or 'strumpets'—were regularly christened with their mothers' names, such as 'Dowsabella Allyn, daughter to one Margaret Allyn, a strumpet, delivered in the street,' and 'Margaret Francis, daughter to one Susan Francis (a common strumpet) dwelling with her father William Francis, a cobbler near the Minories'. However, even these were not always given the mother's name, even when the father was unknown, as was the case for 'George, a bastard, son reputed to one ———, the mother's name Anne Day, a lewd strumpet and singlewoman in Rosemary Lane'.[63]

When women accused men of sex without evidence of pregnancy, their targets were far less likely to suffer consequences. John Boyes, who admitted that 'he being a married man hath lewdly heretofore forgetting his duty towards God and the world... hath lewdly used the company of Elizabeth Polsted', was pardoned on his promise to reform, while Elizabeth 'had correction'. Katherine Neale and her master, Andrew Woodcock, were sent to Bridewell on suspicion of illicit sex. Andrew and his wife both denied that anything had happened, but Katherine confessed 'that Andrew Woodcock, butcher, had the use of her body in his hall

---

[60] The matter later went to arbitration. See BRHA, BCB 2, fos. 54r, 57r.
[61] Ibid. fo. 91r.
[62] Ibid. fo. 58v.
[63] GL MS 9220, fos. 137r, 141v, 176v, 140r, 166r, 141r.

when he came from the watch and that he had divers times before sought to have the use of her body, whereof she told his wife being her mistress'. She 'for her confession had by order correction'. Woodcock, who suggested that Katherine had been encouraged to accuse him falsely, was admonished and released.[64] In the absence of a pressing economic incentive, the double standard flourished.

Even if legal penalties could be avoided, pregnant maidservants could not simply be put out of the house without social repercussions. When a Mistress Hodgson threw out a servant who had been gotten with child by her lodger, she was criticized in a local apothecary's household, where one maidservant 'took the said wench's part and seemed to complain that [Mistress Hodgson] was too severe and rigid against her', because she 'refused to take her unto her house or relieve her'.[65] Similarly, when Humphrey Richardson turned away a pregnant maidservant, his neighborhood credit suffered. A local girl named Agnes Call testified that she and her parents, like other neighbors, 'in pity of . . . Anne Foster gave her a piece of an old blanket to put about her to keep her warm, and they sometimes gave her victuals as others did while she lay in the streets or else she might have been starved'. Agnes' mother Mary Call 'took in her apparel and gave her house room for it' so the servant would not lose what little she had. Another neighbor, Anne Gates, who 'took part with' the girl, publicly rebuked Richardson, calling him 'nitty breeches and Welsh runt'.[66]

THE LIMITS OF THE LAW

Although magistrates' willingness to believe paternity accusations discouraged sexual exploitation, it did not halt abuses. Women's vulnerability depended on the strength of their social networks as well as their exposure to unmarried, masterless men. Fortunate maidservants had mistresses or kin who would leap aggressively to their defense, like Margaret Inman, who harangued William Coop in front of a crowd of parishioners leaving church, saying: 'Thou . . . art a knave and thou wouldst have been naught with my maid . . . and didst rend her apron', leaving his reputation 'much impaired and stained' so that he was 'likely to be called in question before the ecclesiastical judge'.[67] However, women who knew the law or had friends who did were more likely to make public complaints than comparatively isolated and ignorant servants. The whip, too, was a powerful deterrent. Fear of punishment encouraged maidservants to seek out private arrangements whenever possible, but women who wished to avoid publicity were easier for their seducers to ignore. Moreover, sexual abuse did not necessarily result in pregnancy. The second

[64] BRHA, BCB 2, fos. 61v–62r (Polsted case), and fos. 71v–72v, 75 (Neale case).
[65] John Prudden, *Hodgson c. Alice Stanley*, 1639 (LMA, DL/C/235, fo. 267v).
[66] Agnes Call, Anne Castle, and John Clerkson, *Anne Gates c. Humphrey Richardson*, 1610 (LMA, DL/C/219, fos. 113v, 114v, 110v).
[67] Mistress Inman's charges were likely to stick because she was 'a woman of good life and conversation and no brabbler or slanderer of her neighbours'. Robert Mussell and John Judde, *William Coop c. Margaret Inman*, 1611 (LMA, DL/C/220, fos. 498r, 806r).

case study below, the rape of Isabel Burroughs, makes the limits of the protections afforded by bastardy legislation all too clear.

'He had his pleasure of her'

Jane Woodhouse's testimony about her experiences with her master provides a bleak view of the fate of a seduced maidservant lacking legal knowledge or friends. Jane, a maid of about 26, was serving a widow who lodged in the King's Head by Charing Cross when she met Christopher Percy. He 'did oftentimes solicit and move' her to leave her mistress and work for him, 'for that he had a good liking of her, seeing she could dress meat well, as he said, and promised to give her forty shillings a year for her wages'. Shortly after, Percy offered to marry her, 'saying unto her that he had been a widower twelve years, and if she would promise him marriage and love him, he would apparel her according to his ability and maintain her like a woman'.[68] Percy was a landed gentleman, and Jane should have known better than to take his promises seriously: former sheriffs and justices of the peace were unlikely to wed penniless maidservants casually hired at inns. However, she 'was contented and did yield to him to be his wife'. Predictably, no formal contract was made and Percy was careful to avoid witnesses to his promises.

On the strength of their engagement, Jane testified, he 'would have her to come to his bed and lie with him', and she consented, so that 'he had his pleasure of her as well those two night as divers times after in the said house of the King's Head as often as he desired'. Within a month, Jane discovered that she was with child. Seeing 'that the said Mr Percy had kept no promise nor married with her, nor appareled her, but only gave her twelvepence in money all that time, she cried forth and said that she could complain of him', but Percy put her off by claiming that his rents would come in soon, and 'then he would both apparel her and provide for her to go into the country to his house in Dorsetshire'.

Like his previous promises, this was not kept, and Jane's situation began to deteriorate. Percy fell ill and decided to go live with a surgeon in Bramford. Before his departure, he tried unsuccessfully to marry Jane off to the innkeeper. He

> called for Bennyland, the goodman of the said house, and said unto him that he, being a widower, might do very well to marry [Jane], saying that she was a very good servant. 'Nay,' quoth Bennyland, 'she is no fit wife for me nor for you neither. And I do not like of your doing.'

After Percy had lain ill at the surgeon's house for a fortnight, he sent for Jane to 'come and look to him'. She spent two weeks there, but refused to sleep with him: 'he would have had his pleasure of her, and she would not let him for that he had not kept promise with her.' Displeased, Percy sent her back to the inn, saying that in three days he would send his man with money and apparel. However 'she never

---

[68] Jane Woodhouse, *Margery Percy alias Gore c. Christopher Percy*, 1590 (LMA, DL/C/213, pp. 806–7). The following quotations are all from these two pages.

heard neither from the said Mr Percy nor his servant, and so the goodman of the house would not let her stay there any longer'.

Jane returned to Bramford again 'to have somewhat of him to comfort her', but was informed that Percy had left for Dorset. She needed money urgently, so 'she came and dwelt at Westminster with one Mistress Maye eight weeks'. Having 'gotten a little money of her for her service' she returned to Bramford, and this time was able to discover where Percy lived from 'one Hope dwelling at the Phoenix in Bramford' who had served him. The anxious woman made her way to Percy's country house, but 'coming thither he was not within'.

> And then she making a piteous moan how that she was with child by the said Mr Percy, one Mistress Frances, his daughter, took her into the house and kept her there a fortnight, in which time of her being there she never did see the said Mr Percy, but the daughter made her believe, that her father was at London.

Frances Percy wrote to her father for instructions and 'he sent her answer back again that she should rid her forth of his house'. Jane thought he was angry because she 'was come down to have him in his country'. Frances obeyed, and Jane 'was immediately put forth'. Jane's situation was now desperate: her pregnancy was increasingly visible and she had spent her meager savings on her trip to Dorset. She 'was fain to come to London again by foot', and continued her enquiries for Mr Percy, but although she discovered where he was, 'she could never speak with him'. Percy was anxious to avoid her, in fact, because he was in the process of courting a wealthy London widow. Jane did not mention making a public complaint, although she may have done so in the end. We do not know what became of her or her child, but by the time she testified in the subsequent suit between Percy and his new wife, she was living in Westminster again.

Legal and cultural prohibitions on fathering bastards failed to protect Jane Woodhouse for a variety of reasons. Christopher Percy was not only generally unscrupulous—as his subsequent behavior to Margery Gore confirmed—but was also traveling away from home, away from an interested and informed community of neighbors and parishioners, when he seduced his maid. For her part, Jane did not secure witnesses to her supposed marital contract with Percy before agreeing to consummate the relationship, nor did she seek legal redress once she became pregnant. She seems to have lacked supportive friends, and those who knew of her plight—the innholder, the servant Hope, and Percy's daughter Frances—were in no position to force Percy's hand. Although Jane could probably have made a formal complaint and obtained some maintenance from Percy, she was either ignorant of the law or, like Susan More, frightened of it, and willing to face considerable uncertainty and discomfort for the chance of an informal solution.

'Very ill dealt withal'

While authorities believed women who accused men of fathering their illegitimate children, their confidence in testimony about rape—a crime without implications for the poor rates—was very weak indeed. The difficulty of proving lack of consent meant that only the rapists of girls under the age of consent and especially under the age of 10 were regularly convicted.[69] Consequently, victims were left with few options. At best, the case of Isabel Burroughs and William Gould suggests that a semi-formal committee of matrons could establish that a woman had been wronged and identify the man responsible.

Described as a 'young girl', Isabel was probably in her early teens when she was assaulted by her mistress's lodger, William Gould. After the rape, Isabel's mistress, the widow Burnett, brought her to a neighboring tailor's house to board. The tailor's wife noticed that she looked very sad, and asked Isabel what was wrong. 'With much ado privately together the said Isabel with weeping eyes' told her that Gould had sent her up to his chamber on an errand, but 'so soon as she was gone up, he followed her and there striving with her had to deal with her, and therefore she was so sad'.[70] When Isabel's mother found out what had happened to her daughter, she took immediate action to establish the facts. She collected a group of matrons of good credit and a midwife, and brought them to the widow Burnett's house in St John's Street to examine Isabel. The women went up to the chamber where the rape had taken place, and told the widow to fetch Isabel. When the girl arrived, the midwife

> took the said Isabel and set her upon the bedseat which stood in the chamber and looked upon her together with all the rest and did well perceive that the said Isabel had been very ill dealt withal and strained in the *partibus secretis*. And then asking the said Isabel who did so hurt her, she said: 'Mr Gould had make [*sic*] her so, and none but he had had the use of her body and that he did it against a bedside.'[71]

The case was brought to the attention of the Bridewell court, but unfortunately, the records of that year have not survived, and Isabel's fate remains unknown. In similar cases of men having sex with young girls, the men, and sometimes the girls as well, were punished. When John Turner was brought to Bridewell in 1574 for sex with a 12-year old, he was corrected 'with whips' while the girl was corrected more gently 'with rods'. William Gorton was 'corrected' 'for abusing himself with a wench of twelve years of age' who did not appear in Bridewell.[72] It seems likely that Gould was whipped; perhaps the efforts of the matrons to treat the matter as a violent rape saved Isabel Burroughs from being treated as a willing participant. However, whatever punishment Gould received did not deter him from suing his accusers for defamation to silence them. The fact that Isabel did not apparently become pregnant meant that local authorities were unlikely to take a strong interest in punishing her attacker.

Some maidservants whose masters violently assailed their chastity found the strength to resist both literally and legally. Susan Turton, for example, physically thwarted her master, then lodged a public complaint against him. Several witnesses

---

[69] See Capp, 'The Double Standard Revisited' 92; Martin Ingram, 'Child Sexual Abuse in Early Modern England', in Braddick and Walter (eds), *Negotiating Power in Early Modern Society*.
[70] Margery Sacheverell, *William Gould c. Katherine Socklyn*, 1586 (LMA, DL/C/213, pp. 125–6).
[71] Juliana Marsh, 1586 (LMA, DL/C/213, pp. 126–7).
[72] BRHA, BCB 2, fos. 72r (Turner case), 46v (Gorton case).

testified that Susan, accompanied by another woman, had come before Sir Thomas Bennett, a justice of the peace, to complain about sexual harassment. She told him, with considerable exasperation, that 'she and her fellows could not be at quiet for... William Holmes, for he would be tousing and mousing of them and urging them to folly, and take up their clothes and would have had the carnal knowledge of their bodies'. He 'would find her out in any room of the house (she being his servant) and come where she had been making of the beds', and 'touse her so that she was sometimes out of breath to resist him and did throw her upon the bed and strived with her by pulling up of her clothes but had not the use of her body'. Sometimes he 'did pull out his prick and did put it into her hand'. The case does not record the result of Susan's complaint, and Holmes sued her for defamation, but the fact that she felt able to put her master's private behavior into public, discrediting words indicates that if some masters felt entitled to harass their maids, some maidservants also felt sufficiently comfortable with the machinery of the law to deploy it against their superiors.[73]

UNNATURAL MOTHERS

While many maidservants who found themselves with a big belly were able to negotiate private maintenance or risked punishment to obtain formal support, not all were able or willing to do so. Some women attempted abortion, while a few abandoned their infants shortly after birth, or were driven to infanticide. These desperate strategies were dangerous. Abortion was nearly impossible to prove, but, mindful of the link between the shaming and punishment of bastard-bearers and the destruction of illegitimate children, English authorities strove to identify mothers so heartless as to forsake or murder their children, and to subject them to the full weight of the law.

Londoners believed in the possibility of abortion, mostly by the consumption of unspecified 'physick' or 'purgations', although successful abortions may have been rare.[74] In 1575, for example, an alleged prostitute, Cicely Stedman, told the governors of Bridewell that after a sexual encounter, her bawd 'willed her to go take the wench's groat, for that she said she had no money to buy a purgation to kill the child, and therefore she bought coliquintum, and took the same'.[75] The uncertainty surrounding early pregnancy[76] made it easy for women to accuse maidservants of abortion, but difficult for them to prove it. For example, Elizabeth Bowles looked pregnant 'by reason of the roundness and bigness of her belly' when she began to

---

[73] Meredith Broughton, William Coxe, and John Riche, *William Holmes c. Susan Turton*, 1624 (DL/C/229, fos. 88–9).
[74] For example, savin was known to 'bring down the menses with force, draw away the after-birth, expel the dead child, and kill the quick'. It could also be fatally toxic. John Gerard, *The herball or General historie of plantes* (London, 1633), 1378.
[75] This frugal remedy did not have the desired effect. BRHA, BCB 2, fo. 199r.
[76] See Gowing, *Common Bodies*, 111–48.

serve Mr and Mistress Ramsey around 1635. However Mistress Ramsey was 'satisfied by some infallible signs that appeared in her' that her servant was not pregnant; although she was too discreet to elaborate, presumably Elizabeth showed her evidence of menstruation. A neighbor, Mary Heale, was less easily convinced. She visited one day and 'after some salutations', said 'she would tell her a thing if she would not take it unkindly': namely, that Elizabeth was with child. Matilda Ramsey did not believe it, and defended her maid as 'an honest wench'. A few days later, Mary Heale enlarged her accusations: 'I . . . will take it upon my salvation that she is with child, and that she hath but eight weeks to go,' and added that Elizabeth was 'cunning . . . if we did not look to her . . . she would destroy it and had taken things to that purpose but was too far gone.'[77] Indeed, Elizabeth had been taking some medicine: she had sought the advice of a physician for a tympany (a swelling). Mistress Ramsey 'showed the said Mistress Heale some seeds and said . . . that her maid did boil and drink the same, and . . . Mistress Heale replied that those seeds were given many times to women in labour.' The usual test of squeezing Elizabeth's breast was inconclusive: 'there came forth of her breast some water or liquid substance.' In the end, though the Ramseys professed to believe in Elizabeth's innocence, they put her out nonetheless, 'by reason of this report raised on her and because she was otherwise unfit for her service'.[78]

If abortion failed, women determined to keep their pregnancies secret might also abandon their infants. These then fell on the mercy of the parish, to the great disapproval of civic authorities who in 1615 issued an order 'for the finding out of Queanes that leave their children in the streets . . . whereof some by reason of the cold and lack of sustenance have died'.[79] Without a foundling hospital, a woman who wished to discreetly dispose of an unwanted infant would simply leave it in the street, on a church porch, or at a rich man's door. Fear of being saddled with pauper infants led officials to regard pregnant single women with deep suspicion; they often bribed or coerced them to cross into the next parish.[80] The unlucky parish that gained the foundling was then left to seek out the parents for punishment and to force them to take back the child, if it could find them.[81] If not, parish officials could only vent their disapproval in baptism registers. The clerk of St Botolph Aldgate recorded the christening of the occasional foundling with considerable indignation. One of these was 'Dowsabella Portsoken, a child so named, because it was found at Goodman's gate in the Minories street in our ward of Portsoken, the wicked parents unknown'. Another

---

[77] Matilda and Robert Ramsey, *Elizabeth Bowles c. Mary Heale*, 1635 (LMA, DL/C/630, fos. 333v, 334v, 331r).
[78] Elizabeth Bowles, 1635 (LMA, DL/C/194, fos. 151v–152v) and Matilda Ramsey (LMA, DL/C/630, fo. 335).
[79] LMA, Journals, Court of Common Council 29/177a, cited in Beier, *Masterless Men*, 54.
[80] See the strenuous efforts of Christopher Fawcett in St Saviour's, Southwark. Laura Gowing, 'Giving Birth at the Magistrate's Gate: Single Mothers in the Early Modern City', in Stephanie Tarbin and Susan Broomhall (eds), *Women, Identities and Communities in Early Modern Europe* (Bodmin, 2008), 140–41.
[81] See Archer, *The Pursuit of Stability*, 220; Gowing, 'Giving Birth', 145–6.

was named 'Elizabeth Lion (a child so named because it was found in Red Lion Alley in the Minories street, the wicked and hard hearted parents unknown)'. Christ's Hospital only reluctantly accepted the foundlings who made up about 10 per cent of its admissions around the end of the sixteenth century, and on occasion banned them entirely.[82] While the numbers of foundlings horrified city authorities, however, they were minute in comparison to the epidemic of abandonment that later strained the resources of the Foundling Hospital. In addition, most foundlings were already several months old, which suggests that they were more likely to be the legitimate children of pauper parents than the secret offspring of single women.[83]

Finally, in the most desperate cases, an unwed mother might conceal her lapse by giving birth in secret and murdering the child or leaving it for dead. Thus the clerk of St Botolph Aldgate recorded the short life of 'Elizabeth—the reputed daughter of one ———, the mother named Joan Thacke, a lewd strumpet, servant to Thomas Newton a broker in Houndsditch, which said Joan cast her child into a privy and fled away, but by good hap it was heard to cry and was saved and christened in the said Newton's house the eleventh day of May 1615, and died about a week after'.[84] Much though civic authorities deplored bastardy, they did not wish to encourage infanticide, and in 1624, an assumption of guilt was introduced for unwed mothers who gave birth in secret to infants subsequently found dead. Those who suffered under the law were usually maidservants.[85] However, prosecutions were rare even before public will to convict women for infanticide waned in the late seventeenth century.[86] The Middlesex Sessions include only four indictments for the murder of newborn infants during the reign of Elizabeth, and four more from the period from 1603 to 1667. The spinster Joan Bulte, for example, was sentenced to be hanged for having 'in a certain place called "a house of office" . . . between two and three a.m. of the said day . . . assaulted a female infant to which she had given birth, and murdered the same infant by crushing its head with her hands and strangling it with a girdle'.[87] Her savage act may have resulted from deeper troubles than simple fear of punishment. Few pregnant servants were driven to such extremes.

---

[82] GL MS 9220, fos. 163v and 167r; Archer, *The Pursuit of Stability*, 157–9.
[83] Valerie Fildes, 'Maternal Feelings Re-assessed: Child Abandonment and Neglect in London and Westminster, 1550–1800', in Fildes (ed.), *Women as Mothers in Pre-Industrial England* (London, 1990), 149–52.
[84] GL MS 9220, fo. 151v.
[85] 21 Jac.I, c.27 (1624); Susan Dwyer Amussen, *An Ordered Society: Gender and Class in Early Modern England* (New York, 1988), 113.
[86] Garthine Walker suggests that the extent of prosecution for infanticide—and, indeed, the incidence of infanticide—in the seventeenth century has been exaggerated. *Crime, Gender and Social Order*, 149. On the decline of convictions, see Peter C. Hoffer and N. E. H. Hull, *Murdering Mothers: Infanticide in England and New England 1558–1803* (New York, 1981).
[87] See John Cordy Jeaffreson (ed.), *Middlesex County Records*, old series (London, 1886–8, repr. 1974), vols. i–iii. Joan Bulte's case appears in vol. i, 285.

FALLEN WOMEN?

While an unwanted pregnancy certainly derailed a maidservant's career at least temporarily, it was not always or perhaps even often the first step on the slippery slope towards prostitution. Although one might suppose that having borne a child would debar a maid from respectable service and marriage, testimony in a 1634 fornication case brought against one Elizabeth Francis shows that female reputation could prove surprisingly resilient. While the young woman suffered the wrath of her outraged father and the humiliation of a bodily search in front of curious female neighbors, she not only obtained compensation from the alleged father of her child, but went on to make a respectable marriage and to regain the esteem of her community.

Anne Layton was 13 around 1621 when one Mistress Elkes came to see her mother, lamenting that she was undone: her daughter Elizabeth was begotten with child. Not long after, Anne heard a frightening tumult next door, 'the said Mr Elkes threatening or beating her the said Elizabeth and demanding of her who had begotten her with child'. Elizabeth and her mother, 'for shelter to avoid her father's anger and choler', took refuge in the house of another neighbor, that of Mistress Middleton, a schoolmistress who taught girls like Anne's sister Rose, 14, how to sew. There, according to Rose Layton, Mistress Elkes bewailed her daughter's pregnancy and Elizabeth was searched by the matrons, who indeed found her breasts milky and her belly great. After intense questioning, Elizabeth admitted that she was with child by a Mr Loeman of the Middle Temple. This was not a case of overenthusiastic courtship: Loeman was 'an ancient tall black man...about fifty years old at that time'. A delegation of local men including Elizabeth's father and Mr Layton visited Loeman, who paid five pounds up front to make Elizabeth amends, with the promise of more. Elizabeth Elkes then disappeared for about a quarter of a year. The Layton girls thought she had been banished by her father, but her absence during the final months of pregnancy made it possible for the Elkes to put the matter behind them. Around 1627, Elizabeth was married to one John Francis and gave birth, after a respectable interval, in her mother's house.[88]

By the time the matter came to court, all the facts were hotly disputed. Some quarrel must have arisen between the Laytons and the Elkes, because Mr Layton was the moving force behind the *ex officio* case against Elizabeth. A first group of witnesses, four women including the Layton sisters, testified that she had indeed been pregnant, while a second group attacked their credit and cast doubts on the existence of the mysterious Mr Loeman, now long gone from the Temple.[89] It is

---

[88] Anne Westcott alias Layton and Rose Jones alias Layton, *Office prom. Layton c. Elizabeth Francis alias Elkes*, 1634 (LMA, DL/C/630, fos. 292r, 290, 291v).

[89] None of the original witnesses was of flawless credit. Margery Durham was a 'quarrelsome and contentious woman', known for 'excessive or inordinate drinking', who kept a 'disordered' victualing house. Her husband had spent time in Newgate and she herself was known to blaspheme the holy name of God. Elizabeth Worthington was one 'that liveth idly and goeth up and down tipling and drinking from alehouse to alehouse and cellar to cellar', and the Layton sisters had both given birth too soon after their marriages. Elizabeth Middleton denied that any physical search had taken place in her

difficult to discern the truth of the matter, but it seems likely that the detailed story of Elizabeth's being gotten with child was true. The convenient forgetting of the past shame of an accepted and well-liked neighbor seems more plausible than the malicious manufacture of an ancient scandal. In addition, all the first witnesses admitted that with the exception of her youthful error, Elizabeth Francis was a woman of good life and conversation, which they would hardly have done had they invented the story to discredit her. If Elizabeth had indeed borne a child before going into service and making a respectable marriage, the fact that several women testified in her favor serves as a useful reminder of the interdependent nature of early modern female respectability. Since no one was entirely pristine, London women had much to gain by upholding one another's honor and assuming innocence in the absence of absolute proof to the contrary.

Elizabeth Elkes was hardly the only young woman to recover from illicit pregnancy. A number of consistory court witnesses had borne children out of wedlock before continuing in service or marrying. Joan Buffrawe had 'had a child begotten and born of her body about half a year past' before her testimony in 1622, and had subsequently entered the service of a widow in St Giles in the Fields. The maidservant Elizabeth Nixon, who had borne an illegitimate child about a year before she testified in 1637, declared: 'she liveth by her service and so hath done these seven years last past.'[90] Emma Bennett, a bookbinder's wife, was widely known to have had at least one illegitimate child: one witness reported that she 'had a base child born of her body before she came out of the country', while another specified that the child had been born at Whitecliffe close to Ludlow in Shropshire. Emma 'being then married ... to an honest man she had acquainted him therewith and ... her said husband took it very patiently'. She had behaved herself honestly since her marriage, the witness conceded.[91] A young mariner's wife had 'had a base child born of her body about four years sithence', a neighbor reported in 1615, but her credit had not suffered overmuch: 'being sworn before a judge she will not anyways forswear herself.' Elizabeth Lamberson, the wife of 'one of the bag bearers to Sir Henry Fanshaw, knight, of the court rolls to Westminster', had been married for a little over a year when she testified in 1608. Previously she had served the rector of St Faith the Virgin, but despite her clerical situation she confessed that 'she was begotten with child before she was married and she was delivered of that child at Lambeth'.[92]

---

house, and Frances Morris, a laundress in the Middle Temple, did not remember any Mr Loeman. Anne Gibbons, Mary Jenks, Elizabeth Middleton, and Frances Morris, 1634 (LMA, DL/C/234, fos. 17–20r, 15–16).

[90] Joan Buffrawe, 1622 (LMA, DL/C/228, fo. 298); Margaret Deane and Elizabeth Nixon, 1637 (LMA, DL/C/235, fos. 12v, 14–15).

[91] She missed the child: one witness saw her 'play with and make much of a young child of one Mr Lancelot Barrett dwelling in London who had a red head, and ... he hath heard one Elizabeth then servant to the said Mr Barrett say she ... loved the said child for that it was like the child of the said Emma.' Thomas Gibbons, John Searle, and Richard Hayton, 1616 (LMA, DL/C/224, fos. 169v, 158v, 178v).

[92] Mary Stronginthearme, 1614 (LMA, DL/C/223, fo. 206v) and Elizabeth Lamberson, 1608 (LMA, DL/C/218, p. 320).

Prostitution was a thriving trade in London, to be sure, but it was not the inevitable result of bastardy. A more common route may have been that of Anne Jackson, a poor apprentice, who 'did cozen and deceive her mistress' and was consequently dismissed and ended up living in a bawdy house in Turnbull Street.[93] Maidservants out of service were unlikely to be able to live on their savings for more than a few days or weeks, and might fall into vagrancy and thievery if they could not find work. For them, prostitution may have been a necessary makeshift. Arrested for whoredom with one Thomas Smith in 1575, Judith Tailor, a 'lame creature' from Essex, explained pitifully to the Bridewell governors that 'she lay in Shoreditch under a stall. And there the said Thomas Smith came between three and four of the clock in the morning and found her lying there under a stall of whom she sayeth she was afraid. And then the said Thomas asked her what she did there, and she told him that she could get no lodging, whereupon she [*sic*] willed her to go home with him.' Homelessness, more than anything else, had put her and her virtue at risk.[94] While pregnant maids did sometimes end up on the streets, many other offenses and misfortunes could also lead to a servant being turned away.

Other young women entered prostitution as a variety of service rather than an alternative to it. At the worst extreme, Emme Finch's service with the victuallers Alice and Richard Robinson amounted to virtual slavery. When Emme escaped and took refuge with a widow, Joan Burges, Alice Robinson was questioned by the Bridewell governors. She told a conventional tale of a misbehaving servant: while her husband was out, 'one Thomas Casey, a plasterer in Gutter Lane, came into her house, herself and her husband being forth, and one Emme Finch her maid being in the house a-washing, and there and then the said Thomas Casey had the use and carnal knowledge' of Emme's body. When Emme became pregnant, Alice reported, Richard Robinson dutifully 'took £3 of the said Casey which was to discharge the parish', in the presence of two witnesses. Emme Finch herself told a very different story. She testified that 'Alice Robinson her mistress would oftentimes force her to go up into a room to be naught with divers men'. For example:

> a bricklayer who resorted to the house came in and asked if he should drink a pot of beer, and [she] answered 'Yes, if he would,' and bade him sit down in the one of the rooms below; but he refused so to do and would have gone up, then [she] perceiving his lewd intent said her master and mistress were both asleep on the bed; then the said bricklayer was presently going forth of the house, and turning him about he espied [her] master and mistress coming indoors; and he said 'Are these they that were on the bed asleep?' Then the bricklayer sent for an eel pie which they ate and then he would have a pint of wine, which [her] master himself went for, and in that time when her master was gone for the wine, her mistress caused her to go up with the bricklayer, and there the said bricklayer had the use and carnal knowledge of [her] body, and he gave her eighteen pence which her mistress took from her as soon as the bricklayer was gone away.[95]

---

[93] John Lawrence, *Katherine Wilkins c. Joyce Patrick*, 1614, LMA, DL/C/223, fo. 35r.
[94] BRHA, BCB 2, fo. 117r.
[95] BRHA, BCB 5, fos. 25v, 26v.

If Emme's story was true, by finding a father for their maid's child the Robinsons may have hoped to deflect official attention from their sordid business. The Bridewell governors were not convinced, however: they took sureties of the Robinsons and, after keeping her prisoner for a few days, released Emme back into Joan Burges's custody.

Emme Finch's case was unusually bleak: in most cases, maidservants who entered prostitution at their mistresses' behest kept at least part of their earnings. The story of Judith Vincent, who was 'most wickedly betrayed' into sin by her mistress, Dorothy Cleveley, provides a more balanced picture of coercion and enticement. As Judith told the Bridewell governors in October 1575, her mistress requested her 'to go with one Mr Bishop being a priest...saying that he should bring her to a place where she should be retained into service'. Dorothy 'willed her before she went to wash her feet, to put on a clean smock of her said mistress, saying that if she tarried all night at the place where he would bring her, she should peradventure lie with some gentlewoman of the house, and that such another one would be loath to lie with her if her feet were foul and her smock not clean'. At five o'clock, the priest led Judith to a house in Beard Alley where he locked her in a room, and shortly thereafter one Mr Edmund Verney 'willed her to sit down by the fire and to tarry there till he came again, bidding her not to be afraid till he came, for it would be towards nine of the clock'. He returned as promised, bringing Judith 'bread, meat, and drink and a caudle, and willed her to eat and drink, and after desired to look at her feet, and then giving her fair speech willed her to go to bed and so lay with her all that night'.

The following morning, Verney gave Judith four shillings and promised that Bishop would buy her a petticoat. She returned home, explaining to her master (as her mistress had suggested) that she had spent the night at her godmother's. Mistress Clevely 'asked her if she had pleased the gentleman, saying that if she pleased him well, she should find a friend of him'. She took the money, but Judith received the promised petticoat. Shopping with Mistress Cleveley and Judith, the priest bought 'as much red frysadowe as made her a petticoat, and after they bought an upperbody of tufted mocadowe red and black with fringe'. While they were drinking at a tavern afterward, Mistress Cleveley 'threatened her if she did disclose this matter, she would cause her to be so punished as all others should take example by her'. Judith held her tongue for two weeks, but eventually temptation grew too strong and she told another maid in the house. Her mistress then denounced her as a whore, 'wherewith she held herself much offended, because she was brought to folly by her mistress's conspiracy, and being betrayed by her policy'.[96]

Prostitutes who catered to a wealthy clientele fared well enough that a young woman's own family might place her in the service of a well-connected bawd. This was the case for Alice Partridge, a London native who failed to thrive as a conventional maidservant. Alice had formerly served a Lady Hobby, but as she confessed in March 1598, 'because she could not work well the Lady Hobby put

---

[96] BRHA, BCB 2, fos. 179v–180v.

her away'.[97] Agnes Wilkinson, the bawd, told the Bridewell governors that 'the mother of the said Alice and another man which came with her to [Agnes's] house... desired [Agnes] to help the said Alice her daughter to a service or to help her to some friends of [hers]'. The bawd instructed Alice 'to change her name from Partridge to Alice Woodstock, saying else it would be a discredit unto her', and dressed her in 'a gentlewoman's gown left in pawn'. She then sent Alice and another 'servant' of hers, Barbara Allen, to Mr Brooke, Lord Cobham's brother, where they collected hefty fees: Barbara was paid thirty shillings, of which the bawd claimed half. This was apparently her usual practice: 'divers other men who did resort to the house of the said Wilkinson had the use of the body of [Barbara Allen], and... the said Wilkinson's wife had always half of all such sums of money which was given to [her] when any had the use of her.'[98] A prostitute who often earned ten or fifteen shillings could amass savings far beyond those of 'honest' maids, although the pox was a serious occupational hazard, and the illegal nature of the work was a constant danger.[99] Even the more moderate average fee of 4s. 3d. would add up if a prostitute were able to keep a reasonable percentage.[100]

While evidence is scanty, one consistory court case hints that successful prostitutes did on occasion retire to live more conventional lives. Alice Newsham alias Fawkes, who came before the court in a disciplinary case in 1616, was suspected by several witnesses to have been a whore before her marriage. A haberdasher said that she had formerly lived in bawdy houses like that of Mistress Barnaby in Southwark. Thomas Shaxton claimed that Alice had 'boasted and bragged... in most impious manner' of her lewd occupation, saying that 'she had gotten thereby more money than with her hands... She could by prostrating her body... get winter and summer apparel.' Once, Alice had 'famed herself to be with child, and... [Mistress Barnaby] had procured such gentlemen as resorted to her house to give the said Alice some monies, telling the said gentlemen that the said child wherewith she was great was gotten amongst them'. Eventually, she had become pregnant in earnest while maintaining a liaison with one John Lodwicke. Arrested and brought to Bridewell, she was punished, and the child was kept by its father. About four years later, Alice married a different man; it is probably around this time that she 'desired' one Isaac Bostocke 'to be a means to the said Lodwicke that she herself might have the keeping of the said child'. Bostocke 'talked with the said Lodwicke thereabouts', and he answered that she 'should have the said child so as she would keep the same well'. Married, Alice saw no reason why she should not take custody of her

---

[97] If this was indeed the pious and exacting Margaret who married Sir Thomas Posthumous Hoby in London on 9 August 1596, it is hardly surprising that Alice Partridge was found wanting.

[98] BRHA, BCB 4, fo. 8r.

[99] Agnes Wilkinson herself was nearly drowned as a result of a quarrel with another go-between over Alice's fee. He 'offered to stab Agnes if she would not be quiet' but she 'was more earnester' and so he thrust her into the Thames, from which she was rescued by her husband. Later, Agnes' house was invaded by the watch, and while some of the clients 'scaped away', Agnes, Alice, and Barbara were all arrested, even though they hid in a secret hiding place. BRHA, BCB 4, fo. 8r.

[100] Apprentices paid an average of 1s. 10d. and non-apprentices paid 5s. 8d. in Paul Griffiths' sample of 111 payments. 'The Structure of Prostitution in Elizabethan London', *Continuity and Change* 8.1 (1993), 47.

illegitimate child: at the time of the trial John Lodwicke junior was 6 years old and presumably lived with his mother and stepfather.[101]

Fathering an illegitimate child was a grave offense against the social order: it created a material problem—a pauper infant—that burdened the household finances of all those rich enough to pay parish rates, and siphoned scarce aid away from the existing poor. Accordingly, magistrates sacrificed the sexual double standard to economic expediency by allowing pregnant single women to assign their children's paternity. Many men made private arrangements to avoid the scandal of a public resolution, and the expectation that pregnant single women would obtain some support surely tempered maidservants' vulnerability to abuse. Of course, for men at the very top and the very bottom of the social hierarchy, the risks of fathering an illegitimate child may have been negligible. It was hardly the most expensive vice practiced by wealthy gentlemen, while poor servants and vagrants with little to lose could simply run away.[102] Transient single masterless men may have been relatively unswayed by moral or legal concerns. For the middling sort, however, the risks of illicit sex loomed large. An apprentice's career could be upset and his freedom jeopardized by the discovery of premature fatherhood. Married men, too, could be forced to pay the charges of childbirth and putting the children out to nurse, either secretly, or in the jaundiced gaze of resentful neighbors. As the low rates of London illegitimacy suggest, the consequences of bastardy were severe enough to protect most maidservants from casual seduction or rape, reinforcing the moral strictures that condemned such abuses as unacceptable breaches of patriarchal duty.

---

[101] Thomas Shaxton and Isaac Bostocke, *Office prom. Brettingham c. Alice Newsham alias Fawkes*, 1616 (LMA, DL/C/224, fos. 196v–197r, 195v–196r).

[102] For example, the gentleman John Darrell dealt with his own indiscretions by marrying his pregnant maidservants to his menservants. See Francis Knight's testimony about his sister Sybil in *Anne Darrell c. John Darrell*, 1619 (LMA, DL/C/225, fos. 47r–49r).

4

Household Mistresses

Marriage radically transformed a London woman's life. No longer a dependent maidservant or daughter, she was mistress of her own family. In the neighborhood, this entitled a married woman to a new level of respect, as Samuel Rowlands' Bride proudly reminded her erstwhile companions:

> I am your better now by *Ring* and *Hat*,
> No more plain *Rose*, but Mistress you know what.[1]

Married women were addressed with titles like 'goodwife' or, more commonly in London, 'mistress' instead of the bare first names to which servants were entitled, and the rings and tall hats they wore visibly proclaimed their rank. Even a poor woman was subject to no one's domestic authority save that of her husband. If her family comprised servants, apprentices, or children, they were all firmly subject to her. It was important for the husband to support and maintain his wife's dominance over the rest of the household: for him to treat his wife with disrespect might enhance his sense of authority temporarily, but would ultimately subvert the rules of authority and deference that governed relations with servants and children. If they learned not to respect the mistress, the master too would inevitably suffer.

Married women's responsibilities were not limited to ruling servants and children. London wives also shared responsibility for keeping their households on an even economic keel. While women performed unpaid domestic labor and many wives helped provide for their families by working for the market as well, increasing revenue was not their only contribution to household economies. They were also assigned the task of 'saving' or preserving household resources, and often this included restraining their husbands' spending. While the patriarchal order—with children, servants, and the wife ultimately governed by the man who combined the roles of father, master, and husband—was intended to maintain harmony and economic stability, the surest way for an early modern household to fall into economic disarray was through the patriarch's misbehavior. Drinking, gambling, and whoring—the traditional vices of carefree bachelors—posed a serious threat when adult men refused to abandon their youthful pleasures for the sober comforts of settled manhood. In theory, wives had no authority to discipline their husbands' behavior. However, a rigid hierarchy that allowed the wife little voice upheld the letter of the law at the expense of its spirit. In practice, as order was the ultimate goal

---

[1] Samuel Rowlands, *The bride* (London, 1617).

of patriarchal household hierarchies, it was considered to be the wife's duty to maintain the economic integrity and stability of the household as well as she could without breaking the rule of wifely subjection.

Jokes, ballads, and stories suggest that it was commonplace—and often necessary—for women to urge their husbands to embrace the responsibilities of manhood by keeping to their labor and avoiding costly temptations. However, achieving the right balance between subjection and responsibility was difficult. Disadvantaged as they were by law, women's influence was largely limited to the power of their tongues, of which they made the maximum possible use, admonishing, advising, rebuking, nagging, and even scolding their erring spouses. The line between praiseworthy advice and unacceptable scolding was thin, and its location open to question. Thus, rather than being rebels against patriarchal order, 'shrewish' wives are perhaps best seen as would-be enforcers of the patriarchal values of sobriety, thrift, and honest labor. Tension between wives' dual roles and conflicting duties as subjects and governors was a major point of conflict in early modern marriages.

Marriage was not just something that happened to early modern women. Rather, wives took on authority and responsibility, ruling and providing for their families. They were subject to their husbands, but also partners with them, bound to guard and govern the younger members of the household. Their tasks were heavy, often thankless, and sometimes even impossible. Nevertheless, to view them as victims or passive subjects—chaste, silent, and obedient—is to ignore women's real efforts to maintain a fragile social and economic order in which they certainly believed they had a stake, and which could not have survived without them.

'THAT SMALL INEQUALITY'

The early modern English household was based on three hierarchies: husband and wife, employer and servant, and parent and child. All three were supposed to consist of benevolent rule on one side and respectful submission on the other. When husband and wife were considered in isolation, the wife's status was clear: she was subject to her husband. However, she also wielded patriarchal authority by ruling her servants and her children. Accordingly, descriptions of the ideal wife stressed her role as a source of household authority as well as her intimate relationship with her husband: 'She commands with mildness, rules with discretion, lives in repute, and ordereth all things that are good or necessary; she's her husband's solace, her house's ornament, her children's succor, and her servants' comfort.'[2]

---

[2] Henry Parrot, *Cures for the itch* (London, 1626), sig. B6r. See also the description of the virtuous wife in William Crompton, *A wedding-ring, fitted to the finger of every paire that have or shall meete in the feare of God* (London, 1632), 4. For the unique position of the wife in the early modern English household, see Susan Dwyer Amussen, *An Ordered Society: Gender and Class in Early Modern England* (New York, 1988), 40–47.

The metaphor that writers found most apt for describing the wife's dual role was political. The clergyman William Whately explained that husband and wife were both 'governors of an house', the husband as God's representative, and the wife as the husband's representative: 'The man must be taken for God's immediate officer in the house, and as it were the King in the family; the woman must account herself his deputy, an officer substituted to him, not as an equal, but as subordinate: and in this order they must govern; he, by the authority derived unto him from God immediately, she, by authority derived to her from her husband'. William Gouge used the metaphor of a kingdom to explain why the wife's role did not threaten the husband's authority: 'We see that in all estates the king or highest governor hath other Magistrates under him, who have a command over the subjects, and yet thereby the king's supreme authority is no whit impaired, but rather the better established, and he the more honoured. So is it in a family'. The same message was preached from the pulpit:

> For even as the King appeareth so much the more noble, the more excellent and noble he maketh his officers and Lieutenants, whom if he should dishonour, and despise the authority of their dignity, he should deprive himself of a great part of his own honour: Even so, if thou dost despise her that is set in the next room beside thee, thou dost much derogate and decay the excellency and virtue of thine own authority.[3]

Just as disobedience to a magistrate dangerously undermined the principle of obedience to the ruler, disrespectful behavior to a wife eroded the same patriarchal bedrock that supported the husband's dominance. It was necessary for husband and wife to be seen to agree, at least in the eyes of their children and servants, 'so they may both maintain each other's authority to the full'. If they presumed to countermand one another's orders, 'they shall also lighten and lessen each other's power in the family, that both at last shall grow into contempt, because of their indiscretion'.[4] Only by maintaining a united front could they govern their family in peace and harmony: 'For the household, when their master and their mistress, or dame, are at debate, can no otherwise be in quiet and at rest, than a City whose rulers agree not, but when it seeth them in concord and quietness, then it rejoiceth, trusting that they will be even so unto them, as it perceiveth them to be among themselves.'[5] Gouge warned that only a fool would countenance disrespect toward his wife:

---

[3] William Whately, *A bride-bush: or, A direction for married persons plainely describing the duties common to both, and peculiar to each of them* (London, 1619), 89; William Gouge, *Of domesticall duties* (London, 1622), 259; 'An Homily on the State of Matrimony', in *Certain sermons or homilies appointed to be read in churches, in the time of Queen Elizabeth of famous memory* (London, 1683), 315. See also Thomas Gataker, *Marriage Duties briefely couched togither out of Colossians, 3.18, 19* (London, 1620), 4.

[4] Whately, *A bride-bush*, 96–7. Rogers wrote that if the children need correction, the good wife 'holds not [her husband's] hand from due strokes, but bares their skin with delight, to his fatherly stripes'. However, he conceded that a wife could play 'the kind mediator'. Daniel Rogers, *Matrimoniall honour: or, The mutuall crowne and comfort of godly, loyall, and chaste marriage* (London, 1642), 299.

[5] Robert Cleaver and John Dod, *A godly forme of houshold government for the ordering of private families* (London, 1612), 174.

By despising the weaker, men grow by little and little to despise the stronger... [I]t tends not to the honour and ease only, but to the safety also of the supreme Magistrate, to have the power and authority of inferior Magistrates respected, and not trampled under feet. It argueth therefore both want of affection, and of discretion and understanding in husbands, to suffer child, servant, or any other in the house, to insult over their wives, who are joint governors with them over the house.[6]

Moralists dwelt lengthily on the status of the wife because her dual role gave scope to misunderstandings, conflict, and negotiation. Although a husband was to govern his wife, 'there ought to be between them such society and fellowship, yea and greater, than is between the father and the son; and not such as is between the master and the servant'. While wives were bound to obey, husbands did not have a general right to command. A good husband 'willingly resigns up his manly authority sometimes, and wisely abridgeth himself of that power to the uttermost, which else he might usurp over his weaker wife'. No such 'resigning up' of authority was permissible for masters ruling servants.[7] In contrast, autocratic husbandly authority was not only undesirable, it was also nearly impossible, due to the close cooperation required to govern the household: 'such husbands as do brag, and think themselves able to rule, and over-rule their wives: by that time they have proceeded and gone a little further, they shall well feel and perceive themselves to be beguiled, and find that thing to be most hard and intricate, the which to be done, they esteemed most light and easy.'[8]

Just as husbands were too apt to tyrannize over their wives, so wives often forgot their subject place. Gouge found it necessary to castigate 'the opinion of many wives, who think themselves every way as good as their husbands, and no way inferior to them'.

The reason whereof seemeth to be that small inequality which is betwixt the husband and the wife: for of all degrees wherein there is any difference betwixt person and person, there is the least disparity betwixt man and wife.... Besides, wives are *mothers* of the same children, whereof their husbands are fathers (for God said to both, *multiply and increase*) and mistresses of the same servants whereof they are masters (for *Sarah* is called *mistress*) and in many other respects there is a common equity betwixt husbands and wives; whence many wives gather that in all things there ought to be a mutual equality.[9]

Because of this 'small inequality', godly writers found themselves preaching very different messages to husbands and to wives. On the one hand, they commanded women to submit themselves obediently and absolutely to their husbands. On the other, they ordered men to love and respect their wives, and cautioned them against

---

[6] Gouge, *Of domesticall duties*, 412.
[7] Cleaver and Dod, *A godly forme of houshold government*, 216; Rogers, *Matrimoniall honour*, 237–8. Gouge even warned 'sheepish' masters against being too polite in giving orders. See *Of domesticall duties*, 651.
[8] Cleaver and Dod, *A godly forme of houshold government*, 215.
[9] Gouge, *Of domesticall duties*, 271.

standing on their authority or jeopardizing their wives' esteem through unworthy behavior.[10]

Indeed, for these writers, the love of the husband for his wife was an essential element in the marital hierarchy, without which proper household relations would be drastically perverted. Husbands should be superior to their wives, they thought, but not by too much, or else the balance would be thrown off. A husband's lack of love was as dangerous a threat to the patriarchal model as a wife's rebellion. 'Their place is a place of authority, which without love will soon turn into tyranny,' Gouge wrote. He did not see love as a threat to proper husbandly authority; rather, he thought it was a crucial check against the abuse of power: 'Because [the husband's] place of eminency, and power of authority may soon puff him up, and make him insult over his wife, and trample her under his feet, if a entire love of her be not planted in his heart. To keep him from abusing his authority is love so much pressed upon him.'[11]

To fan the fires of conjugal love, godly writers reminded their male readers of all they owed to their wives, dwelling especially on the selfless suffering of women in labor and as mothers to their husbands' children. Rogers wrote:

> She is always in grief for thee, and that for thee, and by thy means; what day, week, month is she free through the year, breeding, bearing, nursing, watching her babes, both sick that they might be well, and well, lest they be sick? If she lose a child by the hand of God, or by casualty, her tender heart takes more thought for it in a day, than thy manly spirit can in a month: the sorrow of all lies upon her. She had need to be eased of all that is easable, because she cannot be eased of the rest.

Gouge emphasized the terrible pain of childbirth, pointing to 'the screeks and outcries which not only weak, and faint-hearted women utter in the time of their travail, but also are forced from the strongest, and stoutest women that be, and that though beforehand they resolve to the contrary'.[12] Thoughts of these agonies were sure, the moralists hoped, to awaken tender, grateful feelings in affectionate husbands. Indeed, one could hardly go too far when prompted by marital devotion. A husband was 'so highly to esteem, so ardently to affect, so tenderly to respect her, as others may think him even to dote on her. An husband's affection to his wife cannot be too great if it kept within the bonds of honesty, sobriety and comeliness.' The tenderness of the Song of Solomon, in Gouge's opinion, provided 'a good pattern and precedent for husbands'. A husband was to address his wife by a title suggesting 'kindness, familiarity, love, and delight', neither too respectful nor too familiar, such as 'wife', 'spouse', 'love', or 'dove'.[13] Wives, Gouge noted, were weak

---

[10] It goes without saying that neither spouse was supposed to take advantage of the other's dutiful behavior in order to shirk their own divinely imposed obligations. See *Certain sermons or homilies*, 313.

[11] Gouge, *Of domesticall duties*, 350–52.

[12] Rogers, *Matrimoniall honour*, 244–5; Gouge, *Of domesticall duties*, 400. Similarly, Crompton wrote of the mother's painful, 'sorrowful' work of bearing and caring for infants: 'her nauseous pangs before, and sleepless nights after the birth, when variety of changes cannot alter, nor give content to her tearless crier'. See *A wedding-ring*, 10.

[13] Here Gouge cautioned that the Song of Solomon was not an appropriate guide, because of the endearments' excessively metaphorical and hyperbolical nature. *Of domesticall duties*, 364, 372, 389.

women and tended to have many faults, but these did not release husbands from their duty. When wives offended, husbands were to bear with them as much as possible, meekly admonishing them, removing the irritations that caused them to offend, and forgiving and forgetting as needful.

In addition to prompting a husband to behave courteously and amiably towards his wife, his love was to significantly temper the imbalance of power between the spouses. A loving husband would yield readily to his wife's 'humble suits' whenever possible: 'free, forward and cheerful ought he to show himself in granting his wife's request . . . provided notwithstanding that her desire be of that which may lawfully be granted'. Yielding did not count when done with bad grace: 'their wives must ask, and entreat again and again, yea be forced to use the mediation of others to persuade their husbands to yield to their request before they will yield, if at all they yield. What is this but to proclaim to all the world that there is no affection in them to their wives?'[14] As Capp notes, while conduct books 'taught that a husband must never yield his pre-eminence', this was very far from meaning that husbands were supposed to domineer over their wives.[15] The only example Gouge cited as blameworthy weakness was when husbands gave way against their own moral convictions, as when magistrates were turned from justice by the persuasions of their wives, or when merchants dealt dishonestly to satisfy their wives' avarice. Otherwise, men were advised to yield even when doing so went against their own minds.

While wives were commanded to seek their husbands' consent in all things, husbands were to give that consent freely, and even to volunteer 'a general consent . . . for ordering of household affairs', including the government of children and maidservants, and daily expenditures, as long as their wives were not especially 'ignorant, foolish, simple, lavish, etc.'. Unlike children and servants, from whom strict accounts could be demanded, wives were to be trusted and allowed greater liberty to make their own decisions. In a section entitled 'Of husbands forbearing to exact all that they may', Gouge explained that although wives had a duty to obey, husbands did not have an untempered right to command: 'Husbands ought not to exact of their wives, whatsoever wives ought to yield unto if it be exacted. They must observe what is lawful, needful, convenient, expedient, fit for their wives to do, yea and what they are most willing to do before they be too peremptory in exacting it.' Orders were to be given mildly and rarely, in an 'entreating' tone, and were to be omitted entirely if they offended the scruples or dignity of the wife. She was to be persuaded, not forced, so a wise husband would accompany his instructions with 'just and

---

[14] Ibid. 365–6.
[15] Bernard Capp, *When Gossips Meet: Women, the Family and Neighbourhood in Early Modern England* (Oxford, 2003), 31. For example, Whately argues that the only way for a husband to preserve his superiority in the eyes of his wife was for him to 'endeavour to be garnished with all commendable virtues, and to exceed his wife as much in goodness, as he doth in place'. Using 'big looks, great words, and a fierce behaviour' to subdue a wife was unmanly. Husbands were particularly enjoined to avoid the 'three special and disgraceful evils', bitterness, unthriftiness, and foolishness, all of which were guaranteed to provoke a wife's anger and contempt. Whately, *A bride-bush*, 100–101.

weighty reasons, that thereby his wife may the better discern the meetness, lawfulness, expediency, and necessity of the things commanded'.[16]

This harmonious partnership of lovingly authoritative husband and graciously deferent wife, cooperating smoothly in the rule of children and servants, was an ideal that flesh-and-blood couples often failed to attain. Gouge felt obliged to criticize husbands who had too mean opinions of their wives, slighted and rejected their goodness, were excessively lofty, harsh, too strict, bitter, excessively proud in commanding, peremptory, insolent, niggardly, unfaithful, improvident, unkind, austere, testy, and even violent. Similarly, he lambasted wives who refused to give honor to their husbands, thought them base, used contemptuous gestures, insisted on dressing above their station, interrupted their husbands, called them by excessively familiar nicknames and endearments, answered back, spent money against their husbands' will, refused to come when called, reproached their husbands for their poverty, obeyed sullenly, and so forth.[17] Nonetheless, despite the tensions that made marital power politics so difficult, and the 'chidings, brawlings, tauntings, repentings, bitter cursings, and fightings' that ensued, wives were no mere subjects.[18] Even according to patriarchal theory, wives were 'governors' of their households, magistrates in their micro-kingdoms, entitled to deference from children and servants and to respect from their husbands. Men who loved their wives, sought their advice, and gave them free rein to order domestic affairs did not substitute companionate practice for patriarchal theory; they followed Gouge's instructions to the letter.[19] An autocratic husband who reduced his wife to the status of a servant did not fulfill the patriarchal ideal; he perverted it.

'HONOUR THY FATHER, AND THY MOTHER'

Maternal authority had a firm biblical basis. Robert Pricke, who based his entire theory of social and political organization on the fifth commandment, argued that God had found it necessary to tell his people to honor both parents to prevent bias in both directions. The verse was intended to remedy

> the corruption and partiality of children, who otherwise would either contemn the Mother, and yield all honour and duty to the Father, by reason of his principality: or else because the Mother doth bear them, nourish them, and is most tenderly affected toward them, would be wholly addicted unto her, excluding and making no account of the Father.[20]

---

[16] Gouge, *Of domesticall duties*, 366, 377.
[17] See ibid. 267–426.
[18] 'An Homily on the State of Matrimony', *Certain sermons or homilies*, 309.
[19] Thus Capp notes that in successful marriages, 'couples accepted an appropriate division of responsibilities, discussed major decisions, and operated on the base of mutual trust, in line with the conduct-books' advice'. *When Gossips Meet*, 71.
[20] Robert Pricke, *The Doctrine of Superioritie, and of Subjection* (London, 1609), sig. B3.

Gouge agreed that children were to obey their parents equally: 'Though there be a difference betwixt father and mother in relation of one to another, yet in relation to their children they are both as one, and have a like authority over them. Now children are not to look to that difference that is betwixt their parents in that mutual relation that is betwixt husband and wife, but to that authority which both parents have over their children: and so to carry an equal respect to both'. If mother and father disagreed, the child should follow whichever parent was right; if 'the matter be merely indifferent', however, the child was to in 'no way show any contempt to his mother, but with all reverence and humility make it known to her that it is best both for herself and himself, that his father be obeyed'. Similarly, when Daniel Rogers addressed the question of whether a child could legitimately marry without maternal consent if the father consented, he wrote: 'The mother's consent makes for the better being, but the father's for the being itself thereof: for he is the head of the wife and of the family.'[21]

Consistory court cases dealing with contested parental consent suggest that dispensing with maternal goodwill was not so simple. In one case, a father not only failed to push through a match that displeased his wife, but ultimately combined with his wife to assert to the court that no contract had ever existed. This was George Humble, a wealthy London leatherseller who made a serious attempt to marry his daughter Honor, 19, to the grocer Christopher Barrett despite his wife Anne's disapproval. Barrett was an eligible young man: son of a Norwich alderman and a member of one of the most prestigious London livery companies, he would have been welcomed by most maidens' parents, even those offering attractive portions like Honor's £300. Indeed, Humble was initially delighted with the courtship: Barrett was welcomed to the family house in Lombard Street and dined with them in their country retreat in Deptford. How far the courtship progressed exactly was hotly disputed, but a scrivener was employed to write up the settlement papers, and Barrett and his father alleged that a contract was made.

However, Honor's mother, Anne, 'did altogether dislike' the young man's suit, and her hostility was quickly communicated to Honor herself. The young woman told her father's sister 'that she could not love and affect him... in the way of marriage and that he should never be her husband' because she thought ill of his behavior: 'she had and did take such dislike of him... chiefly upon some reports of the idle and foolish carriage and behaviour of him.' When Honor told her aunt that her mother disliked Barrett, her aunt counseled obedience: Honor should be 'dutiful and diligent unto her mother and no doubt all things would be effected to her the said Honor's good liking'. This was a special kind of filial obedience, however, as it flew in the face of her father's plans. For his part, Humble consulted a clergyman to see 'whether a father might marry his daughter without the consent of the mother'. He was told that it was possible, but only if the mother opposed the marriage without just cause.[22] Despite Humble's preference for the match,

---

[21] Gouge, *Of domesticall duties*, 485; Rogers, *Matrimoniall honour*, 76.
[22] Mildred Addison and Josias Shute, rector of St Mary Woolnoth, *Christopher Barrett c. Honor Humble*, 1628 (LMA, DL/C/213, fos. 251–2, 299).

ultimately the family closed ranks behind Honor and Anne Humble. When Barrett sued to enforce the alleged contract, George Humble testified that although documents had been drawn up dealing with Honor's jointure, he had desisted negotiating with the Barrett family once Honor stated 'that she could not affect him... so far as to make him her husband'. Honor went on to marry a haberdasher named Thomas Hudson about a year later.[23]

A more extreme example of maternal influence appears in a humbler contract suit. In this case, a London maid not only refused to marry her father's candidate for her hand—a suitor vehemently opposed by her mother—but wed a different man in direct opposition to his wishes. Anne Frier, the daughter of Mark Frier, a skinner, had long been fond of her father's apprentice Richard Robinson. Around 1576, a maidservant heard them quietly contracting themselves together, prompting her to 'stand privily to see and hear'. When they were done, she burst out crying that she was 'glad that she... had got them in such a trip', but upon entreaty agreed not to inform her master. When the skinner inevitably got word of the engagement, he was displeased and sent Robinson 'beyond the seas' to Denmark.[24] Frier had a different candidate for his daughter's hand, Peter Richardson, and he 'earnestly' persuaded Anne to accept him 'using some threats... and saying that if she would not yield to his request she... should not have his blessing'. Paternal influence was powerful, and Anne agreed to attend a dinner at her grandmother's house where the match would be discussed. However, her mother, Blanche, the daughter of 'old mistress Barton', Anne's grandmother, was violently set against the marriage. She told her maid that 'she had rather knock her daughter on the head than the said Peter should marry with her', and informed her mother that 'she had rather see [Anne] burned quick than she should marry with the said Peter'.[25]

The dinner was intended by Peter Richardson and Mark Frier to provide witnesses to a new contract, but Anne failed to cooperate. Frier promised Peter a solid portion of 'as much in wares as would be worth between seventeen and twenty pounds by the year for the space of seven years'. Anne deposed that Peter asked for her hand, but she 'knowing and remembering (as she sayeth) that she had long before that time given her right hand with her faith and troth in the way of marriage to Richard Robinson so as she could not again give her right hand, reached forth her left hand to the said Peter'. He promised to marry her, but she 'held her peace'. When her grandmother said, 'Daughter, you have given him your left hand, now you must give him your right hand', Anne obeyed, but still remained silent. When her uncle asked her whether or not she would take Peter, 'neither naming to

---

[23] George Humble, 1628 (LMA, DL/C/231, fo. 246); parish register of St Mary Woolnoth, 8 November 1629.
[24] Joan Nutbrown and Andrew Knight, *Peter Richardson c. Richard Robinson and Anne Frier*, 1579 (LMA, DL/C/629, fos. 94v, 93r).
[25] To be burned quick was to be burned alive. Anne Frier, Joan Nutbrown, and Agnes Barton (LMA, DL/C/629, fos. 100r, 96v, 138v).

120   City Women

husband nor any such words', she answered 'yea'. When Peter asked her for the ring he had formerly given her, wishing to bestow it on her before witnesses, she claimed to have forgotten it at home.[26]

Although this was not a perfect contract, Richardson had a gold ring made for Anne and the banns were published. Meanwhile, Anne and Richard Robinson, back from his travels, planned a quick wedding at the Tower. They invited their old confidante the maidservant Joan, now married to a barber-surgeon: Richard went for 'a trim' to Thomas Nutbrowne's shop, and told Joan that he and Anne would be married the next day, inviting her to come along. Indeed, the next day, Anne and Richard were married at the Tower. Frier was probably ignorant of the plan, but Blanche may have been directly involved: her brother Ralph Barton not only attended the wedding but gave away the bride and helped put up the large sum necessary to obtain an irregular marriage license from the Lieutenant of the Tower.[27]

Mark Frier was surely upset to hear that his daughter and former apprentice had wed in defiance of his will. But since the marriage was settled, the family developed collective amnesia about the dinner where Peter and Anne had supposedly been contracted. Blanche's mother deposed that she saw Peter and Anne holding hands, but 'heard no words spoken by either of them, that she can now remember'. Mark testified that he had told the company 'they were met together there ... to know if Anne Frier could find in her heart to fancy Peter Richardson in the way of marriage', but he simply could not recall whether any contractual words had been spoken. Unsurprisingly, Blanche Frier testified 'by virtue of her oath that she neither remembreth anything that was then done or any speeches which then and there was uttered between the said Peter and Anne', although she more forthrightly added that she 'gave no heed thereto because (as she sayeth) she ... could never be brought to like that her daughter Anne should be married with the said Peter Richardson but did always utterly disagree thereto'.[28] Anne Frier and Richard Robinson were able to marry, it seems, largely because of Blanche's hostility to Peter Richardson. Without her mother's support, Anne would have had a harder time opposing the new contract with Richardson, and without her maternal uncle's help, she would have had a difficult time legally marrying Robinson in the absence of banns or a license.[29]

---

[26] Richard Williams and Anne Frier (LMA, DL/C/629, fos. 144r, 100r).
[27] Joan Nutbrown and Ralph Barton (LMA, DL/C/629, fos. 95r, 98r).
[28] Agnes Barton, Mark Frier, and Blanche Frier (LMA, DL/C/629, fos. 138, 143r, 145r).
[29] Richard Robinson was eventually reconciled to his unwilling father-in-law, for when the astonished members of the House of Commons found him concealed in their midst in 1584, he confessed 'that he was by occupation a skinner and dwelt at the Harts Horn in Gracious-street London, the house of one Mark Fryer a skinner also his father-in-law'. *A compleat journal of the votes, speeches and debates, both of the House of Lords and House of Commons throughout the whole reign of Queen Elizabeth, of glorious memory* (London, 1708), 334.

MISTRESSES AND SERVANTS: DIVIDED LOYALTIES

Mistresses had real authority over their servants, authority they had a moral obligation to wield conscientiously.[30] The poet Patrick Hannay advised his female readers that they could not be too vigilant in monitoring maidservants' work:

> Look thy maids be not idle, nor yet spend
> Things wastingly: for they so oft offend,
> When careless is the mistress; yet with need
> Ne'er pinch them, nor yet let them ere exceed:
> The one doth force them seek thee to betray,
> The other makes them wanton, and too gay;
> It is no shame to look to every thing,
> The mistress' eye doth ever profit bring.[31]

While mistresses had a special responsibility for their maidservants, apprentices and menservants were also subject to their authority. Perhaps few were as domineering as the fictional mistress whose tirade was recorded in a collection of scolding speeches:

> Out you stomachful rogue! Nay, for all your pouting and lowring, I will make you know what it is to be an apprentice. I will hereafter make you earn your breakfast before you eat it. Run away if you will, and complain to whom you please, I will answer them, for I will never keep such an idle lazy rogue under my roof... I will make you learn to say, if I say the crow is white, you shall say so too; whether it be right, or wrong, you must say as I say, and then all shall be well.[32]

Nonetheless, apprentices and menservants could not afford to despise their mistresses, as a ballad of a mother's advice to her son going to be apprenticed in London makes clear: 'Please thou thy mistress best:/For why? thy mirth is very small,/Whereas her friendship fails'. 'The London dames', she said, 'be hasty shrews;/and therefore it is best/to win their favour first of all'. Without his mistress's good opinion, the boy's life would be miserable; with it, he would be safe from his master's wrath:

> But if thy master chance to chide,
> And she remain thy friend,
> The wand shall not come near thy back
> Before she hold the end.[33]

---

[30] Gouge, *Of domesticall duties*, 650.
[31] Patrick Hannay, *A happy husband or, Directions for a maide to choose her mate* (London, 1619), sig C4v.
[32] 'Mistress's lecture' from John Taylor, *A juniper lecture with the description of all sorts of women, good, and bad: from the modest to the maddest, from the most civil, to the scold rampant* (London, 1639), 4–6.
[33] *The admonitions of his mother, and her counsaile at his departing*, in Andrew Clark, ed., *The Shirburn Ballads* 1585–1616 (Oxford, 1907), 345.

Just as children were supposed to obey both parents, servants were instructed to serve both master and mistress zealously. They could not legitimately obey a master's command against a mistress's rights, or vice versa:

> So faithful ought servants to be to their masters and mistresses, that if one of them should labour to use a servant in any manner of deceit to the other, the servant ought not to yield. As if a master should move his maid privily to take away jewels, plate, money, linen, or any such thing as is in her mistress's custody. It skilleth not that the master hath the chiefest power over all the goods: a secret taking of them away without the privity of the mistress in whose custody they are, is in the servant deceit, and a point of unfaithfulness. Much less ought any servants be moved by their mistress privily to take away their master's corn, wares, or any goods for her private use. Of the two this is the greater part of unfaithfulness.[34]

When master and mistress disagreed, servants were supposed to obey whoever was in the right, but this was not always clear. Divorce cases offer several examples of servants who faced a difficult choice between siding with their master or their mistress. In cases of domestic cruelty, servants almost always supported their mistresses, although apprentices were less likely than maidservants to testify against their masters. Even in cases of female adultery, when the master was the injured party, servant loyalties could be divided.

Many servants recounted having braved physical danger to protect their mistresses from violent husbands. Maidservants in particular often reported aiding their mistresses by seeking help from neighbors and even confronting their masters. For example, Isabel Hatchin, who had been Hester Crosse's servant, testified that she thought she might have saved her mistress's life by having 'caused the neighbours to come into the said house to aid and defend' her from her husband's blows. Isabel said that 'if the neighbours had not then come into the house and helped to rescue her from the tyranny of him the said Nicholas, [she] verily believeth he the said Nicholas had killed her or at least had marred her beyond recovery'. As it was, Hester miscarried. On a different occasion, when Nicholas kicked Hester out of bed and 'being naked on the ground the said Nicholas spurned or kicked her', she found refuge in Isabel's trundle bed on the floor of the same room. Another former servant, Elizabeth Hayes, was sick and unable to appear in court, but her nurse-keeper deposed that Elizabeth told the following story: Nicholas fell out with his wife over the value of two pence, and taking up his knife, threatened to 'let out her guts'. Elizabeth demanded to know 'his intent therein' and took 'him by the arm which held the knife'. He replied 'that he would be the death of his said wife', but the maid countered: 'You shall not'. Crosse noted darkly: 'if not now it shall not be long ere I will have my will'.[35]

In a similar case, the maidservant Eleanor Mather thought that her presence restrained John Multhry, a physician whose home life belied his healing profession.

---

[34] Gouge, *Of domesticall duties*, 632.
[35] Isabel Hatchin and Magdalen Atkinson, *Hester Crosse c. Nicholas Crosse*, 1632 (LMA, DL/C/233, fos. 281, 296).

To 'prevent his further fury and mischiefs', she reported often warning him that she would call out 'murder' if he did not stop beating his wife Mary. He sent her out of the house, she said, when he wanted to beat Mary without interference. Eleanor represented herself to the court as a fearless character. On one occasion, she said, when Mary was so badly injured that she had to stay in bed for a fortnight, Multhry 'attempted the chastity of [her] (his then maidservant) and used much violence to have had the use of her body', but she 'spat in his face' and asked him ironically: 'Now you have almost murdered my mistress... would you wrong me?' In repulsing his attacks Eleanor was luckier than two previous maidservants; nonetheless she wisely left the household after less than a year's service there.[36]

Menservants and apprentices also sided with their battered mistresses. David Jones, former apprentice to the cutler William Watkins, reported that he and his fellows had probably saved Anne Watkins' life despite their great fear of their master. One night, when Watkins came home 'drunken and reeling', he 'raged as though he would have killed them all'. The apprentices and their mistress promptly fled: Jones 'and two other prentices ran up into the garret and went out into the gutters and another hid himself in the cellar and the said Anne... locked herself up in her chamber'. After Watkins 'had hunted up and down his house after his servants who ran from him and hid themselves so as he could not find them then he sought for his wife and brake open her chamber door'. Hearing Anne scream, the apprentices 'hasted to her and rescued her', and they all took refuge in the kitchen. However, after a brief interlude Watkins raged again: attacking his wife with a cleaver, he 'struck at his wife therewith and one of [Jones's] fellows that ran between them to rescue his said mistress received a blow on his wrist which his master gave him with the said cleaver which was a great wound and he verily believeth in his conscience that with that stroke his said master had killed his said mistress if she had not been so rescued'.[37]

Although these interventions were risky, it is not hard to see why servants sided with their mistresses: a violent husband was all too likely to be an abusive master as well. All the members of John Frier's household suffered from his cruelty, for example. The young servant Ursula Fisher (Anne Frier's younger sister) complained that they had been given rotten salt fish for their diet, 'not fit to be eaten of any Christian man or woman'. Frier's apprentice went into more detail: he said that they were all given 'very slender diet': 'fish and that was so bad and so unsweet as was too bad to give a dog so as they could not eat one bit of it unless he the same John Frier had stood and looked over them as sometimes he did, when for fear of him they did sometimes strain themselves to eat of that unsavory fish'.[38] The lack of decent food also left an impression on the memory of another maidservant, Alice Andrews, especially as it had ruined the festive season:

---

[36] Eleanor Mather and Anne Bannister, *Mary Multhry c. John Multhry*, 1632 (LMA, DL/C/232, fos. 89v–90v, 84v).

[37] David Jones, *Anne Watkins c. William Watkins*, 1611 (LMA, DL/C/221, fos. 1268v–1270r).

[38] Ursula Fisher and William Lovett, *Anne Frier c. John Frier*, 1602 (LMA, DL/C/216, sl. 772, 967).

And upon Christmas Day last, he demanded that there should be no fire in any room in the house but in the kitchen, and there he commanded the child should be kept and nowhere else, and meat there was none, but only one piece of beef that was such as that it was not fit to be eaten for that it was not sweet, neither was sweet when he the same John Frier brought it into the house, which was on the Thursday before, and no other meat he allowed all that Christmas week for his wife and the household, but they were constrained to buy or provide other meat for themselves, he going abroad, neither would he allow any candles either to dress the child or to have light to do anything else, but such as they provided of themselves, and such as their friends gave them and helped them with.

Even the baby was kept short: Frier told the maid Alice that 'he would not allow one penny a day for the child', claiming it was not his. Alice reported that she had been constrained to buy soap for her mistress, who otherwise would not have been able to wash her clothes and go to church decently: 'sometimes [Anne Frier] stayed at home from church because she could have no soap to wash her own clothes nor starch to starch them, but oftentimes she...hath known clothes lie wet from Monday till Thursday for want of soap, and then [Alice] was fain to buy soap herself to wash them or else they had not been done.' The apprentice had heard Ursula tell John Frier that she had laid out forty shillings for her sister.[39]

The indignation of Frier's servants must have been fed by the fact that he was bent on diverting household resources to his own mysterious purposes: Alice reported that he methodically stripped the household, selling Anne's silk gown, rings, jewels, and even the baby's mantle, and 'then brought into the house with him strangers to look upon his household stuff, telling them he would sell it'. Once the loyal maid was able to prevent a sale of her mistress's clothing: 'he had packed up another gown of hers with a riding safegard, and hid them behind a pair of stairs, which she...finding did tell her mistress of, and she took them away.'[40]

While the servants of cruel husbands sided almost universally with their mistresses, they were more conflicted in suits alleging the wife's adultery. Gouge instructed servants to impartially 'mak[e] known to their master the sin of his wife, and to their mistress the sin of her husband' so that the sins in question could be redressed, but servants did not always find this easy, and may have been loath to disobey their mistresses even when they were commanded to help them carry on illicit affairs.[41] The baker's wife Elizabeth Loder, for example, seems to have implicitly expected obedience and silence from her servants. In addition to baking, the couple kept a tavern, employing a tapster named James Travis. The close friendship between the tapster and his mistress was noted by other members of the household. One servant, Christopher Horsley, noticed that Elizabeth 'went not at all to market or very seldom but sent her maid and went seldom abroad of herself and in that time was very familiar with the said James using unseemly gestures with him'. As a consequence, Travis was put out of William Loder's service. After that, Elizabeth

---

[39] Alice Andrews and William Lovett (LMA, DL/C/216, sl. 777–80, 968).
[40] Alice Andrews (LMA, DL/C/216, sl. 778).
[41] Gouge, *Of domesticall duties*, 633.

abruptly abandoned her habit of staying home, making use of her prerogative as mistress to claim duties outside the house: 'she the said Elizabeth went usually to market herself and was much or often abroad, insomuch that her said husband observing that alteration in her, found fault with her for her being so much abroad.'[42]

Relations between the Loders were already tense when William Loder rode into the country on business. According to the maidservant Joan, Elizabeth Loder spent nearly the whole day abroad, not returning until quite late when the whole household was in bed except for Joan and a servant called Edward Watts. Elizabeth sent Edward to bed and then told Joan to go into the street and fetch Travis, which Joan said she 'by her said mistress's appointment accordingly did'. The two lovers sat by the fire in the kitchen, and drank a quart of wine, also fetched by Joan. Elizabeth then instructed the maid to 'lay a clean pair of sheets upon the bed in a chamber called the Corner Chamber for the said James to lie in and caused her also to make a fire in the same chamber'.[43] Travis was hidden more or less secretly in the house for two days. Horsley was eventually taken into Elizabeth's confidence: she asked him to let Travis out of the house early in the morning on the second day, and he also visited Travis for a drink in his room. Watts discovered the tapster's presence as well, although this was unintended: Travis ventured 'out of his chamber before he was dressed and without a band on' without a convincing excuse. He claimed he was going out, but Watts heard him walking around in his chamber later that day. Watts asked Joan whether his mistress 'lay there with him all night', and she answered that 'she could not tell, but she said that in the morning he had a beastly pair of sheets'.[44]

All the servants must have been well aware that Elizabeth Loder's fondness for Travis was disliked by her husband, but it does not seem to have occurred to any of them to oppose her entertainment of the tapster in her husband's absence. It seems likely that one of them—probably Watts, whom Elizabeth Loder did not trust— acquainted Loder with the matter upon his return. However, the fact that Elizabeth Loder calmly ordered her maid and manservant to help arrange her lover's illicit visit is an apt reminder of the very real authority held by household mistresses.

DOMESTIC ECONOMIES: TAMING THE SPENDTHRIFT HUSBAND

The hierarchical structure of the early modern English household was intended to produce order both within the family and in the broader neighborhood. This order was an end in itself: divine harmony was reflected on earth when the great chain of

---

[42] Christopher Horsley, *William Loder c. Elizabeth Loder*, 1615 (LMA, DL/C/223, fo. 26r).
[43] Joan May, 1615 (LMA, DL/C/223, fo. 25r).
[44] Although Joan did tell the court that she thought her mistress had committed adultery, she did not mention this particular detail in her deposition. Christopher Horsley and Edward Watts, 1615 (LMA, DL/C/223, fos. 27r, 28v).

being stretched unbroken from the Creator to the lowliest stones and when the microcosm mirrored the macrocosm. However, order was also valued for more worldly reasons. Orderly households were self-sufficient, people hoped, in no need of charity or poor relief. The authority wielded by household governors was crucial to the household economy: husband and wife kept servants and children in line, taught them morals and thrifty ways, and made sure that they were housed and fed. The governors shared a joint duty to see to the provision of the family, setting a just balance between getting and spending according to their status. When both spouses did their duty, the household was secure:

> ... he that has a good Wife is happy I say,
>   if he takes pains to labour his Living to get,
> She'll not spend it abroad in an idle way,
>   she'll work the skin off her fingers to keep him out of debt
> She'll give him good counsel, if he will it receive,
> And set him at all times in a way for to live.[45]

For ordinary householders, the battle for solvency was a very real struggle that could only be won when man and wife combined their best efforts. The intimate alliance that pitted the married couple together against a harsh economic world was strongest when labor went hand in hand with love.[46] In a New Year's ballad, when a husband worried about rising prices mourned, 'Gentle wife, I tell thee,/my very heart is done', she consoled her 'sweet husband' with the promise of partnership:

> Go thou and ply thy labour,
>   and I will work with thee...
> I will not be idle,
>   but I will card and spin:
> I will save together
>   that thou bringest in.
> *Husband*
> Dear wife, thy gentle speeches
>   revive me at the heart,
> To see thee take my poverty
>   in such a gentle part:
> If God do ever raise me,
>   thou shalt have thy desert.[47]

---

[45] *The batchelour's guide, and the married man's comfort* (London, 1685–1688).
[46] This economic and emotional alliance is what Joanne Bailey terms 'co-dependency' in her study of secondary complaints in eighteenth-century separation suits. She emphasizes the material aspects of marriage—cohabitation, provision, and the material work of governing children and servants—and argues that 'these material factors forged co-dependency between wives and husbands, which could be intensified by their emotional needs'. *Unquiet Lives: Marriage and Marriage Breakdown in England, 1660–1800* (Cambridge, 2003), 194.
[47] *The housholders new-yeeres gift containing a pleasant dialogue betwixt the husband and his wife* (London, 1640). See also J. A. Sharpe, 'Plebeian Marriage in Stuart England: Some Evidence from Popular Literature', in *Transactions of the Royal Historical Society*, 5th series, 36 (1986), 69–90.

Loving couples might suffer poverty regardless of their industry, but if husband or wife neglected to look to the economic health of the household, disaster was inevitable. William Gouge reminded his readers that neither spouse was to hide away goods, nor to spend prodigally, nor to waste time and goods in idleness:

> For suppose an husband be industrious... and get much abroad, if the wife either by her unthriftiness, idleness, negligence, or the like vices, suffer that which is brought home to be embezzled and wasted; or by her prodigality, bravery, or love of vain company, consume it herself, where will be the profit of the husband's pains? Or on the other side, if a wife should be as painful and prosperous in getting... and the husband by carding, dicing, drinking, reveling, or other like means should waste all away, what fruit would remain of the wife's providence?[48]

Although the behavior of both spouses was theoretically equally important to the household economy, in practice the great weakness of the patriarchal model was its reliance on the good will of the husband. Though husband and wife shared a mutual duty to maintain the household, only he controlled the whole. If she failed to oversee the maids, sank into idleness, or spent too much, her husband could discipline her and take control of the purse strings. As long as he wielded his authority properly, the hierarchies that governed the household kept it safe from the ravages of idleness or prodigality on the part of wife, servants, and children. If he misbehaved, however, by spending too much or failing to earn a living, the welfare of the household was at serious risk.

Although it was the wife's duty to gather and keep household goods, she could not legally protect them from her husband's depredations. As *femes covert*, married women owned nothing, not even their clothes; all belonged to their husbands. The moralists realized that a household cursed with an improvident husband could not hope to thrive no matter how hard the wife labored. Gataker scathingly condemned those who 'live, like drones, on their wives' labours', 'those that spent riotously the portion they have with their wives', and 'all that misspend that though earned with their own hands, or left them by friends, that should maintain house and wife with'. He told them sternly: 'Such must know that they rob wife and children... and so are no better than such as rob by the highway side.'[49] Rogers castigated 'odious' improvident husbands who 'while themselves bearing themselves upon the fidelity and drudgery of the wife at home, go abroad, and open the sluice and floodgates of prodigality and wastefulness, that all the labour of the wife at home, cannot dam up the waters. They spending and spoiling more abroad in one hour, than the woman can patch up or redress at home in a week...' This was truly a perversion of the intended order, for improvident husbands were '[t]hus woefully inverting the method of God, injuriously laying a double load upon the weaker party, till her

---

[48] Gouge, *Of domesticall duties*, 254. See also Cleaver and Dod, *A godly forme of houshold government*, 184; Whately, *A bride-bush*, 14–15.

[49] Gataker, *Marriage duties briefely couched togither*, 46. See also Cleaver and Dod, *A godly forme of houshold government*, 201.

shoulders crack again: who yet undertake it to shun utter debt, and yet at last fall into it nevertheless'.[50]

Misbehavior by married men posed a very real threat to early modern society, particularly when young men failed to make successful transitions from carefree bachelors to responsible adults. As Shepard has shown in her study of Cambridge, bachelors who could not claim the social status of householders consoled themselves by striving to impress their peers instead: 'Youthful rituals of misrule indulged routine aspects of male sociability to excess; misappropriated the authority of adult males; and subverted patriarchal imperatives of order, thrift, and self-control.'[51] Rowdy, hard-drinking bachelors defied the orderly ideals of English society, but their excesses were limited, in theory at least, by the adult men who governed their conduct: apprentices' masters, watchful fathers, and the proctors who supervised the Cambridge students. When men married, however, they were expected to settle down, to leave the ranks of the governed and enter those of the governors. Social order depended on these young household heads.

Wives were expected to encourage their husbands to embrace adulthood and its attendant duties. In a comic story about 'the taming of a wild youth', for example, a newly sober bridegroom introduced an old friend to his wife, '[a] woman proper, fair, wise and discreet':

> And said 'Behold, here's that hath tamed me.'
> 'Hath this' (quoth I) 'can such a wife do so?
> Lord, how is he tam'd then, that hath a shrow!'[52]

A ballad subtitled *The praise of a married life* argued that women's influence was invaluable. The narrator, a young bridegroom comparing his old swaggering habits with his newfound respectability, ascribed the transformation to his bride:

> No constables nor watch scare I,
>   that crieth 'Who goes there?'
> I do not reel, but soberly
>   can pass them void of care:
> I use no caudle in the morn,
>   I drink not out mine eyes,
> My wife hath made me these to scorn.

He no longer lost his money at cards, his credit by keeping bad company, nor his health by excessive drinking: 'my wife hath caused me to turn,' he explained. Moreover, she had lifted his status by bearing him a son: 'By christ'ning of my little lad/I did in credit rise:/All this by my good wife I have.' His wild bachelor pleasures were nothing, he concluded, to the prosperous comfort of married life.

> The babe doth grow, and quickly speak,
>   this doth increase my joy,

---

[50] Rogers, *Matrimoniall honour*, 230–31.
[51] Alexandra Shepard, *Meanings of Manhood in Early Modern England* (Oxford, 2003), 94.
[52] e.g., shrew. Samuel Rowlands, *Humors looking glasse* (London, 1608), 14.

> To hear it tattle, laugh, and squeak,
>   I smile and hug the boy...
> All bachelors I wish you wed,
>   if merry you would live,
> A single man is oft misled,
>   and seldom doth he thrive.[53]

Wives were supposed to smooth men's transition from youth to manhood, yet all too often married men were loath to abandon their carefree habits and 'the camaraderie of misrule'.[54] A ballad misleadingly titled *Lamentation of a new married man briefly declaring the sorrow and grief that comes by marrying a young wanton wife* explored one bridegroom's unwillingness to let go of his bachelor pleasures. In the first part, the 'lamentation' of the young man, he looked back with nostalgia at his youthful pastimes, mourning:

> When I lived single,
>   I knew no cause of strife,
> I had my heart in quiet,
>   I led a pleasant life—
> But now my chiefest study
>   Is how to please my wife,
> I being a married man.
>
> Quoth she, 'You do not love me,
>   To leave me all alone,
> You must go a gadding,
>   And I must bide at home,
> While you among your minions,
>   Spend more than is your own'.

In an 'answer... written most friendly by his gentle wife Nan', she admitted that she criticized his 'gadding', but explained that she had his interests at heart:

> If I do blame your gadding
>   It is for love, be sure,
> Bad company doth always
>   Ill counsel still procure
> The man that will be thrifty,
>   Must at his work endure.

Her husband's youthful escapades must be a thing of the past, she said, but by accepting the burdens of adulthood he would gain both status and power:

> This works his commendations
>   Amongst the very best.
> The chief men of the parish,
>   His quaintance will request,
> And then he shall be called

---

[53] *Tis not otherwise: or: The praise of a married life* (London, 1617).
[54] Shepard, *Meanings of Manhood*, 96.

> To office with the rest...
>
> He shall be made a headborough
>   Unto his credit great,
> At what time all the neighbours,
>   His friendship will entreat,
> And then it is most decent,
>   He should go fine and neat...
>
> Then bareheaded unto him,
>   A number daily flocks:
> To help him by his office,
>   From many stumbling blocks:
> Then comes he to be constable,
>   And set knaves in the stocks.

All these glories would prove ample compensation for the lost pleasures of youth, so instead of resenting her sobering influence, Nan insisted, he should be grateful to her for making an 'honest man' of him:

> A Wife hath won you credit,
> A Wife makes you esteem'd
> An honest man through marriage
> Now are you surely deemed.[55]

The popularity of this theme suggests that husbands' unwillingness to shoulder the burdens of manhood was as great a factor in domestic strife as wives' refusal to accept their assigned roles, if not more so. But recalcitrant husbands posed their wives with a challenge. What could they do to 'tame' their feckless mates? The first line of attack was the wife's advice. A 1630 ballad subtitled *John Jarret's wife's counsell to her husband* consists of a London wife's litany of admonition about her husband's excessive spending. In an affectionate tone, she advised him to leave off his improvident habits:

> Pray gentle John Jarret, give ear to my words,
> It is my true kindness this counsel affords,
> And every good husband to his wife accords:
> If your time you waste away at alehouse boards,
> *I tell you, John Jarret, you'll break.*

This prodigal wasted his money on a slew of immoral pastimes. Much of it went to lewd women: he spent 'an angel and more' on 'a brave whore' at St Katherine's, bought a gown for 'Black Kate' near Billingsgate, and kept a lover 'with the old bawd her mother' at Wapping. He spent his days gambling at shuffle-board, and was further impoverished by paying two shillings a week for 'a bastard at Brainford at nurse'. While he wasted his time and money with 'ill company', Jarret's wife complained, she and the children sat 'sighing at home'. He would become a

---

[55] *The lamentation of a new married man briefely declaring the sorrow and grief that comes by marrying a young wanton wife* (London, 1629).

bankrupt if he did not heed her counsel.[56] The same strategy of loving admonition was successfully employed by 'Kate', the northern heroine of *Robin and Kate: or, A bad husband converted by a good wife*. At first Robin, who loved 'nappy liquor so well,/that he'll be at th'alehouse both early and late', resisted Kate's advice:

> I will go or I'll stay,
>   To be at command
>   of my wife, I do hate,
>   For I must and I will,
>   have my humor sweet Kate.

However, after Kate explained: 'I give thee good counsel,/I do not command', he capitulated.

> Ah now my sweet Kate I perceive very well,
>   thy words do proceed from a hearty affection,
> Now all my delight in thy bosom shall dwell,
>   I'll ever be ordered by thy direction:
> My former ill husbandry,
>   I will repent,
> And in thy sweet company,
>   rest well content:
> Strong liquor no more,
>   shall impair my estate,
> Now I'll stay at home
>   with my bonny sweet Kate.[57]

These messages could have been delivered in any number of ways: the role of the advisor could have been played by a father, neighbor, magistrate, or clergyman. However, balladeers chose to employ wives as counselors because gentle rebukes for excessive spending were a natural outgrowth of their general responsibility for conserving household resources. For a wife to exercise her influence to discipline her husband's spending was entirely proper, though men might grouse. Thus in *Seldome Comes the Better*, a remarried widower advised his listeners to appreciate the wives they have. He himself had scorned his first wife for criticizing his wastefulness:

> She would tell me for my good,
>   that I must leave my vice,
> But I not rightly understood
>   her counsel of high price . . .
> The other *[his first wife]* was a huswife good,
>   when she a penny spent,
> It went from her like drops of blood,
>   to th'alehouse she ne'er went,

---

[56] *I tell you John Jarret, you'l breake John Jarrets wives counsell to her husband* (London, 1630).
[57] Martin Parker, *Robin and Kate: or, A bad husband converted by a good wife in a dialogue betweene Robin and Kate* (London, 1634). See also *A dainty dialogue between Henry and Elizabeth. Being the good wives vindication, and the bad husbands reformation* (London, 1670–77).

> Unless it were to fetch home me
> for which at nought I set her.

His new wife was more permissive, but her laxity was an economic disaster:

> That wife would only me reprove,
> for wasting of my store;
> But this, as well as I doth love
> the good ale pot, and more,
> She'll sit at the alehouse all the day,
> and if the house will let her
> She'll run on the score, and I must pay.[58]

Virtuous wives were not supposed to suffer in silence when the well-being of the family was at risk. This combination of subjection and an advisory role could be a difficult balancing act, but it was normal and expected of wives. For example, when the maidservant Prudence Jervice was considering whether to marry the smith William Cook, she asked his stepbrother if he was an honest man. He replied: 'He was an honest and religious man but she must look to keep him in for that he would sometimes fly out (meaning that company would sometimes cause him to drink and lose his time).' Keeping her prospective husband 'in' would be one of Prudence's duties as a wife. This disciplinary capacity was a challenge, of course, for wives with uncooperative husbands: for them, giving advice was a delicate, thankless, and sometimes dangerous task. Living up to her name, Prudence reconsidered her plan to marry Cook and endow him with her £25 portion: she was heard to say that 'she would suffer any punishment or lie in any prison before she would marry him'.[59]

Wifely admonishment was a crucial means of pressuring married men to live up to their responsibilities, but it went against the grain of the family hierarchy. Godly moralists agreed that rebukes were least likely to provoke resistance when they were presented very gently: 'prayer and tears will prove your best weapons,' Crompton advised.[60] In Robert Snawsel's *A Looking-Glasse for Married Folkes*, the virtuous matron Eulalie explained to the struggling young bride Xantip how she had dealt with her husband's excessive drinking. First she waited until 'his stomach was emptied, and he c[ame] to himself'. Then, alone in bed, she:

> would gently admonish him, or rather entreat him, that he would have a care of the health of his body... telling him of such young men, yea, gallant gentlemen as he knew, who got surfeits by so overcharging their stomachs: also with weeping eyes I would entreat him, to have a care of his estate and credit, children and servants, lest the one should be undone by his spending their portions, and the other by following his unseemly course of life.[61]

---

[58] *Seldome comes the better: or, An admonition to all sorts of people as husbands, wives, masters, and servants, &c. to avoid mutability, and to fix their minds on what they possesse* (London, 1629).
[59] William Smith, *William Cook c. Prudence Jervice*, 1627 (GL MS 9189/2, fos. 141v, 140v).
[60] Crompton, *A wedding-ring*, 34.
[61] The unpleasant lesson over, she would quickly change the topic of conversation to something more amusing. Robert Snawsel, *A looking-glasse for married folkes* (London, 1619), 59.

The physical weakness of the admonishing wife recalled that of men taming wild beasts, so authors made copious use of metaphors from animal husbandry to inform wives how to 'train' their husbands. Dangerous men had to be tamed with gentleness:

> ... if imperious, he should more desire,
> Than due respect doth of a wife require;
> Think not harsh stubbornness will ere procure him,
> To be more mild, (it rather will obdure him).
> The whip and lash the angry horse enrages,
> Mild voice and gentle stroke his ire assuages.[62]

Eulalia told Xantip that her own husband had been 'as cruel as a lion, and terrible as a dragon', so she 'considered what those do that take in hand to tame lions, and elephants, etc. which cannot be mastered with strong hand'. When Xantip expressed her fear that no gentleness could prevail with her husband, Eulalia answered: 'Fear not, woman, there is no wild beast so savage, but by gentle handling it may be tamed.' It would be a lengthy undertaking, but here again animal husbandry provided useful context: 'think with yourself what a great labour you took before you could teach this parrot to pronounce some words ... And doth it seem irksome and tedious unto you to take some pains to make your husband a good man?'[63]

Despite Eulalia's strictures, wives did not always count on gentle persuasion to remedy ill behavior. A more aggressive alternative was shrewish nagging, the vice often thought to accompany frugal huswifery.[64] The energy, inquisitiveness, and watchfulness that made a thrifty housewife and a careful mistress were all too likely to be accompanied by a sharp tongue. Moralists refused to condone nagging, even when used for good ends. As Rogers put it: 'It's true, that a wasteful woman is the bane of her husband in one kind, but so may the thrifty in another by her shrewishness ... [W]hat avails it a man if he must die, that he rather is hanged, than beheaded?' He reminded his female readers that frugality was no excuse: 'Thrifty or unthrifty thou art little accepted, except subject and peaceable. Rather thy one virtue, should make thee more studious of others.' More pragmatically, a popular ballad encouraged husbands to accept the occasional tongue-lashing as the inevitable complement of good huswifery:

> A wife that's indifferent between good and ill,
>   is she that in huswifery shews her good will,

---

[62] Hannay, *A happy husband*, sig. C in 'A Wife's Behaviour'.
[63] Snawsel, *A looking-glasse for married folkes*, 52, 70, 79. See also Gouge: 'though her husband should be of an harsh and cruel disposition, yet by this means might he be made meek and gentle. For the keepers of Lions are said to bring them to some tameness by handling them gently and speaking to them fairly.' *Of domesticall duties*, 278.
[64] This interpretation of shrewishness from the female perspective contrasts with the usual focus on male reactions in studies like Anthony Fletcher, *Gender, Sex and Subordination in England 1500–1800* (New Haven, Conn., 1995), 12–13; and Lynda E. Boose, 'Scolding Brides and Bridling Scolds: Taming the Woman's Unruly Member', *Shakespeare Quarterly* 42.2 (1991), 179–213. It corroborates that presented in Capp, *When Gossips Meet*, 86–7.

> Yet sometimes her voice she too much elevates,
>   is that the occasion for which her he hates?
> A sovereign remedy for this disease
>   is to hold thy tongue, let her say what she please.[65]

Many wives did no doubt say what they pleased, confident that right was on their side. The gentle persuasions of John Jarret's wife, held up as a pattern of virtuous wifely advice, could slide easily into 'shrewish' tirades like this satirical example:

> In troth husband, I can hold no longer, but I must speak: I see you still follow this vein of ill husbandry, never keep at home: Is the house a wild-kat to you? Here I sit all the day long with the children, sighing, and looking every minute when you will return home: i'faith this course of life must be left; Do you think I can sell your wares, or know the prices of them when your customers come? Let them look to your shop that will, for I will not: keep your shop, and then it will keep you... You begin the week well, for this day, and no longer, so soon as you were up, and ready, then to the alehouse to your companions, to some game or other for your morning's draught of strong liquor... I would I had been made a man, for women are nothing but your drudges and your slaves, to make you clean, and to wash and starch your clothes: when you go whither you please, and take no care at all for anything.[66]

Conflict was inevitable when husband and wife disagreed about what level of male sociability was acceptable, and abuses were possible on both sides. The irate wife browbeating her sheepish spouse was a common figure in the popular imagination and the inspiration of much social satire.[67] While the fictional travails of those men who were too weak or too good-natured to quell their shrewish spouses amused their contemporaries, the misery of the husbands of overbearing wives was real enough. Unlike mistreated wives, they could not even appeal for neighborly aid without losing face: skimmington rides directed at dominant wives shamed the unmanned victims of marital abuse as well as the perpetrators. Most 'henpecked' husbands probably preferred to hide their humiliations from the public eye.[68]

When husbands *were* able and willing to take brutal measures to assert mastery, marital conflict could have dire outcomes, even in fiction. Misogynistic tales about the taming of shrewish wives generally take the wife's complaints about her husband's drinking as a starting-point, like the 'railing' of this smith's wife:

> Thou sittest at the alehouse here,
> While I at home do spare:
> Not caring so thy guts be full,
> How thy poor wife doth fare.

---

[65] Rogers, *Matrimoniall honour*, 295; Martin Parker, *The marryed mans lesson: or, A disswasion from jealousie* (London, 1634).

[66] John Taylor, *A juniper lecture, With the description of all sorts of women, good, and bad: from the modest to the maddest, from the most civil, to the scold rampant* (London, 1639), 8–14.

[67] See e.g. John Taylor, *Divers crabtree lectures Expressing the severall languages that shrews read to their husbands, either at morning, noone, or night* (London, 1639), 77–9.

[68] See Martin Ingram, 'Ridings, Rough Music and the "Reform of Popular Culture" in Early Modern England', *Past and Present* 105 (1984), 86; Shepard, *Meanings of Manhood*, 136.

> Thy servants do even what they list,
> Thy children they may starve,
> Hanging's too good for such a rogue,
> Far worse thou dost deserve,
> Out filthy beast I loathe thy looks,
> And hate thee like a toad.

The smith, offended, broke one of his wife's arms to teach her a lesson. After he ostentatiously paid the surgeon in advance for the cost of healing the other, his wife became 'most gentle, quiet, meek,/Guiding her tongue so sure' that the victorious husband 'had her ever at his command'.[69] Though Jarret's wife and bonny Kate were praised for their counsel and the smith's wife received a brutal beating, the difference between praiseworthy advice and irksome nagging was one of tone, not of message. Wives' double obligation to obey their husbands and to prod them toward good behavior forced them to walk a very fine line.

DESTRUCTIVE HUSBANDS AND THE RHETORIC OF ORDER

The worst husbands, drunkards who devoted their energies to gambling away their goods and beating their wives, were amenable neither to gentle admonition nor to nagging. If destitution threatened, a prudent wife might be forced to subterfuge or outright resistance. Some moralists were sympathetic to these strategies. Gouge noted that 'it oft falleth out that a wise, virtuous, and gracious woman, is married to an husband destitute of understanding, to a very natural (as we say) or a frenzy man, or to one made very blockish, and stupid, unfit to manage his affairs through some distemper, wound, or sickness. In such a case the whole government lieth upon the wife, so as her husband's consent is not to be expected.' Daniel Rogers thought that wives should not be compelled to obey their husbands in cases 'such as extend to the hazard of estate, children, yea liberty and life itself'. He provided a reasonably extensive list of exceptions to the general rule of wifely subjection, situations in which 'the woman is like to share as deep in the sorrow, if not more, than the husband'.[70]

Earlier moralists were more likely to think that a provident wife could justly hide household goods from her husband. Gouge, who ordinarily prohibited wives from disposing of goods without their husbands' consent, made an exception for women whose husbands' prodigality threatened the well-being of the household:

> Thus a faithful provident wife observing her husband to riot, and to spend all he can get in carding, dicing, and drinking, may without his consent lay up what goods she can for her husband's, her own, her children's, and whole household's good. This is no

---

[69] From 'A she-devil made tame by a smith' in Samuel Rowlands, *The knave of clubs* (London, 1609).
[70] Gouge, *Of domesticall duties*, 287–8; Rogers, *Matrimoniall honour*, 264–5.

part of disobedience, but a point wherein she may show her self a great good help unto her husband; for which end a wife was first made.[71]

Rogers thought that a husband might, 'being a man carried by his inordinate lusts, and feeling himself to suffer his estate to decay ... permit [his wife] to look into the affairs of the family', but for this female stewardship, his consent was required. In general the wife 'must not distract the common stock from her husband's hand, into her own' but this did not relieve her from responsibility: if the husband were unable to provide for his family, she was 'to set to her shoulders to the uttermost, rather than the state of the family be perverted'. She was encouraged to rely on her own talents: 'being endowed with a gift and skill in some mystery, which her husband is not, especially the husband being idle and slothful to improve his own stock, or perhaps having embezzled it already: [she] may be occupied in that calling of hers: provided that she be comptable to her husband, whose stock she occupies.'[72] This was an imperfect solution, as the industrious wife was obliged to resign the profits of her labor to her idle husband. However, in London and other cities where custom gave married women the right to trade as *femes sole*, a wife could theoretically escape almost all financial obligation to her husband by setting up business with borrowed capital: 'For, if she occupy a borrowed stock, she is praiseworthy for her industry, but comptable only to her creditors: in such a case, if she share with him so far as to keep him from beggary, it's enough, for she aims at the support of her family.'[73]

In contrast with Gouge, who in 1622 praised hiding money from destructive husbands, and Rogers, who in 1642 suggested circumventing the rigors of coverture, Thomas Hilder wrote in 1653 that a married woman with an improvident husband could only use gentle persuasion in hopes of reclaiming his affections. He suggested: 'the more expensive thy husband is abroad, the more sparing be thou at home, that if possible the estate may hold out to be a means to bring up thy children, until (under God) they can shift by good ways for themselves.'

> But for thy own condition ... thou mayest not (contrary to thy husband's allowance) lay by one penny (as we say) against a wet day; and the reason why I thus think, is, because thy husband alone hath the propriety in his estate, unless some agreement between you before marriage, or between thy friends and him have altered the case.[74]

Indeed, by the publication of Hilder's book, the law had moved firmly against wives. A Chancery case from around 1639 dealt with a wife 'with an unprovident husband' who 'had, unknown to him, by her frugality raised some monies for the good of their children'. The court initially acted in her favor, but later reversed

---

[71] Gouge, *Of domesticall duties*, 292.

[72] Rogers, *Matrimoniall honour*, 270–71.

[73] Ibid. 271. It is unclear, however, whether *sole* traders were in practice able to shield their businesses from their husbands or their husbands' creditors. See Margaret Hunt, *The Middling Sort: Commerce, Gender, and the Family in England 1680–1780* (Berkeley, Calif., 1996), 138–42.

[74] Thomas Hilder, *Conjugall counsell, or, Seasonable advice, both to unmarried, and married persons* (London, 1653), 112.

the decision 'as being dangerous to give a *feme* power to dispose of her husband's estate'.[75]

A wide gap separated the precepts of common law and popular understandings of wives' roles in governing the household economy. Although Gouge's advice went contrary to the law in giving women the right to hide goods from their prodigal husbands, it was still too rigid to please his parishioners in the Blackfriars. In the preface of his text, Gouge remembered 'that when these *Domesticall Duties* were first uttered out of the pulpit, much exception was taken against the application of a wife's subjection to the restraining of her from disposing the common goods of the family without, or against her husband's consent'. However, he pleaded, 'surely they that made those exceptions did not well think of the cautions and limitations which were then delivered, and are now again expressly noted: which are, that the foresaid restraint be not extended to the *proper goods of a wife*, no nor overstrictly to such *goods as are set apart for the use of the family*, nor to *extraordinary cases*, nor always to an *express consent*, nor to the *consent of such husbands as are impotent, or far and long absent*'. What was more, he was willing to add to the list: 'If any other warrantable caution shall be shewed me, I will be as willing to admit it, as any of these.' Far from being perceived as a dangerous proponent of wives' property rights, Gouge found himself apologizing for not defending women's rights more: 'This just apology I have been forced to make,' he wrote, 'that I might not ever be judged (as some have censured me) *an hater of women*.'[76]

For ordinary people, concerns about economic stability counterbalanced common law restrictions on wives' property rights. Women suing their husbands for the restitution of conjugal rights or divorce and witnesses on their behalf commonly appealed to the rhetoric of order to bolster their cause. They explained that the unchecked destruction—both physical and economic—wrought by irrational husbands would inevitably shipwreck domestic economies. When men failed to fulfill their duties, their families and the broader communities in which they lived paid the price: '[S]pendthrift dissolute husbands . . . not only neglect all endeavours to maintain their own families, but prodigally pawn and spend what the industrious wife hath earned and provided, and so unnecessarily and inevitably bring misery upon themselves, and a charge unto the parish in which they inhabit,' one pamphleteer explained.[77] Neighbors testified that *they* had been burdened with the care of providing for troubled households: when husbands failed to provide, and, worse, undermined the efforts of wives to do so, charity paid for household necessities. Domestic harmony was undone when husbands attacked their wives, children fled their fathers, and servants—to save their mistresses' lives—raised

---

[75] *Scot c. Bargrave*, cited in *Pridgeon c. Pridgeon*, *The English Reports*, 91 vols (Edinburgh: William Green & Sons, 1900–1932), vol. xxii, p. 721, cited in Amy Louise Erickson, *Women and Property in Early Modern England* (New York, 1993), 125.
[76] Gouge, *Of domesticall duties*, preface.
[77] Rice Bush, *The poor mans friend, or A narrative of what progresse many worthy citizens of London have made in that godly work of providing for the poor* (London, 1650), 13–14. For neighborly self-interest, see also Capp, *When Gossips Meet*, 109–10.

hands against their masters. Neighborhood harmony was shattered by the curses of drunken husbands and the shrieks of battered wives.

Men could even be barred from exercising their legal rights to their wives' property, as was the case for George Rye in 1633. Soon after they were married, Rye had absconded to St Albans with the contents of his wife's trunks and chests. Bridget's friend William Silke, a middle-aged turner, went after him and rebuked him, but though Rye agreed to come home, he fled the next morning to Ireland. Rye eventually reappeared in London, but his return was prompted by love of his wife's money rather than her person. One summer day, Bridget's neighbors heard a tumult coming from her house, and 'a little girl that she... kept in her house came running forth into the court and cried out that her aunt... was murdered'. The neighbors rushed out and Bridget Rye 'in great fear and trembling and much affrighted' called for help out of the window. George Rye and 'three others of his ruffianly company' were attempting to convey away 'her' household goods. Bridget entreated her neighbor Anne Benning to call the watch; the officers and the watchmen soon arrived 'and rescued her the said Bridget and resisted the said George and his company in their lewd attempts'.[78]

In a similar case, when Anne Evans strove to divorce her husband Christopher Evans, neighbors cited his determination to retain control of 'her' goods as evidence of his cruelty. An embroiderer's wife testified that she had seen Evans 'misuse' his wife, and that among other things she had seen 'the purse and keys and apparel of the foresaid Anne Evans locked up and kept from her by the said Christopher Evans, and when she the said Anne prayed him to give her them again saying that she would pay his debts, he refused to give them unto her.'[79] One Mary Jones' landlady testified, as part of a divorce case for cruelty, that Mary's husband Charles Jones stole 'her' goods. He would 'take from her her keys and having unlocked her chests and coffers carry away with him whatsoever he found there and likes of which she had provided by her own industry and he consumed and wasted the same abroad from the company of the said Mary'. These witnesses spoke as though the goods in question belonged morally to the wives, whatever the law had to say on the matter.[80]

Unlike Rye, Evans and Jones also attacked their wives. They may have considered that by enforcing their own brute dominance they were defending patriarchal order: Christopher Evans explained that he struck his wife, Anne, because she behaved 'in unseemly manner' with Humphrey Pritchard, and provoked him 'by throwing stools and chambers pots and such like things at his head'. On one occasion, she stayed out all night, he said, and when he asked her where she had been, 'she bade [him] "go look," whereupon he did beat her the same Anne with his girdle'. Similarly, one William Greene stated tersely that 'upon the misdemeanours

---

[78] Anne Benning and Agnes Muddin, *Bridget Rye c. George Rye*, 1633 (LMA, DL/C/630, fos. 130r, 129).
[79] Mary Habort, *Anne Evans c. Christopher Evans*, 1613 (LMA, DL/C/221, fo. 1497r).
[80] Alice Tursett, *Mary Jones c. Charles Jones*, 1614 (LMA, DL/C/222, fos. 70v–71r). See also Craig Muldrew, *The Economy of Obligation: The Culture of Credit and Social Relations in Early Modern England* (New York, 1998), 97.

of...Margaret Greene he hath given her moderate correction'.[81] However, their actions were seen differently by disapproving neighbors. Evans and Green were unable to produce witnesses corroborating their stories.[82] Instead, neighbors described Evans 'beating...Anne his wife with the hoop of a barrel and dragging or drawing her about the house by the hair on her head in very cruel manner' and throwing 'divers things at her head in very cruel and furious manner'. Elizabeth Kingston reported that one evening when she was lighting Margaret Greene home to her house, William attacked them savagely. He tripped Margaret, a woman of good parentage and behaviour, causing her to fall into the fire, whence she was rescued by a maid, then, taking a knife in one hand and a candlestick in the other, 'thrust the knife very furiously at the breast of his said wife but the whalebones that were in the bodice of her petticoat would not suffer the knife to enter her body, then...with the knife he raced her throat, neck, and breast and made it bleed extremely.' When Elizabeth intervened, he hit *her* with the candlestick 'and cut her a great gash in the eyebrow that the blood ran down grievously'.[83]

Husbands who beat their wives to the extent of causing serious injury were considered to be beyond reason. This was the case of the tailor John Young, who one night nearly killed his wife, Anne. Their maidservant Sara ran to Edward Coles' house and asked for help: '"I fear", quoth she, "that he will kill her or do her some great mischief, he hast thrust me out of doors."' Indeed, by the time the neighbors arrived, Anne Young

> was not able to speak nor go nor stir any of her limbs to help herself, and her jaws were displaced or otherwise so hurt with beating that she was not able to stir them, and the gristle of her nose was so bruised that until by the help of a surgeon it was raised...she could not well fetch or take any breath at the nose, but seemed as though she were more like to die of that beating than to recover and live.

Another woman thought Anne would never recover fully, for 'ever since she hath used to have such strange fits of shaking and quaking as that she is for the time when the fit cometh blind and senseless very strange to see'.[84] Margaret Bonefant confronted John Young, who explained 'that he did think [his wife's] estate had been better when he married her than he did then find it'. She told him that 'that

---

[81] Christopher Evans (*Anne Evans c. Christopher Evans*, 1613, LMA, DL/C/221, fos. 1210v–1211) and William Greene (*Margaret Greene c. William Greene*, 1607, DL/C/217, p. 225). For the patriarchal arguments employed by violent husbands in separation cases, see Laura Gowing, *Domestic Dangers: Women, Words and Sex in Early Modern London* (Oxford, 1996), 208, 219, 220, 230.

[82] This was typical. A rare example of a witness favorable to the allegedly cruel husband was Francis Bridge, who testified on behalf of his brother that John Bridge's wife, Margaret, had 'much wasted the goods of her said husband by her unfitting ways'. Other witnesses accused John of cruelty, forcing his wife to live in great want, and trying to bribe them to prove her a whore. See Francis Bridge, *Margaret Bridge c. John Bridge*, 1616 (LMA, DL/C/224, fo. 34v), and other depositions (fos. 35, 102v–104r, 105v–106r, 107v–108r).

[83] Agnes Man and Mary Gladin (*Anne Evans c. Christopher Evans*, 1613, LMA, DL/C/221, fos. 1494r, 1484v–1485r); and Elizabeth Kingston (*Margaret Greene c. William Greene*, 1607, LMA, DL/C/217, p. 201).

[84] Anne Coles and Margaret Bonefant, *Anne Young alias Lyngham c. James Young*, 1608 (LMA, DL/C/218, pp. 53, 50–51, 54).

was not the way to know or understand of her estate, but if he would know that it must be his kind usage of her and not that severity for that was the way to make an end of them both', but he answered bleakly: 'Ay . . . I am told I shall be hanged if she die within a year and a day, but if I be, there is but one out of the way.'[85]

Young soon gave further proof of his dark frame of mind by stabbing himself. The surgeon called by the neighbors first 'espying him to have wounded himself in two places on his breast with a knife looked for the knife and threw it out of the way', sent a neighbor, Ursula Lucas, for sugar to stanch the blood, then, 'seeing there was no danger of death in it let him feel the more smart'. Mistress Lucas, seeing Young 'walking up and down his chamber in his shirt without any other clothes upon him being very exceedingly bloody', saw 'that he had so hurt himself with a knife' and 'asked him how it happened that he had done that to himself'. Young answered: 'Only unkindness,' and, she noted, 'that was all the answer and speech that she . . . could have of him'. When a male neighbor visited Young and asked him 'what he meant so to do to himself, he answering said it was a thing that should have been done before'.[86]

Witnesses testified that Young, a poor tailor, had bragged of his estate and boasted that 'by laying out two shillings he can make five shillings of it', so it seems likely that he had fallen into debt through speculation.[87] However, John blamed all on his wife's unkindness. When she threatened to hit him with a wooden bowl, he said, he beat her face black and blue. She consequently 'forsook' his bed and 'that night and the next following lay by herself'. When he visited her chamber, he 'seeing her purse lying there took out two rings of three that was in it'. This annoyed her so much that she 'became so sullen that she counterfeited herself sick and went to bed, and kept her bed a week after', forcing him 'to spend forty shillings in keeping of her in that her counterfeit sickness'. Her refusal to sleep with him and evident desire to be rid of him were the cause, he said, of his attempted suicide:

> such hath been and was the unkindness of [his wife] towards him . . . as that she hath divers times when he . . . hath gone out at doors she hath fallen down of her knees and prayed to God that he . . . might never come in at the doors again, whereby he . . . was in a desperate mind . . . for which he is now heartily sorry and desiring Almighty God to forgive him, as that in the morning when he arose out of his bed (he lying alone as he had done long before and after his said wife's refusing his company) he did stab himself with a knife which he carried to bed with him in the breast in two places.

If only she would dutifully 'be quiet and live quietly with him in the fear of God', he would 'get much more and be better able to keep and maintain both himself and her than now he is to keep himself, his mind is so unquiet by reason of this trouble'.[88]

---

[85] Margaret Bonefant, LMA, DL/C/218, p. 51.
[86] William Watson, Ursula Lucas, and Nicholas Roberts (LMA, DL/C/218, pp. 58, 56–7, 61).
[87] William Watson (LMA, DL/C/218, p. 59).
[88] John Young (LMA, DL/C/218, pp. 88–9).

None of the witnesses agreed with Young's interpretation of events; instead they supported Anne's claim that she could not safely live with her husband. Their sympathy for her was bolstered by self-interest, for Anne Young fell on the charity of her neighbors when her husband refused to relieve her. When Margaret Bonefant went to visit Anne during her recovery, she found her 'in such want as that [Margaret] did see Mistress Coles and others that came to see her give her money and send for drink, wood and coals and for meat and likewise for ointment for her and for divers things that was fit for her comfort she having no money herself but being in great want and need'.[89] This theme of economic irresponsibility was often repeated in divorce testimony; witnesses tarred abusive husbands as shiftless, spendthrift, and wantonly destructive of both goods and health.

In 1615, several witnesses testified in support of Margery Newbury's suit for separation against her husband, Thomas. They painted a stark picture of a husband hell-bent on destroying his family and a wife who strove desperately to compensate for her husband's ravages. Margery, a widow, had made a terrible mistake by marrying Newbury, a sadler in his early 30s. Witnesses insisted that her conduct had been irreproachable: she behaved 'as an honest sober wife ought to do', 'honestly and modestly in all things'.[90] Newbury, on the other hand, had 'called her whore and bitch...beaten and kicked the said Margery...trod upon her with his feet and broken her head with bedstaves and with a jug...pulled her up and down the house by the hair of her head...torn the ruff from off her neck'. Elizabeth Sturley, Margery's maidservant and sister of her previous husband, noted that Newbury had 'altogether given himself over to a lewd and dissolute life, following and keeping the company of lewd women, common drunkards, and other wicked and evil livers'. He was suspected of adultery: Thomasine Skarlett, who treated Margery's 'broken head', 'seeing in what state of body the said Thomas Newbury was forbade the said Margery not to come into his company for fear of infection of the said disease called the pox'. At Margery's request she gave him an ointment; it made his hair fall out.[91]

Witnesses laid special emphasis on Newbury's failure to live up to his financial responsibilities and his insistence on thwarting Margery's efforts to support the family. He 'being a sadler by his trade refuseth to labor therein', would 'not take any manner of pains to get his own living or to maintain his said wife, children or family, but hath wasted his estate in riotous manner' and 'carried out the money out of his house that his said wife hath procured and gotten by her pains and industry'.[92] Margery had taken over the traditional role of the provider: 'Margery Newbury hath been the only maintainer of her said husband and hath provided meat, drink, and apparel, and all other necessaries fitting a man of his degree and also by her labour kept and maintained her children and family without the aid of

---

[89] Margaret Bonefant (LMA, DL/C/218, p. 51).
[90] Daniel Peale and Elizabeth Sturley, *Margery Newbury c. Thomas Newbury*, 1615 (LMA, DL/C/223, fos. 273r, 275r).
[91] Elizabeth Sturley and Thomasine Skarlett (LMA, DL/C/223, fos. 275, 280r).
[92] Ibid. fos. 275v, 280r. See also Faith Petts (LMA, DL/C/223, fo. 279r).

her husband.' She 'for these eight years last past hath been the only maintainer of her said husband's children and family by her industrious means and painstaking'. Her work was constantly undermined by Newbury, whose 'lewd life' was such that he would 'not work nor take pains for his living nor for the maintenance of his wife and children, but carrieth and conveyeth the goods which his said wife had gotten by her industry and honest labour out of her house and consumeth the same in lewd and drunken company'. Margery was 'a very painful woman and provident for the getting of the maintenance of herself, husband and her children', but Newbury in her absence 'sold away twenty barrels of beer which the said Margery had provided to furnish her house withal'.[93]

Newbury seemed determined to cast his family on the parish. He repeatedly voiced the intention of ruining Margery and the children entirely, saying he 'would never leave them until he had brought them to an hospital', and that he would 'turn her and her children out of doors a-begging'. After years of this life, Margery had been brought to the edge of her endurance. Elizabeth Sturley reported that she had 'to shun the violence of her said husband run up to the top of the house upon the leads and cried out very fearfully, at which times [Elizabeth] hath very much feared that she would leap off the said leads into the street'. Margery had also 'been fain to leap out at a window'.[94]

The rhetoric of order was a double-edged sword. If men were able to draw on patriarchal discourse, so were women. Margery Newbury's witnesses consistently deployed patriarchal ideals to demonstrate how utterly Thomas Newbury had failed to live up to his obligations as husband and father, provider and guide, and how admirably Margery herself had fulfilled the role of the provident wife, mistress, and mother.[95] Margery fed and clothed her family, keeping them off the poor rates; Thomas threatened to cast his wife and children into the hospital, to make them beggars, dependent on parish charity. Margery worked hard to stock her house with provisions; Thomas sold them and spent the proceeds on whores and drink. Margery behaved modestly; Thomas brought a loathsome disease into the household. On one side, as the witnesses put it, the wife strove for order, economic stability, health, and domestic harmony, and on the other, the husband threatened to destroy his own household and to weaken the broader social fabric. The conservative virtues of thrift, moderation, sobriety, honesty, modesty, and industry were entirely on her side. If Thomas Newbury had called witnesses of his own, it is possible that they would also have made appeals to patriarchal discourse, but like the vast majority of allegedly cruel husbands, he was unable to produce any neighbors to shore up his case. Men's right to bring their families to ruin was not

---

[93] Elizabeth Sturley, Daniel Peale, and Faith Petts (LMA, DL/C/223, fos. 276r, 273r, 272v, 278v–279r).
[94] Elizabeth Sturley (LMA, DL/C/223, fos. 276r, 275v).
[95] Similarly, Walker finds that in Cheshire, abused wives described their husbands' violence as 'the willful destruction of the household's economic, social and moral integrity, in spite of their own noble efforts to maintain it'. Garthine Walker, *Crime, Gender and Social Order in Early Modern England* (Cambridge, 2003), 65.

a popular rallying cry in early modern London. Even putting aside sympathy for Margery's 'black, bruised, and swelling face', it is not difficult to see why male and female neighbors sided with her: among the specters that menaced the community, poverty, alcoholism, and the pox far outweighed the milder and largely abstract threat posed by headstrong women.[96]

In a 1619 separation suit, we are able to compare the testimony of the wife's witnesses with the story the husband told to justify himself. Like Margery Newbury, Mary Perks was the breadwinner for her household. She took 'extraordinary pains to get a penny by her needle' and also took in bands for starching; she was observed to 'labour and take pains very much ... to earn and get her a poor living'.[97] Thomas Perks, on the other hand, lived idly 'up and down a careless man' and sold his working tools as well as the lease of his house to finance his pleasures. Like Newbury, he spent his substance in drunken carousing: he was arrested by the watch at least once for being out late 'beastly drunk' and came home with his clothes so dirty that he seemed to have been 'wallowing in the street'. In his rage he targeted both people and possessions. The Perks' former maidservant Anne Breache reported that he came in drunk one night threatening to kill her, and to pin her mistress to the bed where she lay with his bare knife. The maid,

> seeing his outrage and dreading that he would do mischief that night, did use all the sleight she could to put him out of her mistress's chamber and having done so, shut the door against him, and being prevented of his intended mischief he went down into the kitchen wherein he did break and batter to pieces some implements of household stuff and cut the rope of the jack[98] into many shivers and pieces and there he remained all that night until the next morning.[99]

He could even be said to have destroyed his own child, since he caused Mary to have a 'mischance' or miscarriage. His violence was most harshly directed towards his wife but overflowed to the greater neighborhood: once, when the maidservant Anne Frost came to his house to collect some bands from Mary for her mistress, she found Mary 'sitting in a chair in her kitchen crying and bleeding at the nose, and her husband standing over her with a naked knife in his hand and saying that he would kill her, and further saying that it were as good for him to be hanged for her now at the first as hereafter, "For," quoth he, "I will kill her."' When Anne asked him to leave Mary alone, he 'flew' at her, called her 'whore', and beat her out of the house with a wooden candlestick, inflicting injuries that took seven weeks to heal.[100]

Like Newbury, Perks also consorted with lewd women. He abandoned his wife, disappearing for a year without a trace, then returned 'in mean bare apparel' with a suspicious female companion and importuned his former maidservant and her

---

[96] Daniel Heale (LMA, DL/C/223, fo. 273v).
[97] Anne Frost and Christian Harris, *Mary Perks alias Fuller c. Thomas Perks*, 1619 (LMA, DL/C/226, 4th series, fos. 45r, 44r).
[98] This may refer to a device for turning the spit or some other household machine.
[99] Anne Frost and Anne Breache (LMA, DL/C/226, 4th series, fos. 45r, 7th series, 18r, 17v).
[100] Anne Frost (LMA, DL/C/226, 4th series, fos. 45v–46r).

husband to take her as a lodger, promising to pay the charges. Anne Breache, the same woman who had shut Perks out of Mary's chamber a few years earlier, now married to a musician, soon perceived that this lodger was great with child, and visited Mary to inform her of the situation.[101] For Mary Perks, her husband's adultery appears to have been the last straw, for she soon began divorce proceedings.

As in the Newbury case, Mary's witnesses drew a contrast between her industry and good behavior (she demeaned herself 'lovingly and kindly' towards her unrewarding spouse) and Thomas's destructive, irresponsible idleness and violence.[102] One was a paragon of patriarchal virtues, and the other was a threat and a burden to everyone around him. In the Perks case, however, we are fortunate enough to hear Thomas Perks' side of the story. As we might expect, he attempted to shift blame onto his wife, but did so in surprising ways. Rather than countering the accusations of violence and adultery—which he simply denied—Thomas blamed Mary for his failures. He recounted that he had maintained her pretty well for six years, but when his trade failed, she had abandoned him, 'and took away with her of his proper goods plate and other implements of household stuff, and at her said departure vowed with some oaths never to return thither again'. Perks explained that his ensuing idleness and haunting of alehouses was due to her absence: he 'in grief of hurt at her departure and for want of a guide to look unto his house grew careless of himself and his welfare, so that he was constrained to sell the remainder of the years he had to come in his house . . . to his great hindrance and almost utter undoing'. He admitted that he had 'not of late since her departure been so careful of his thriving as heretofore he had been', but this was 'by reason of his wife's unkindness in not cohabiting with him as she ought by law to do'.[103]

Perks' story was a narrative of weakness, not of strength, of hurt feelings rather than authority. He argued that without his wife's labor, guidance, and affection, he was unable to fulfill his responsibilities and to act as a man should. Perks—like James Young—glossed over accusations of cruelty, and instead depicted himself as being desperately in need of his wife's love and companionship. If their wives were allowed to live apart, Perks and Young argued, they would be financially and emotionally ruined. In making these appeals, Young and Perks seem to have hoped that the court's desire to keep households stable and economically independent would outweigh their concern for the danger facing Anne Young and Mary Perks. The two wives and their witnesses made the opposite argument. They also appealed to the court's love of order and stability, but argued that no efforts, no labor, no loving wifely conduct could redeem their impossible husbands or restrain their fury. Unless the marital bonds were severed, they suggested, their families would sink into misery and beggary.

Both violent men and battered wives could make impassioned appeals to the ideal of the orderly household. To succeed, they had to persuade onlookers and

---

[101] Ibid. 7th series, fos. 18v–19r.
[102] Christian Harris (LMA, DL/C/226, fo. 43). For complete testimony, see LMA, DL/C/226, 4th series, fos. 43r–48v, and 7th series, fos. 15v–19r.
[103] Thomas Perks (LMA, DL/C/192, fos. 103v–104).

judges that they were indeed in the right. While men were undeniably privileged by virtue of their sex and their better access to institutional power, these advantages could be weakened or negated by the disapproval of the neighbors. For example, in 1611 Thomas Charles, a constable, arrested his own wife, telling onlookers that he had a warrant to bring her to Newgate. Legally, Frances Charles had little recourse, leading one scholar to interpret the case as an illustration of the 'very real possibility of men's manipulation' of legal institutions to abuse their wives. However, a full understanding of the incident must include the reaction of the crowd. A goldsmith saw Charles

> pull and hale his said wife in the street in Holborn in most inhuman and cruel manner upon pretense that he had a warrant to carry her to Newgate ... calling her 'whore' and using her so hardly by pulling her in the street as the people who flocked about them to see the event of that manner cried shame of the said Thomas. And one Mr Prescod, a man of good note and authority, did much rebuke him for so handling and entreating his said wife, and at last (he saith), one Mr Wetherhead a constable ... seeing the cruel and inhuman usage of him the said Thomas towards his said wife, and pitying the case, using first means to get away a warrant from the said Thomas which he then had against his said wife, afterwards took away his said wife from him and so freed her from his cruelty.[104]

Not only did the people exclaim at Charles's abuse of his authority, but even the forces of order stepped in to put a stop to his outrageous behavior.

Violent husbands lost sight of the forest for the trees: their obsession with one element of patriarchal order—the subjection of wives to their husbands—led them to sacrifice the whole.[105] When men beat their wives, the patriarchal household structure was thrown into disorder as servants fled for help or confronted their masters, and neighbors and watchmen were forced to enter private houses to set things right. It was torn apart when abused wives took refuge, temporarily or permanently, in the houses of neighbors or kin.[106] As clergymen regularly read to their flocks:

> Who can worthily express the inconvenience, that is, to see what weepings and wailings be made in the open streets, when neighbours run together to the house of so unruly a husband, as to Bedlam-man, who goeth about to overturn all that he hath at home? Who would not think that it were better for such a man to wish the ground to open, and swallow him in, than once ever after to be seen in the market?[107]

Violence was associated with a failure of patriarchal responsibility: abusive husbands were often drunkards who neglected their trades and spent their money on gambling rather than food for their wives and children, forcing neighbors to provide aid instead. Their brawling disturbed the peace and diminished the credit

---

[104] Gowing, *Domestic Dangers*, 227. Robert Bartholomew, *Frances Charles c. Thomas Charles*, 1611 (LMA, DL/C/220, fo. 602v).
[105] See also Elizabeth Foyster, 'Male Honour, Social Control and Wife Beating in Late Stuart England', *Transactions of the Royal Historical Society* 6 (1996), 217.
[106] See Amussen, *An Ordered Society*, 167–8.
[107] 'Homily on the State of Matrimony', *Certain sermons or homilies*, 315.

146   *City Women*

of the neighborhoods in which they lived. Thomas Wilson's abuse of his wife, kicking her and dragging her around a tavern near their home, 'made all the neighbours a-weary of their lives to dwell near unto them' according to one fed-up local. Domestic chaos went hand in hand with economic disorder, threatening parish rates. While husbands' violence did not dishonor their wives as women's adultery dishonored their husbands, such men did ultimately discredit themselves.[108]

It is difficult to know what marriage was like for ordinary people. The sources used here—conduct books, ballads, divorce testimony—all suffer from their own biases. Most couples resolved their marital difficulties, if they had any, without resort to the courts. The typical early modern English husband was not a rampaging beast, nor was the typical wife a long-suffering saint. Similarly, images of bullying shrews and henpecked husbands should be taken with several grains of salt. However, the focus on the household provided here allows us to imagine how ordinary marriages differed from the sober harmony advocated by Gouge and his fellows. Complaints in popular literature about scolding wives and drunken husbands suggest that many wives felt that their husbands spent too much time and money in alehouses and taverns, and told them so. Men resented the irksome demands made on them by their wives; they may have seen alehouse sociability as a precious reward for a life of toil. In hard times, when rising prices threatened household economies, these tensions may have been especially severe. When resentment erupted into outright conflict, the fact that both spouses could feel that they were defending traditional order added fuel to the fire. In most marriages, however, this tension, while real, was probably not overwhelming. Irritation was balanced by affection; recklessness by responsibility. While few marriages were immune from occasional disputes, in many cases they were surely resolved, as they were in this ballad, with mutual forgiveness and a renewed will to face life's hardships together:

Wife: Well, come, sweetheart, let us agree.
Husband: Content, sweet wife, so let it be.
              Where man and wife do live at hate
              The curse of God hangs o'er the gate.
              But I will love thee as my life,
              As ever man should love his wife.[109]

If economic anxieties could drive husbands and wives apart, they could also draw them closer together. The consolations of conjugal affection rivaled those of the alehouse, and they were affordable even for the poor, as one wife suggested: 'What thou want'st in riches,/I will supply in love./Thou shalt be my honey,/and I thy

---

[108] Joan Simpson, *Bridget Wilson alias Winter c. Thomas Wilson*, 1622 (LMA, DL/C/228, fo. 193r). See also Foyster, 'Male Honour, Social Control and Wife Beating in Late Stuart England', 219.

[109] M. P., *Merry dialogue betwixt a married man and his wife concerning the affaires of this carefull life* (London, 1628).

turtle dove.'[110] Love, as balladeers and clergymen taught, was an essential ingredient in the marriages of the laboring poor and middling sort, not a luxury. It was the honey that sweetened the wife's reproofs, the gravitational force that drew the husband home from the tavern, the veil with which married people covered one another's faults. Without it, even paragons of duty would live sunless lives; with it, the most flawed of mortals could hope to muddle through.

---

[110] *The housholders new-yeeres gift containing a pleasant dialogue betwixt the husband and his wife* (London, 1640).

5
Public Lives

Early modern London women led intensely public lives. Although moralists instructed them to remain within doors and mind their own business, city wives preferred to sit at their doors or in their shops, where they could work and mind the house while chatting with their neighbors. 'Gadding' might be a vice, but neighborliness was a virtue. Moreover, social engagement was essential to neighborhood order: inquisitive neighbors identified suspicious newcomers liable to fall on parish charges, and played a central role in supervising troubled households and intervening in domestic disputes. Informal public life was particularly important for women. While men might derive their identities from livery companies, parish government, and office-holding, women looked to the neighborhood for public roles. As 'honest matrons' attending women in childbed, they asserted their difference from men and maids. On their way to attend births, they could walk the streets after dark with a sense of entitlement only shared by members of the watch.[1] After births, they shared exclusive gossip and festive consumption. Despite male complaints about female talk, women gained influence through their tongues. 'Public fame' could be a powerful weapon to correct abuses of power.

The neighborhood could be a crucial source of support and aid for vulnerable women. Wives and widows came together to attend, comfort, and assist women in childbed, and to ensure that husbands were treating their wives with consideration and providing special foods and other 'necessaries'. Neighbors eyed one another's comportment closely and did not hesitate to intervene in cases of domestic violence to protect or, as they usually put it, to 'rescue' endangered wives. But while neighbors restored order by halting beatings, they worried, too, that marital separation was another form of disorder. Once immediate danger was averted, neighbors privileged reconciliation over separation, striving to restore harmony against all odds. Civic authorities took the same tack: while sympathetic to battered women and hostile to abusive husbands, they advised reconciliation whenever remotely possible. The same emphasis on reconciliation also appears in cases of female adultery. Though one might expect unfaithful wives to be cast out, penniless, in fact neighbors urged forgiveness, and divorcing an unfaithful wife was difficult without her cooperation, evidence of desertion, or incontrovertible

---

[1] This right could be abused: in 1614, Anne Chamberlaine told her servants she was going to 'a woman in travail', and instead kept company with a philandering clergyman all night long. See James Clerk, *Office c. Francis Holliday*, 1614 (LMA, DL/C/222, folio between fos. 79 and 80).

proof. Social order tended to take precedence over both women's safety and men's honor.

The intensely public nature of London life could also strain order, and neighborhood harmony often needed to be restored through arbitration and drinking ceremonies. Women competed with one another for status, and gossip could be maliciously destructive. Men feared that women's desire to impress one another with gorgeous attire led to reckless spending and even to adultery as a means of acquiring desired adornments. Women, on the other hand, worried when their husbands spent time and money on female neighbors, and did not hesitate to attack their rivals viciously in hopes of shaming them and their own husbands into fidelity. Neighbors of both sexes, but perhaps especially women, stressed by endless battles against urban filth, poverty, and illness, were too often overcome by unquenchable irritation and anger that tore at the fabric of neighborhood harmony. Indeed, the precariousness of social and economic order had much to do with the value placed on it by ordinary Londoners and magistrates alike.

THE NEIGHBORHOOD

While London women attended festive guild suppers and crossed the city to go to market and to visit kin and friends, their social lives were primarily organized around their neighborhoods.[2] Not only did neighbors meet in church on Sundays—at least in theory—but women also spent many of their waking hours sitting at their doors or in their shops, where they could see and hear what happened in the street and sometimes in neighboring houses.[3] Given the expense and bad quality of candlelight, sitting by the door may have been a necessity for eye-straining needlework. In addition to this advantage, however, the threshold simultaneously favored domestic order and sociability. A woman sitting there could keep an eye on her maidservant and see that the apprentice was at work, stand up to serve a customer, watch her children playing in the street, observe any interesting passersby, hail a hawker, and pass the hours of tedious labor gossiping, joking, and quarreling with her neighbors.

Hundreds of depositions situate London wives at their own doors or those of their neighbors, working, chatting, and wrangling. A tailor's wife in Shoe Lane was 'sitting at her own door at work' during a quarrel.[4] Christian Armett of St Sepulchre was sitting at her door with her husband, a haberdasher, when they heard a woman accuse Dorothy Williams of having had 'four or five husbands in one year'. Christian Day was 'sitting a-working at her door' when a man called Margaret

---

[2] See Bernard Capp, *When Gossips Meet: Women, the Family and Neighbourhood in Early Modern England* (Oxford, 2003), 267–319.

[3] See Laura Gowing, '"The Freedom of the Streets": Women and Social Space, 1560–1640', in Paul Griffiths and Mark Jenner (eds), *Londinopolis: Essays in the Cultural and Social History of Early Modern London* (Manchester, 2000), 134–5, 137.

[4] Susan Clarke, 1617 (LMA, DL/C/225, fo. 23r).

Banbury a whore. A Stepney clothworker's wife was sitting at her own door when she heard Mary Reene call Susan Chaddock a 'fat-arsed sow'. Sara Bond, a carpenter's wife, was sitting at her door when Marcie Barwick told Alice Ansley that her husband wore 'privy horns'.[5] At the threshold, London wives could monitor the street and interfere if need be. When Beatrice Vicars 'saw and heard a great sort of people gathered together about Thomas Harrison's door' and understood him to have 'beaten his wife', she 'sitting at her own door in the same lane went towards Harrison's door'. The man soon found himself subject to disapproving female scrutiny. Another neighbor, Margaret Trott asked: 'Mr Harrison, why do you beat your wife in this sort?' When he insulted her, Margaret promptly fetched her husband to back her up.[6]

Women who did not have their own doors at which to sit might sit at those of their friends or lodging places. An ostler's wife was 'making of bone lace' at the door of Joan Atkinson when Ellen Tompkins called Joan a 'gilliflower whore'. Another woman sat 'at the door of the house where ... she lodged' where she overheard two local women quarrel over a kettle.[7] Women also sat at one another's doors for companionship. A young widow explained that she brought her distaff over to a vintner's house 'to spin and keep company with his ... wife as she was wont divers times to do for neighbourhood's sake'. One long summer evening, Elizabeth Jacob, a chandler's wife, sat at Dorothy Mitton's door, 'talking neighbourly' with some men and women.[8]

Not all neighbors felt equally 'neighborly' together, however: threshold groups embodied both inclusion and exclusion. Frances Price knew that Mary Bird and Helen Steed were friends because she had 'seen them sitting in the street working together very lovingly and friendly', and another neighbor had seen them sitting and working 'together at their doors and in one John Beech's shop'.[9] Usually women sat or stood at their own doors or those of their friends, but if they ventured into hostile territory, retaliation could ensue. Mary Ball was standing by Mistress Kiddey's door sewing a shirt when Joan Gibson found fault with her for standing there. '"Why," quoth Mary Ball, "will you let me to stand in the Queen's highway?"' Joan was 'greatly moved' at her and 'took a dish full of water and threw it in Mary Ball's face'. Angry words followed, to the great annoyance of Agnes Hunter, who was mending stockings in her shop nearby. Agnes left 'because she would not have heard their scolding as she sayeth and she being away a good while came again

---

[5] Christian and William Armett, 1592 (LMA, DL/C/214, p. 302); Christian Day, 1587 (LMA, DL/C/213, p. 158); Alice Harford, 1613 (LMA, DL/C/221, fo. 1395v); and Sara Bond, 1606 (LMA, DL/C/217, p. 108).

[6] Beatrice Vicars and William Clerke, *Henry and Margaret Trott c. Thomas Harrison*, 1600 (LMA, DL/C/216, sl. 169, 156).

[7] Jane Sanmon, 1615 (LMA, DL/C/223, fo. 343v) and Mary Clemence, 1629 (LMA, DL/C/231, fo. 402r). See also Sara Morgan alias Faggo, 1633 (LMA, DL/C/630, fo. 55r) and Ruth Chamberlaine, 1627 (LMA, DL/C/230, fo. 434r).

[8] Agnes Garrett, 1572 (LMA, DL/C/211/1, fo. 48r) and Elizabeth Jacob, 1591 (LMA, DL/C/214, pp. 95–9).

[9] Frances Price and Catherine Ward, *Mary Bird c. Helen Steed*, 1607 (LMA, DL/C/217, pp. 61, 58).

thinking all had been quiet then, and then at her coming again she found them still in chiding'. Mistress Kiddey threw more water at Mary, while Joan Gibson 'took a loaf of bread of the baker's stall and struck Mary Ball therewith'.[10]

Neighbors knew much about one another's lives, and newcomers were subjected to intense questioning. Anne Talbot was grilled about her solitary state in the places where she moved after she left her husband, a dyer, around Easter in 1619. First, she kept Alice Warren in childbed, looking after her and living in her house in Stepney for the month after Alice's delivery. Later, she rented a chamber in Petticoat Lane where she lived with her father, then moved with him to Selbey's Alley in St Botolph Aldgate. By that time Anne was heavily pregnant, and soon she gave birth to a girl who was baptized by the name Elizabeth. Anne's neighbors in Selbey's Alley were inquisitive: 'the said Anne being demanded at her first coming thither to dwell what her husband was, she said sometimes he was a seafaring man and was at the East Indies, and sometimes a dyer's wife whose husband dwelt about Mark Lane, insomuch as the neighbours thought very hardly of her.' They had their suspicions about the paternity of her daughter:

> Robert Mason coming often to the house of her the said Anne and keeping her company much, she was asked the question by some of her neighbours who that man was, and sometimes she would say he was her brother and sometimes her cousin insomuch as the neighbours did suspect him that he came thither for some ill pretense in regard she did give him such extraordinary entertainment at his coming.[11]

Selbey's Alley became uncomfortable for Anne Talbot, so she moved again, this time to Brick Lane, close by but in a different parish. There, Anne tried to appear respectable. When her neighbors 'demanded of her where her husband was and what profession he was', she told them 'that her husband was a thread dyer, and lived at Ipswich, who sent her up money as she said to buy her necessaries'.[12] However, the neighbors there still noted that Anne frequently met with Mason at her house or in taverns, where 'they have been merry together and he hath embraced her about the middle very kindly'.[13] Anne had little talent for discretion. A Brick Lane woman reported:

> Anne Talbot making the said child ready on Sunday morning, she took up the said child's leg in her hand, and speaking to her father who then lived with her, said: 'Here is Mason's own leg, viz. a bow leg like him, that child was not wrong fathered.' And thereupon her father winked at her and bade her hold her tongue.[14]

Anne made no attempt to hide her liaison with Mason from her old employer Alice Warren. After being churched, she visited her to invite her to come see the baby, and when Alice did come, she saw Anne 'lay the said child in his the said Mason's

---

[10] Katherine Parvis and Agnes Hunter, *Mary Ball c. Joan Gibson*, 1601 (LMA, DL/C/216, sl. 313, 312, 314).
[11] Anne Marten, *Robert Talbot c. Anne Talbot*, 1623 (GL MS 9189/1, fo. 53v).
[12] The first part of this answer was true, because Robert Talbot did move to Ipswich for a period.
[13] Anne Ensall (GL MS 9189/1, fo. 75v).
[14] Joan Blackborne, ibid. fo. 76v.

lap, saying to him, "It is yours and it is like you for the child hath bow legs and so have you."' Mason laughed, and gave her money for the baby's maintenance.[15]

Neighbors' interest in one another's lives extended even to the deathbed. When William Oliver was ill in Thomas Barrett's house, Cicely Simthorpe declared that she 'for neighbourhood's sake used often times to go to the said Barrett's house to visit the said William Oliver in his sickness'. Her husband, Edward, a joiner, went there as well to 'comfort' Oliver. This was a brave act, for William Oliver lay dying of the plague. The scrivener who was called to write his will nearly fled when he heard 'a whispering among such as were there about the breaking of a sore', and insisted on working in the hallway, later reading the will out loud to the dying man from a gingerly distance. It was Edward Simthorpe who helped poor Oliver hold the pen to make his mark; the local curate had refused to come.[16]

Good neighbors or gadding gossips?

Sociability could be equally well praised as 'good neighbourliness' or condemned as 'gadding'.[17] Gossip could be seen as harmless recreation and a means of pressuring misbehaving neighbors into reformation, or as domestic treachery and the root of social discord. The results of sociability shaped its interpretation: it was good when it strengthened communal bonds, bad when it weakened household and communal harmony. Of course, both effects could coexist: female talk was widely perceived as strengthening neighborly bonds at the expense of the marital one, while critical gossip about an absent neighbor could be a bonding experience for those present.[18] Festive eating and drinking was another area of contention: it strengthened neighborly bonds but strained household budgets. Married people tended to justify their own festive consumption—at gossips' feasts for women, in taverns and alehouses for men—in terms of custom and neighborliness, while criticizing that of their spouses as harmful waste. Similarly, wealthy citizens who feasted respectably at taverns looked askance at the disorderly merriment of their poorer fellows in alehouses.

Citing texts like Samuel Rowlands' *A crew of kind gossips*, historians have tended to suppose that women's gossip was problematic in a way that men's gossip was not, as it was considered to pose a threat to patriarchal order. In the satire, six wives drinking in a tavern complain about their husbands, and the six husbands refute the complaints and bemoan their wives' bad behavior. For example, the sixth wife laments her husband's lewdness:

> There's not a whore in London, nor about,
> But he hath all the haunts to find her out.

---

[15] Alice Warren, ibid. fo. 50v.
[16] Neither Cicely nor Edward Simthorpe was named as a beneficiary in the will, although Oliver did ask Edward to make him a coffin. Cicely and Edward Simthorpe, and Philip Barton, 1578 (LMA, DL/C/629, fos. 47r, 43r, 13r). For neighborly visiting of the sick, see also Ian Archer, *The Pursuit of Stability: Social Relations in Elizabethan London* (Cambridge, 1991), 76.
[17] See Capp, *When Gossips Meet*, 27.
[18] See ibid. 57–9.

> He knows the panders that can fit his turn,
> And bawds that help good fellows to the burn.

Her husband, in turn, defends his jaunts as innocent recreation:

> I never was in bawdy house but twice,
> And there indeed a friend did me entice
> To see some fashions; only there we drank,
> And saw a gallant queane, her name was *Franke*,
> In a silk gown, loose bodied, so was she:
> Not that I tried her, but as they told me.[19]

His wife, he maintains, is the one at fault for her 'devilish nature' and 'accursed jealous eye'. Fletcher describes this text as having a 'thoroughly patriarchal' message. 'The men's faults, taking the defenses they offer into account, are portrayed as venial... The women, by contrast, are portrayed as universally shrewish and variously spendthrifts, idle and violent.' As Capp puts it, 'Rowlands expresses disgust at the women's disloyalty in criticizing their husbands in public, but then depicts the six "honest husbands" discussing and damning their wives' behavior, with no hint of disapproval. Women's talk was stigmatized as gossip not because it differed in character from men's, but because it was perceived as the subversive behavior of subordinates.'[20]

In accepting Rowlands' distinction between women's unacceptable gossip and men's harmless talk, however, we risk ascribing universality to men's opinions, and ignoring those of women. The evidence does not suggest that women shared in men's condemnation of female gossip. Nor can we assume that husbands' talk about their wives did not bother women. Husband and wife were supposed to protect each other's good names abroad, not to attack them. Gouge condemned spouses who betrayed one another:

> By blazing abroad one another's infirmities: as when tattling gossips meet, their usual prate is about their husbands, complaining of some vice or other in them: 'My husband,' sayeth one, 'is covetous: I cannot get of him anything almost: he maketh me go as nobody goeth.' 'And my husband,' replieth another, 'is so furious as none can tell how to speak to him': so one after another goeth on in this track, some discovering such infirmities as should be concealed; others (which is worse) plainly belying their husbands. In like manner also husbands when they meet with their boon companions, make their wives the common subject of all their talk: one accusing his wife of one vice; another his, of another.[21]

Popular literature depicts male sociability—in taverns, alehouses, bowling alleys, and so on—as a common grievance for frustrated wives.

---

[19] Rowlands, *A crew of kind gossips, all met to be merrie complayning of their husbands, with their husbands answeres in their owne defence* (London, 1613).
[20] Anthony Fletcher, *Gender, Sex and Subordination in England 1500–1800* (New Haven, Conn., 1995), 20; Capp, *When Gossips Meet*, 62–3.
[21] William Gouge, *Of domesticall duties* (London, 1622), 251.

Wife: As I am a sinner I am ashamed of thee, thou art such a noted tavern haunter...
thou art bewitched to the tavern, and to such base company that have no regard or care of their wives and family at home.
Husband: Good wife, forbear your violent and raging speeches, I confess I am in a fault, but it shall be so no more; I am sorry for it, I will take a new course with myself and forsake all ill company...
Wife: I scorn to be a good wife to such a perpetual drunkard, that is drunk ordinarily twice a day, and never comes home, unless it be to sleep, and then out again... Come sirrah, tell me first in what company you were in yesterday, from nine of the clock in the morning, till twelve at night. Then secondly, tell me what tavern you were at. Then thirdly what wine you drank. Then lastly, what it cost you all the day in expenses; and what you had to eat, for it is impossible you could be all that while at a tavern, and eat nothing.[22]

The expense of same-sex sociability compounded the anger of the excluded spouse, who shared in the cost but not the pleasure.

When the betrayal of marital secrets was not at stake and gossip was friendly, the difference between 'good neighborliness' and 'gadding' was largely economic: when all was well at home, servants orderly, children obedient, and family finances sound, few criticized friendly sociability. Even the strictest moralists conceded that women had a right to pay neighborly and charitable visits. Although Rogers criticized 'gadding' wives, he advised a husband to 'yield [his wife] the indulgence of all decent and sober refreshings, and recreations of body and spirit, which may ease the tediousness of body and spirit, through the incessant and never ceasing yoke of family businesses... allowing her the converse of her friends'. Wise husbands allowed a 'genial liberty' to their wives in 'the meetings and lawful merriments of their kind, which it were a poor thing for a husband curiously to enquire after'.[23]

On Sundays, once religious duties were fulfilled, decorous amusements such as walking in the fields, visiting friends or family, or eating and drinking in neighborly company did no harm to women's reputations. Thomas Platter, a German traveler, was struck by the presence of women in taverns:

[W]hat is particularly curious is that the women as well as the men, in fact more often than they, will frequent the taverns or ale-houses for enjoyment. They count it a great honor to be taken there and given wine with sugar to drink; and if one woman only is invited, then she will bring three or four other women along and they gaily toast each other.[24]

Around Christmas especially, merry meetings in mixed company were to be expected. In 1599, some neighbors met at Katherine King's house one Sunday

---

[22] John Taylor, *Divers crabtree lectures Expressing the severall languages that shrews read to their husbands, either at morning, noone, or night* (London, 1639), 133–9.
[23] Daniel Rogers, *Matrimoniall honour: or, The mutuall crowne and comfort of godly, loyall, and chaste marriage* (London, 1642), 248, 251.
[24] *Thomas Platter's travels in England, 1599*, ed. and trans. Clare Williams (London, 1937), 170.

'to be merry in the evening after supper'. In addition to drinking and gossip they 'had some Christmas games and suchlike sports'.[25]

There are few indications that alehouses were off-limits to respectable women, as long as they were with their husbands or in neighborly company, and did not drink or spend too much. When Elizabeth Aldeworth saw a family friend sitting with two other men in an alehouse, she 'came into the said house to them and sat down by them at the board's end to drink' and to talk business.[26] When Jane Smith was accused of being a common drunkard, a witness said in her defense that she was 'no ways addicted or given to drinking more than is fitting for a well governed woman to do'.[27] In contrast, neighborly drinking was largely off-limits for maids. In a rare example, the spinsters Jane Boone and Anne Malabourne, both migrants in their late 20s or so, faced disapproval for drinking in Thomas Buttock's tavern with their single friend Elizabeth Bagg. After downing a pint or two of burnt wine, the young women asked for the reckoning and went to the bar to pay, but their host, angry to learn that his servant had served them, said they would have no wine in his house. When Elizabeth insisted that they could pay for it, he called her a jade and added that 'they were all jades that kept her company'.[28]

Adult women could be disparaged for spending too much time abroad, but such attacks—in the absence of evidence of excessive drinking, lewdness, or idleness—were likely to be contested. The widow Mary Drane cited her landlord's criticism of her as evidence against *him*. Though he was 'a man that doth profess religion in outward habit and guise to the world', she thought him a hypocrite: 'she is persuaded in her conscience that he is not the man inwards as men do repute him.' She recounted how she had once spent an hour in a tavern with a countryman of hers who was planning to ride into Essex and asked her whether she wished to send anything by him to her mother. Although Mary had been home by ten, 'she was condemned by [Hopper] and his wife for keeping out of doors so much'. She considered this one of the 'many wrongs and injuries' that she as 'a silly poor woman and a widow' had suffered at his hands.[29]

Drinking in alehouses and taverns may not have fallen within the moralists' definition of sober recreation, but it was an essential element in the fabric of neighborhood life, strengthening friendships and salving differences. One Sunday around midsummer, Katherine Ward and her husband joined their neighbors in Francis Price's victualling house, where they witnessed the reconciliation of Helen Steed and Mary Bird. First, John Steed sent for his wife, who was at another alehouse. When she arrived, he said: 'Come on, Nell, what, shall we have Goodwife Bird and you fall out for a few brabbling words? I will make you friends if all the ale in this house will make you friends.' He called for drink, and 'then all the company drank and were merry'. The two women forgave one another and Helen drank to

---

[25] Katherine King and Williams Hills, 1599, (LMA, DL/C/215, sl. 841, 843).
[26] Thomas Clatterbuck, 1572 (LMA, DL/C/211/1, fo. 136v).
[27] Mary Drane, *Jane Smith c. John Hopper*, 1620 (LMA, DL/C/227, fo. 195v).
[28] Jane Boone and Anne Malabourne, *Elizabeth Bagg c. Thomas Buttock*, 1631 (LMA, DL/C/233, fos. 181–2). See also Peter Clark, *The English Alehouse: A Social History 1200–1830* (London, 1983), 131–2.
[29] Mary Drane, 1620 (LMA, DL/C/227, fos. 195v–197r).

Mary. Seeing some drink left in her glass, John Steed rebuked her: '"Nay, Nell," quoth her husband, "you shall drink all to her", whereupon she drank of all the whole glassful of ale (it being bottle ale)'.[30] Draining the glass was essential, because the drink symbolized the ill will that the drinkers hoped to overcome. Thus when Rachel Cheeresley and Anne Haynes reconciled themselves in a victualling house after a dispute in which the former had defamed the latter as a base and barren whore, the mistress of the house reported that after an initial round of drinking, Anne poured 'a glass of beer, and holding the same in her hand spake to the said Cheeresley: "I drink to you ... and all the malice or hatred I bear to you I put into this glass."' After Rachel repeated the ritual, 'the two went forth of the house together very lovingly and friendly'.[31]

While friendly toasts were a valued part of neighborhood life, excess left both women and men open to criticism. Magdalen Lewis remarked snidely to Mary Warner: 'I said as I say still, I ... was never an old man's whore nor a young man's whore nor I was never brought home drunk in a chair.'[32] Going idly up and down from alehouse to alehouse was a sure sign of disorder and vice. One John Coppin, a tobacco-seller, was prosecuted in an *ex officio* case for his affair with Margery Clerke, a married woman. According to a tailor's apprentice, their alcoholic perambulations were extensive. Leonard Huckleton met with Margery one day, and was invited to accompany her to Coppin's house. 'Having drunk a pipe or two of tobacco they all three went to one Bartholomew Daniel's house, victualler, in the Minories where likewise they did drink, and they the said Coppin and Margery Clerke were very familiar together.' From there, the company 'went to the Sun Tavern in the Minories where they stayed there by the space of a hour', by which time Coppin and Margery were 'very extraordinarily familiar together'. Finally, they moved on to 'one Sweetman's house a victualler in Aldgate and there stayed half an hour' before Huckleton 'went privately away' and Coppin and Margery adjourned to her bed.[33]

Drinking was harshly disparaged when it was associated with excessive spending. Jane Hallilay railed at the victualler Thomas Willis: 'Thou art a common drunkard and a whoremasterly slave and thou dost keep other men's servants in thy house in the night drinking.' It was wrong of Willis to 'harbour other men's servants to spend their masters' goods'. Willis had aspirations to local office, but, Jane threatened: 'I ... will see thee hanged before I will have a drunkard or a whoremaster churchwarden'.[34]

---

[30] Katherine Ward, *Mary Bird c. Helen Steed*, 1607 (LMA, DL/C/217, pp. 57–8). See also *Elizabeth Duckett c. Jane Williams*, 1610 (LMA, DL/C/219, fos. 124v, 156v–157r); *Elizabeth Howell c. Eleanor Tipsley*, 1613 (LMA, DL/C/223, fo. 31); *Jane Bellie c. Richard Worrall*, 1615 (LMA, DL/C/223, fo. 333).

[31] Elizabeth Pratt and Winifred Ryder, *Anne Haynes c. Rachel Cheeresley*, 1621 (LMA, DL/C/228, fos. 108r, 140r).

[32] Hanna Knowling, *Mary Warner c. Magdalen Lewis*, 1634 (LMA, DL/C/630, fo. 167r).

[33] Huckleton, beset by curiosity, snuck away to Margery's house, and, when no one answered his knock, lurked outside until she and Coppin emerged. In Margery's defense, her husband had been absent in 'some country unknown' for about two years. Leonard Huckleton, *Office prom. Birch c. John Coppin*, 1620 (LMA, DL/C/227, fo. 95).

[34] Thomas Oliver, *Thomas Willis c. Jane Hallilay*, 1628 (LMA, DL/C/231, fo. 203r).

Despite complaints about 'gadding' wives,[35] it would have been impossible for an early modern London woman to gain a good reputation by keeping entirely to herself, because one of the most salient markers of local status was associating with other women 'of the best sort'. Neighborhood women were the collective arbitrators of female status,[36] and good associations could and did trump discrediting facts. In 1608, for example, one Frances Hearne was asked about the reputation of her neighbor Dorothy Charleton, who had two years earlier been subjected to one of the most discrediting punishments early modern England had to offer, a public carting.[37] While Frances mentioned the carting in passing, she went on to say that 'Dorothy Charleton hath kept company with women of the best sort amongst her neighbours and hath been and so is at this time commonly accounted an honest woman and hath demeaned herself very soberly, discreetly, and honestly amongst her neighbours'. An engraver's wife testifying in the same case made the connection between Dorothy's good associations and good credit even more clearly, saying she did not think Mistress Charleton had been carted for bawdry or perjury, and 'the reason she sayeth which maketh her think so is that both before that time of her being carted and ever since she hath kept company with the best sort of women of citizens' wives and tradesmen's wives . . . and hath been always well accepted of in their company'. However, according to a witness who had given evidence against Mistress Charleton at the Sessions, she had indeed been convicted of bawdry and perjury for lying under oath about an incident in which a man had been killed, and had been both carted and set in the stocks.[38]

Keeping company with the right sort of women was as crucial to good neighborhood reputation as keeping company with ill-livers was harmful. Snobbish unsociability could have negative repercussions, as when Anne Wade told a neighbor that 'Anne Holloway was a bold-faced queane and thought herself so good that no woman of the parish where she dwelt was worthy to be her fellow'.[39] Respectable London women believed that birds of a feather flocked together, and they were as anxious to belong to the right flocks as they were to ensure that their own circles remained free of suspicious plumage.

CHILDBED: COMPANIONSHIP AND SUPPORT

Childbirth had meaning far beyond the immediate household: labor, christenings, gossipings, churchings, and burials were important events for neighborhood matrons. As guild processions theatrically displayed the corporate body of the male London citizenry, so the rituals of childbirth gathered together assemblies of

---

[35] See e.g. *Matrimoniall honour*, 277–8.
[36] See Gowing, '"The Freedom of the Streets"', 137.
[37] Carting, usually reserved for bawds or other sexual offenders, was so shameful that a mere reference to it could prompt a defamation case.
[38] Frances Hearne, Elizabeth Pierce, and Thomas Greene, 1608 (LMA, DL/C/218, pp. 75–6, 77–8, 44–5).
[39] Anne Hume, *Anne Holloway c. Anne Wade*, 1617 (LMA, DL/C/225, fo. 71r).

women with membership in a different kind of community. While the strength and inclusiveness of these communities has been debated,[40] evidence from the consistory court and popular literature suggests that childbed rituals were indeed expressions of female solidarity, at least for married women, while male grumblings about gossips' feasts reflected resigned resentment rather than a serious threat. Childbed communities should not, however, be romanticized. Matrons attended women in childbed because they thought it their right and duty to see things done properly: aid and moral regulation were inextricably intertwined. Moreover, the solidarity of female childbirth communities was hampered by midwives' and matrons' inability to reliably safeguard laboring women and their children. Celebratory accounts of 'traditional' childbirth must be tempered by consideration of the challenge that frequent maternal and infant deaths posed to female bonds.

Being 'big with child' was a more or less constant status for young wives: average intervals between births were as low as twenty-three months in richer parishes and twenty-seven months in poor ones.[41] Although pregnancy was no death sentence,[42] childbirth was a frightening experience for early modern London women. Maternal death rates were especially high in the disease-ridden capital: the London Bills of Mortality recorded 21 maternal deaths per 1,000 baptisms for the period 1657–99 in contrast to Schofield's national estimate of 10 deaths per 1,000 births.[43] In St Botolph Aldgate, where the parish clerk regularly recorded causes of death between January 1582 and September 1593, childbed was the most frequent cause of death after plague and consumption for wives under the age of 46, accounting for about a

---

[40] Some historians celebrate the protective atmosphere of childbed rituals and the temporary demotion of the husband to fetcher of food and drink, while others see a culture of shame in the seclusion of the mother and emphasize tensions between mothers, midwives, and matrons, and the social criticism of female consumption in gossipings. See Adrian Wilson, 'Participant or Patient? Seventeenth Century Childbirth from the Mother's Point of View', in Roy Porter (ed.), *Patients and Practitioners: Lay Perceptions of Medicine in Pre-Industrial Society* (Cambridge, 1985), and *The Making of Man-Midwifery: Childbirth in England, 1660–1770* (Cambridge, Mass., 1995); Linda A. Pollock, 'Childbearing and Female Bonding in Early Modern England', *Social History* 22.3 (October 1997); Laura Gowing, *Common Bodies: Women, Touch and Power in Seventeenth-Century England* (New Haven, Conn., 2003) and 'Ordering the Body: Illegitimacy and Female Authority in Seventeenth-Century England', in Michael J. Braddick and John Walter (eds), *Negotiating Power in Early Modern Society* (Cambridge, 2001); Gail Kern Paster, *The Body Embarrassed: Drama and the Disciplines of Shame in Early Modern England* (Ithaca, NY, 1993).

[41] Roger Finlay, *Population and Metropolis: The Demography of London 1580–1650* (Cambridge, 1981), 142. See also Chris Wilson, 'The Proximate Determinants of Marital Fertility in England 1600–1799', in Lloyd Bonfield, Richard Smith, and Keith Wrightson (eds), *The World We Have Gained: Histories of Population and Social Structure* (New York, 1986), 205.

[42] Schofield argues that in the context of high background mortality rates, childbirth was a relatively minor additional risk: mothers died in about 1% of births in early modern England, and faced a 6% or 7% lifetime risk of dying in childbirth. Roger Schofield, 'Did the Mothers Really Die? Three Centuries of Maternal Mortality in "The World We Have Lost"', in Bonfield, Smith and Wrightson (eds), *The World We Have Gained*, 259–60.

[43] The two figures are not directly comparable. Registers of baptisms did not include stillbirths, which accounted for a large proportion of maternal deaths. See Schofield, 'Did the Mothers Really Die?', 232–3, 235.

fifth of all 199 deaths.[44] Indeed, this may understate the proportion of women's deaths from childbirth for London as a whole, because the years included a plague epidemic and the parish was poor and crowded. In the richer parishes of the center of the City and the more rural outskirts, plague and consumption may have played a lesser role, and deaths in childbed may have been correspondingly more significant, particularly as richer women married younger and gave birth more often than their poorer counterparts.

Fears of death ran strong, especially for first-time mothers. One macabre way of insulting a bride was to suggest that she would not die of her first pregnancy. For example, when two women quarreled on the road to London, Elizabeth Luke said that Thomasine Rogers 'was but a broken vessel and that her husband...should not need to fear that she should die of her first child'. In 1633, Anne Tarleton defamed her former maidservant Jane Prince, who was to marry William Browne: she asked him: 'Are you the man that should marry my maid Jane Prince?' When he said he was, she continued: 'Then you shall be sure your wife shall never die of her first child, for she...hath had a bastard in the country.'[45] The danger of childbirth made it an especially meaningful time for oaths and curses. As we have seen, single women were questioned during childbirth because they were considered unlikely to tell a falsehood at that perilous moment. Married women might also believe that successful deliveries were dependent on speaking the truth. When one Christian Greene, in labor, accused her former mistress of bawdry, a witness thought her motives were innocent of malice: it was, she said, 'only a conceit that she had that she should not be delivered of her child except she had uttered the same'.[46]

While childbirth was a life-threatening ordeal, London women did not face it alone. Their husbands, servants, and female neighbors all played important roles in the alleviation and management of the inevitable pain and fear. Throughout pregnancy, conduct books instructed husbands to treat their wives with special consideration:

> When thy wife is great, and full of anguish with the labour of breeding and bearing: when she is in travail, or lieth in (as they term it), and begins to recover the strength, that pains in travail had diminished; then comfort her with loving speeches, then cheer her with affable countenances... then see that she want no looking to, no good fare, no good usage that thou canst help her unto.[47]

---

[44] GL MS 9221, Register General of St Botolph Aldgate, 1571–93. In contrast, for thirteen non-London parishes, Schofield finds that childbirth caused a fifth of deaths only for women between the ages of 25 and 34, while it accounted for a lower proportion of deaths (about one in eight) for younger and older women. 'Did the Mothers Really Die?', 259.

[45] Malen Clarke, *Elizabeth Luke c. Thomasine Rogers*, 1619 (LMA, DL/C/226, 6th series, fo. 36r); John Stocke, *Jane Prince c. Anne Tartleton*, 1634 (LMA, DL/C/630, fo. 168r).

[46] Alice Parsons, *Mary Philips c. Christian Green*, 1607 (LMA, DL/C/217, pp. 212–14).

[47] William Whately, *A bride-bush: or, A direction for married persons plainely describing the duties common to both, and peculiar to each of them* (London, 1619), 69.

Some men considered these duties excessive. In a satire warning young men what to expect in marriage, Dekker described how a man's wife's pregnancy 'breeds him new cares and troubles':

> if she let fall but a pin, he is diligent to take it up, lest she by stooping should hurt herself... And oft times through ease and plenty she grows so queasy-stomached, that she can brook no common meats, but longs for strange and rare things, which whether they be to be had or no, yet she must have them there is no remedy. She must have cherries, though for a pound he pay ten shillings...[48]

'In this trouble and vexation of mind and body', Dekker went on, 'lives the silly man for six or seven months, all which time his wife doth nothing but complain, and he, poor soul, takes all the care, rising early, going late to bed, and to be short, is fain to play both the husband and the huswife.' Once a wife's pangs began in earnest, her husband's demotion to general dogsbody was complete.

> then must he trudge to get gossips, such as she will appoint, or else all the fat is in the fire. Consider then what cost and trouble it will be to him, to have all things fine against the christening day, what store of sugar, biscuits, comfits and carroways, marmelade, and marchpane... with a hundred other odd and needless trifles... Besides the charge of the midwife, she must have her nurse to attend and keep her, who must make for her warm broths and costly caudles.[49]

Indeed, Gouge lectured husbands about their duty to procure such items, reminding them that 'the want of things needful is at that time very dangerous: dangerous to the health and life of the woman and child also'. To deny the wife her choice of nurse and midwife was evidence, he said, of 'inhumane and more than barbarous unkindness'.[50]

With the onset of labor, women took charge of the delivery. A laboring mother could expect to be attended by a midwife and several matrons: only the most unfortunate 'lewd' women gave birth alone. Newly delivered mothers continued to be surrounded by female companions for several weeks as they were repeatedly visited in celebratory 'gossipings'. During his wife's lying-in month, Dekker complained, not only did the husband have to bear the cost of providing her with 'dainties' such as 'partridge, plover, woodcock, quails', he also had to furnish his house with refreshments.

---

[48] Thomas Dekker, *The batchelars banquet* (London, 1603), sig. B4. Medical theory held that pregnant women's fancies were to be taken seriously. William Gouge wrote that husbands were to obtain whatever their pregnant wives longed for 'to the uttermost of their power and ability... For it is well known, that it is very dangerous both for mother and child to want her longing: the death sometimes of the one, sometimes of the other, sometimes of both hath followed thereupon.' *Of domesticall duties* (London, 1622), 399.
[49] Dekker, *The batchelars banquet*, sig. B4.
[50] Gouge, *Of domesticall duties*, 400–401.

[S]undry dames visit her, which are her neighbours, her kinswomen, and other her special acquaintance, whom the goodman must welcome with all cheerfulness, and be sure there be some dainties in store to set before them: where they about some three or four hours (or possibly half a day) will sit chatting with the child-wife.[51]

Rather than being grateful for his hospitality, the gossips did nothing but berate the beleaguered husband, 'accusing him of little love, and great unkindness to his wife', and filling her head with notions of entitlement. This, too, was hallowed by tradition. Gouge cited as an example of covetousness and unkindness how 'there be many that when the time that their wife should be delivered approacheth near, carry her from all her friends into a place where she is not known, lest her friends should by importunity draw him to expend and lay out more upon his wife than he is willing'.[52] Gossips' influence was hard to withstand. In practice, wives were less pampered than Dekker's satire claims. In poorer households, mothers' caudles were probably made of sweetened ale rather than spiced wine, while chicken—if that— substituted for game birds. Nor did all mothers benefit from the services of a drynurse during their lying-in month, although, as we shall see in the following chapter, nurse-keeping was a common occupation for poor women. Nonetheless, in its broad strokes Dekker's narrative corresponds to the reversal of ordinary power relations described by Adrian Wilson.[53]

The practices that so irked Dekker were important for the health and comfort of the mother, as a 1626 account shows. Anne Mindge's experience was described to the consistory court because it contradicted cultural expectations: rather than playing the traditional role of the helpful and unobtrusive husband, Richard Mindge evinced nothing but hostility to his wife. This account, inflected by the indignation and concern of Anne's neighbors and friends, suggests that Anne would have been very much worse off without the forceful intervention of female neighbors and sympathetic men.

The Mindges were newcomers in London, having spent the first turbulent months of their marriage in Kent living with Anne's mother.[54] The story begins when Anne invited a neighbor, a grocer named John Stair, to accompany her and her husband shopping in Cheapside for childbed linen and other 'necessaries'. After 'Anne made choice of and bargained for suchlike necessaries together with two waistcoats for herself' the illusion of domestic tranquility was destroyed: Richard 'in a froward and willful humor refused and would not pay for the said necessaries'. Anne fell to weeping in the street, and Richard cursed her, while the embarrassed grocer requested him to refrain. When they came home again, Anne 'went up into a chamber to put off her hat' and Richard followed her, shut the door, and struck her.

---

[51] Dekker, *The batchelars banquet*, sig. B4v.
[52] Gouge, *Of domesticall duties*, 401.
[53] Wilson, *The Making of Man-Midwifery*, 29.
[54] See Anne Walters and Joan Idgitt, *Anne Mindge c. Richard Mindge*, 1626 (LMA, DL/C/230, fos. 72v–78v).

Hearing Anne's cries, Stair ran up, broke open the door, and again calmed the violent man.[55]

Despite Mindge's unwillingness to pay, Anne managed to acquire the linens she needed: the day before she fell into labor, Mindge found her in their chamber sorting and preparing them. He angrily threw the cloth down the stairs and into the chimney, then threatened to cast Anne herself down the stairs. Mindge's apprentice Robert Kettle stepped between Richard and his heavily pregnant wife, then, as he testified, 'held down the said Mr Mindge on the bed in the said chamber until he the said Mr Mindge fell asleep'. After the danger had passed, Kettle went down to the kitchen where Anne was sitting, and told her that her husband was asleep. Anne 'went up without her shoes fearing her said husband should awake and lay that night with her maid in a trundle bed'.[56]

The next day, Anne was very ill; a midwife was sent for and the neighborhood matrons assembled in her chamber for a long vigil. Kettle provisioned the women: he 'was called up by the nurse to fill beer for the women there'. Mindge, on the other hand, disregarded the rule of male exile from the childbed chamber: scandalizing those present, he walked into the room and lay on the bed, resting his arm heavily on Anne's exhausted body. Kettle reported that 'thereupon the said women and the nurse did by force thrust him out of the said chamber', and Kettle, with the help of a neighboring servant, 'did by force carry him into a shop of the same house'. Mindge slept that night on Kettle's own bed in the shop. The next morning, he again attempted to enter his wife's chamber, asking whether she had not 'lain a-bed long enough', but was not suffered to do so.[57] Despite these continual interruptions, Anne was at length safely delivered of her first child. Later on, the interventionist stance of the neighbors continued: when Richard bolted his doors and beat his wife, the neighbors hammered at the door and called the constable. When he arrived and distracted Richard, Anne 'was got or pulled out of a window of the said house together with her said child', and the constable took them to the house of a local widow, Dorothy Maddox, to spend the night.[58] The couple, married in the summer of 1624, were separated by 1626. By the time he testified, Robert Kettle had left Richard and found a new master.

This drama shows how the female domain of childbed took precedence over the usual household hierarchy. Women and even Mindge's own apprentice unhesitatingly used force to restrain and expel him from the couple's chamber after he repeatedly broke the rules that dictated consideration and support for a laboring wife. His exclusion was explicitly described as a matter of health and safety rather than shame.[59] The forthright behavior of the matrons neatly illustrates Wilson's argument that 'the presence of other women may have served to police the

---

[55] John Stair (LMA, DL/C/230, fos. 94r–96v).
[56] Robert Kettle (LMA, DL/C/230, fos. 69v–70r).
[57] Ibid. fo. 70v.
[58] Dorothy Maddox (LMA, DL/C/230, fo. 80v).
[59] Kettle deposed: 'Mr Mindge ... laid his arm on his said wife insomuch as the said Anne called to the nurse, and it was feared by [Kettle] and the women then and there present that he had or would have done the said Anne some harm.' LMA, DL/C/230, fo. 70v.

lying-in—to ensure that the husband respected the norms' of a childbed ritual that 'was constructed and maintained by women *because it was in the interests of women*'.[60]

Although custom and companionship protected laboring mothers from unruly interlopers, accounts of early modern childbirth before the rise of man-midwifery must acknowledge the inability of midwives and matrons to effectively prevent the deaths of infants and mothers. Margaret Pelling notes that the 'complexity and high intensity of medical care' in early modern societies compensated for 'the limited efficacy of therapeutic procedures'.[61] Similarly, the energy with which London women threw themselves into rituals of childbirth reflected their desire to conquer danger rather than actual control. When practices and rituals failed, laboring mothers could feel betrayed, and tensions grew. This was the case when Agnes Fisher's infant died soon after birth in 1631. While the matrons refrained from blaming either Agnes or her midwife, Elizabeth Besey, Agnes herself thought that she had been neglected and that the midwife had not tried hard enough to save the baby's life. She accused Elizabeth of having failed to exercise her office appropriately, and the midwife in return blamed Agnes's passivity for the death. The female alliance crumbled in the face of medical disaster.

Elizabeth Besey, a licensed midwife since 1618, was called to Agnes Fisher's labor early in the morning in August 1631, and came there directly from a different delivery. By the time a neighboring widow named Joan Bourman arrived, about twelve hours later, Agnes was in extreme pain, but the baby had not yet been born, nor would it be until the following morning. There was some question about whether the midwife did all she could to hasten the delivery. Anne Wardener said Mistress Besey did not use methods that she had 'seen other midwives use in the like case in that she did not give her hot or warm drinks to hasten her delivery'. On the other hand, Joan Bourman reported that Mistress Besey 'did administer her the said Agnes' husband's urine unto her the said Agnes when her throws were strong upon her to further her delivery'.[62]

At some point during the night's vigil, Mistress Besey, who was sitting in front of Mistress Fisher, herself apparently seated on a birthing stool, succumbed to exhaustion and fell asleep, laying her head in Agnes's lap. She had probably been awake for well over twenty-four hours. Agnes Fisher, suffering and frightened, 'crying then out and . . . imploring her aid and help, saying that she wanted her help and nothing else', lifted up Mistress Besey's head and said: 'What, are you asleep and I want your help?' Upon this 'calling and jogging' Elizabeth immediately roused herself and 'was ready and did help her'. At this point Joan Bourman, sitting nearby, 'felt with her hand the head of the said child'. It was born 'very weak and feeble and nearer death than life', suffering from some bruising around the head, and in an effort to save it, Mistress Besey left Agnes to the care of the matrons

---

[60] Wilson, *The Making of Man-Midwifery*, 29; emphasis original.
[61] Margaret Pelling, 'Medical Practitioners', in Charles Webster (ed.), *Health, Medicine and Mortality in the Sixteenth Century* (Cambridge, 1979), 235.
[62] Anne Wardener and Joan Bourman, *Office prom. Fisher c. Elizabeth Besey*, 1633 (LMA, DL/C/630, fos. 90v, 93v). For Besey's licensing, see the Vicar-General's Book (LMA, DL/C/342, fo. 70v).

while she looked to the child.[63] Despite being wrapped in clothes that had been heated by the fire, the baby died within an hour.

Agnes herself was more fortunate. The widow Wardener thought that she 'after her delivery was indifferent well and not anyways in danger of death nor had other weakness than women in that case usually have'. When the widow visited her a day or so later, Agnes was sewing in bed. She rose from her bed after three days. Margaret Ingram visited a week later, and said that Agnes then 'was reasonable well and sate up in a chair in her chamber'.[64] For the midwife, Agnes's survival was a qualified success: Elizabeth callously tried 'to cheer her up', saying 'jestingly... that she might give God thanks for sparing her for if she had not as many lives as a cat she might have died too'. Agnes, for whom the experience had evidently been traumatic, was unconsoled and accused her of being an unfit midwife. In her defense Elizabeth blamed Agnes for the death of the child, testifying that she was 'so dull and slow in her pains and so unapt or unwilling to help herself and to set forward the production of her child' that the infant was fatally weakened by the day-long labor. However, the other women, while acknowledging Mistress Besey to be a careful and experienced midwife, testified that Agnes had done 'as much as she then could or her strength would permit'.[65]

Midwives and matrons did what they could for women in childbed. They asserted that these women required special foods, extra warmth, and care. They encouraged the hiring of drynurses to attend the mother for up to a month, relieving her of normal household duties. If 'necessaries' were not forthcoming, neighboring matrons might provide these out of their own pockets. They attended women in labor, offering help and comfort, often for hours on end. In crowded London houses, they enforced inconvenient rules of privacy, demanding extra space for laboring mothers. These female communities could not reliably protect mothers and their infants from exhaustion, infection, and death, however, and tragic outcomes could leave lasting bitterness.

THE TROUBLED HOUSEHOLD: SUPERVISION, INTERVENTION, RECONCILIATION

When violent men cast their households into disorder, neighbors intervened to help women at risk. They shared food and other 'necessaries' with women whose husbands denied them sufficient maintenance, and strove to prevent brutal beatings. They did not hesitate to enter one another's houses in cases of need, and their own houses served as temporary refuges for terrified wives. Neighbors, especially self-appointed committees of matrons, also took the lead in appealing to constables

---

[63] Margaret Ingram and Joan Bourman (LMA, DL/C/630, fos. 89, 92v, 90r, 92v).
[64] Anne Wardener and Margaret Ingram (ibid. fos. 91v–92r, 90r).
[65] Elizabeth Besey and Margaret Ingram (LMA, DL/C/195, fos. 84r, 83v, and DL/C/630, fo. 91v).

and magistrates to halt domestic violence.[66] However, Londoners' conservative love of order was a double-edged sword for abused wives. While violent husbands found little support in their neighborhoods, there was considerable resistance to permanent marital separation. Neighbors who intervened in troubled households usually attempted to reconcile husband and wife even in the most hopeless cases. Magistrates and aldermen, too, were loath to recommend formal separation. While a few cases of marital breakdown reached the consistory court, many more were mediated or came to uneasy truces as husbands were bound over to keep the peace towards their wives. Even divorce cases were rarely carried to sentence: suing for divorce could be a means of pressuring an erring husband to reform. Many women were left in danger because it was difficult for people to come to terms with the idea of breaking the marital bond and dismantling the household.

Concerned neighbors counterbalanced the authority of abusive husbands and alleviated the plight of their wives. Informal charity could be an important safety net. Anne Frier 'was often constrained to have meat of her friends abroad for her necessary food', and when she gave birth to a child and her gossips saw that 'they wanted many necessaries which had been fit for a woman in childbed as she was at that time, as fire and divers things', the lack was discreetly remedied.[67] Neighbors who physically intervened between angry men and their victims could put themselves in real danger. A husbandman who stopped Richard Wade from cutting his wife's throat by grabbing the blade 'received much hurt, and continued in surgery for a long time'.[68] A cordwainer's wife testified that when Anthony Soda beat his wife Mary, she 'hath gone into their said chamber at some of those times to rescue her the said Mary and hath stood betwixt them to keep the said Anthony from beating his said wife'. Dorothy Rance was less heroic. When she heard Anthony 'in a great rage with his wife throwing things about the chamber', she 'arose and went up intending to have persuaded him to peace and quietness but when she came at their chamber door she saw the said Anthony Soda with a knife in his hand threatening to kill the said Mary...whereupon [she] durst not go in to rescue the said Mary, fearing he should do her...some hurt, but went down to her own chamber.'[69]

Some brave neighbors were credited—or credited themselves—with saving women's lives. When one Mistress Russell walked her friend Ellen Groome home to Tuttle Street one night, Ellen's husband Michael with 'devilish hatred and cruelty' took 'a pair of tongs in his hand and lifting them up to his head with

---

[66] See Capp, *When Gossips Meet*, 105–9; Susan Dwyer Amussen, '"Being Stirred to Much Unquietness": Violence and Domestic Violence in Early Modern England', *Journal of Women's History* 6.2 (1994), 70–89. As Margaret Hunt has argued, in early modern England, domestic violence had yet to become 'unspeakable', so it may have been psychologically easier for outsiders to intervene than is the case today. 'Wife Beating, Domesticity and Women's Independence in Eighteenth-Century London', *Gender and History* 4.1 (1992), 23.
[67] Alice Andrews and Agnes Webb, *Anne Frier c. John Frier*, 1602 (LMA, DL/C/216, sl. 777, 954–5).
[68] George Lucke, *Ragael Wade c. Richard Wade*, 1616 (LMA, DL/C/224, fo. 280r).
[69] Alice Ford and Dorothy Rance, *Mary Soda c. Anthony Soda*, 1622 (LMA, DL/C/228, fos. 343r, 342r).

great violence swore he would knock out his said wife's brains and threw them very fiercely at her head'. He would have slain her, according to the maids, 'had not the said Michael been prevented and she the said Ellen defended by... Mistress Russell'.[70] Providing a refuge was one of the most effective ways for neighbors to protect endangered wives. Once, Ellen Groome fled to the house of a neighboring tailor, William Bradshaw, saying that 'she durst not remain in her own house'. Groome demanded that she be surrendered to him, but the Bradshaws instead hid Ellen and persuaded him to go to bed there, since he refused to return home. Once he was in bed, Ellen quietly returned to her own house and locked the door. Groome rose and 'perceiving her to be gone to her own house ran after her in his shirt having no other clothes on him', but although he broke the windows and swore that he would kill her, he could not get in.[71] At another moment of extremity, Ellen escaped with the help of the neighbors: she was 'enforced to run from her said husband and was conveyed out of her house in Westminster by some of her neighbours... on a great and high pale'. A maid named Goulde 'did help the said Ellen Groome on the said pale', she reported.[72]

Even after the fact, neighbors could assist battered women. Jane Collett, an elderly marketwoman, reported that the Vulcombes' maid 'came one evening to [her] sitting in Cheapside selling of fruit', and cried that her master 'had killed her said mistress'. Jane 'made all the haste she could' to Richard Vulcombe's house, where she 'found him... standing at the door'. When she tried to enter, she 'was repelled by him yet at length... got into the house'. The widow found Winifred Vulcombe 'lying all along by a fireside bleeding very freshly and that exceedingly', with her head 'so gashly cut that one might then have turned their two fingers in it and at the same time was in great peril and danger of her life and [she] for her part thought she would then have bled to death'. Jane sent the maid, Abigail Gibbs, 'to go for Mr Tomlinson a chirurgeon to come to her said mistress and use his skill, who came and did apply some herbs to her to cure her wounds and stop the bleeding'. Later, when Jane visited Winifred during her convalescence, 'they did agree together to set a bolt on the inside of her chamber door to keep him out'. Unfortunately the bolt was weak, and Richard 'with great violence pulled the door open and in furious manner ran unto his wife and taking her with both his hands by the neck said: "Ah thou whore, I have not done with thee yet."' Jane Collett 'stepped to him and used all the means and strength she could to pull him away from her'.[73]

Once immediate danger was past, neighbors tried to bring violent husbands to their senses, castigating their intemperance and pointing out the good qualities of their wives. Once a husband repented, it was time to bring the couple to loving agreement and to persuade them to put the past behind them. Thus relatives and

---

[70] Goulde Pettie and Jane Lewis, *Ellen Groome c. Michael Groome*, 1615 (LMA, DL/C/223, fos. 299r, 292r).
[71] Richard Clerk (LMA, DL/C/223, fo. 290).
[72] Jane Lewis and Goulde Pettie (LMA, DL/C/223, fos. 316r, 292v, 299v).
[73] Jane Collett and Abigail Gibbs, *Winifred Vulcombe c. Richard Vulcombe*, 1620 (LMA, DL/C/227, fos. 180, 212v, 180v).

neighbors did their best to reconcile Mary Multhry with her husband, a physician given to drink and adultery, despite compelling evidence that the marriage was doomed. Multhry had coerced two maidservants into sex and attempted to rape a third. He had fathered a child with the 'harlot' Margaret Townsend, and 'by reason of his evil course of life was infected with the foul disease of the running of the reins'. He kept his wife short of 'necessaries' (a neighbor lent her money) and struck her with a brickbat, leaving her as ill as though she had been 'in travail of child'. Nonetheless, the neighbors tried to patch things up. Grace de Crete, who came by to ask Multhry for advice concerning her sick child, found the couple quarreling and tried to persuade Multhry to 'use his wife more lovingly, for that she was a good and loving wife unto him'.[74] Margaret Wilde accompanied Mary Multhry on an unsuccessful visit to try to persuade Margaret Townsend to father her child on another man.[75] Once, after Multhry had badly injured his wife, he fetched her sister Anne Bannister to look to her. Anne told Multhry of his cruelty, but when he said he was sorry and would not do it again, she insisted on reconciling the couple even though Mary was unwilling to cohabit with her brutal husband.[76]

When local attempts at reconciliation failed, neighbors might appeal to higher authorities or suggest that wives seek out their aid. In 1592, when Margaret Danvers 'fell a-weeping' in fear during an argument with her sister-in-law, a neighboring woman asked her what was wrong, and Margaret answered: 'that wicked woman...would have her husband to beat her'. '"Why," quoth [the neighbor], "there is remedy for that. You may complain to the higher powers, my Lord Mayor or somebody to get thy redress."'[77] However, formal attempts at reconciliation were not necessarily successful. Anne and John Frier were 'reconciled' at least once by an alderman before Anne began divorce proceedings: the servant Anne Andrews deposed that they 'were both sent for to Mr Alderman Banning's house one day and thither they both went, and come home friends at night'. Anne told Alice 'and the rest in the house to have special care not to displease him the same John Frier her husband, for that then they were made friends as she said, and so they seemed to be friends at that time'. However, within a week, Frier 'fell out again with his said wife, saying he did not go to Alderman Banning to be made friends but to be separated from her and so railed upon her as formerly he had done, telling her that he would sell away all he had and slit her nose, and give her a whore's mark'. A neighboring woman tried to reconcile them again when Anne Frier came to her shop 'with her handkerchief before her nose bloody, saying unto her...: "Look you here how my husband hath misused me." "Marry, God forbid,"' she answered, and went to John, 'and desired him to go...to his wife.' But Frier obdurately answered 'that he would see her damned first before he would come at her'. When Anne heard the news, she made a final

---

[74] *Mary Multhry c. John Philip Multhry*, 1632 (LMA, DL/C/232): Eleanor Mather (fo. 90v), Anne Clerke (fo. 89r), Anne Bannister (fo. 85r), Anne Andrews (fos. 91–92r), and Grace de Crete (fo. 94).
[75] They obtained a warrant for the woman's arrest, but she refused to change her story. Margaret Wilde (LMA, DL/C/232, fo. 93).
[76] Anne Bannister (ibid. fos. 85v–86r).
[77] James Pratt, *Helen Keller c. Mary Foster*, 1592 (LMA, DL/C/214, p. 312).

attempt to make peace with her husband with the help of a female delegation, then departed:

> she the same Anne herself and a sister of his the same John Frier's whom Anne Frier had sent for being a man's wife about Moorgate and [Agnes Webb] and one Mistress Harris went all together to him the same John Frier to persuade him to be friends and quiet with his said wife, but they could not prevail with him. There was at that time many ill words between him and his said wife but no persuasion could prevail with him to quietness. And so at last she the same Anne took her child up, and went home to [Agnes Webb's] house and there stayed a while and then departed with her sister named Mistress Lyon.[78]

Even divorce suits could serve as impetus for arbitration or as part of long-term marital negotiations. Winifred Vulcombe and her husband were first mentioned in the context of a divorce suit in 1616, when an elderly cutler testified that a prior case had been abandoned because the couple had been poor and 'unfit to continue'. As an alternative, the cutler, Jane Collett, and a neighbor named Peter Needham had arbitrated between the two: Needham wrote out an agreement that they all signed.[79] The unhappy couple was back in court in 1617, however, when witnesses testified that Richard had left his wife, and that her goods were being seized to pay his debts.[80] In 1620, yet another suit was begun, and Jane Collett and the maid Abigail Gibbs testified that Richard had nearly killed his wife. This was the last instance of proceedings between the Vulcombes in the consistory court, but in 1622 and, over a decade later, in 1633, Winifred herself was sued for defamation, having, among other things, called a neighboring woman 'an old rotten witch, an old jade and a queane'. Astonishingly, she and Richard were still married.[81]

Case study: *Sara Porthouse c. William Porthouse*

Testimony from the suit brought by Sara Porthouse against her husband illustrates the pattern of neighborly intervention: material aid and physical protection, followed by attempted reconciliation. Wed in 1592, William and Sara Porthouse spent part of their first years of marriage lodging in the house of a tailor, John Michael, and his wife, Anne. The fact that William denied his wife sufficient maintenance made them costly lodgers. Michael testified that Sara 'would still make her moan unto [his wife], being in great want and necessity both for her misusing by her husband with strokes, and for want of meat and drink and other necessaries, as [his] wife would always tell him . . . and [his] wife hath given unto her meat and drink such as she had'. The Michaels, sympathetic towards Sara, were eager to represent her as the passive victim of William's violence: one revision made

---

[78] Alice Andrews and Agnes Webb, *Anne Frier c. John Frier*, 1602 (LMA, DL/C/216, sl. 778–9, 955).
[79] Christopher Bowe, 1616 (LMA, DL/C/224, fo. 288v).
[80] See LMA, DL/C/225, fos. 90v–93v.
[81] See *Mary Swift c. Winifred Vulcombe*, 1622 (LMA, DL/C/228, fos. 268–269v, 301–302r, 327); and *Magdalen Dossett c. Winifred Vulcombe*, 1633 (LMA, DL/C/630, fos. 55, 79v–80r, 155, 159v, 163r, 166v).

in Anne's deposition suggests that when the deposition was read over to her, she altered it to make it clear that she was referring to one-sided violence:

> [She] and her husband being in bed together, heard a great noise and bustling in the next chamber where... William Porthouse and Sara Porthouse his wife used to lie, and thereupon [she] heard the same Sara Porthouse cry out, whereupon [her] husband rose out of his bed and went ~~to part them~~ into the chamber to keep him the said William Porthouse from striking the said Sara.[82]

Porthouse's attempts to isolate his wife angered the neighbors, who may have felt that in forbidding his wife from seeking their company, he was making an implicit attack on their credit. Petronella Ayre reported that Sara told her

> that her husband William Porthouse had forwarned her of her [Petronella's] company, and likewise of her going to the neighbors' houses where she used to go at such times as her husband was abroad, for she sayeth she hath heard her the same Sara say that her husband would lock up the victuals in the house and go forth and then would be angry with the neighbors that did relieve her.

Little could be more calculated to raise the ire of the neighbors than Porthouse's leaving his wife short of maintenance and then quarreling with them when they supplied the lack. Frances Offwood, a girl from Essex who spent some time lodging with the Porthouses at their own house in Aldermanbury around 1598, described how 'she did see and know... Sara Porthouse to be in great want both of meat and drink and the necessaries of her body, and she... hath let her have money to help her necessity which money she never had again'. Frances reported with some heat that 'Sara bought... eggs with some of that money, and when she had dressed them and was about to eat them, he the same William Porthouse came into the house and reviled her and cursed her and brake all the eggs upon her'. Frances admitted that she once told Porthouse 'that she would do him all the hurt she could if she should be brought to depose against him for that he kept away her money', but, she insisted, 'she sayeth no more than she knoweth to be true for all her so saying so'.[83]

In St Andrew Holborn, where the Porthouses first dwelt, the trouble between them came to a head when William allowed his brother to hurt his wife. The neighbors, hearing 'a great rush', called to Sara to learn what had happened, and heard her reply: 'Oh this dwarf [Porthouse's brother] hath thrown me down the stairs!' This, a neighbor noted, 'was not well done'. The local matrons took action; a constable testified that 'Mistress Michael, Mistress Ayre and divers other women of very good account' visited him at his home 'and desired him for God's sake to come and see the peace kept betwixt... William Porthouse and Sara his wife, for that as they then told him... Sara Porthouse was in very great danger of her life'. The constable, John Livesey, procured a warrant and brought the couple 'before divers

---

[82] John and Anne Michael, *Sara Porthouse c. William Porthouse*, 1599 (LMA, DL/C/215, sl. 468–9, 416).
[83] Petronella Ayre and Frances Offwood (LMA, DL/C/215, sl. 410, 439–40).

justices who at the same time sat in judgment at the Castle in Smithfield', and when Justice Skivington had questioned the couple and their neighbors, 'they committed the said William Porthouse to Newgate and sent her the said Sara to an uncle of hers dwelling in London'.[84] This crisis took place about five years before the 1599 suit. It seems that after the separation mandated by Skivington, the couple was reunited, but to no good effect. John Michael reported 'that William Porthouse hath removed sundry times his dwelling within this half dozen years last past, and ... his neighbors in every place do give him the same William Porthouse a hard report for misusing his wife'.[85]

Faithless wives

Social resistance to marital separation also hampered husbands who wished to divorce their wives for adultery. Although women's adultery was deeply threatening to a sexual order predicated on female chastity, it was a milder problem for community economies, and provoked more disapproval than serious action. Reconciliation remained the ideal. If husband and wife remained together, no illegitimate children would fall upon the parish and no divorced adulteresses— stripped of dower rights and maintenance—would prey on other women's husbands or burden their own kin.

Around Candlemas in 1613, Elizabeth Loder, the wife of a baker and tavern-keeper in St Botolph Bishopsgate, hid her lover in her house for several days during her husband's absence. William Loder ultimately sued her for divorce, but only after the couple's friends and neighbors had tried and failed to reconcile the two. Detailed evidence presented in court illustrates the complex and conflicting demands of honor, Christian duty, and family obligation, as the Loders and those who knew them struggled to resolve the crisis created by Elizabeth's adultery. The outraged husband, permitted by religion, law, and honor to cast out his faithless wife, found that in practice a clean break was hard to make.

Convinced that his wife had betrayed him, Loder called two married couples to witness her confession: his sister Rose Haycroft and her husband, Joseph, and Elizabeth's kinsman George Blundell with his wife, Alice. The two pairs gave very different accounts of what ensued. Rose Haycroft reported that William said: 'Oh Lord, I would I had never lived to this day for my wife hath undone me.' How, Blundell asked innocently, 'hath she lost you any leases or writings?' William answered that 'she had disgraced him and stained his house by playing the whore with his tapster'. 'It may be it is some mistrust you have of her,' Blundell suggested. 'No mistrust,' William answered, then asked Elizabeth: 'How say you, Bess?' She (according to William's sister) answered: 'I will never deny it for if I should I cannot ask God forgiveness'. Joseph Haycroft told a similar story, adding that Elizabeth

---

[84] Petronella Ayre and John Livesey (LMA, DL/C/215, sl. 410, 414–15). John Michael said that only the brother was imprisoned but that the magistrate would have done the same to 'Porthouse himself if he might have been gotten at that time' (sl. 469).
[85] John Michael (LMA, DL/C/215, sl. 469).

sorrowfully but freely declared 'they could do her no good; she had more need of the company of a preacher than of them.' The Blundells, in contrast, neither heard nor were willing to hear incriminating details. George reported that Loder complained that 'his bed was defiled' and ordered Elizabeth to confess. However, Blundell explained, he 'prevented the said Elizabeth's answer by saying that he would not meddle with it nor believe any thing was said and bidding her therefore hold her peace'. Alice similarly could not recall any damning admissions.[86]

In search of advice, Loder told the clergyman Thomas Sottiford that his wife had committed adultery with his man, and asked 'if he might not put her away for this offence'. Sottiford answered that 'our saviour Christ said no man may put away his wife except it be for adultery, but for adultery a man may put away his wife, which is but a word of permission and not of command, leaving it to the discretion of the husband'. He advised Loder to forgive his wife: 'first he should use all gentle and good persuasions to reclaim her, rather than to put her away for one fact, if she might be reclaimed.' Loder asked the clergyman to come and speak with Elizabeth, which he accordingly did a few days later. Sottiford reported that William instructed his wife to confess the truth, then left them alone together. Sottiford 'signified unto her how great an offence the sin of adultery was both to God and to her husband, and gave her particular instance of the plagues and judgments of God executed on divers persons for such sins and signified to her that her husband had reported that he took her committing of adultery with her man and exhorted her to repentance'. Elizabeth was moved to confess in guarded terms that she had been 'too familiar' with John Travis. However, she told Sottiford that she and her husband had reconciled and slept together after the initial accusation, and 'that since that time she had given her husband no cause of offence but the fault was in him that there was now no better agreement between them, "for," said she, "he is very cruel to me."' She 'seemed very penitent and sorrowful', and 'seeing her so heavy and weeping much, and conceiving good hope of her penitency', Sottiford went down to speak with William Loder. Now it was William's turn to be lectured: since he had promised Elizabeth not to upbraid her any more, he must now 'take his wife into his favour again and pardon that which was past, upon hope of her amendment'. Loder balked at first, but after some exhortation, the clergyman was glad to see husband and wife drinking to one another amicably, 'each of them forgiving the other'.[87]

While Elizabeth Loder broke her marriage vows, dishonored her husband, and defied the patriarchal order, she was not immediately cast out by her husband, rejected by her kin, or faced with the hostility of the local clergy. Instead, pressure was put on the outraged William Loder to forgive his wife so that the household might be patched together: maintaining female chastity took a back seat to preserving the family. Indeed, while female infidelity posed a grave threat to sexual order, in other respects it was far less threatening. It almost never produced

---

[86] Rose and Joseph Haycroft, and George and Alice Blundell, *William Loder c. Elizabeth Loder*, 1615 (LMA, DL/C/223, fos. 22, 21v, 23v, 24).

[87] Thomas Sottiford (LMA, DL/C/223, fos. 29v–30).

illegitimate children in the eyes of the law, for example. In fact, divorcing an unfaithful wife may have been more harmful to community economies than the tacit acceptance of adultery: because divorced adulteresses did not receive maintenance and were unable to remarry, they were apt to burden their kin, rely on charity, or fall into a life of crime.[88]

Loder's difficulties help explain why so few men in London brought divorce suits against their wives for adultery. In most cases, reconciliation or unofficial separation may have obviated the need for a legal remedy, and husbands were probably aware that in the absence of indisputable guilt, judges were disinclined to relieve husbands of their marital obligations. As a result, the cases that did come to the court tended to be open-and-shut or the formalization of existing separations. For example, when husbands and wives were parted for lengthy periods, inexplicable pregnancies greatly facilitated divorce. These cases, occurring most often in the seafaring communities of Stepney and Whitechapel, account for many of the adultery suits brought against London women. Edith Buckham gave birth to a child while her husband was on a voyage to Virginia. She named Albert Johnson as the father; he was subsequently arrested and forced to take paternal responsibility.[89] Similarly, Mary Holder had a baby while Ephraim Holder was away on a long voyage. She acknowledged to the midwife that Richard Fisher was the father. The whole parish had suspected them of adultery, and Fisher paid the costs for the child.[90] Testimony in *Peter Andrews c. Susan Andrews* describes Susan's attempt to conceal a pregnancy during the absence of her husband, master of the East India Company's ship the *Mary*.[91] Using a false name and claiming that her husband was in the country, she hired a chamber from a Westminster widow, but her subterfuge was discovered.[92] It was usually, but not always, the husband who traveled: Elizabeth Hawkins left her husband soon after their marriage, 'and dwelt with the Lady Montgomery and traveled with her into Ireland and there she remained... two or three years together'. Returning to London, Elizabeth admitted to her brother-in-law 'that a serving man that is since dead begot her with child of that child which she now hath and nurseth herself being a girl near the age of sixteen or seventeen weeks old'.[93]

In some cases, suits for divorce followed the more or less consensual break-up of the household. When Mary alias Alice Stanley alias King alias Morley alias Glascock

---

[88] This is how Martin Ingram explains the paucity of *ex officio* presentments for adultery, as opposed to fornication. *Church Courts, Sex and Marriage in England, 1570–1640* (Cambridge, 1987), 253.

[89] In her defense, Edith claimed to have been raped. See *Richard Buckham c. Edith Buckham*, 1626 (LMA, DL/C/230, fos. 57v–58v, 90r–94r); and Edith's statement, 1625 (LMA, DL/C/193, fo. 217r).

[90] See *Ephraim Holder c. Mary Holder*, 1626 (LMA, DL/C/230, fos. 58v–67r).

[91] Peter Andrews left England on the *Mary* in March 1626, sojourned in the East Indies for over two years, returned most of the way on the *Hart*, and finally arrived back in England on the *Hopewell* in December 1629. His wife may well have wondered what had become of him. Robert Collins, *Peter Andrews c. Susan Andrews*, 1630 (LMA, DL/C/231, fo. 535).

[92] Mary Wronggrey, Ellen Ashley, and Mary Pybus, 1630 (ibid. fos. 562v–563v, 563v–564r, and 564).

[93] John Hawkins, *William Hawkins c. Elizabeth Hawkins*, 1625 (LMA, DL/C/229, fos. 139v–140r).

came to court for a bigamous marriage to William Stanley in 1598, her first husband testified that their marriage had ended that way: he had married her when they were fellow-servants and she was 16, but after half a year she had left him, taking some of his goods. When he found her living in London six or seven years later, he had offered to take her again as his wife, but she had refused.[94] Anne Francis lived with her lover, Thomas Fox, in a victualling house for two weeks and allegedly attempted to go to Holland with him, only prevented by a prohibition of ships in June 1627; she openly told the court that she was cohabiting—and sleeping—with Fox, not her husband.[95] Alice Jones testified in 1588 that after thirteen children—apparently having had enough—she had left her husband and gone with her servant Robert Plover to Newport, where, she specified unrepentantly, 'he had company of her body at his pleasure'.[96]

Some wives may even have committed adultery on purpose to free themselves. Jane Burre, who confessed to having sinned 'divers times with one Thomas Sames a carpenter', told the court for good measure that she had been married to her husband Robert 'against her will' and that she 'could never of herself love and fancy him'. She explained that she 'extremely hated the said Robert Burre and by reason thereof they have lived together very unquietly and with much sorrow and grief by reason of the brawls that have been between them'. They could not, she said, 'safely and without peril and danger live together', because she 'being weary of the unquiet life that she and her said husband led together did think and intend to rid and free herself from her said husband by poisoning of him'.[97] Adultery was a relatively peaceful way of dissolving an unbearable marriage bond. Joan and Tobias Daniels were also incompatible. The two were often 'at very hot words together reviling each other in most odious manner', and Joan told a witness 'that she was weary of her life to live with him . . . she could not tell what course to take to live in peace with him.' She sued Tobias for divorce for beating her with a shovel, but told a friend that if that failed, she would have him divorce her for adultery: 'she could not endure to live with him and rather than she would live with him, she would come into the court and acknowledge herself to be a whore.' Tobias was equally miserable, complaining to friends that his wife pawned his clothes for drinking money; witnesses thought he would 'mischief himself or her' if they were forced to live together.[98]

---

[94] She made several illegal marriages, resulting in such a confusion of names that the court was relieved to be able to identify her on the basis of a slight deformity: although the young girl King had married had grown to be 'a tall woman with somewhat a swart color in her face', she was still recognizable when she removed her glove to show the court 'the little finger of her left hand grown crooked bowed down to her hand, the same having been cut in two'. Richard King, 1598 (LMA, DL/C/215, sl. 177–8).
[95] *Thomas Francis c. Anne Francis*: Thomas Hunt, 1627 (GL MS 9189/2, fos. 170v–180r); Anne Francis, 1627 (LMA, DL/C/193, fo. 246).
[96] Alice Jones, *John Jones c. Alice Jones*, 1588 (LMA, DL/C/213, p. 339).
[97] Jane Burre, *Robert Burre c. Jane Burre*, 1611 (LMA, DL/C/220, fos. 481v–482).
[98] Marlin Colstocke, Humphrey Taylor, and Leonard Bagley, *Joan Daniels c. Tobias Daniels*, 1622 (GL MS 9189/1, fos. 29v–31r).

Even more than men, women who sued their spouses for adultery alone were only likely to bring cases with indisputable evidence or when *de facto* separations had already taken place. Lady Isabel Young brought her husband, Sir Robert, to court in 1615 because he had not lived with her for ten or eleven years and had recently been known to consort with Eleanor Hickman, alias the Spanish Lady, alias the Miller's Wife, in Turnbull Street. There was no shortage of evidence: a constable searching the house (a suspected brothel) had seen the two together in a suspicious manner, and a tailor's wife coming to collect a debt had seen them 'in one another's embrace... between a pair of sheets lying in naked bed together', as had a maidservant in the house. Beyond noting that he had left his wife 'for some causes best known between themselves', Sir Robert did not dispute the facts.[99] In a humbler social sphere, Abigail Hawkins of Stepney sued her husband, William, for divorce in 1607 because he had committed adultery with Susan Digby, a local married woman. The two had done public penance for adultery, dressing in white sheets for the whole parish to see and asking for forgiveness, so no detailed evidence was required. A witness specified that Abigail had ceased to cohabit with her husband 'so soon as the adulterous life between him and Susan Digby was discovered'. After thirteen years of marriage and five children, Agnes Thomas alias Evans sued her husband, Evan Thomas, for separation in 1591 on the basis of past legal records. An elderly governor of Christ's Hospital recounted that according to the register of illegitimate children, Thomas had confessed nine years before to fornication with his maidservant. In 1620, Jane Crodie asked for divorce on the grounds that there was a common fame in Oxford that her husband had lived in adultery with one Elizabeth Taylor, fathering a base child that was maintained by Elizabeth's parents; she produced a certificate from an Oxford justice of the peace to this effect, and the erring husband could not deny his fault.[100] Given the difficulty of obtaining separation without indisputable proof or a confession, women with unfaithful husbands were more likely to try to pressure them and their lovers into better behavior, as we shall see below.

RIVALS AND ENEMIES

Londoners valued communal harmony, but they did not find that harmony easy to maintain. Competition, jealousy, and cramped, dirty, living conditions posed a constant challenge to the ordered ideal. Anxious about their status and their children, London women were all too apt to speak sharply. While popular practices like mediation and arbitration helped resolve many disputes, neighborliness was always a work in progress.

---

[99] Robert Lavecock, Joan Edwards, Alice Anion alias Wyn, and Sir Robert Young, *Lady Isabel Young c. Sir Robert Young*, 1615 (LMA, DL/C/223, fos. 264, 262, 265r).
[100] Peter Fairlambe, *Abigail Hawkins c. William Hawkins*, 1607 (LMA, DL/C/217, pp. 134–5); Evan Thomas and William Norton, *Agnes Thomas alias Evans c. Evan Thomas*, 1591 (LMA, DL/C/214, pp. 88–9, 160–61); Henry Brignall and Edward Crodie, *Jane Crodie c. Edward Crodie*, 1620 (LMA, DL/C/226, 5th series, fos. 43v–44r, and LMA, DL/C/192, fo. 133v).

Status disputes

Neighbors were often rivals. Women usually had a clear idea of where they stood in local estimation, and strove energetically to raise their rank or at least to protect themselves against any lowering attacks. Thus the clergyman William Crompton noted disapprovingly: 'we see many contend for superiority in place, who shall stand, sit, and go before; we may observe women strive with their neighbours, who shall excel in decking and trimming their bodies, adorning and setting forth their houses, following new fashions, and out-stripping one another in excessive feasting.' Why, he mourned, could they not compete for virtue instead?[101] Sexual reputation was only a part of the status calculation, which also drew on economic worth, hard work and skill, fertility, cleanliness, looks, health, and a host of other measures.

To claim higher status, quarreling women and men switched fluidly from measure to measure: an advantage on one count might be construed as a disadvantage on another. Thus three different sorts of measures, wealth, maternity, and sexual honesty, all came into play in one 1611 quarrel. In Chancery Lane, Elizabeth Chare and Elizabeth Jacob fell out 'about some building which the said Elizabeth Chare her husband had erected near to her the said Elizabeth Jacob's house and had thereby hindered her light of her house'. Mistress Jacob threatened Mistress Chare with the law, claiming that she had £20 to spend in the suit. Mistress Chare immediately changed the topic to a different kind of worth, telling her opponent that 'she was as good a woman as she was though she had not £20 to spend', and perhaps even 'something better'. 'Wherein art thou so good as I?' inquired Mistress Jacob. Mistress Chare declared: 'I . . . have ten children and thou hast never a one.' 'Ay,' her childless rival replied, not missing a step, 'you . . . have ten children indeed but who got them? Your husband . . . got not of them, but alas, poor ninnyhammer, he . . . is fain to father them.' A snide remark about one of Mistress Chare's daughters then prompted the outraged mother to storm inside, retorting that 'Elizabeth Jacob had never such a jewel'. A maid came out and 'asked the said Mistress Jacob sitting still at the window . . . what she meant so to disquiet her mistress'. 'She . . . said she was a better woman than I,' Mistress Jacob explained. 'Why, what do you make of my mistress,' the maid asked, 'is she not an honest woman?' 'Yes,' admitted Elizabeth, but unwilling to concede superiority went on: 'she . . . sayeth that she is honester than I because she hath had ten children . . . She . . . hath had ten children indeed, but every whore may have a child!'[102]

Social competition often focused on dress, a costly element of household expenditure for all ranks and a highly visible measure of status.[103] The continental visitor Thomas Platter was struck in 1599 by the care London women gave to their

---

[101] William Crompton, *A wedding-ring, fitted to the finger of every paire that have or shall meete in the feare of God* (London, 1632), 29.
[102] Mary Barton, Roger Dade, and William Gray, *Elizabeth Chare c. Elizabeth Jacobs*, 1611 (LMA, DL/C/220, fos. 815–820r).
[103] See Jeremy Boulton, *Neighbourhood and Society: A London Suburb in the Seventeenth Century* (Cambridge, 1987), 147.

clothes: 'They lay great store by ruffs and starch them blue, so that their complexion shall appear the whiter, and some may well wear velvet for the street —quite common with them—who cannot afford a crust of dry bread at home.'[104] This was surely an exaggeration, but indeed, clothing was important. There was nothing wrong with a seemly level of display, but critics worried about the expense of female competition. Gouge's condemnation of immodest dress had far more to do with *economic* display than with revealing attire:

> it well beseemeth all women, so wives after a peculiar manner, namely, in attiring themselves, to respect rather their husbands' place and state, than their own birth and parentage, but much rather than their own mind and humour. A wife's modesty therefore requireth that her apparel be neither for costliness above her husband's ability, nor for curiousness unbeseeming his calling.[105]

Women's desire to 'hunt after new fashions' was not only frivolous, commentators thought, but a threat to economic order. Since fine clothing was no longer reserved for the ladies of the court, all women were becoming embroiled in a fashionable arms race, Edward Hake mourned:

> They must not go as other do.
> Wherefore, they must devise
> To have them known from common sort
> By some newfangled guise.[106]

To bankroll these vanities, husbands and fathers wasted their substance and shut their ears to the pleas of the hungry poor. Dekker imagined that 'if at a feast or some other gossips' meeting whereunto she is invited, [a wife] see any of the company gaily attired for cost, or fashion, or both... she forthwith moves a question in herself, why she also should not be in the like sort attired'. Consequently, she would complain to her husband in bed:

> on Thursday last, I was sent for, and you willed me to go to Mistress M's churching, and when I came thither I found great cheer, and no small company of wives, but the meanest of them all was not so ill attired as I, and surely I was never so ashamed of myself in my life... alas I speak not this for myself, for God wot I pass not how meanly I am appareled, but I speak it for your credit and my friends.[107]

The poor husband was obliged to pawn the lease of his house for a new gown. Women's passion for apparel could even lead them to adultery, Dekker warned, giving the example of a woman who had married beneath her and felt deprived of both attire and status. Her maid suggested that she take a lover to 'furnish and maintain you gallantly what garments soever you will have: and what color and fashion soever you like best, you shall presently have it'.[108] Excessive consumption

---

[104] Williams, ed. and trans., *Thomas Platter's travels in England*, 182.
[105] Gouge, *Of domesticall duties*, 280.
[106] Edward Hake, *Newes out of Powles Churchyarde* (London, 1579), sig. D4v.
[107] Dekker, *The batchelars banquet*, ch. 1, sig A3r.
[108] Ibid. ch. 5, sig. D4v.

was the root of all evil: it led inevitably to poverty, sin, and crime, as prodigal spenders sank into beggary or prostitution or stole to finance their sinful lifestyles.

These themes were echoed on London streets, where splendid apparel could be admired as a sign of wealth and status, or derided as evidence of dishonesty. Gold lace in particular was a contested symbol. Elizabeth Smith told Phyllis Wood: 'Thou art a painted queane and a doctor doth maintain thee in gold lace.' As a result, Mistress Wood, whose fine attire had occasioned local resentment, was 'mocked and scoffed at by some of her neighbours'.[109] At the Talbot tavern in Westminster, Thomas Sincock attacked Joan Evetson, asking: 'Thou alewife whore, who gave thee that lace on thy coat?' 'Not thou!' she replied. 'I would it were cut from thy bum and then a man might see what a curtailed whore thou art,' Thomas continued, 'I have known thee to be a whore and a bawd of seven or eight years standing and that I will prove.'[110] In Allhallows Barking, Christian Hedges came to Elizabeth Mole's house, struck a pan to make a disgraceful noise, and said: 'Though thou camest over from Ireland with a little gold lace on thy tail, it is well known thou wert Captain Desmond's whore and so continuest.' 'I had rather be an Englishman's whore than a captain's whore,' she clarified, lest any benefit accrue from Elizabeth's association—however dishonest—with a man of high rank. In St Dunstan in the West, a maidservant made a scene in the street, crying out: 'Mistress Pothecary can never let me alone, a pox on her for a whore.' When a woman passing along the street looked at her curiously, the maid responded angrily: 'Do not look for it is I, and I will say as much to her face.' Finally, she explained what had upset her: Priscilla Harris, an apothecary's wife, had 'found fault with her... for wearing of gold lace'.[111]

Just as gold lace could be countered by accusations of dishonesty, and evidence of fertility could be attacked with insinuations of adultery, so women who lost face because their husbands misbehaved were apt to accuse their rivals of 'wearing the breeches'. The affection between two friends was strained around 1607 when their husbands 'went forth together', presumably to an alehouse, and while one husband came home at a suitable hour, the other 'did not come home when as it seemed his wife would have had him'. The frustrated wife tried to turn the embarrassing situation around by remarking snidely to her erstwhile friend 'that her husband was in awe of her, he durst do no other but as she would have him'.[112] Maids favored a similar strategy in quarrels with married women. When a conflict arose between the maidservant Elizabeth Edwards and one Alice Baker around 1613, Alice mocked Elizabeth, calling her a whore and a 'saddle-nosed queane', and saying that her 'nose

---

[109] Anne Lad, *Phyllis Wood c. Elizabeth Smith*, 1635 (LMA, DL/C/234, fo. 147).

[110] Joan riposted: 'I am as honest a woman as thy wife and if I am a whore she is a whore.' 'Dost thou call his wife whore?' a bystander inquired. 'No,' Joan explained warily, 'but I am a honest woman and so I think is she.' John Smith, *Joan Evetson c. Thomas Sincock*, 1614 (LMA, DL/C/222, fos. 242v–244).

[111] Mary Johnson and Henry Foster, *Elizabeth Mole c. Christian Hedges*, 1614 (LMA, DL/C/222, fos. 280–281r); Nathaniel Knightly and Nathaniel Love, *Katherine Wyn c. Priscilla Harris*, 1617 (LMA, DL/C/224, fos. 404, 406v).

[112] Frances Price, *Mary Bird c. Helen Steed*, 1607 (LMA, DL/C/217, p. 62).

turned up like a drab's tail'. To retaliate, the maid remarked: 'I would be ashamed to have a husband and to wear the breeches'.[113]

Both men and women were apt to bring up sexual behavior when they were unable or unwilling to pay their debts, thus changing the topic from economic honesty (where they were at a disadvantage) to sexual honesty (where they could take the offensive). When a man tried to collect a debt from Thomas Thompson, the latter said: 'Thou art a cozening knave, a whoremaster, and a whoremasterly knave, go thy ways like a whoremasterly knave as thou art!' Eleanor Wright, attempting to collect money from an elderly goldsmith, was attacked by his ally Elizabeth Merrick, who asked her: 'What was the rogue or the fiddler that thou wenst running up and down the country withal?' Elizabeth, 'pulling up her own coats before in a shameful manner', said that 'the fiddler had fiddled her', crying mockingly: 'Come buck me fiddler, come fuck me fiddler!'[114]

Sexual honesty was invoked by the losers of all sorts of economic disputes. When two butchers argued over buying cattle, one of them concluded: 'Thou art a pander unless thy neighbours do belie thee.' When Robert Robinson lost the purchase of a ship's load of salt to William Chislett, he burst out: 'Thou art a whoremaster and thou wilt have another bastard brought home to thee one of these days, and if thou hadst had thy right, thou shouldst have stood in a white sheet before now.' This was apparently quite true, as Chislett had fathered a bastard four years before and had paid twenty nobles for the poor of the parish to avoid penance. Similarly, when two women quarreled over who would have the lodging of Joan Russell, 'a very honest maiden', the loser tried to devalue the victory by attacking Joan's credit, saying that she had slept in naked bed with a married man for a year (and consequently was not a desirable lodger after all).[115] With such richly varied measures of worth at their disposal, quarreling Londoners were rarely at a loss for words.

'My husband's whore'

A more bitter kind of competition took place when wives thought their rights to their husbands' earnings and affection were threatened by other women. Given their lack of direct control over their husbands and the difficulty of suing for divorce, many wives sought to shame their rivals into good behavior.[116] Thus Alice

---

[113] 'Thou art an arrant whore to say that I wear the breeches,' replied Alice. The next day, a maidservant saw 'Alice Baker's husband's prentice pull from off a post near her...door a paper wherein as [she] hath heard was written that Alice Baker aforesaid did wear her husband's breeches'. Joyce Taylor and Robert Crosheowe, *Elizabeth Edwards c. Alice Baker*, 1613 (LMA, DL/C/221, fos. 1542v, 1422v, 1543r).

[114] William Walker, *Thomas Shepherd c. Thomas Thompson*, 1610 (LMA, DL/C/219, fo. 125r); Katherine Barnely and John Winne, *Eleanor Wright c. Elizabeth Merrick*, 1639 (LMA, DL/C/235, fos. 241v, 251v–252r).

[115] John Honson, *Pitt c. Meredith Jones*, 1631 (LMA, DL/C/233, fo. 59r); Jeffrey Corne and Michael Nicholls, *William Chislett c. Robert Robinson*, 1602 (LMA, DL/C/216, sl. 1002, 1004, 999); Jane Seabright and Eizabeth Morgan, *Joan Russell c. Elizabeth Morgan*, 1602/3 (LMA, DL/C/216, sl. 819, 911).

[116] See Capp, *When Gossips Meet*, 95–7.

Rochester called Jane Lilham 'a whore, an arrant whore, and a common carted whore', and said: 'My husband hath kept thee a great while at Newcastle and all that he got he spent on thee . . . Thou hast lain oftener with him than he hath done with me.' One Elizabeth Hodgkins had a warrant served on her suspected rival and triumphantly cried: 'Now I have thee, whore', further declaring her 'the bastard-bearing whore who hath made my husband . . . spend ten pounds on her since Lent began'.[117] When the marital bond was threatened, women acted swiftly to humiliate their enemies. In 1611 when Elizabeth Frier found her husband drinking with Margaret Yard in a Turnbull Street tavern, she struck her violently on the back, saying: 'Thou art Stephen Yard's wife but thou art my husband's whore. He can be contented to spend ten shillings on thee but he will not spend twopence in my company!' Similarly, Mary Nicholson went hunting for Florence Bastwell in Red Cross Street in 1612. She asked Florence's daughter where her mother was, and upon hearing that she wasn't home, declared: 'She . . . is gone a-whoring again, is she not? She . . . hath had one bastard by my husband already and now she is gone to get another one.' Later, when she met Florence in person, Mary insulted her: 'Thou art a whore and thy child is a bastard and my husband's bastard and thou didst marry thy husband to cloak thy knavery!'[118]

This shaming strategy did not mean that the husband was considered free of blame. Wives might scold their husbands, but this would not come to court except as circumstantial evidence. For example, Elizabeth Frier of the Turnbull Street incident railed at her husband: 'Go thy way to the next house to thy whore.' Thomas protested, 'God is my judge, I know no dishonesty by her', and Elizabeth replied contemptuously: 'Hang thee, rogue.'[119] In 1576 a cobbler sheepishly told the Bridewell governors that one 'Baker's wife came and sat in his lap and kissed him with her hands about his neck and his wife came and took them and knocked their heads together'.[120]

Some wives defamed other women as 'my husband's whore' after their attempts to reform their husbands had failed. For example, a victualler's wife heard a noise through the wall, 'and harkening thereunto did perceive that John Styles was beating of his wife Elizabeth Styles'. Afterwards, Elizabeth told him: 'Now thou hast beaten me for a whore', referring to Mary Fairfax, who was standing in the street. Since Elizabeth was unable to persuade her husband to stop the affair, she concentrated on attacking her rival, referring to her in public as 'that filthy whore that kept my husband so late and his own door so near'.[121] Dorothy Hove of Great

---

[117] Both Alice Rochester and Jane Lilham lived in Wapping, where many immigrants from Newcastle settled: probably Alice's husband was a sailor who sailed between Newcastle and London. Elizabeth Cooper, *Jane Lilham c. Alice Rochester*, 1610 (LMA, DL/C/219, fo. 198); Elizabeth Stursaker, *Pomfrett c. Elizabeth Hodgkins*, 1640 (LMA, DL/C/235, fo. 334r).
[118] Thomas Shepherd, *Margaret Yard c. Elizabeth Frier*, 1611 (LMA, DL/C/219, fo. 437); Agnes Atkinson and Margaret Britton, *Florence Bastwell c. Mary Nicholson*, 1612 (LMA, DL/C/221, fos. 1270v, 1271v).
[119] John Sly, *Margaret Yard c. Elizabeth Frier*, 1611 (LMA, DL/C/219, fo. 438r).
[120] BRHA, BCB 3, fo. 86r/p. 223.
[121] Orphania Startupp and Ellen Cuthbert, *Mary Fairfax c. Elizabeth Stiles*, 1600 (LMA, DL/C/216, sl. 275, 250).

Burstead, Essex, came to a similar conclusion. Dorothy, described by the local clergyman as 'somewhat curst of her tongue if she be moved yet far from outrage', jealously rebuked her husband, saying: 'You whoremaster, a pox take you for a whoremaster! Go to your whore yonder upon the hill!'[122] However, it proved safer for Dorothy to attack Jane Hartford, the 'whore on the hill'. A local woman saw John Hove break two sticks in beating his wife in an orchard 'most unreasonably' until she fell down, and then kick her until Dorothy 'was in a swound'. He then

> took her up and bowed her forward until he had revived her and when she was revived he then beat her again with a third stick, saying unto her: 'Are you dead you whore? I will fetch you again and revive you.' Whereupon she the same Dorothy said: 'I am no whore. Go you to your whores if you will! Go to your whore on the hill.'[123]

When the neighboring women fetched the constables, Hove was pacified, but the trouble between him and his wife continued. On a different occasion when Hove, a baker, was tending the fire, Dorothy bitterly told some other women who had come to the bakehouse: 'Come, let us all be whores for they are better beloved than honest women: yonder is my husband's whore on the hill better beloved than I am. I fare the worse for her fine tail. She is a whore and a bitch.' Various people, including the vicar, tried to reconcile Dorothy and Jane, but Dorothy wouldn't consent: 'I will never be friends with such a brazen-faced whore as she is... She hath stolen away the love of my husband from me.'[124]

Honest wives might band together to counter suspected predators. In Stratford Langthorne, a slanging match erupted between several backyards as two women attacked their neighbor Elizabeth Boswell. They told her: 'Thou art Browne's whore, and Browne's wife while she lived led an ill life with her husband by reason of thee so following him.' The defamers had fears for their own husbands as well. Margaret Hopkin, accused of saying, 'Thou art a whore, thou runnest after other women's husbands', claimed in court that Elizabeth 'sate all night at cards with other women's husbands'.[125] Elizabeth Boswell's alleged sexual predation was compounded by the fact that she kept an alehouse where other women's husbands gambled away the money they ought to have taken home to their wives.

The strategy of publicizing their spouses' infidelity was not open to men, who were expected to be able to put a halt to their wives' adultery: cuckolds could even be prosecuted as panders. Men who were unable to reform their wives and unwilling to sue for separation were in a pitiable case, like John Poulter, who complained plaintively to a local clergyman that his wife was unfaithful to him with Bradford Berry and that 'the place of their usual meetings was worn bare'. A gentleman deposed that Poulter 'wept to [him] for that he said he could not have the company of the said Mary', and another witness said that Poulter had

---

[122] William Pease (LMA, DL/C/219, fo. 58r) and George Underwood (LMA, DL/C/218, p. 403), in *Jane Hartford c. Dorothy Hove*, 1609.
[123] Mary Sell, 1609 (LMA, DL/C/218, pp. 428–9).
[124] Alice Heard, 1608 (ibid. p. 345) and John Feltham, 1609 (ibid. p. 615).
[125] Cicely Wright, Margaret Hopkins, and Joan Debney, *Elizabeth Boswell c. Joan Debney*, 1620 (LMA, DL/C/219, fos. 261, 292v).

asked him to persuade his wife to live with him. When Berry said he would lie with her as long as she came to his house, the witness recounted, Poulter 'with grief of heart said that he... would be contented that she the said Mary should play the whore with Berry if she would refrain the company of others'.[126]

The unbearable irritations of urban life

While London women found diversion, comfort, and aid in the company of their neighbors, the close terms on which they lived could lead to quarrels as well as friendship. Existing rivalries could be inflamed by small incidents, and in the crowded city these came easily. Many consistory court cases bear witness to the anger that seethed in urban neighborhoods, occasionally erupting into unquenchable rage. The difficulties of keeping one's household clean, in particular, often fueled neighborhood quarrels. Laundry and sweeping out the house were both women's tasks, and set them continually at odds with the muck of the early modern city. Dirt, foul odors, and worse annoyed women as they sought to keep their houses, persons, and possessions free of the filth that threatened both reputation and health.[127] The struggle was in part a zero-sum game that pitted neighbor against neighbor: removing garbage from one's own space often meant putting it next door instead.

The intensity of one woman's reaction to dirtied laundry hints at the frustration of the never-ending struggle with filth. Around 1620, Grace Stanley had 'clothes then hanging out to dry' where she lived in Martin's Court in the parish of St Sepulchre. Her neighbor Joan Wood's manservant passed by and, according to an onlooker, 'against his will... did besmear them with his clothes'. Grace acted with instant fury: she 'took a forkstaff which women use to hold up their linen from falling to the ground, and with that struck so vild [sic] a blow that she laid him almost for dead'.[128] The servant recovered, but Grace's relations with Joan, never very warm to begin with, did not.

Disgusting odors could poison neighborliness as well as the air. An open sewer running down Spur Alley 'did cause the stink in that alley to savour so evil that it was very offensive to them that lived there', according to a local woman.[129] One woman tried to rid her section of the alley of the waste by sweeping the sewer downward 'as all the rest who dwell there do', but a brawl erupted when Grace Hittan, living downstream, 'finding herself aggrieved swept the channel upwards contrary to the stream of the water to the annoyance of all the neighbours'. In an attempt to regulate the stink, several members of the Jury of Annoyances for the

---

[126] Samuel Purchas, John Vassall, and John Jones, *Office prom. Valentine c. Mary Poulter*, 1615 (LMA, DL/C/223, fos. 46v, 192, 193).
[127] See Keith Thomas, 'Cleanliness and Godliness in Early Modern England', in Anthony Fletcher and Peter Roberts (eds), *Religion, Culture and Society in Early Modern Britain* (Cambridge, 1994), 72–3.
[128] Anne Butler, *Katherine Partridge c. Grace Stanley*, 1620 (LMA, DL/C/225, fo. 166v).
[129] Isabel Dickson, *Elizabeth Stedman c. Grace Hittan*, 1620 (ibid. fo. 16v).

Liberty of Westminster were called in to view the inadequate sewer, but by the time the case came to court, the malodorous problem had not yet been rectified.[130]

Private convenience and public health often came into conflict, especially during visitations of the plague. In Vinegar Yard in St Martin's in the Fields, for example, Elizabeth Gaddard, the wife of a coachman for hire, worried that his customers might be deterred by the plague padlock on Christian Burrow's house. She obscured it with a 'pull of leather', to the ire of one Giles Clement, who called her 'queane and bitch'.[131] The management of human waste was a continual area of contention. In 1621, Peter Hill, who kept a tobacco and acquavita shop in St Alphage Cripplegate, offended his neighbors by 'pissing at a sink near unto his own door'. One Thomas Bradshaw 'took some sniff thereat and told him that he would wash him further off'. Hot words ensued, and Hill ultimately sued Bradshaw for calling him a 'panderly rogue' and accusing him of keeping a bawdy house.[132] In St Andrew Holborn, two maids were sitting by a doorway one morning in 1627 when Elizabeth Morton threw 'out a pot of water or piss which did fall upon' them and 'did much annoy [them] the same water or piss having long stood or been in the said pot as [they] conceived by the filthy smell or strength thereof'. One of them called Elizabeth 'filthy dirty slut and dirty sow', and she riposted by accusing the girl of having had 'a bastard by an old man in the country'.[133]

Women also quarreled fiercely on their families' behalf. In Green Dragon court in St Sepulchre, Alice Fulham's son William was sweeping 'of the yard before his mother's door' when he 'sprinkled or dashed some puddle water by chance upon [Ellen Alsop's] child being playing thereabouts'. Mistress Alsop rebuked him, saying: 'Away you filthy bastardly rogue, do you misuse my child?' Another woman asked Alice Fulham 'what she meant to suffer her child to be so abused', so Alice looked out of the window, and asked: 'Is my child any more bastardly rogue than yours is?' Ellen clapped her hands scornfully and replied: 'Away, away, thou filthy queane! The cart and the basin is more fit for thee than thine own house! Ting, ting, ting!'[134] Her derisive words implied that Alice deserved to be forced to follow a cart to the sound of ringing pots and pans, the traditional punishment for bawds.

Children were frequent objects of contention. Early modern London's high death rates took a huge toll on infants and children, especially those of poor parents: poor households in the Boroughside in Southwark contained only 1.6 children on average, but in wealthy parishes as well, mortality rates outstripped those of rural England.[135] Even in the absence of epidemics, minor distempers or parasites could prove fatal, and burial registers record many examples of children

---

[130] Elizabeth Osborne, 1619 (LMA, DL/C/226, 3rd series, fo. 40r). *Dorothy King c. Jane Galloway* in 1622 also deals with a quarrel over 'the sweeping down of the channel in the street'. See William Rabbett (LMA, DL/C/228, fo. 322v).
[131] Helen Gardener, *Elizabeth Gaddard c. Giles Clement*, 1631 (LMA, DL/C/232, fo. 171v).
[132] Isaac Swan, *Peter Hill c. Thomas and Sara Bradshaw*, 1621 (LMA, DL/C/228, fos. 58–9).
[133] Jane Etherington, *Margery Hale c. Elizabeth Morton*, 1627/8 (GL MS 9189/2, fos. 159v–160v).
[134] Ursula Roberts, Elizabeth Broome, and Isabel Scillicorne, *Alice Fulham c. Ellen Alsop*, 1611 (LMA, DL/C/220, fos. 592, 594r, 597v).
[135] Boulton, *Neighbourhood and Society*, 125.

who succumbed to 'teeth', 'pining', and 'worms' along with other diseases and accidents. London parents fretted over their children, and the ubiquity of illness and death did not necessarily make them easier to take. When Frances Frost, a wax chandler's wife, looked out of her window around 1638 and saw the parish sexton digging a grave close by where she had lately buried two children, she rushed out, 'being fearful that the bones or corpse of her children might be removed'. Indeed, to her grief she found a mangled remnant cast out on the ground. In 1626, a silkweaver defended himself against a charge of blasphemy by explaining that 'in the time of the late visitation of the plague [he] upon the death and burial of a child of [his] was somewhat troubled in his mind by overmuch grieving'. He had taken the tragedy 'much to heart', leading him to speak unadvisedly.[136]

Parental anxiety and childrens' vulnerability fueled bitter quarrels. In 1608, an altercation began when Elizabeth Hollinshed's sick child was woken up by a neighbor chiding next door. The mother 'spake unto Winifred Bland to be quiet and not disturb her child that was sick, saying unto her that she did not know what it was to have such a child'. This was provocative because Winifred was childless and apparently barren. Stung, she responded: 'Ay, thy child is punished for thy sins.' Elizabeth told her angrily that 'she would never be worth the hair of the head of such a child'.[137] 'Bess, Bess, when I have any children I will have but one father to them,' Winifred replied.[138] In Foxwell's Court in the parish of St Sepulchre, Anne Sills' husband Henry, a wheelwright, rented out old coaches for hire. One day in 1620 when his workmen were pulling a coach into the yard, one Anne Chambers suspected (mistakenly, a witness said) that they had injured a child of hers, and consequently 'spake her pleasure of Anne Sills'.

Conflicts over discipline appeared frequently, as parents resented any interference with their children. When William Gunter's little girl fell out and fought with another child in the street, Mistress Gunter chid 'her own child and the other', but when the other mother came over and 'would have stricken' Gunter's daughter, William Gunter 'would not suffer her', at which point another neighbor took offense and called him a cuckold. A suit between Joan Jarvis and Christian Fossett in 1628 was prompted by a falling-out

> about a little boy of [Joan Jarvis] who was then playing with a cat and dog in the street near the door of the said Christian Fossett, who taking offense thereat said she would burn the child's cat if he did not play farther from her door. Unto which [Mistress Jarvis] said she had better let the boy's cat alone, and thereupon [Mistress Fossett] did fall to railing.[139]

---

[136] Frances Frost, 1640 (LMA, DL/C/235, fo. 320v) and Anthony Scarborough, 1626 (LMA, DL/C/230, fo. 100r).
[137] Jane Carter and Margaret Barrett, *Elizabeth Hollinshed c. Winifred Bland*, 1609 (LMA, DL/C/218, pp. 312, 409).
[138] Elizabeth Buck, *Winifred Bland c. Elizabeth Hollinshed*, 1608 (ibid. p. 267).
[139] Elizabeth Spencer, *Anne Sills c. Anne Chambers*, 1620 (LMA, DL/C/227, fo. 228r); Christopher Palmer, *William Gunter c. Mistress Dawson*, 1607 (LMA, DL/C/217, p. 39); Anne Robins, *Joan Jarvis c. Christian Fossett*, 1628 (LMA, DL/C/231, fo. 190r).

Servants also quarreled about the discipline and care of local children. In Chick Lane in 1631, a chandler's little daughter wandered over towards the house of a neighbor, Elizabeth Baker. The chandler's maidservant, Joan Goldsmith, called the child back, threatening to whip her if she went into Elizabeth's house. The latter took offense and told Joan she 'was a queane in forbidding the child to come to her house, for that she never wronged that or any other child', and insisted that she 'loved a child better than [Joan] did'.[140] In 1606 when an apprentice spanked a little girl who had struck his master's daughter, a female neighbor, 'somewhat discontented', made an offensive remark about his excessive familiarity with taking up of women's clothes. The youth told the court that he had only acted to protect his master's child, and in any case his intention was 'more to fright it than to hurt it'.[141]

Anyone who infringed local standards of good behavior could expect retribution. In 1620, two residents of Foxwell's Court quarreled over a matter of charity. According to a neighbor, 'a poor fellow coming into the same court and requesting a cup of beer of [Julian Duckett] was denied it, and he going from her to... Elizabeth Mayd, had a cup of beer at her hands, and having the cup in his hands he did drank to her the said Duckett'. Seeing the beggar's sarcastic gesture, one Anne Tyson called out an insulting pun on Julian's name: 'Do not drink to her for she is a gentlewoman and her name is Mistress Duck-arse.' Mistress Duckett, nettled but less verbally adept, settled for calling her opponent an arrant whore. In a similar incident, when Elizabeth Bacon was chiding with Thomas Skerry, 'being a man of almost a hundred years old', about a broken pot in Swan Alley, Joan King looked out a window and remarked: 'What a hard heart thou hast so to misuse an old man.' Elizabeth responded with an accusation of incest.[142]

Having a sharp tongue did not necessarily harm a woman's reputation. A witness asked about the character of Elizabeth Hollinshed reported neutrally that she was 'quiet enough so long as she is pleased but when she is angered she will be shrowish as other women will'.[143] However, some individuals gained bad reputations by disrupting communal harmony. The conduct of Margaret Samborne, a young goldsmith's wife, was just on the edge of what was considered tolerable: she had friends and allies within the neighborhood but many thought ill of her. One witness criticized her impiety and disrespect for authority: 'she hath little or no religion in her for this respondent hath heard her say that she did not go to church to hear the foresaid Mr Simpson her pastor preach or his sermons but only for fear that the law should take hold of her for not coming to church.' She abused the parson 'behind his back in saying that he was a bald priest and a bald-pated rascal'. A tailor's wife complained that Margaret swore and blasphemed 'in very fearful and

---

[140] Thomas Westcott and William Ball, *Elizabeth Baker c. Joan Goldsmith*, 1631 (LMA, DL/C/232, fos. 31v, 32v).
[141] Richard Cracoft and George Layton, *Hester Savile c. Elizabeth Hudson*, 1606–7 (LMA, DL/C/217, pp. 7, 142).
[142] Anne Sheffield, *Anne Tyson c. Julian Duckett*, 1620 (LMA, DL/C/227, fo. 163v); Margery Buckley and Clatworth Cheney, *Joan King c. Elizabeth Bacon*, 1620 (ibid. fos. 207, 206).
[143] Ellen Steed, 1609 (LMA, DL/C/218, p. 587).

outrageous manner in the daytime out of her own house and in the night time so bitterly that she hath caused this deponent when as she hath been in her naked bed to rise out of one bed and go lie in another bed in another chamber to avoid the hearing thereof, besides she abuseth her neighbours in words insomuch as that her neighbours careth [sic] little for it'. Margaret was given to drink, according to one neighbor, but not excessively, according to a clothworker's wife who said: 'Margaret Samborne loveth to drink a cup or two of white wine but not more than will do her good.'[144]

Only five of the most disruptive women were condemned to being ducked as scolds, of whom only two were successfully punished.[145] Lucretia Gunter, a young porter's wife and a lifelong resident of St Sepulchre's parish, was said by her own sister to be 'a woman of a turbulent and hasty disposition and one that hath and doth wrong her husband sometimes in words'. She had been bound over for the theft of some clothes from Judith Stokes' child, although she settled the matter privately before the Sessions. She would 'scold very courageously with her neighbours seldom suffering some or one of them to be at quiet for her', for which they 'laboured to have had her cucked', but she thwarted them by temporarily 'removing herself out of that place'.[146]

Joan Honey was supposed to have been ducked three years before she appeared as a witness, but she had avoided punishment by keeping away from home for three weeks. A pavier's wife in her early 30s and an immigrant from Edmonton in Middlesex, Joan had probably lived in St Giles Cripplegate for most of her London career. She was known to be a scold, a brawler, and a drunkard, sometimes 'so drunk that she hath been led home and sometimes she hath tumbled in the dirt in the street by reason of her drunkenness'. Her ducking was commanded by Sir Stephen Soame as punishment for having 'set her boy to set a libel at Elizabeth Crowder's door and to defile her door with dung and filth most loathsomely in envy and malice to her'.[147] Joan's partner in this neighborhood feud was Martha Watkins, married to a painter stainer in Allhallows in the Wall, and in her late 20s, born in Westminster. Martha, 'a scolding and very unquiet woman', was also

---

[144] *Anne Levans c. Constance Waller*, 1622–23 (LMA, DL/C/228): Joan Penny (fo. 240), Joan Wood (fo. 228v), Margaret Foxley (fo. 348v), Mary Turke (fo. 229v); Katherine Robinson (GL MS 9189/1, fo. 43r).

[145] Having been condemned as a scold is just the sort of thing that witnesses might be expected to bring up, either to demonstrate that a woman accused of defamation was known for scolding, or to injure a witness's credit. The examples here corroborate other research finding that rather than symbolizing a 'crisis in gender relations', the cucking stool was reserved for women who severely strained communal harmony, and that the punishment was rarely inflicted. Walker finds little meaningful difference between the portrayals and punishments of female 'scolds' and male 'barrators', for example. See Martin Ingram, '"Scolding Women Cucked or Washed": A Crisis in Gender Relations in Early Modern England?', in Jenny Kermode and Garthine Walker (eds), *Women, Crime and the Courts in Early Modern England* (Chapel Hill, NC, 1994); Garthine Walker, *Crime, Gender and Social Order in Early Modern England* (Cambridge, 2003), 108, 110–11.

[146] GL MS 9189/1, 1622: Margaret Webster (fo. 94r), John Parfey (fo. 95r), Abraham Thomas (fo. 93v), Thomas Whitacre (fo. 96r). 'Cucking' and 'ducking' appear to be used interchangeably.

[147] Mary Morris and Mary Turner, 1608 (LMA, DL/C/218, pp. 232, 246).

to have been punished, but 'she was so unruly as that the constable could not get her to it and so she was not ducked at that time'.[148]

Two women were actually subjected to the cucking stool. Ursula Griffin, 40, was a tailor's wife from Somerset and lived in St Botolph Aldersgate. She was a petty thief, having been known to purloin 'a pothook, a pewter basin, a piece of bacon and other things'. She earned her living carrying water, and was 'very often distempered in her wits', so that she 'hath many times fought and brawled with her neighbours...and hath fought with a woman in Cheapside at the conduits there and brake her head and drew blood of her'. Ursula was 'ducked in the cucking stool' for slandering two women.[149] Margaret Herring, 57, was the oldest of the group, a migrant from Essex and a resident of St Michael Wood Street. She deposed that her husband, Simon, was a goldsmith, but others reported that he was a poor waterbearer who received a parish pension. Indeed, 'Margaret Herring, wife of Simon Herring, waterbearer', had appeared in Bridewell about ten years before she testified for the consistory court in 1614.[150] Margaret was thought to be a 'very unquiet and troublesome woman amongst her neighbours', but her ducking five years before, ordered by Sir Thomas Bennett, was the result of words she had spoken against some more elevated figures, Sir Baptist Hickes, Sir William Stone, and Hugh Blackhurst, goldsmith and constable.[151] Social order, rather than sexual order, was at stake.

ARBITRATION, MEDIATION, RECONCILIATION

Communal harmony, strained by quarrels and rivalries, was renewed by the same mechanisms of arbitration and reconciliation that were used to restore order in troubled households.[152] Defamation cases often reached the consistory court only after local arbitration had failed. This could range from casual mediation to formal meetings with designated arbitrators. Women, like Barbara Warsapp, a 40-year-old cooper's wife, were more likely to take the lead in informal mediation. When two sisters-in-law fell out, one told the other: 'For what I have had a child before I was married thou hast had two or three since thou wert married when thy husband was out of town, which the cuckold thy husband knowest.' The offended woman, Susan Stanner, told Mistress Warsapp, who said: 'I will not have you two being sisters fall out together. I pray go with me together and I will make you friends together I hope.' They assembled a small party of neighbors, and Barbara talked with Elizabeth Stanner, 'very earnestly persuading her to be friends' and not to

---

[148] Robert Hunch and Mary Morris, 1608 (ibid. pp. 231–3).
[149] Ursula Griffin, 1614 (LMA, DL/C/222, fo. 9r) and Margaret Brookes, 1615 (LMA, DL/C/223, fo. 144).
[150] Margaret Herring, 1614 (LMA, DL/C/222, fo. 154r); BRHA, BCB 5, fo. 3v.
[151] Edward Brogden, 1613 (LMA, DL/C/222, fo. 90r).
[152] See J. A. Sharpe, '"Such Disagreement betwyx Neighbours": Litigation and Human Relations in Early Modern England', in John Bossy (ed.), *Disputes and Settlements: Law and Human Relations in the West* (Cambridge, 1983).

make further trouble between Susan and her husband. Unfortunately, the more they talked, 'the more cross and froward she the same Elizabeth Stanner was saying she would not be friends'.[153]

In formal cases of neighborly mediation, both parties chose arbitrators. The neighbors would then convene in a tavern, alehouse, or private house to see an agreement made. When two girls, Sara Powell and Mary Crompton, fell out, their fathers chose Owen Dobbies, a 60-year-old clothworker, and Robert Gravener, a 40-year-old ironmonger, to arbitrate. The stature of arbitrators was essential to their ability to enforce agreements, so mature, prosperous men of long local residence were in high demand, and some specialized in neighborly reconciliation. In 1597, George and Elizabeth Boreman defamed their neighbor John Randall, saying: 'If there be ever a whoremaster in the lane from the one end to the other thou art he, and thou keepest a whore under thy nose.' William Allen, 60, deposed that as soon as he heard about the quarrel, he 'sent for the same Boreman and his wife to the church to talk with them and to see if he could reconcile them and make them friends (as he sayeth he useth to do whensoever he heareth of any of his neighbours so to fall out)'. While neighborly arbitrators lacked formal coercive powers, the quarreling parties usually agreed to abide by their settlements. After Philip Clark defamed the maid Elizabeth Moore, saying that there was no baser whore in the strews, a neighbor reported that Clark paid her the sum 'which was allotted unto her upon an award or arbitration made by some neighbors'.[154]

Though arbitration did not always succeed, it was an attractive alternative to litigation. Griffith Hinton, a middle-aged grocer, did his best in a serious case: Geoffrey Wilson had accused Katherine Povey, the wife of Hugh Povey, a leatherseller, of being his whore or at least of having been willing to be his whore. Legal action had already been begun, but lawsuits were expensive, so Wilson asked Hinton to 'be a means to make an end' of the dispute. Accordingly, Hinton visited Povey's house. Povey was not at home, so he asked Katherine herself if she were willing to consider arbitration. 'She seemed very willing thereto and said she would acquaint her husband with the motion', and the next day, when Hinton returned, Povey also pronounced himself eager to make an end of the quarrel. Hinton and Povey went together to Dr Price in St Olave Silverstreet, and 'after much conference together and relating to them by the said Povey of the injury done by the said Wilson and his wife to the said Povey and his wife', Price asked Povey whether he would 'refer the cause to him . . . to arbitration'. Povey agreed, and Price stipulated that Hinton should also be an arbitrator.

They met together at the Three Tonnes in Newgate Market. There, 'the said Hugh Povey and Geoffrey Wilson did both of them as well for themselves as for their wives make choice of the said Dr Price and [Hinton] to be arbitrators' and 'did refer themselves wholly to be ordered by' them and 'to abide and perform their

---

[153] Barbara Warsapp, *Susan Stanner c. Elizabeth Stanner*, 1598 (LMA, DL/C/215, sl. 145–6).
[154] Owen Dobbies and Robert Gravener, *Sara Powell c. Mary Crompton*, 1629 (LMA, DL/C/231, fos. 486v–487r and 524); William Allen, *John Randall c. George and Elizabeth Boreman*, 1597 (LMA, DL/C/215, sl. 64–5); Mary Griggs, *Elizabeth Moore c. Philip Clark*, 1631 (LMA, DL/C/233, fo. 194r).

orders'. Nasty speeches on both sides were recounted and the clergyman persuaded them to unity, peace and love. The verdict was that 'they should be friends and drink each to other and that Geoffrey Wilson should pay to the said Hugh Povey thirty shillings in money'. Povey insisted that the sum be paid immediately, and Wilson sent home for it. The wives were sent for too, and Wilson's wife came, but to the arbitrators' dismay, Katherine Povey 'would not come to them'. That is, she would not come into the tavern, but spoke to her husband privately outside, derailing the agreement: when Wilson offered the money, 'Povey having in the mean time spoken with his wife refused to receive the same'. Price spoke with her privately, and concluded that she was 'an unreasonable woman'. Arbitration having failed, the case proceeded in the consistory court.[155] In most cases, mediation was probably more successful, but successful arbitration did not enter the legal record. It was nonetheless essential to the delicate balance of neighborly life in early modern London.

While women played a very limited role in formal institutions and moralists encouraged them to remain secluded from public life, London wives and widows were active participants in a very public social world—that of their neighborhoods. Neighbors, both men and women, were deeply invested in a concept of social order that went far beyond the simple dichotomy of male authority and female subordination. They observed and commented on their fellow-residents, and maintained standards of seemly behavior through gossip, direct intervention, arbitration, reconciliation, and recourse to figures of authority. Neighbors and magistrates tempered the seemingly unrestrained power of household heads, deterring and limiting abuses. However, while Londoners generally agreed on the value of social order, they disagreed vehemently on where they stood within it. While women could employ their sharp tongues against abuses, they were equally apt to battle one another in corrosive verbal contests that endangered the ideal of communal harmony, necessitating further interventions. Order, always prized, was never secure.

---

[155] Griffith Hinton, *Katherine Povey c. Geoffrey Wilson*, 1616 (DL/C/224, fos. 162r–163v).

6
Her Honest Labor

Conduct books prescribed separate economic roles for men and women, with men bearing responsibility for 'getting' income, and women for 'saving' it through thrifty housekeeping. In the precarious households of poor Londoners, however, necessity ensured that women worked for money whenever they could. Throughout this study, we have seen how neighbors' and authorities' desire to maintain social and economic order shaped women's lives in early modern London, taking precedence over sexual anxieties; this pattern also holds true for female labor. Women's industry was not condemned either for taking them out of the house or for weakening wives' dependency upon their husbands. Rather, the dominating priority of making ends meet meant that women gained social credit in their neighborhoods for their work, and took pride in their contributions to the household economy. City law, too, supported their economic endeavors: wives who exercised trades independently of their husbands could trade as *femes soles* with the right to borrow money and rent shops.

Women's work was valued only when it was seen to contribute to the larger public good, however, and women faced severe restrictions when they were suspected of destabilizing London's larger economic order. While women's earnings shored up their households, they were readily construed as a threat when women competed with men for work. By the mid-sixteenth century, female apprenticeship in the guilds had already largely disappeared in London,[1] and in the pinched years of the end of the sixteenth century, when overloaded labor markets steadily drove down artisans' earnings, women were cast, like aliens, as unwelcome competitors whose willingness to undercut prices impoverished honest freemen and their families.[2] Unlike aliens, women did not benefit from organized lobbies or the sympathy of politicians anxious to aid religious refugees and improve the quality of English manufactures. As a result, with the exception of a few

---

[1] Marjorie Keniston McIntosh, *Working Women in English Society, 1300–1620* (Cambridge, 2005), 135.

[2] One of the grievances of the Weavers against aliens in 1595 was that 'they set women and maids at work' who not only mastered the trade themselves, but then taught it to their husbands, thus bringing 'that which should be our livings to be the maintenance of those that never deserved for it'. Weavers' Company, Book 3, fos. 125–38, quoted in Frances Consitt, *The London Weavers' Company* (Oxford, 1933), 313. See also Christine Peters, *Women in Early Modern Britain, 1450–1640* (New York, 2004), 51–2; and, for the exclusion of women from guilds in Germany, Merry E. Wiesner, *Working Women in Renaissance Germany* (New Brunswick, NJ, 1986), 149–85, 193–4.

freemen's widows, women were almost totally excluded from the vast majority of crafts and trades, except when unofficially assisting their husbands.

The occupations that remained open to women were limited. Women spun, sewed, knitted, and made lace for shopkeepers. They retailed food and drink, on the street or in shops and victualling houses. Women's skills in laundry, cleaning, and nursing were readily converted to waged labor performed for neighbors or almshouses, livery companies, or the Inns of Court. A few women claimed professional status as midwives, or through teaching or surgery. However, their work was nearly always ill paid. Skilled or unskilled, any occupation open to women was swamped by poor wives and widows willing to work for a pittance to help make ends meet. Even in the narrow range of occupations open to them, women were apt to find their profits characterized as private gain that damaged the common good. Thus civic authorities made constant if unavailing attempts to restrict the numbers of fishwives and hucksters, whom they painted as unnecessary intermediaries whose profits came at the expense of high prices for poor customers, even though itinerant sellers undercut the prices charged in shops. Alehouses and victualling houses, often run by women, were also the target of energetic regulatory drives: they were condemned as lewd, disorderly places where undesirable consumption strained the economies of poor families.

MARKET WORK AND REPUTATION

It is sometimes thought that women's paid labor posed a problem for the early modern English patriarchal order. By drawing women out of doors and into the marketplace and public establishments, we are told, work eroded distinctions between public and private spheres, exposing women to lascivious eyes and disapproving gossip.[3] Women's meager earnings were thus counterbalanced by the discredit their forays brought to their households, and by the threat that their nascent independence posed to their husbands' authority. Indeed, moralists like Cleaver and Dod drew a stark contrast between the economic roles of men and women: 'The duty of a husband is to get goods: and of the wife to gather them together, and save them. The duty of a husband is to travel abroad, to seek living: and the wife's duty is to keep the house. The duty of the husband is to get money and provision: and of the wife's, not vainly to spend it.'[4] Labor was the man's right and responsibility; chaste dependence was proper to the wife.

For most Londoners, of course, this division was impractical. Strict spatial distinctions between public and private were more easily maintained in print

---

[3] McIntosh, *Working Women*, 123; Michael Roberts, '"Words They Are Women, and Deeds They Are Men": Images of Work and Gender in Early Modern England', in Lindsey Charles and Lorna Duffin (eds), *Women and Work in Pre-Industrial England* (London, 1985), 153–4.

[4] Robert Cleaver and John Dod, *A godly forme of houshold government for the ordering of private families* (London, 1612), 167–8.

than in versatile urban houses, and fragile household economies could not afford to do without women's earnings. In these communities, rather than being rejected as a threat to sexual order, women's paid labor was accepted as an essential ingredient in the self-sufficiency of poor and middling families.[5] Like men, women derived credit from their contributions to family economies. For a wife to sit idly by while her family foundered and fell upon the poor rates would not be considered dutiful respect for her husband, but rather near-criminal negligence of her own responsibility for the family's welfare.

Wives who described their maintenance in court showed no shame for their 'labour', 'painstaking', and 'industry'. For example, Ellen Dickon testified that her husband, 'a very poor man', was a porter and that she was a water-bearer, so that the couple 'by his labour and [her] industry and painstaking in carrying of water to her neighbours do live'. Mary Parker lived 'by the labour and pains of her husband (being a journeyman butcher) together by her own pains'. Elizabeth Browning was 'maintained partly by her own labour and industry in the working of caps and such things, and partly by her husband's wages being a seaman'. Margaret Bellamy, a young wife who lived with her husband in lodgings, deposed that 'by the space of these seven years last past she hath been maintained by her husband and by her own honest endeavours'. Elizabeth Gardner reported: 'she liveth partly by the means of her poor husband being a blacksmith, and she getteth somewhat herself by doing any honest labour she is able to do.'[6]

Poor women sometimes even placed greater emphasis on their own work than that of their husbands. Anne Bentley put her work first in 1621: 'she liveth partly of herself by her honest endeavours getting a penny by her needle by working unto shop folks and partly by her husband who is a servant vintner.' Anne Lee, a painter's wife in Stepney, deposed: 'she windeth raw silk from the throsters and thereby getteth her living', and, she added, 'hath some maintenance from her husband'. Mary Hare, a spurrier's wife, said: 'she liveth by helping to wash where she can, yet works and helps her husband sometime in his shop.' Luce Guppie, a weaver's wife in St Bride's, claimed: 'she is maintained partly by her husband and partly by her own labour in sempstry by which she hath the greatest part of her maintenance.' Indeed, Luce's neighbors agreed that she supported her family, for her husband 'would and did use when he could procure any money from his said wife which she had gotten with great pains he would frequent bowling alleys and alehouses until he had spent the same and would not take any fit course to get his living'.[7]

---

[5] See Alexandra Shepard, *Meanings of Manhood in Early Modern England* (Oxford, 2003), 195–6; Bernard Capp, *When Gossips Meet: Women, the Family and Neighbourhood in Early Modern England* (Oxford, 2003), 45.

[6] Ellen Dickon, 1619 (LMA, DL/C/225, fo. 210v); Mary Parker, 1624 (LMA, DL/C/230, fo. 15v); Elizabeth Browning, 1629 (LMA, DL/C/231, fos. 419v–420v); Margaret Bellamy, 1634 (LMA, DL/C/630, fos. 244, 256v); and Elizabeth Gardner, 1619 (LMA, DL/C/227, fo. 232v).

[7] Anne Bentley, 1621 (LMA, DL/C/228, fo. 112); Anne Lee, 1617 (LMA, DL/C/225, fo. 78r); Mary Hare, 1610 (LMA, DL/C/219, fo. 284r); Luce Guppie, 1615 (LMA, DL/C/223, fo. 318v); and Thomas Hanson, 1616 (LMA, DL/C/224, fo. 132r).

Some female witnesses laid claim to professional status. Midwives were particularly likely to do so. Elizabeth Parkhurst, a hosier's wife, reported that she was 'a midwife by her profession', and Elizabeth Baylie said: 'she useth to do in her calling or profession as other midwives of the city of London.' However, they were not alone in claiming a professional identity. Alice Warren of Brick Lane omitted any reference to her husband, a drover, when explaining how she lived, explaining that 'she getteth her living by piecing and mending of stockings which is her profession'. The widow Hester Allen was 'by profession a dry nurse', and Anne Brand, a cheesemonger's wife, was 'a butter woman by profession'. The elderly widow Katherine Ames explained: 'She useth the trade or mystery of a broker in buying and selling apparel and thereby maintains herself.'[8]

Honest labor was a source of credit for poor men and women because it implied independence from alms: beggars who relied on the charity of their neighbors could not be trusted to tell the truth.[9] Even if poor women could not survive without alms, they were expected to do their best to make what money they could. Katherine Osborne insisted that she 'helped to get her living by her labour by carrying of water, washing and scouring', but Elizabeth Evans testified scornfully that Katherine 'spent what was gotten by her husband in drunkenness and would not take pains to help to get her livelihood for herself and children through her drunkenness and idle course of life never kept and clothed in rags and was relieved by the alms of the parish'. A neighbor cast doubt on the testimony of a bricklayer's wife by deposing that she received free bread at the parish church. Depending on charity was shameful: when a household received alms, an earning wife might disassociate herself from a dependent husband. Margaret Buckley, 80, testified: 'she getteth *her* living by winding of silk and her husband is a poor old man and hath a pension of the parish towards his maintenance.'[10] Individuals avoided admitting receiving alms if they could, so most references to charity were provided by opposing witnesses. Elizabeth Roberts, a shoemaker's wife, admitted that she was poor, but it was a female neighbor who pointed out that she had 'sometimes some relief in the parish'. Joan Goddin mentioned that she worked seasonally gathering peascods, but another witness noted that she had 'a pension of twelvepence a week' from her parish and had 'gone to great men's houses within the said parish begging for victuals'. Conversely, Edward Snowden buttressed the testimony of Joan Helme, 'an honest poor woman', by arguing that she was 'well able

---

[8] Elizabeth Parkhurst, 1630 (LMA, DL/C/232, fo. 6v); Elizabeth Baylie, 1617 (LMA, DL/C/225, fo. 41); Alice Warren, 1623 (GL MS 9189/1, fo. 51r); Hester Allen, 1629 (LMA, DL/C/231, fos. 507v–508r); Anne Brand, 1618 (LMA, DL/C/225, fo. 327r), and Katherine Ames, 1629 (LMA, DL/C/231, fos. 407v–408v).

[9] See Alexandra Shepard, 'Poverty, Labour and the Language of Social Description in Early Modern England', *Past and Present* 201 (2008), 58–60.

[10] Katherine Osborne, 1635 (LMA, DL/C/630, fo. 365v); Elizabeth Evans, 1635 (LMA, DL/C/234, fo. 93v); John Smith, 1634 (LMA, DL/C/630, fo. 178r); and Margaret Buckley, 1620 (LMA, DL/C/227, fo. 207v; emphasis added).

to live by means of her own industry and of her husband's labour being a gardener by his trade'.[11]

Even the clergyman Daniel Rogers conceded that wives might make money. He described the wife's duty as 'first getting, then storing, and lastly dispensing those things which are committed to her charge':

> The first of these three, is proper only to those women, who sell their husbands' commodities, or are allowed to be chapmen of their wares, (which is the case of few) or such as by reason of some special skill in any crafts or manufactures, have some stock allotted them by their husbands, to trade and traffic withal... Besides the huswifery of many tradesmen's wives, who learn their husbands' skill, serve to the making of sundry wares, which serve to the upholding of the family, and estate.[12]

Thus as long as they did not neglect their central duty of governing the house, it was good for women to earn money by retailing their husbands' goods, helping them in their workshops, or engaging in a different line of business. Rogers' advice was particularly suited to urban households: baking, malting, dairying, and keeping poultry, all traditional female enterprises, were impractical in an urban setting where bread and cheese could be more readily purchased from bakers and chandlers. The wives of London artisans and laborers were more likely to keep shop, do piecework, sell in the market, clean and nurse for wages, or run victualling establishments.

When women worked for money, their labor often took them into the streets: not only was needlework often done on the threshold, but water-bearers, porters, hucksters, and marketwomen all spent their days outside. Capp even suggests that the street was a predominantly feminine space because men were likely to be toiling in workshops or at work in the fields.[13] How was this public movement reconciled with the idea that women were to remain inside? Some scholars suggest that household honor was put at risk when women roamed abroad. Cases in which women accused their neighbors of pranking around town, living loosely and carelessly in and about the city, and going from alehouse to alehouse are taken to show that Londoners internalized the identification of female mobility with sexual dishonesty, a common trope in pamphlet literature.[14] However, 'gadding up and down' was less of a sexual sin than an economic one. The opposite of 'gadding' was not remaining enclosed within doors, but working and living thriftily—which often entailed being outside. Thus when one witness refuted a negative description of a neighbor, she stated that Catherine Hambleton 'liveth no idle life for she liveth with her mother an ancient woman where she taketh great pains to maintain her

---

[11] Elizabeth Roberts and Alice Neale, 1609 (LMA, DL/C/218, pp. 442, 441); Joan Goddin and William Weaver, 1634 (LMA, DL/C/630, fos. 126r, 177v); and Edward Snowden, 1619 (LMA, DL/C/192, fo. 79r).
[12] Daniel Rogers, *Matrimoniall honour: or, The mutuall crowne and comfort of godly, loyall, and chaste marriage* (London, 1642), 291.
[13] Capp, *When Gossips Meet*, 53.
[14] See Laura Gowing, '"The Freedom of the Streets": Women and Social Space, 1560–1640', in Paul Griffiths and Mark Jenner (eds), *Londinopolis: Essays in the Cultural and Social History of Early Modern London* (Manchester, 2000), 139–40.

said mother and doth not live up and down so carelessly as is expressed'. The identification between gadding and idleness was made for both sexes. Margery Noble 'lived idly and carelessly up and down the court', a witness said. 'William Swaine is by trade a carman but followeth it not himself but keepeth a man that doth it for him, and liveth himself idly, using much to frequent alehouses,' a disapproving neighbor reported.[15]

A closer look at pamphlets like Edward Hake's *Newes out of Powles Churchyarde* reveals that authors who fretted about women on the street were largely concerned about consumption: Hake's aim was to reprove 'excessive and unlawful seeking after riches, and the evil spending of the same'. All sorts of people, he complained, were flaunting unseemly splendor, blurring social boundaries:

> The rascals now must roam abroad
> like men of honest port:
> And strumpets stately in attire
> like ladies must resort
> To places where themselves think best.[16]

Gadding about the streets was identified with showing off fancy attire, not with working. In contrast, there is little evidence that going abroad for work had negative repercussions for women's reputations. The only women who sometimes had to defend themselves for going out for their work were butchers' and poulterers' wives who made business deals in alehouses and taverns. For example, Mary Wharton, a butcher's wife, was defamed by a tavern hostess for being locked in a room alone with one Mr Pierson. As the hostess told the story, she had feared that the room was on fire, and broke open the door to find Mary and Pierson 'in great sweats'. However, a witness deposed that Mary's neighbors did not consider her conduct unbecoming, because as a butcher's wife she was obliged to go to alehouses and taverns with her husband's customers.[17] Her husband may have been too tied to his shop to conduct such negotiations.

LABOR ON THE MARGINS

Women did whatever work they could get. Many, perhaps most, worked in the textile crafts that were not restricted to citizens. Midwifery and especially nursing employed many women, while others sold fresh foods and other wares, either as marketwomen or as hucksters or fishwives. Poor wives and widows dominated heavy laundry, while others specialized in starching. Poor charwomen washed and scoured for their neighbors. The victualling trades employed many women along with their husbands or independently, and a handful of women ran shops, retailing

---

[15] Elizabeth Edwards, 1624 (LMA, DL/C/229, fo. 30r); Martha Booth, 1622 (GL MS 9189/1, fo. 92r); John Shawe, 1608 (LMA, DL/C/218, p. 22).
[16] Edward Hake, *Newes out of Powles Churchyarde* (London, 1579), sig. D1r.
[17] Anne Usher, *Mary Wharton c. Elizabeth Barret alias Barwicke*, 1617 (LMA, DL/C/230, fo. 426r).

fresh foods, ruffs and points, and everyday necessities such as bread and coal. While coverture theoretically barred married women from entering into financial agreements, hindering female shopkeepers, according to the custom of London, wives could adopt *feme sole* status and trade apart from their husbands: 'Where a woman that hath a husband useth any craft by herself only, wherewith her husband doth not meddle: such a woman shall be charged as a *sole* woman for all that which toucheth her said craft.'[18] In addition, the wives of tradesmen who sold food—cheesemongers, butchers, poulterers, bakers, and so on—usually worked with their husbands, as did the mistresses of inns, alehouses, and taverns. Their labor was essential to these establishments.

Table 6.1 shows the number of occurrences for different varieties of work in women's London consistory court depositions. The data is taken primarily from witnesses' answers to the question of how they were maintained or what they did for a living, but also includes some circumstantial references in depositions. Because the question of maintenance was not universally asked, or fully answered (many women said simply that they were wives), the figures should be taken as an impressionistic indication of the sectors in which women worked, not a statistical measure. Women who could credibly claim to be maintained entirely by their husbands—an indication of wealth and hence of credit—were likely to do so. For example, Anne Berk, a bookseller's wife, said 'she is a wife and liveth of her husband', though we know from other sources that she wove silk points and employed a maidservant to do so as well.[19] Mistress Berk appears as a silk-point weaver in the table, but there is no way of knowing how many other wives failed to mention their own paid employment.[20] Being poor and hardworking was more creditable than being poor and idle, but being rich and not having to work was best of all.

Some important sources of income for women were unlikely to be mentioned in this context. No women mentioned keeping lodgers for a living even though many Londoners lived in lodgings: the work of looking after lodgers seems to have been subsumed in women's domestic tasks, unworthy of special notice. Where 'inmates' received disapproving scrutiny from parish officials intent on removing potential burdens, lodging-house keepers may also have been unwilling to draw attention to themselves.[21] Wet-nursing was dependent on the particular circumstances of

---

[18] *The city-law, or, The course and practice in all manner of juridicall proceedings in the hustings in Guild-Hall, London* (London, 1647), 40–41. Few married women took on *feme sole* trader status, however, preferring the legal flexibility of coverture. When spouses were of good credit and on good terms, the drawbacks of separating their finances may have outweighed the benefits. Marjorie McIntosh, 'The Benefits and Drawbacks of *Femme Sole* Status in England, 1300–1630', *Journal of British Studies* 44 (2005), 410–38.

[19] She may have sold her wares to the same chapmen who peddled her husband's books. Anne Berk, 1608 (LMA, DL/C/218, p. 167).

[20] See Amy Louise Erickson, 'Married Women's Occupations in Eighteenth-Century London', *Continuity and Change* 23.2 (2008), 274.

[21] On lodging-houses, see Bernard Capp, 'The Poet and the Bawdy Court: Michael Drayton and the Lodging-House World in Early Stuart London', *The Seventeenth Century* 10.1 (1995), 27–37; Lena Cowen Orlin, 'Temporary Lives in London Lodgings', *Huntingdon Library Quarterly* 71.1 (2008), 219–42.

Table 6.1 Wives' and widows' work, 1570–1640

Work	No. of witnesses	Work	No. of witnesses
Craftswomen	89	*Hucksters and marketwomen*	45
By her needle	18	Shop with fruit, herbs	3
Winding, twisting silk	17	Herbs, herbwoman	5
Weaving silk points	2	Fruitwoman	3
Spinning silk	1	Applewoman	1
Knitting silk stockings to shopmen	1	Apples and pears	1
Making silk flowers	1	Strawberries and other fruits	1
Silkweaver, silkwoman	1	Red currants	1
Working of caps	1	Roots and fruits	1
Mending of stockings	4	Artichokes	1
Stocking-mending stall	1	Fishwife	3
Spinning	7	Trading in fish and oysters	1
Spinning cotton for chandlers	1	Oysterwoman	1
Knitting	7	Keeps cattle, sells milk	1
Hosier, knits hose	2	Sells milk	2
Making bone lace	3	Butterwoman	4
Making gold and silver bone lace	1	Poulterer, sells poultry ware	2
Making gold and silver fringe to shops	1	Tripewoman, sells tripe	2
Stitching of bodies for shops	1	Sells hides at Leadenhall	3
Sempster, keeps sempster's shop	11	Oaten cakes	2
Tailor	1	Oatmeal	1
Embroiderer	1	Tobacco	1
Making thread	1	Candles	1
Carding	1	Lace	1
Making buttons	2	Other wares, marketwoman	2
Hand labor	1	Sells fruit at Red Bull playhouse	1
Making up gloves with husband	1		
Laundresses and charwomen	37	*Medicine and nursing*	63
Washing, washing abroad, at divers men's houses, for gentlewomen, for neighbors	11	Keeps sick folk, nursekeeper	21
		Keeps women in childbed, drynurse	13
Helping to wash, helping to wash and starch, washing for richer kin	5	Wetnurse	9
		Midwife	16
Laundress, washing and laundering	3	Midwife's deputy	1
Starching ruff bands to shops	3	Surgeon, treats pox	1
Starching to gentlemen	1	Surgeon, dresses sores	1
Making starch	1	Nurse for old men in Charterhouse	1
Washing and scouring, washing starching and scouring, charwoman	10		
Works for cook in Serjeant's Inn	1		
Works (laying the cloth, etc.) with her husband, who is butler at Serjeant's Inn	1		
Dressing dinner abroad for neighbors	1		

Victualling trades	56	Other trades and services	44
Victualling house, alehouse	31	Servant[a]	19
Tavern hostess	6	Keeping playhouse doors	4
Inn hostess	7	Placing maidservants	1
Draws beer	1	Matron of Bridewell	1
Cook's shop	2	Selling books	1
Sells drink from her cellar	2	Folding books into quires for binding	1
Chandler's shop	7	Porter, letter-carrier	2
		Teaching children	5
		Teaching gentlewomen to play the virginals	1
		Broker, selling old clothes	1
		Weeding	1
		Bawd	1
		Waterbearer	6

[a] The number of married and widowed women who said that they were servants should not be compared directly to the numbers of women who said they did other sorts of work, because being a servant—unlike being an alewife or a nurse—was a status rather than an occupation. Women almost always gave their status, but rarely described their work.

having excess milk, and was unlikely to be described as a regular means of maintenance. Understandably, no woman claimed to do illegal work, although one witness was credibly described as a professional bawd. The sex trade thrived in London, however, and petty crime may have subsidized many struggling households.

On the other hand, many women mentioned several different kinds of work, like Magdalen Holmes, who said that she 'for the most part useth her needle and knitting and sometimes washing or starching and by these means helps to get her own living'. Mary Watkins used to 'keep a cellar wherein she sold drink but she hath now put it off', and got 'her living by her washing and laundering' as well as occasionally serving as a wet-nurse. Helen Edwards said she maintained herself 'sometimes as a nurse, sometimes as a charwoman, and in washing and scouring'.[22] Competition for work was fierce, and women who restricted themselves to one occupation risked finding themselves unemployed.

Craftswomen

Many women testifying for the consistory court mentioned working with textiles. In addition to the women who reported making money through their handwork, casual references to 'work' are ubiquitous: women often described themselves 'sitting at work' by their doors, in their shops, and in the houses of

[22] Magdalen Holmes, 1620 (LMA, DL/C/226, fifth series, fo. 13); Mary Watkins, 1633 (LMA, DL/C/234, fos. 4v–5r); and Helen Edwards, 1631 (LMA, DL/C/232, fo. 173r).

their friends and kinswomen. Nearly all early modern London women were at least occasionally engaged in sewing, mending, knitting, making lace, winding silk, or spinning, much of which could be done while minding children and keeping an eye on a husband's shop if he were absent. For example, Jane Damport, the wife of a poor tailor, mentioned 'sitting at work in her husband's shop' in St Botolph Aldgate; she may have been sewing for her husband's business.[23] Women with their own shops probably also kept busy while waiting for customers.

Whereas some of women's textile work was destined for household consumption, much of it was oriented to the market. London women specialized in more complicated manufactures than the basic carding and spinning of village women. They described themselves living 'by their needles', knitting hose or silk stockings, and making silk thread, caps, and lace. In addition to filling individual orders, women might do piecework for tradesmen. Elizabeth Jordayne, a middle-aged widow, said 'she getteth her living by stitching of bodies [bodices] for the shops and otherwise by her needle'. Mary Drane, widowed at 30, had inherited something from her mother: 'of that and upon her own industry and painstaking which she employeth herself with her needle by working to the shops, she maintaineth herself and sayeth she is worth at least £10 her debts paid.' Luce Hitchcock, married to a laborer, lived 'by knitting of silk stockings to shop men'.[24]

Craftswomen often made products that had only recently been introduced into England, and that were accordingly less likely to be regulated by the guilds. Knitting stockings, making bone-lace, making buttons, and weaving points were all relatively new manufactures introduced in the later sixteenth and early seventeenth centuries. These 'projects' were designed to shore up the English economy by providing employment and obviating the need to import finished goods from abroad.[25] The lack of regulation that characterized these new projects opened up opportunities for working women, but also ensured that wages remained low: because so many women were desperate for work, any occupation open to them was flooded with labor. Women's low wages were the product of an artificially crowded labor market, not the natural compensation for unskilled or semi-skilled work. Historians have been apt to describe women's work (in implicit comparison to that of men) as low-skilled.[26] However, women who knew how to make the newest luxury goods like 'gold and silver bone lace of several sorts and fashions' could charge for teaching their skills.[27] Moreover, it is a mistake to equate formal training with skill and difficulty. London artisans and tradesmen served long apprenticeships, but these

---

[23] Jane Damport, 1601 (LMA, DL/C/216, sl. 473).
[24] Elizabeth Jordayne, 1619 (LMA, DL/C/227, fo. 246v); Mary Drane, 1620 (LMA, DL/C/227, fo. 195); and Luce Hitchcock, 1619 (LMA, DL/C/226, 2nd series, fos. 11v–12r).
[25] Joan Thirsk, *Economic Policy and Projects: The Development of a Consumer Society in Early Modern England* (Oxford, 1978), 6.
[26] See McIntosh, *Working Women*, 122; Katrina Honeyman and Jordan Goodman, 'Women's Work, Gender Conflict, and Labour Markets in Europe, 1500–1900', *Economic History Review* 44.4 (1991), 610.
[27] See Elizabeth Barton and Elizabeth Dover, *Helen Wigmore c. Sara Webb*, 1631 (LMA, DL/C/232, fos. 27r, 26v).

were not solely designed to teach the complexities of the craft.[28] They also served to regulate and restrict entry into labor markets, bolstering citizens' earnings. Once young men gained the 'freedom' of London, they were free to practice whatever trade they found fit, and some switched from trade to trade.[29]

Although the independence of the medieval London silkwomen was a thing of the past, many women worked with silk, especially in the eastern parishes where the silk manufactures were concentrated: Stepney, Whitechapel, and St Botolph Aldgate. Winding and twisting raw silk was largely their concern, and this industry grew as more and more raw silk was imported in the sixteenth and seventeenth centuries.[30] Male silkthrowsters who put out silkwinding to women earned praise for 'employing the poor... who otherwise would unavoidably be burthensome to the place of their abode'.[31] For their part, silkwinders competed fiercely for work. One silkthrowster, Thomas Becke, testified in a 1634 defamation case between two women who worked for him. He explained that Mary Crouch came to his house 'for work as she usually had done being one that did wind silk for [him]'. Bridget, his wife, deposed that Mary 'fell into discourse' with her husband about Edith Butcher, 'and demanded wherefore he would employ such a woman as she was in his work', because (Mary alleged) she was a whore who had sold herself for a kirtle and a waistcoat.[32] Winding silk may still have been one of the more lucrative occupations open to women. One silkwinder, Hester Peacock, was reported to earn 'her six or eight or nine shillings a week according as the silk falleth out in goodness' in 1620. If she were able to find consistent work, this would have provided her with an annual income of more than £15, well beyond the fifty-two shillings a year suggested by Archer as a widow's earnings.[33]

Although most craftswomen worked 'to shops' or for their own household use, a few kept their own shops. Elizabeth Chare ran a sempster's shop and employed a maidservant who said she was 'a sempster and getteth her living by buying and selling and by her work now under [Mistress Chare]'. Margery Downham, a young tailor's wife, kept a sempster's shop in Chancery Lane. Her husband's trade and her own previous service with a Lady Platt before her marriage may have helped her to establish a clientele. Anne Hawes, 50, said that 'she keepeth a sempster's shop and her husband is a musician and by that means they get their living'. She sold

---

[28] For most crafts, three or four years of training was thought sufficient. See Ben-Amos, *Adolescence and Youth*, 123.
[29] See Alexander Thurston, 1614 (LMA, DL/C/223, fo. 17r); Thomas Williamson, 1617 (LMA, DL/C/225, fo. 49); Henry Wood, 1619 (LMA, DL/C/225, fo. 215v); Richard Okeley, 1618 (LMA, DL/C/226, 1st series, fo. 34v); William Ward, 1619 (LMA, DL/C/226, 6th series, fo. 32v); Edmund Hawes, 1610 (LMA, DL/C/219, fos. 134v, 137v); and Thomas Young, 1619 (LMA, DL/C/226, 8th series, fo. 9).
[30] Linda Levy Peck, *Consuming Splendor: Society and Culture in Seventeenth-Century England* (Cambridge, 2005), 85.
[31] 'Charles II, 1662: An Act for regulating the Trade of Silk throwing', *Statutes of the Realm* vol. 5: 1628–80 (1819), pp. 407–9.
[32] Thomas and Bridget Becke, *Edith Butcher c. Mary Crouch*, 1634 (LMA, DL/C/630, fos. 221v, 220r).
[33] Richard Brewton, 1620 (LMA, DL/C/227, fo. 121v). Ian Archer, *The Pursuit of Stability: Social Relations in Elizabethan London* (Cambridge, 1991), 194.

'shirtbands and such other linen wares' with the aid of her daughter and an apprentice, a Welsh girl. In addition to employing maidservants, female shopkeepers also put out piecework. Dorothy Smith, a sempster, was fetching work to do at Margery Thimblethorpe's shop when she overheard Ellen White accuse Margery of being a bawd.[34]

Marketwomen, fishwives, hucksters

Women dominated the sale of fresh produce and also dealt in fish, meat, and poultry. Hugh Alley's 1598 illustrations of London food markets show women sitting at stalls selling fruits and vegetables, eggs, baked goods, tripe, sausages, pigs' heads, live and dead ducks, and more. Others are depicted walking by with baskets on their arms or balanced on their heads, while yet more marketwomen are shown riding side-saddle on horses laden with panniers. In the drawing of Billingsgate, fishwives sit by their baskets hawking fish, eels, and shellfish. Men are not absent from these pictures—they too are shown selling from stalls or from heavy baskets strapped to their backs, and herding sheep and cattle to the butchers.[35] Both buying and selling, however, women maintained a large presence in London's markets. Women who sold food on the street can be roughly divided into two groups: the village marketwomen who came in from the countryside to sell farm produce, and the London-dwelling marketwomen, shopkeepers, and hawkers who retailed victuals from other suppliers.

Country marketwomen were farmers' wives and their maids from nearby villages who rode to London on market days to sell their wares. Anne Quicke of Chigwell, Essex, explained that she had incurred no charges in coming to court to testify: 'by reason she keepeth London market and cometh usually to the city, it is no great labour nor charge for her to come and pleasure a neighbor in a matter of truth.'[36] Anne Sibley, a husbandman's wife of Theydon Garnish, Essex, heard defamatory gossip while she was 'riding up to London upon a market day as she useth often in the summertime to do'. In the same case, Jane Casse of Stapleford Tawney was overtaken by the defamer, Elizabeth Lake, as she was 'upon a market day riding from her own house to London to sell her commodities', and said she had been 'glad of her company' on the ride. Mary Heard, a young wife from Theydon Mount, was also riding to London that day.[37] These trips were grueling, with early rising and long journeys: Chigwell was over ten miles from the City, while Theydon Mount was about twenty miles distant, perhaps a five-hour ride each way, just possible in the long days of summer. Even shorter distances were tiring:

---

[34] Mary Barton, 1611 (LMA, DL/C/220, fo. 816r); Margery Downham, 1609 (LMA, DL/C/218, p. 394); Anne Hawes, 1610 (LMA, DL/C/219, fo. 154v); Mary Griffin, 1610 (LMA, DL/C/219, fo. 146r); and Dorothy Smith, 1618 (LMA, DL/C/225, fo. 159r).
[35] Hugh Alley, *Hugh Alley's Caveat: The Markets of London in 1598*, eds. Ian Archer, Caroline Barron, and Vanessa Harding (London, 1988).
[36] Anne Quicke, 1591 (LMA, DL/C/214, p. 20–21).
[37] Anne Sibley, Jane Casse, and Mary Heard, *Elizabeth Lake c. Thomasine Rogers*, 1619 (LMA, DL/C/226, 8th series, fos. 37r, 38r, 6th series, fo. 35).

Alice Wilson struck a maid of hers 'that rode upon a horse asleep' home to West Ham, five miles from the City, the women having sold their peasecods one spring.[38]

Marketwomen were a regular link between the country and the city. After a day's work in the market, they might resort to a tavern for a drink and some gossip before returning homeward, picking up the news, if they had not already done so on the street. For example, a few women from West Ham were drinking 'a pint of wine or two' at the King's Head near Leadenhall when they quarreled about the paternity of Elizabeth Pomfrett's red-headed daughter.[39] It was through marketwomen that Leonard Carter of Acton, Middlesex, found his missing daughter Elizabeth in 1623. Elizabeth had gone into service in a neighboring gentleman's household, and was soon seen to be with child. When the authorities found out, her master, one Hall, told them that the girl had fled, much to her parents' dismay. They became suspicious, however, when Hall's neighbor's maidservant saw Elizabeth looking out from an upper window. 'Within a day or two after', Carter 'went to the house ... and standing in an upper chamber of the said house likewise saw the said Elizabeth standing or sitting in an upper chamber of the said Hall's house at a window'. Before they were able to act, however, Elizabeth 'was conveyed away from the said Hall's house'. Nothing more was heard of her until Goodwife Poudle and Goodwife Blanck, 'dwelling in Acton who usually on market days resort to London with wares', told Carter that they had seen Hall and Elizabeth near Charing Cross. He went to town to make enquiries, 'and so found her in service with a linen draper dwelling at the sign of the Golden Lock near York House in the Strand'.[40]

Village women were not alone in selling in the London markets. In outlying parishes, some men worked as market gardeners, and their wives often retailed their produce, like Margaret Hart, 40, who sold herbs in the street. Dorcas Clingdove, a Stepney gardener's wife, said: 'she is a laundress and by that means getteth her living as also by selling of herbs for her husband in the summertime.'[41] In addition, while the wives of butchers and cheesemongers usually worked in their shops,[42] on market days they were often found in the market. Anne Brand, a cheesemonger's wife, said she was 'a butter woman by profession and tending on the market held at Leadenhall'. Anne Taylor deposed that she was 'at Leadenhall a-selling of certain hides (as usually she and other butchers' wives use to do)' when Christian Readmore gossiped to her about another butcher's wife, saying: 'Goodwife Taylor, how farest thou by that whoremaster knave and that bawdy knave Ralph Kibley? This day sevennight he stood watching at Leadenhall ... until Nan Lawne had sold her

---

[38] Margaret Stanton, 1601 (LMA, DL/C/216, sl. 307).
[39] Joan Pragle, Elizabeth Wilson, and Alice Whiskyn, 1623 (GL MS 9189/1, fos. 60r–61r, 74r–75r).
[40] Leonard Carter, 1623 (GL MS 9189/1, fos. 115–16r).
[41] Margaret Hart, 1601 (LMA, DL/C/216, sl. 518–19); Dorcas Clingdove, 1623 (GL MS 9189/1, fo. 52r).
[42] The Butcher's Wife's outburst in a collection of wives' lectures is prompted by 'an honest butcher gently admonishing his wife, that she neglected the looking to her shop ... by which he was much hindered'. John Taylor, *Divers crabtree lectures Expressing the severall languages that shrews read to their husbands, either at morning, noone, or night* (London, 1639), 89.

hides, and then they went together to the tavern. I would wish Nan Lawne to take heed of him, for he is both a bawdy knave and a whoremaster knave.'[43]

The retail of fruits and vegetables was a largely female concern. Some women kept market stalls, like the elderly widow Jane Collett, who sold fruit in Cheapside. Others kept their own shops. Elizabeth Charter, a pewterer's wife, kept 'a shop under the stall of the dwelling house of Joan Toogood' where she got 'her living by selling of fruit and herbs and other commodities'. Beatrice Philips, married to a merchant tailor, witnessed an incident of defamation while selling apples. Anne Johnson, the 28-year-old wife of the pewterer Henry Johnson, told the court: 'she liveth by selling of fruits and herbs and such commodities in Fleet Lane where she hath a shop.' A young widow named Isabel Leonard had a shop in Shoe Lane 'where she sold fruits and other commodities'. Poultry and eggs also sometimes came under women's purview: Dorothy Freeman, a grocer's wife, 'kept a shop in Newgate Market where she sold poultry ware'.[44]

Advantageous locations were in high demand in Leadenhall and Cheapside, and marketwomen with legitimate stalls distinguished themselves from the hucksters who stood where they could. They grouped together with sellers of similar goods: when Katherine Fayermanners defamed the butterwoman Aveline Grace, the incident was witnessed by two other butterwomen and a chandler's apprentice who sold butter as well as by two passers-by. The incident illustrates the ways in which marketwomen claimed and contested status as honest traders. One Mistress Griffon grabbed Aveline by the sleeve, and told her to get down to the end of the market like a whore and a thief, while Katherine asked the other butterwomen why they, honest women, let Aveline stand among them, insisting that she should go to the lower end of the market. Aveline, who may have been suspected of selling stale wares or using false weights, was a 'baggage', Katherine added, for whom Newgate was more fit than Cheapside; she hoped a cart would come and take her away. The insulted woman took this abuse coolly, saying only: 'it was no matter, she would do well enough with the said Fayermanners.' She may have lost her cool, however, when she realized that a cutpurse had taken advantage of the crowd to steal her butter money.[45]

The status of hawkers and hucksters, who sold itinerantly from baskets, was lower than that of marketwomen, who paid rent—sometimes substantial sums—for their stalls. Hucksters, who made small profits by purchasing victuals from producers and reselling them for higher prices, also came into conflict with regulations against forestalling, engrossing, and regrating. These were, respectively, buying up goods before they reached the open market, buying up large quantities

---

[43] Anne Brand, 1618 (LMA, DL/C/225, fo. 327r); Anne Taylor, 1574 (LMA, DL/C/211/1, fo. 262r).

[44] Jane Collett, 1620 (LMA, DL/C/227, fo. 180r); Elizabeth Charter, 1619 (LMA, DL/C/226, 2nd series, fos. 3v, 15r); Beatrice Philips, 1630 (LMA, DL/C/231, fo. 539r); Anne Johnson, 1618 (LMA, DL/C/226, 4th series, fo. 29r); Isabel Leonard, 1618 (LMA, DL/C/225, fo. 277v); Dorothy Freeman, 1620 (LMA, DL/C/226, 7th series, fo. 33r).

[45] Elizabeth Newman and John Mahne, *Aveline Grace c. Katherine Fayermanners*, 1591 (LMA, DL/C/214, pp. 102–3).

of goods with the objective of raising prices, and reselling goods bought at one market in another.[46] These activities were not always illegal: reselling certain foods was permitted at certain times and in certain places. However, hucksters always occupied a marginal and suspect position. In his *Caveat*, a text promoting market regulation, Hugh Alley made them a central target of his reforming zeal, calling them a 'lewd, covetous, greedy, and evil disposed people':

> inhabiting in and about the city, and suburbs of the same, called hagglers, hawkers, and wanderers, up and down the streets, in buying into their own hands, to raise the prices, for their own lucre and private gain, all kind of provision, and victuals, used and exercised, in the same city, to be bought, or sold, and presently selling the same again to others in the same markets, the inconvenience whereof, in these few late years, hath bred this great dearth and scarcity.[47]

Women hucksters appear in an unfavorable light in the records of the Cornhill wardmote, partly because they were among the large and varied group of people who tarnished the dignity of the Royal Exchange. No sooner was that monument to high commerce founded, it seems, but it was invaded by very low commerce indeed. In 1579, a request was made 'that such lewd women as commonly resort to the Exchange in the night at the breaking up thereof and thereabouts continue until eight of the clock in the night may be avoided from thence which otherwise may be hurtful to divers men's apprentices and servants and to divers others that pass thereby'. In 1590 the wardmote listed 'certain women, maidens, and others, presented for selling oranges, apples and other things at the Exchange gate in Cornhill and abusing themselves in cursing and swearing to the great annoyance and grief of the inhabitants and passers-by'. In 1594 the list of wares had expanded, and the wardmote listed 'women presented for selling of oranges, lemons, fruits, unwholesome poultrywares and other things at the Exchange gate, noisome to the inhabitants and offensive to the merchants thither resorting'. In the next century the situation was no better, and the wardmote found it necessary to mention:

> the annoyance presented by such as sell apples and other fruits at the Exchange whereby the street is obstructed with baskets and other things that coaches and carts cannot well pass and divers young women and maid servants live in that idle course of life and sit there at unlawful hours in the night time and entice apprentices and servants to waste their monies unduly and are the occasion of many brawls to the disquieting of the neighbors.[48]

Women were not the only targets of the wardmote's ire. Another perennial problem was that of the 'great numbers of boys and children with divers young rogues who as well in the forenoon as in the afternoon make such shouting hallowing and playing at the ball with their caps and other games that neither the honest citizens who walk there for their recreation can quietly walk nor one hear another speak'.

---

[46] Ian Archer, Caroline Barron and Vanessa Harding, 'The London Food Markets', in *Hugh Alley's Caveat*, 5.
[47] *Hugh Alley's Caveat*, 42–3 (fos. 2v–3r). Modernized from facsimile edition.
[48] GL MS 4069/1, fos. 26v, 51v, 118v.

'Footballers' were particularly destructive: 'most men's wares who keep open shops are thereby sore spoiled and great hurt done, and also many persons' glass windows thereby broken.' What was worse, an even more unseemly contingent had moved in to keep the orange-sellers company: birders had appeared as early as 1596, and in 1621 the wardmote lamented '[t]he great abuse and annoyance presented done before the south gate of the Exchange (especially at Exchange time) by rat-catchers, sellers of dogs, birds, plants, trees and the like in selling their said commodities there being very much offensive and troublesome to the neighbors and inhabitants thereabouts'. This motley group was still there in 1623 and 1639.

These male targets of official disapproval suggest that the wardmote's hostility towards the orange-sellers was not a simple desire to exclude women from the public sphere of the Royal Exchange. In fact, one of the accusations cited against the rat-catchers and pet-sellers was that they impeded the access of wealthy women to the Exchange: they troubled the 'merchants, gentlemen, ladies and others resorting as well to the Exchange as to the pawn above the Exchange'. Merchants wanted the Exchange for themselves and their wives, for sedate walking, grave conversation, high commerce, and luxury shopping, while children, fruitwomen, and animal-sellers seized upon the open space for their noisier pursuits.[49]

While the orange-sellers were criticized for their disorderliness, not simply their sex, the targeting of street-selling fell hard on women: barred from the guilds, women were disproportionately pushed into the casual occupations most likely to be subjected to official condemnation, and least likely to be protected by corporate rules. For example, the Cornhill wardmote repeatedly complained of women selling yarn. They first appeared in 1582 in the high street, where their objectionable presence prompted a petition to the Lord Mayor to find a better place for them: 'The women sellers of yarn presented for that they stop and hinder the passage in the Queen's high street and forestall the inhabitants thereabouts and besides that if foul weather happen they be very troublesome to the inhabitants, most humbly craving that some place may be appointed for them by your honour and worship's discretion.' Evidently they were assigned to sell their yarn in Leadenhall Market: in 1590, the clerk of the market was 'presented for permitting the women which sell yarn to stand in the street to stop the common passage and to forestall the inhabitants in this ward: And for that they have not placed the same women in Leadenhall as hath been appointed.' The clerk was presented again for the same fault in 1593, and in 1596 a petition was repeated for 'a necessary place for those who sell yarn'. By the next decade, the yarn-sellers were successfully moved to Leadenhall, to the displeasure of the shopkeepers there. In 1615, a complaint was made about 'the annoyance done by yarn-sellers in forestalling the shops near Leadenhall', and in 1629, women were again presented 'for forestalling of linen yarn in the market at Leadenhall'.[50] It is difficult to believe that the yarn women

---

[49] Ibid. fos. 19r, 21v, 157r, 160r. For shopping at the Royal Exchange, see Peck, *Consuming Splendor*, 42–7.
[50] GL MS 4069/1, fos. 40r, 51v, 60r, 67r, 140r, 191v. For similar complaints a century later, see Beverly Lemire, *Dress, Culture and Commerce: The English Clothing Trade before the Factory, 1660–1800* (London, 1997), 102–3.

had sufficient clout to forestall the Leadenhall shops. It seems more likely that the low costs of itinerant selling and female labor were considered to be unfair competition by the respectable tradesmen who made up the bulk of the ward's solid citizenry, and that hucksters served as convenient and visible scapegoats in hard economic times.[51] Without an official voice, the yarn-sellers were left with little choice but to irritate local sensibilities wherever they went.[52]

Despite incessant efforts by civic authorities, the number of hawkers and hucksters was on the rise. The failed campaign against fishwives, uncovered by Paul Griffiths, illustrates this trend. The fishmongers were a powerful guild, and they made intense efforts to restrict the sale of fish by 'foreign' fishermen and women hawkers. From the 1550s, aldermen complained about the 'great and superfluous numbers' of fishwives who bought fish from the boats at Billingsgate and resold it around the city. A plan was made to regulate the fishwives by setting a limit to their numbers and issuing them badges. Badges were supposed to be reserved for women over 30, the wives and widows of London citizens, although elderly fishwives sometimes gained approval to employ deputies, like Joan Lambert, 'a lame and aged woman', who obtained permission to have one Judith Coleman sell fish for her instead.[53] Fishwives were also forbidden to compete directly with fishmongers by setting up shop in fixed locations: instead they were to 'go up and down' the streets crying their wares. Though fewer than fifty authorized fishwives were working in 1568, by 1596 their numbers had swelled to 160, with more presumably circumventing the rule. From 1612, Bridewell had responsibility for issuing fishwife badges at sixpence apiece and keeping track of the names and numbers of authorized fishwives. None of these efforts were successful in eliminating unregulated fish-selling: by 1625 or so, the authorized fishwives themselves were petitioning the aldermen to stop 'foreign fishwives' employing an estimated 'two hundred wenches' from encroaching on the territory of the 'ancient poor fishwives'.[54]

Loud-mouthed fishwives were known for scolding and quarreling, although in this they were hardly unusual among London women. Rebecca Chandler and Elizabeth Oxenton, for example, were described as 'persons of a very quarrelsome and contentious disposition... blasphemers of God's holy name' by a male colleague.[55] Nonetheless, despite their bad reputations and the opprobrium heaped on their heads by aldermen and City Councilors, hucksters played an important role in London commerce. They offered cheap wares and convenience to customers who

---

[51] Archer suggests that as a result of the social polarization of the 1590s, London aldermen focused their disciplinary initiatives on petty traders rather than the profiteering wholesalers that had previously been targeted. *The Pursuit of Stability*, 202–3.

[52] This is not to say that male craftsmen and tradesmen were never censured by the wardmote. However, these were usually guilty of taking up the streets for their work, cheating their customers, or making too much noise, rather than illegitimate competition. See GL MS 4069/1, fos. 14r, 24r, 27v, 216r.

[53] BRHA, BCB 4, fo. 11r.

[54] Paul Griffiths, *Lost Londons: Change, Crime and Control in the Capital City 1550–1660* (Cambridge, 2008), 128–30.

[55] Abraham Orton, 1635 (LMA, DL/C/234, fo. 123v).

could wait for them to pass in the street rather than fighting through market crowds. The range of goods sold by hucksters seems to have steadily increased, and they became iconic figures of London life, with their distinctive 'cries' immortalized in popular literature. In addition to the oatmeal-cakes, artichokes, roots, fruits, and currants mentioned in the consistory court records, in seventeenth- and eighteenth-century plates, women were depicted selling cherries, matches, mops, brushes, baskets, biscuits, cooked pears, singing birds, and more.[56]

Fishwives and other female hawkers symbolized the irrepressible growth of consumer London in a way that the stately aldermen, bedecked with beards and gold chains, did not. While civic responses to fishwives were unfailingly critical, some Londoners, like Daniel Lupton, took a certain tolerant pride in their loud women:

> They are easily set up and furnish't, get something, and spend it jovially and merrily: 'Five shillings a basket,' and a good cry, is a large stock for one of them. They are merriest when all their ware is gone: in the morning they delight to have their shop full, at even they desire to have it empty. Their shop's but little, some two yards' compass, yet it holds all sorts of fish, or herbs, or roots, strawberries, apples, or plums, cowcumbers, and such like ware. Nay, it is not destitute some times of nuts, and oranges, and lemons. They are free in all places, and pay nothing for shop-rent, but only find repairs to it... They change every day almost, for she that was this day for fish, may be tomorrow for fruit; next day for herbs, another for roots: so that you must hear them cry before you know what they are furnished withal.[57]

A 1635 ballad recounted how the Devil set up shop as a landlord in London, attracting all sorts of clients with his offer of eternal life—rich farmers, city dames, gentry gallants, usurers, craftsmen, and so on—only to be forced to flee by 'the poor women,/that cry fish and oysters':

> ...when these came hither,
> they kept such a noise,
> Each brabbled with other,
> which first should have choice,
> As that their noise frighted
> the Devil of Hell,
> No more he delighted,
> such bargains to sell.[58]

While some scholars have suggested that hucksters' work exposed them to an informal campaign of harassment as unchaste 'public' women, men who defamed

---

[56] See *The Cries of the City of London*, 1655, Bodleian Library, Douce Portfolio 139, fos. 6–10; M. Laroon, *Cryes of the City of London*, 1711, Folger Shakespeare Library; and *The Old pudding-pye woman set forth in her colours* (London, 1670).
[57] Daniel Lupton, *London and the Country Carbonadoed and Quartered into Several Characters* (London, 1632), 91–4.
[58] Thomas Dekker, *An excellent new ditty: or, Which proveth that women the best warriers be, for they made the devill from earth for to flee* (London, 1635).

them seem to have been more motivated by economic rivalry.[59] This was the case in the quarrel between Joan Granger and William Dawson around 1609. Both Joan and William sold 'artichokes and roots' in St Clement Danes, usually standing by one William Wood's house, and 'by reason of their so standing together to sell their wares, they did oftentimes fall out about serving one another's customers'. When Dawson complained that Joan should 'keep her own parish and not take away his customers', she replied that 'the street was as free for her as for him'. Not so, Dawson answered: 'she lived like a queane for he paid scot and lot in the parish and she paid none.' 'Thou liest like a drunken knave as thou art', returned Joan, and Dawson cried: 'thou liest like a drunken whore!' Joan sued him for defamation, but a local maid said that her reputation had not suffered: 'her neighbours do not think the worse of her for them but do think they are both to be blamed for brawling in the street.'[60] Even disapproving men might think twice before harassing a huckster: rather than venturing timidly into public spaces, fishwives and fruitwomen claimed the streets as their own.

The victualling trades

London authorities were dismayed to find their city all too well supplied with establishments where men and women could spend money on drink. In 1592, they resolved to restrain the disreputable practice of selling of drink from cellars. In 1612, the Lord Mayor was informed that 'that there is almost no house of receipt, or that hath a back door, but when it cometh to be let it is taken for a tavern', a situation in dire need of reformation. He estimated in 1613 that there were more than a thousand tippling and victualling houses in London, encouraging the waste of corn in brewing, and a count found more than 400 taverns in 1620.[61] Dekker warned that 'all trades, all professions sit tippling all day, all night, singing, dancing (when they can stand), laughing, cursing, swearing, fighting. A whole street is in some places but a continued alehouse.' Small wonder, when it was 'an easier life, a lazier life, a trade more gainful'. While victualling might enrich those who kept alehouses, it threatened the broader order: 'These quaffings hurt thousands, and undo many poor men who would else follow their labour, but now live in beggary; their wives (unless they tipple hard too, as for the most part they do, by their evil examples) starving at home, and their ragged children begging abroad.'[62]

Official disapproval and Dekker's consternation were powerless to purge London of drinking places. As with the hucksters, the aldermen's continual failure to reduce the numbers of taverns and alehouses reflected the importance of these establishments for city life. They were a mainstay in the practical and social life of the

---

[59] Gowing, '"The Freedom of the Streets"', 143; McIntosh, *Working Women*, 132.
[60] William Barnes, Elizabeth Smith, and Elizabeth Reynolds, *Joan Granger c. William Dawson*, 1609 (LMA, DL/C/219, fos. 7–8, 9v).
[61] See *Analytical index, to the series of records known as the Remembrancia. Preserved among the archives of the city of London A. D. 1579–1664* (London, 1878), 539–49.
[62] Thomas Dekker, *English villanies six severall times prest to death by the printers* (London, 1632), ch. 16, sig. K3–K4.

capital: sociable drinking was important to both sexes, and business agreements, marriage contracts, and the reconciliations of quarreling neighbors all took place in alehouses and taverns. Few Londoners brewed their own ale, and therefore this staple had to be fetched from the local alehouse. In addition, thousands of lodgers and inmates did not keep house; if they did not diet at their hostess's table, they were bound to rely on victualling houses for their everyday nourishment.

Women kept all sorts of eating and drinking establishments, usually working with their husbands. While a large majority of licensed victuallers were male, their wives took on much and sometimes even all of the work of running the alehouse, especially when victualling was their husbands' second trade.[63] Indeed, victualling and innkeeping were natural extensions of women's roles as household mistresses. Alehouses and victualling houses were usually designated by the names of their proprietors, and differed little from private houses except that they contained many seats in their main room, and perhaps in other rooms as well: a typical alehouse was described as having 'a room full of seats or place for men and women to sit and drink'.[64] Taverns were larger and equipped with bars, and inns had extra bedchambers, but in all cases the hostess lived there: it was her house.

The wives of victuallers, vintners, and innholders worked in their husbands' trades. Mabel Gomersall, a young victualler's wife in St Sepulchre, mentioned 'going up and down serving of her guests'. Anne Sedgewick described herself and her husband John 'drawing drink in the cellar of the house'. Keeping the bar was a usual duty for a vintner's wife or tavern hostess. Elizabeth Prichard was 'sitting at the bar in her house being a tavern and known by the sign of the Mermaid' when she heard two women 'brabble and fall out about some pears' in the street outside. Anne Laurence, a victualler's wife, was also sitting at the bar when she heard one of her customers call another a 'base beggarly whore'.[65] A lone man could hardly run a victualling house by himself. Because vintners', victuallers', and innkeepers' wives were full partners in the family business, they routinely kept them going during widowhood and after remarriage. Bridget Bolton, the wife of a clothworker who kept the inn at the sign of the Swan with Two Necks, inherited the house when he died in 1609. Thirty years old and a prosperous businesswoman, the widow was much courted. Three months after Bolton's burial in March, a quarrel arose in the inn when a woman suggested that one Robert Powell was not worth her consideration.[66] Bridget evidently agreed, for when she next appeared as a witness in 1622, she had been married to one Edward Norton for thirteen years. She lived in the same parish and described him as an innholder, so they were probably still keeping the Swan.[67]

[63] Peter Clark, *The English Alehouse: A Social History 1200–1830* (London, 1983), 74, 78–9, 82–4.
[64] Richard Allen, 1619 (LMA, DL/C/192, fo. 87r).
[65] Mabel Gomersall, 1602 (LMA, DL/C/216, sl. 1074); Anne Sedgewick, 1622 (LMA, DL/C/228, fo. 181r); Elizabeth Prichard, 1611 (LMA, DL/C/220, fo. 607v); Anne Laurence, 1632 (LMA, DL/C/233, fo. 313v). For women keeping the bar, see Mary Prior, 'Women and the Urban Economy: Oxford 1500–1800', in Prior (ed.), *Women in English Society 1500–1800* (London, 1985), 98.
[66] Bridget Bolton, 1609 (LMA, DL/C/218, pp. 517–19); register of St Lawrence in the Old Jewry.
[67] Bridget Norton, 1622 (LMA, DL/C/228, fo. 218v).

Women also kept victualling on their own. This could be a useful way to diversify a household economy, as an entrepreneurial smith in a ballad thought, who told his wife: 'I will shoe horses, and thou shalt sell ale.'

> By selling of ale some money is got,
> If every man honestly pay for his pot:
> By this may we keep the wolf from the door,
> And live in good fashion though now we live poor.

His wife agreed, and by that means the smith 'got him two strings to his bow'.[68] Although the alehouse went to ruin, thereby proving the superior merit of honest, masculine labor, in real life sometimes the wife's trade was more profitable than the husband's. William Neave reported: 'until within a year last past he . . . did follow his trade of making guns as a smith but [his] wife hath of long time kept an alehouse, and so they both do at this present.' His wife, Jane, corroborated the statement: 'she liveth by her keeping an alehouse and victualling and by brewing and means of that her husband hath gathered besides.'[69] Keeping an alehouse was deemed particularly appropriate for widows and 'very aged and poor people and whose labours are past and have no other means of living', like Margery Durham, who had 'in her younger time got her living by washing, starching, and scouring, but she now doth get her living by selling of drink'. She was 50 or so and had not heard from her husband in years. Younger widows kept alehouses as well, like Alice Neale, 40, in Southwark and Anne Evans, 44, who kept a victualling house in St Martin Ludgate.[70]

There was nothing inherently disreputable about running a victualling house; in fact, women who did so were particularly anxious to defend themselves from defamation. When Thomas Gardener defamed Judith Neale, saying 'Why, what is she but a whore? . . . Or else why did her husband run away from her if she were not a whore?', a local woman testified that Judith was much hurt 'because she usually entertaineth in her house shipmasters and men of good rank and quality'. Mistress Neale had to clear her name of imputations that might keep good customers away. Dank cellars and establishments offering more exotic fare had more dubious reputations. Rose Sergeant, who dealt in 'tobacco and strong water', attracted the wrong sort of customer. As she told a neighbor, 'a man having spent a quantity of sixpence in her house in drink, he did request her to lend him her knife whilst she went for some beer, and in that time and with that her knife he cut his own throat'. Rose was imprisoned, though she protested that

---

[68] Humphrey Crouch, *The industrious smith wherin is showne, how plain dealing is overthrown* (London, 1635).
[69] William and Jane Neave, 1610 (LMA, DL/C/219, fos. 164r, 166r).
[70] Letter to the Privy Council, 1608, quoted in Sue Wright, '"Churmaids, Huswyfes and Hucksters": The Employment of Women in Tudor and Stuart Salisbury', in Lindsey Charles and Lorna Duffin (eds), *Women and Work in Pre-Industrial England* (London, 1985), 110. Margery Durham, 1634 (LMA, DL/C/630, fo. 288r); Alice Neale, 1609 (LMA, DL/C/218, pp. 334, 441); Anne Evans, 1616 (LMA, DL/C/224, fos. 125v–126v).

'the same man before his death did acquit her from having any hand in that wicked act'.[71]

More frequently, hostesses had to deal with unruly customers. When some chapmen came to Hester Frank's house to drink, she asked them not to disturb the house, but instead they called her 'old whore and arrant whore', and the constable had to be called 'to make peace amongst them'. John Grissall ordered drink in Margaret Copthwaite's house, but when she demanded payment, he said 'Out you whore! What have you to do with it?' He 'did lay his hand upon her bosom and thrust her from him', calling her 'whore' several times, though the neighbors thought nothing the worse of her for it. Margery Taylor in Islington faced attempted rape when 'George Webb came in her house to drink, she keeping a victualling house, when her husband was from home, and nobody at that time in the house, and he the said George Webb would have had the carnal use of her body and have lain with her, and used such means to that end "as that", quoth she the same Margery Taylor, "I was fain to leave my own house"'. When Webb, nothing abashed, subsequently sent his maid to her house to fetch ale, Margery asked the girl incredulously: 'What, is thy master mad? He is but a whoremaster knave!'[72] Hostesses also risked incurring the wrath of their customers' resentful wives, who mourned:

> I would these whores that trust such knaves,
> Might ne'er be paid their score,
> They never knew what sorrow meant,
> But griefs to others give,
> A mischief light on hostesses,
> That do by drunkards live.[73]

When Joan Higgett came to a victualling house in Stepney looking for her blacksmith husband, she 'fell into a passion', and told the hostess that she kept a bawdy house and that her daughter and her maids were all whores.[74]

Women also kept chandlers' shops, selling bread, beer, coals, and other staples. These were crucial for the poor as they dealt in small quantities and gave credit to neighbors: one couple was identified as being poor because they did 'fetch their victuals of chandlers and others as poor folks do by the penny'. Mary Parker lost eleven shillings on a bad debt when some poor people 'did fetch bread, drink, cheese, and coals' at her house, and failed to pay.[75] The proprietors of such shops were not much richer. Mary Ticer, a mariner's wife in Holborn, kept a chandler's shop in her husband's absence, but was thought to rely on illicit earnings. Alice

---

[71] Anne Usher, *Judith Neale c. Thomas Gardener*, 1639 (LMA, DL/C/235, fo. 253r); Judith Bowde, *Rose Sergeant c. Katherine Cooke and Margaret Webster*, 1620 (LMA, DL/C/227, fo. 204).
[72] Margaret Hatrell, *Hester Frank c. Francis Laman*, 1633 (LMA, DL/C/630, fo. 68v); Elizabeth Smith, *Margaret Copthwaite c. John Grissall*, 1613 (LMA, DL/C/221, fo. 1489r); William Coles and Anne Hawkins, *George Webb c. Margery Taylor*, 1602 (LMA, DL/C/216, sl. 812, 810).
[73] Samuel Rowlands, *The knave of clubbs* (London, 1609), sig. F3.
[74] Katherine Bailey, *Elizabeth Dalling c. Joan Higgett*, 1633 (LMA, DL/C/630, fo. 80v).
[75] Anabella Kelloway, 1624 (LMA, DL/C/229, fo. 82); Mary Parker, 1624 (LMA, DL/C/229, fo. 88).

Ithill reported that after Mary's husband had been gone for 'almost a whole year... Mary Ticer did complain herself and make her moan unto her... being as it seemed in some want of money, saying that she knew not how to do. "But," quoth she, "if I would play the queane I should quickly furnish my shop."' Shortly afterwards, Mary 'did furnish her shop very well and took in sea coals and other things'.[76] Local women suspected her of preying on their husbands. The wife of one Dickon, a poulterer, told Mary 'that her name might well be called "Ticer" for she had ticed away her husband from her'. '"Well," quoth the same Mary, "content yourself. I will make your husband as kind a husband to you as any husband in this town and I assure you I will not keep him company more but if he cometh on one side of the street, I will go on the other."'[77] However, local resentment festered and Mary Ticer was soon involved in no fewer than three separate defamation cases.

Other women with chandler's shops were more successful in avoiding scandal. Grace Rudd, a cutler's wife in St Giles in the Fields, kept a chandler's shop to supplement her husband's income. A middle-aged widow, Anabella Kelloway, sold bread, beer, and faggots in St Clement Danes. Anne Gibbons' husband was described as a chandler, but she herself said: 'she keepeth a chandler's shop... whither divers and sundry people resort for several wares daily and hourly.' Indeed, it was customary for chandlers' wives to serve clients as it was for butchers' and bakers' wives. When a clergyman entered Alice Brickland's shop, she 'wished him to get him out of her shop or else she would throw the knife (which she then had in her hand which she usually cutteth cheese withal, her husband keeping a chandler's shop) at his head'. He had, she claimed, run away with another man's wife.[78]

Cleaning houses and clothing

Dekker joked that charwomen got their name by sitting 'by a good fire, in easy chairs', but in reality they worked hard for meager livings and lowly status.[79] They did the heaviest domestic work and had to call their employers 'mistress', a painful concession for adult women, but did not enjoy the relative security of maidservants, who received meals and lodging.[80] Women who reported washing and scouring abroad were accordingly among the poorest witnesses, and could claim little credit. Katherine Osborne reported: 'she hath helped to get her living by her labour by carrying of water, washing, and scouring.' She and her husband lived in lodgings, and her landlord said she was 'scare sober two days in a week'. Elizabeth Clarke, an elderly widow, said: 'she getteth her living by carrying the water tankard and by

---

[76] Alice Ithill, *Mary Ticer c. Alice Bishop*, 1599 (LMA, DL/C/215, sl. 820).
[77] Jane Overbury, 1599 (LMA, DL/C/215, sl. 834).
[78] Thomas Stanick, 1619 (LMA, DL/C/226, 1st series, fo. 7v); Grace Rudd, 1620 (LMA, DL/C/225, fo. 13v); Anabella Kelloway, 1624 (LMA, DL/C/229, fo. 82v); Anne Gibbons, 1634 (LMA, DL/C/234, fos. 17r–18v); and Etheldreda Emerson, *Baines c. Alice Brickland*, 1619 (LMA, DL/C/226, 3rd series, fo. 17v).
[79] Dekker, *English villanies*, ch. 15, sig. K2v.
[80] In 1629 Frances Rice testified that she called Frances Ireland 'mistress as she doth the mistresses of other houses where she works' (LMA, DL/C/235, fo. 197r).

washing abroad at goodmen's houses and is little or nothing worth.' Katherine Humphrey, a tailor's wife, was 'a poor woman and that which she hath she earneth by her honest labour in getting a penny by washing and starching', and Mary Hare, who lived 'by helping to wash where she can', acknowledged that she was 'poor and nothing worth'.[81]

The plight of Jane Carter, 'a poor woman' who lived 'by washing and scouring of vessels for others at home at their houses', illustrates the precariousness of a charwoman's existence. Jane had left service just over three years before her testimony at the age of 40; her late marriage suggests that she had struggled to find a spouse, and indeed her husband was no prize. Joseph Carter, a glazier, was noted for 'his often and extraordinary frequenting the alehouses in Pudding Lane... very much drunken and his senses overcome with drink'. Jane had 'come thither to the alehouses in Pudding Lane... [and] complained of her husband for his misusing of her and she hath been oftentimes much misused by having both her face and shoulders black and blue which she hath said was by her husband's beating of her and he hath confessed the same.' Her domestic troubles came to the attention of the court because her independence was questioned when she testified in a case involving Elizabeth Hollinshed, whom she had known for twelve years, and for whom she did 'use to wash clothes every month'. A neighbor said Jane would not venture to testify against Elizabeth, who was 'a very good friend and one of her best friends... Jane Carter dare not offend or displease Elizabeth Hollinshed'. For women in Jane's difficult situation, such friendships were valuable sources of employment and support.[82]

Friendly relationships with employers also helped charwomen to veil their lowly status by framing their labor as neighborly help. Jane Shepherd, a mariner's wife, said she was maintained partly by her husband and partly 'by her own labour washing abroad or dressing dinner or supper for her friends and neighbours'. A widow in St Botolph Aldgate said she was 'a laundress to a gentlewoman and to other her near neighbours'—not to the world at large. Upon report that 'she seemed to be so needy and so poor a woman as a little pail of suds being by chance spilt, she cried out saying she was undone', she protested that she had been 'something grieved and disquieted by the spilling of her water which was to make an end of her washing and by reason it was then night when she could get no more, and for spilling the same in her house having but one room... but not in respect of that neediness she had of a penny or twopence to buy more'.[83]

While McIntosh suggests that it was considered scandalous for charwomen to work in men's houses,[84] the regulations ordering charmaids to find live-in

---

[81] Katherine Osborne, 1635 (LMA, DL/C/630, fo. 365v); Francis Rule, 1635 (DL/C/234, fo. 93r); Elizabeth Clarke, 1616 (LMA, DL/C/224, fo. 256); Katherine Humphrey, 1622 (LMA, DL/C/228, fo. 128r); Mary Hare, 1610 (LMA, DL/C/219, fo. 284r).

[82] Ellen Steed, Jane Carter, and Frances Price, *Elizabeth Hollinshed c. Winifred Bland*, 1609 (LMA, DL/C/218, pp. 585–6, 311, 588).

[83] Jane Shepherd, 1629 (LMA, DL/C/231, fo. 421r); Sara Carew and Edward Erbie, 1608 (LMA, DL/C/218, pp. 292, 287).

[84] McIntosh, *Working Women*, 75. For hostility to charmaids, see Wright, 'Churmaids, Huswyfes and Hucksters', 104–5.

services did not apply to adult women. Charmaids were objectionable because of their youth and maiden status; their work could be seen as a cover for prostitution. Charwomen, on the other hand, were as respectable as their poverty permitted, and did not hesitate to admit to their occupation. One might object, of course, that wives and widows were also capable of prostitution, but city authorities were pragmatic. While forbidding adult women from working outside the home might protect their virtue, it also risked throwing their households on the parish. A consistent aversion to increasing the poor rates encouraged officials to reconcile married and widowed women's charring with their consciences.

Most charwomen did whatever work they could get, but some women specialized in washing and starching. While maidservants often did the laundry, clothes could be sent out to professional laundresses. Thus Mary Turke's servant Joan said 'she doth not do all her ordinary work as an ordinary servant, doth for her said mistress having but a little household putteth all her clothes forth to washing'. This spared maidservants, but heaped the heaviest work on washerwomen. Continual exposure to caustic soaps and hot water, the manipulation of heavy wet cloth, and the carrying of unwieldy burdens made washing an arduous way to get a living. Nor was the work well paid. Young Anne Lambe, newly married to a husband she described as a yeoman, cannot have received much maintenance from him because she reported: 'she is a poor woman and hath nothing but that she earneth very dearly by washing and starching and other work such as she can get.'[85]

Laundry was also dependent on the weather, as the drying of clothes required sunshine, or at least dry weather or wind. One maidservant described herself starching in the courtyard, 'it being a sunshine day'.[86] Finding a place to dry clothes might present problems. They could be hung in a courtyard, or spread out indecorously in a churchyard, or brought to Moorfields, where a 1559 copperplate shows women sitting by laundry spread out to dry. In 1607 a dialogue praising London civic sentiment noted that the fields were designated 'for citizens to walk in to take the air, and for merchants' maids to dry clothes in, which want necessary gardens at their dwellings'. There were even rumors of 'the building of certain houses for shelters for maidens having their clothes lying there a-drying, if at any time it should chance to rain'.[87] However, just as merchants tried to evict orange-sellers from the Royal Exchange, the warders of Moorfields came into conflict with the laundresses, and forbade the use of walls and rails as clotheslines in 1609.[88] When spread to dry in public, linens had to be guarded because they were tempting bait for thieves; laundresses, who were responsible for the clothes they took in, could not afford losses. Jane Sandford recounted a near escape from professional disaster: 'about half a year past' there had been 'some controversy between Mistress Bruskin' and herself. Jane had 'before helped Mistress Bruskin to wash and starch',

---

[85] Joan Penny, 1622 (LMA, DL/C/228, fo. 241); Anne Lambe, 1621 (LMA, DL/C/227, fo. 283v).
[86] Mary Williams, 1599 (LMA, DL/C/215, sl. 473).
[87] Richard Johnson, *The pleasant walkes of Moore-fields* (London, 1607), sigs. A2–B1.
[88] Griffiths, *Lost Londons*, 93.

and in her absence, she 'being gone into the country', Mistress Bruskin 'slandered' her, claiming that she 'had stolen some of her linen'. However, 'since that time she hath denied those reports' and employed the laundress once again.[89]

Most women would be expected to have some facility with washing and starching, but especially in the cases of delicate and valuable fabrics, the procedures could be complex. The aristocrats of laundry were the women who specialized in starching ruff bands, the gorgeous, impractical frills of stiff linen that adorned the necks of everyone who was anyone in Elizabethan and Jacobean London. These could be very fine, to the pamphleteer Philip Stubbes' stern disapproval:

> The women there use great ruffs, and neckerchers of holland, lawn, cambric, and such cloth, as the greatest thread shall not be so big as the least hair that is, then lest they should fall down, they are smeared and starched in the devil's liquor, I mean starch: after that dried with great diligence, streaked, patted and rubbed very nicely, and so applied to their goodly necks...[90]

Starching a ruff band was complicated. They were made of long strips of material, ranging from about one and a half yards long, for an apprentice's modest ruff, to a full six yards for one belonging to Queen Elizabeth. A mass of tiny pleats was sewn into one side of the ruff, and every time it was washed, these had to be reset. Starch of varying colors would be worked into the delicate fabric, then the starcher, wielding a hot 'poking stick', would carefully set the pleats one by one. Starching an elaborate ruff was risky because of the great number of pleats and the delicacy of the fabric. A starcher who tore or scorched her ruffs might not be able to afford to replace them.[91]

According to John Stow's *Annals*, the art of starching was first introduced to Englishwomen in 1564 by a Flemish refugee, Dinghen van den Plasse, who 'professed herself a starcher, wherein she excelled, unto whom her own nation presently repaired, and employed her, and paid her very liberally for her work'. Spotting a business opportunity, London wives 'began to send their daughters, and nearest kinswomen, to Mistress Dinghen, to learn how to starch', paying substantial fees: 'her usual price was at that time, four or five pounds, to teach them how to starch, and twenty shillings how to seethe starch'.[92] Whatever the accuracy of the *Annals*, it seems likely that London women were eager to learn the comparatively lucrative skill. By the seventeenth century, knowledge of starching had become more widespread, but it was still one of the more rewarding occupations open to women. Frances Andrews, a self-professed 'starcher', claimed that she lived by 'starching of ruff bands to shops'. Frances, whose husband had lived from her 'these four years last past', worked in a partnership with Anne Allen, a yeoman's wife, who similarly reported: 'she starcheth ruff bands for shop folks and by that

---

[89] Jane Sandford, 1610 (LMA, DL/C/219, fo. 62v).
[90] Philip Stubbes, *The anatomie of abuses* (London, 1583), sig. F4v.
[91] Liza Picard, *Elizabeth's London: Everyday Life in Elizabethan London* (London, 2003), 123–5.
[92] John Stow, *Annales, or a generall chronicle of England* (London, 1632), 869.

means she getteth her living.'[93] Starching was also the chosen occupation of Elizabeth Hamlyn, a gentleman's wife, and the Welshwoman Margaret Strowde. She was able to afford a maidservant, and before her marriage had served in the household of Sir Samuel Saltonstall, a relatively good position, so although she said she was 'little worth of herself', this may have been simply a literal understanding of coverture. Alice James, an elderly widow, said: 'she is a laundress and useth to starch to gentlemen in London, and thereby liveth with some other means of her own and is worth £10 her debts paid.'[94] Even skilled starchers were subject to the vagaries of politics and fashion, however. Starch-makers like the widow Ellen Webb occasionally found themselves the target of legislation driven by worries about the wasteful use of wheat.[95] Even more seriously, as starched ruffs went out of fashion during the reign of Charles I, the starchers' livelihood disappeared.

Curing and caring for the body

A rich historiography has explored medical practice in the early modern period. Physicians, barber-surgeons, apothecaries, midwives, quacks, and cunning-folk[96] competed in a world where the limitations of medicine did nothing to dispel the eagerness of the population to be cured.[97] Nearly all the day-to-day work of *caring* for the sick, however, fell to the lot of ordinary women who worked as dry-nurses or nurse-keepers, who have been almost entirely omitted from accounts of early modern medicine. For example, when a vintner's young sister fell dangerously ill around 1595, she was nursed for six weeks until she recovered by Katherine Foxley, a poor carpenter's wife, who stayed in residence and was in charge of buying any 'necessaries' her patient needed.[98] In fact, the nursing of sick people—the provision of warmth, company, cleanliness, and digestible foods—may have been the single greatest factor in their relief.

It is well known that parishes employed pauper women to nurse other sick poor, elegantly gaining maximum poor relief for minimum cost. Nurses also worked in London's hospitals, and wealthy households routinely included nurses to look after childbearing mothers and children as well as sick people.[99] However, historians are only just beginning to realize how many women were employed as nurses in

---

[93] Frances's divorce was formalized a few years later: witnesses deposed that in her husband's absence, she consorted with other men and eloped with his goods. *Thomas Andrews c. Frances Andrews*, 1622 (GL MS 9189/1, fos. 3r–6r, 16v–17r, 86v–89v, 91v–92v); Frances Andrews, 1618 (LMA, DL/C/226, 4th series fo. 38r); Anne Allen, 1618 (LMA, DL/C/226, 4th series, fo. 30r).

[94] Elizabeth Hamlyn, 1624 (GL 9189/1, fo. 200v); Margaret Strowde, 1617 (LMA, DL/C/225, fo. 156); Alice James, 1615 (LMA, DL/C/223, fo. 315r).

[95] Ellen Webb, 1635 (LMA, DL/C/234, fos. 55r, 56v).

[96] Folk magicians, also known as wise men and wise women.

[97] Margaret Pelling estimates that, not counting midwives and nurses, about 500 practitioners were working in early modern London at any one time. 'Medical Practitioners', in *Health, Medicine and Mortality in the Sixteenth Century* (Cambridge, 1979), 188, 235.

[98] Katherine Foxley, 1599 (LMA, DL/C/215, sl. 409).

[99] Diane Willen, 'Women in the Public Sphere in Early Modern England: The Case of the Urban Working Poor', *Sixteenth Century Journal* 19.4 (1988) 559–75; Pelling, 'Medical Practitioners', 187.

ordinary private homes.[100] Large numbers of women were employed as nurses in the sixteenth and early seventeenth centuries: their comforting services were affordable for all but the poorest patients. Many women reported keeping sick folk or keeping women in childbed, but the two were not typically combined. Thus in the first category, a candle-maker's wife said she engaged in 'keeping of sick folk', and the widow Joan Robinson, 'a drynurse', kept a broker in Long Lane around 1621. In the second category, Frances Bea, a brewer's wife, explained: 'she getteth her living by keeping women when they lay in in childbed.' Anne Ealbank got 'her living by keeping women in childbed as a drynurse'. Joan Duste, a middle-aged widow, reported: 'she doth sometimes keep women in childbed and liveth of her own.'[101] Childbed nurses, who looked after mothers in the weeks following childbirth, should not be confused with midwives: the two occupations were entirely separate. The widow Winifred Smith's nursing, for example, was a long-term, live-in occupation: 'She liveth by keeping women in childbed and when she is not so employed she liveth with her brother-in-law Christopher Richardson sometimes and sometimes with her own brother named Edward Smith a plumber in Tower Street.' Katherine Clowdestey, 32, the wife of a poor glover, reported keeping one Elizabeth Denham for a month in childbed. She was still living there when Elizabeth was about to be churched, which would have taken place about a month after childbirth, so she had been hired around the time of Elizabeth's delivery, as was standard practice.[102]

Both sick-nurses and nurses who kept women in childbed usually lived with their patients, which would have made nursing a difficult occupation for women with heavy household responsibilities or young children. However, it was ideal for poor childless women whose husbands were at sea, since nurses were provided with room and board besides their wages. Eleanor Eartson, accustomed 'to keep women in childbed', said that her husband was at sea. Nursing was also a common occupation for widows like Jane Martin, 35, who kept one Elizabeth Masham until she succumbed to the plague and followed her husband, George Masham, to the grave.[103]

---

[100] McIntosh's study of women's work in England between 1300 and 1620 lumps nursing together with midwifery, charring, laundry, and prostitution in a 13-page discussion of 'non-residential household employment, sex work, and health care'. In contrast, finding that in 1695–1720 over 12% of female workers were involved in medicine and nursing, Earle surmises that 'more women earned their living by medicine than ever before or since'. While Erickson suggests that nursing is over-represented in church court records because sick-nurses testified about wills, most nurses deposed about other matters. McIntosh, *Working Women*, 72–84; Peter Earle, *A City Full of People: Men and Women of London, 1650–1750* (London, 1994), 131; Erickson, 'Married Women's Occupations', 278.
[101] Agnes Harling, 1588 (LMA, DL/C/213, p.420); Joan Robinson, 1622 (LMA, DL/C/228, fo. 209v); Frances Bea, 1610 (LMA, DL/C/219, fo. 232v); Anne Ealbank, 1618 (LMA, DL/C/225, fo. 304); Joan Duste, 1613 (LMA, DL/C/221, fos. 1214v–1215r).
[102] Winifred Smith, 1601 (LMA, DL/C/216, sl. 263); Katherine Clowdestey, 1599 (LMA, DL/C/215, sl. 316).
[103] Eleanor Eartson, 1601 (LMA, DL/C/216, sl. 514); Jane Martin, 1626 (LMA, DL/C/230, fo. 50v).

Wet-nursing, in contrast, was less of a regular occupation than an occasional sideline, as in the case of a Lambeth woman who reported: 'she liveth by and upon her husband's means for the most part and that she also helpeth to get her livelihood by nursing a child.' Joan Johnson, a Whitechapel woodmonger's wife, got 'her living by being a midwife's deputy and by nursing children'. One Mary Watson only mentioned her work as a wet-nurse when questioned about her infrequent attendance at church: 'she...doth go sometimes once a fortnight or three weeks on Sundays to her parish church to hear divine service which is as often as she can do, she being a nurse and having a young child till within this fortnight last.' Only women who nursed the children of the gentry were likely to support themselves solely on that basis, like Agnes Wincheley, who explained that her husband, a fustian dresser, 'liveth of his trade and keepeth house by himself, and [she] keepeth with Sir Paul Banning and nurseth his child in the said Sir Paul Banning's house'.[104]

Neighborhood connections were essential in linking wet-nurses with hungry infants. In 1616, Susan Gurden, a baby's godmother, found a woman in Southwark to nurse the infant, and handed over the child when it was a fortnight old. However, the first wet-nurse later said 'that by reason she had a little child of her own which she gave suck unto she thought she should not have sufficient milk for them both'. Instead, she suggested 'another woman which she had provided and brought with her being as she said an honest woman and dwelling near unto her'. The new wet-nurse, Ellen Finch, was then given five shillings for a fortnight's wages.[105] Anne Talbott, having left her husband and borne an illegitimate daughter, put her plight to good use by asking a neighbor, Dorcas Clingdove, 'to help her to a nurse child, for that she then had a child of her own being a female child about the age of twelve months which she intended to wean'. Dorcas 'did do her best endeavour and by chance did hear of a gentlewoman named Mistress Smith that was destitute of such a one, that lived in St Bartholomew the Less, whose child she did nurse about sixteen weeks'. After that, Dorcas 'did hear of a better place for her, and told her thereof, and meant to have sent her down into Kent where she was willing to go for her preferment'.[106] Dorcas Clingdove was a laundress who also sold herbs in the summertime for her husband, a gardener: in the course of her daily work, she may have come into contact with many London gentlewomen.

While most women who provided medical care were nurses, London was home to a few female surgeons and cunning-women as well as many midwives. One specialty that occasionally fell within the purview of female practitioners was curing the pox. It was probably one of these experts to whom an irate lodger referred when she scathingly invited her landlady to 'send for your doctrice which healed you of your ill disease', clarifying: 'which if you will have it in English is the French pox.' One Margery Wiltshire, previously married to a surgeon, testified in the divorce

---

[104] Alice Galway, 1633 (LMA, DL/C/630, fo. 95); Joan Johnson, 1635 (LMA, DL/C/234, fo. 138r); Mary Watkins, 1633 (LMA, DL/C/234, fo. 5r); Agnes Wincheley, 1617 (LMA, DL/C/225, fo. 86v).
[105] Susan Gurden, *Office c. Joyce Gurden*, 1616 (LMA, DL/C/192, fo. 17).
[106] Dorcas Clingdove, 1623 (GL MS 9189/1, fos. 51v–52r).

case against Robert Partridge that he had committed adultery. Partridge had come to her house eight or nine years before:

> to have a chamber there, for to be cured of a grief or a disease, which he then had gotten and was infected withal, and she sayeth that the disease wherewith the said Robert was then infected was a very loathsome noisome disease of [her] sight and knowledge, he having his head all over and his forehead and likewise his privy and secret parts ulcerated and full of sores and broken out with issues running out of them in most filthy and loathsome manner.

Margery had taken an active role in his treatment and those of others similarly afflicted. She said she was sure of the diagnosis, 'having dressed him for three days together for the same disease', and affirmed that it was 'such a kind of disease as men usually get by committing adultery or fornication with lewd women of her knowledge having been a surgeon's wife and cured many such diseases'.[107]

Another woman, Thomasine Skarlett, worked under her own name 'professing surgery and using to cure the infectious disease called the pox', which caused her to be summoned no fewer than six times before the College of Physicians between 1588 and 1611 for irregular medical practice. When Thomas Newbury's wife, Margery, asked her for help with her husband's disease, she gave her some ointment and 'directed her the manner how to use or apply the same to her husband'. When Mistress Skarlett visited a month later, Newbury complained that the ointment had made his hair fall out. Thomasine 'then seeing in what state of body the said Thomas Newbury was forbade the said Margery not to come into his company for fear of infection'.[108] Newbury was under the care of two male surgeons as well, but perhaps Margery thought that 80-year-old Thomasine might have some additional wisdom to impart. The old woman's insistence on Margery's sexual abstinence suggests that female practitioners may have been especially attuned to the dangers facing the wives of diseased men. Mistress Skarlett did not only treat the pox. Seventeen years before she testified for the consistory court, she had made a brief appearance in Bridewell for treating the pregnant widow Agnes Brisley. Agnes had been washing windows for a fishmonger when she 'fell out of the window and bruised her side'. She went to Mistress Skarlett 'who professed physic, to help her' and the surgeon told her that she must take a purgation. Agnes thought fit to mention: 'I am with child and ... Mr Thickens is the father', and Mistress Skarlett scolded: 'What a naughty fellow is he. Couldst thou not keep thyself from him?' However, she gave her the purgation anyway, and said that three more purgations would cleanse her.[109] Suspected of abortion, Thomasine was summoned to explain herself before the Bridewell Governors, but nothing seems to have come of it.

---

[107] Thomas Pitches, *Margaret Powell c. Bridget Adland*, 1633 (LMA, DL/C/630, fo. 101v); Margery Wiltshire, *Rose Partridge c. Robert Partridge*, 1611 (LMA, DL/C/220, fo. 720v). See also Thomas Atherton, 1616, *Luce Guppie c. Amy Andrews* (LMA, DL/C/224, fo. 268r).

[108] Thomasine Skarlett, 1615 (LMA, DL/C/223, fo. 280v). For Thomasine's troubles with the College of Physicians, see Margaret Pelling, *Medical Conflicts in Early Modern London: Patronage, Physicians, and Irregular Practitioners, 1550–1640* (Oxford, 2003), 199.

[109] BRHA, BCB 2, fo. 29v.

No witnesses described themselves as cunning-women: to do so would only invite trouble. However, an adultery case provides evidence of the continued appeal of folk medicine even in the face of learned authority. Margaret Debuck fell seriously ill of smallpox around 1600. During or shortly following her illness, she confessed to her husband that she had maintained an illicit love affair with her own brother for several years. The vicious suit that ensued cast John Debuck and his friends against Margaret's family: Margaret's mother, Juliana Wood, energetically maintained that her daughter was innocent, and had been cunningly manipulated by her husband (a Frenchman) and unscrupulous physicians. Debuck, on the other hand, described Mistress Wood as a shady character who drank and dabbled in theft and even witchcraft. Defending his care of his wife, he appealed to learned authority:

> the opinion of divers physicians were used, as namely the opinions of Mr Doctor de Lawney, Mr Doctor Palmer, Mr Doctor Argentine and Mr Doctor Barnard. And the said Mr Doctor Barnard and a surgeon and a midwife came to [his] said wife and there the said Mr Doctor Barnard, being a man very learned and skillful... did direct that [his] wife should be let blood under the tongue by reason of some dangerous sickness that [she] was then in her tongue being swelled in her mouth and rolled up as it were in a lump that she would not speak but a while after [she] had the use of her speech again.[110]

Mistress Wood described this treatment as being tantamount to the deliberate torture of her daughter: she was in the house when Margaret was bled, 'but could not find in her heart to see her to dealt withal'. Afterward, Juliana 'did see eighteen boxes put upon her between the nape of her neck and her shoulders, whence she became extreme sore'. While these painful and ineffective means were employed, Margaret's more basic needs were ignored; she 'never had any good nourishing broth made for her', so Juliana 'went again into the market and bought two great chickens to have dressed for her'. However, this maternal offering was rejected: 'John Debuck's sister and other French folk in the house made talk with him in French and then he would say that Mr Doctor said that chickens were not good for her.' Juliana countered that when she had accompanied Debuck to Doctor Argentine with Margaret's urine for inspection, the doctor had told them that Margaret should be kept warm. But when Juliana nursed her daughter in Debuck's house, he 'would never suffer her to have any fire in the house in the night time whereby to warm anything for her said daughter'. What was more, Debuck forbade her to minister to her daughter: 'seeing her... to come so often to his said wife... and to have such a motherly care of her as she had, seeking to comfort and relieve her as much as in her lay', he told her 'to come no more'. He would not even allow her to appoint 'an honest woman of Croydon, who had kept [Margaret] in her childbed'

---

[110] John Debuck, *John Debuck c. Margaret Debuck alias Winstanley and John Winstanley*, 1601 (LMA, DL/C/216, sl. 335).

as a sick-nurse,[111] instead insisting that only two women Juliana thought had never loved Margaret should care for her.[112]

Juliana admitted that she had consulted an unorthodox source of medical authority: while in the market at Croydon talking with her neighbors about Margaret's illness, she had heard of a woman in Holborn who had helped 'a man...taken suddenly lame in the fields', and accordingly arranged for her to visit her daughter. The woman 'took her by the hand, saying "Alas poor woman, God help thee."' Juliana did not think she was a witch, but Debuck apparently disagreed, as a local woman reported: 'Margaret Debuck's mother came thither and brought with her two women which John Debuck did not like of, but said "Do not you bring any such women hither to my wife", meaning thereby that they were witches as she...understood him, for he said that he would take any *good* means for the recovery of his wife'.[113] Debuck himself referred to the illicit healer as 'a cunning woman...who practiced by sorcery'.[114] Given the pain and expense of learned medicine, it is hardly surprising that patients sometimes preferred the more comforting—if no more effective—ministrations of women and cunning-folk.

Unlike cunning-women, midwives were both respected and respectable. Their fees, ranging from one to five shillings for delivering paupers to several pounds for wealthier clients, made midwifery one of the most lucrative occupations open to women, and midwives prided themselves on their achievements.[115] Some midwives had years of experience. Elizabeth Baylie, the daughter of an Italian merchant and the wife of a coppersmith, testified in 1617 at the age of 59 years. She had been licensed in 1608, and at that time had claimed fourteen years of experience, producing a committee of six matrons as satisfied customers. Producing six or eight testimonials and asserting a certain number of years of experience was the usual procedure for midwives seeking to be licensed. They may have first trained as midwives' deputies, like Joan Johnson, a 36-year-old woodmonger's wife in Whitechapel. Some were never licensed.[116]

Licensed midwives swore to attend women whether rich or poor, and to refuse to consent to immoral acts such as giving birth in secret. Nonetheless Anne Stockdale, licensed in 1616, confessed in 1619 that she had secretly attended Anne Darrell, a gentlewoman living in London with her lover. Thomas Stevens visited Mistress Stockdale once or twice to arrange for her services, and when Anne Darrell went into labor, Stevens sent his man to fetch the midwife, who found Anne 'very sick and in great pain and travail'. Stevens requested Mistress Stockdale 'to use her best skill', offering her the munificent sum of eight pounds. The midwife safely

---

[111] A rare instance of mixed sick- and childbed-nursing.
[112] Juliana Wood (LMA, DL/C/216, sl. 397–8, 393–5).
[113] Juliana Wood and Winifred Smith (LMA, DL/C/216, sl. 400–401, 360); emphasis added.
[114] John Debuck (LMA, DL/C/216, sl. 334).
[115] One anonymous London midwife earned £50 for 37 deliveries in 1704. See Doreen Evenden, *The Midwives of Seventeenth-Century London* (Cambridge, 2000), 125–30.
[116] Elizabeth Baylie, 1617 (LMA, DL/C/225, fos. 40v–41r); Vicar-General Book 10, 1607–1611 (LMA, DL/C/339, fo. 55v); Joan Johnson (LMA, DL/C/234, fos. 138r, 139r). On the training and licensing of London midwives, see Evenden, *The Midwives of Seventeenth-Century London*, 24–78.

delivered the baby, with no help but that of two maidservants equally sworn to secrecy, in contravention to the custom that demanded that only matrons attend births. The baby girl was spirited away, wrapped in a cloak, to Anne Stockdale's house and was privately baptized 'Anne' by the curate of St Sepulchre with two servants as godparents. Mistress Stockdale found a wet-nurse, Goodwife Gurnett, to nurse the child. When this scheme was unravelled by a watchful beadle, the midwife landed temporarily in Newgate.[117]

Elizabeth Besey's testimony from 1633 illustrates the long hours and stress involved in safely delivering women in childbed. Mistress Besey, 63, was a widow and had been licensed since 1618 when her husband, the gentleman Thomas Besey, was still alive. Agnes Fisher, a former client, instigated a suit against Elizabeth after her infant died, and the midwife was at pains to explain that she had acted responsibly. She claimed that she had come to Agnes' labor

> so soon as she had notice thereof or could well leave such other women as she had then in labour or were under her hands to be delivered and remained and continued with her at times needful, duly helping and assisting her in her labours until such time as she was well and safely delivered of her child, which was as [she] believeth the next morning after [she] came to her as aforesaid, she coming unto her (*ut credit*) about six of the clock in the morning.

During this ordeal, Elizabeth explained, she 'did sometimes (being wearied with labour and her former watching with other women) take a short nap', but only 'whilst the said Agnes was without pain', and, she said, she was 'very wakeful' and could assist Agnes whenever necessary. The midwife's involvement did not end after the birth. Since Agnes's baby died soon after birth, Elizabeth attended the infant's burial, at which time Agnes 'grudgingly and reprovingly' accused the midwife of carelessness, saying that the 'child might have lived'. Elizabeth reported that she 'without malice or any discontent and thinking rather to cheer her up than to dishearten her did jestingly reply that she might give God thanks for sparing her for if she had not as many lives as a cat she might have died too'. She sent her daughter to check on Agnes six days after the delivery, and was pleased to hear that she was 'in good health and strength of body and up about her household employment'.[118]

In another case involving the death of a child, the midwife was more to blame. In 1598, an infant of Robert and Anne Payne died within a fortnight after birth, and the gruesome injuries sustained to its skull led to an inquiry into the competence of the midwife, Katherine Herman. Two barber-surgeons and another midwife were called as expert witnesses. At the examination of the child's body, the surgeon William Foster was asked by the women there whose fault it was, and he replied ambiguously that it was a 'hard question'. He explained to the judge later that

---

[117] Vicar-General Book 12, 1616–1623 (DL/C/341, fo. 26). Anne Stockdale, *John Darrell c. Anne Darrell*, 1619 (LMA, DL/C/226, 2nd series, fos. 13–14).

[118] Elizabeth Besey, *Agnes Fisher c. Elizabeth Besey*, 1633 (LMA, DL/C/194, fos. 83–4). For Elizabeth Besey's licensing, see LMA, DL/C/342, fo. 70v.

though he was convinced that the midwife had been at fault, he had been unwilling to answer for fear of frightening the other pregnant women: 'there were divers women there and some of them with child and he knew not but did suspect that they would take some contempt or doubt of themselves and of their own children.'[119] This prudent silence was also adopted by the other midwife called in as an expert witness. Katherine Scolt alias Henrick, a native of Antwerp who had practiced in cases of 'danger and extremity' for over twenty years, had no qualms about condemning Herman to the court. She noted that Mistress Herman's missing forefinger was a serious impediment, and said that she was deficient in both knowledge and skill. Mistress Henrick had been sent for before to repair Mistress Herman's handiwork, and had visited Payne's child a week after birth. The women there had asked her what ailed the child and how to help it, but she hadn't answered for fear of causing problems for herself as an alien: she 'would not tell where the fault was especially for that it was an Englishwoman that had delivered Mistress Payne of that child'. It seems doubtful that Katherine Henrick herself was licensed, which may account for both her unwillingness to challenge Mistress Herman directly and her insistence that she practiced mostly among her friends 'and especially upon urgent occasions and in cases of necessity'.[120] Maintaining good relationships with potential clients, other practitioners, and the authorities was an aspect of the profession that no midwife could afford to overlook.

Other occupations

A very few women returned to service after marrying: it was contrary to custom, and any wife who lived away from her husband in service could expect to have to justify herself. Women with children were also unattractive to employers. A tailor reported that 'Rose Morris about Christmas last was a twelvemonth... was his household servant'. She had 'affirmed and reported that she was a married wife and had a husband living', and this had apparently been no impediment, but ultimately her master 'suspecting the said Rose Morris to be with child displaced her out of his service'. Rose's unusual marital situation was considered to be in keeping with her generally shady reputation.[121] Married servants also had divided loyalties, and might not keep their employers' secrets. Dorothy Tawton served a ship's captain and his wife. When her husband (a barber-surgeon 'nothing worth') visited her, she asked him: 'William, who dost thou think is in bed with my mistress?' 'I cannot tell,' he replied. 'Mr Chapman,' she answered, and when he did not believe her, she led him 'to the top of the stairs and looked into the chamber and then and there saw the said Chapman and... Jane Heley in naked bed together' at two o'clock in the afternoon.[122]

---

[119] William Foster, *John Payne c. Katherine Herman*, 1598 (LMA, DL/C/215, sl. 405–6).
[120] Katherine Henrick, 1598 (LMA, DL/C/215, sl. 387–8).
[121] When she had worked for a widow, drawing drink in her cellar, she once asked one Luce Thomas to take her place while she ran an errand. She borrowed Luce's hat and went out, never to return. William Richardson and Luce Thomas, 1617 (LMA, DL/C/224, fos. 365v, 345r).
[122] William Tawton, 1633 (LMA, DL/C/630, fo. 156).

Nonetheless, some women did go back into service, because their husbands were at sea, or had left them, or because of poverty. Those who did so tended to be young, still within the normal age range for servants, like Joan Penny, 28 or 29, who reported: '[she] doth not live with her husband neither hath done these two or three years last past, and the occasion why they live apart is for that they have no means to live and keep house together and for no other cause and her husband now liveth as a servant at the Red Lion tavern near Billingsgate who is by trade a vintner and there draweth wine.' Joan seemed anxious to present herself as being superior to a common maid of all work: 'she doth not do all her ordinary work as an ordinary servant doth for her said mistress having but a little household putteth all her clothes forth to washing, insomuch as [she] doth not wash... neither doth scour.' Anne Smith and her husband, Thomas, a harness-marker, illustrated the risks of early marriage. Anne, 23, had been married for eight years already, but 'although she be a wife yet she is constrained to get her living by any lawful means as she can to maintain her and by being a servant to other men'. Thomas Smith may have been an apprentice, unable to acknowledge his marriage.[123]

Widows could also go back to service, although few would find willing employers. No widowed servant over the age of 50 appeared as a witness, and the average age of the ten widowed servants who did testify was barely over 40, lower than the average age of nearly 49 for the 354 widows out of service. Charitable or civic institutions may have been more likely than individuals to employ widows, doing so as a means of poor relief. Agnes Basely, 40, servant to the master of King's Hospital in Islington, said she had 'formerly been sent to the aforesaid hospital by the masters of St Bartholomew's hospital in London, and hath her maintenance from the said Hospital of St Bartholomew's aforesaid and thereby liveth'. Mary Adams reported serving the Master Lieutenant of the Tower. One widowed servant, Elizabeth Ratcliffe, a recent immigrant from Warwickshire, may have entered service in London in order to be nearer to her son. She reported that she had borne 'a base child born of her body begotten by her deceased husband before her... marriage', and another witness specified: 'it was a boy and is about fourteen years old and is an apprentice here in London about Pye Corner with a saddler.'[124]

Other institutions also employed women. The fees playgoers paid every time they entered a finer enclosure were collected by women like Audrey Beeston, 29, who had been 'appointed by the company of players of the Red Bull... to see what monies were taken at a twopenny gallery or room in the same playhouse'. She was married to the player Robert Beeston, and noted that she had 'a share thereof in her own right'. Customers could be difficult: when Joan Hewes demanded money from Luke Bryan, he refused: '"Pay?" quoth the said Bryan, "you are a scold." "A scold?" quoth the said Hewes, "it would set your kitchen on fire to keep many such

---

[123] Joan Penny, 1622 (LMA, DL/C/228, fo. 242r); Anne Smith, 1623 (GL MS. 9189/1, fo. 146).
[124] Agnes Baseley, 1615 (LMA, DL/C/223, fo. 129r); Mary Adams, 1573 (LMA, DL/C/211/1, fo. 170v); Elizabeth Ratcliffe, 1618 (LMA, DL/C/224, fo. 331r); William Manley, 1618 (LMA, DL/C/225, fo. 230r).

scolds."'[125] Although one man said 'there could no woman keep a playhouse door but she must be a whore', the women who worked in playhouses were often elderly. Mary Wells, who sold fruit at the Red Bull, was a 60-year-old widow, while Audrey Beeston's colleague Juliana Harrison was 64.[126] The Inns of Court provided employment for couples like Elizabeth and William Chapman: he was a porter, and she was 'likewise employed at the same Inns in carrying of letters and such like'. Mary Lee testified: 'both she ... and her husband belong to Serjeant's Inn in Fleet Street where [her] husband is butler there and [she] doth help him to lay the cloths and such like business.'[127]

A final contingent were teachers. Some catered to the upwardly mobile, instructing children and gentlewomen in music and dancing. Frances Gooche, the wife of a poor clerk in Chancery, 'a little low woman somewhat crooked-shouldered', lived 'partly by teaching gentlemen's children to work and play of instruments and good behaviour and such things as are fit for gentlewomen to learn'. A surgeon thought she 'had very good skill in music and in dancing and was a modest woman', so seeing 'that she went sometimes abroad to teach music and to dance, he ... spake unto her to teach his children'. She agreed and 'took a lodging' close to his house 'where his children went unto her to learn the space of four or five months and likewise his ... father's daughters (that were young) were her scholars, she going home to his ... father's house to teach them'. She taught 'his daughters both to sing, play on instruments and dance and likewise to work with the needle and to read'. Other schoolmistresses taught children of humbler status to sew and to read. Their own level of education was not necessarily high. Mary Swanie, a cooper's wife, said she got her living by her husband's trade and 'by teaching of children', but her signature was composed of a single (albeit nicely formed) 'M'. Elizabeth Burroughs, a scrivener's wife who kept a school, managed two hesitant initials. Of course, an inability to write did not mean that a woman could not read. Elizabeth Ellel said that she taught 'young children to read and work with their needles', but she signed with a mark.[128]

Crime and prostitution

Although many poor women claimed to live by their honest labor, not all labor was 'honest'. Some women dabbled in prostitution or crime to supplement their meager earnings, while others relied entirely on the sex trade, cozening, or theft to support themselves. The capital offered many opportunities for women willing

---

[125] Audrey Beeston and Mary Wells, *Joan Hewes c. Luke Bryan*, 1618 (LMA, DL/C/225, fos. 341r, 340v).
[126] Laurence Johnson, *Mary Philips c. Richard Christopher*, 1607 (LMA, DL/C/217, p. 192); Mary Wells and Juliana Harrison (LMA, DL/C/225, fos. 340, 342).
[127] Elizabeth Chapman, 1629 (LMA, DL/C/232, fo. 278v); Mary Lee, 1624 (GL MS 9189/1, fo. 149r).
[128] Richard Worme, Alice Jones, and Alexander Baker, 1608 (LMA, DL/C/218, pp. 81, 114, 118–19). Mary Swanie, 1611 (LMA, DL/C/220, fo. 463); Elizabeth Burroughs, 1634 (LMA, DL/C/630, fos. 212–13); Elizabeth Ellel, 1616 (LMA, DL/C/224, fo. 82).

or desperate enough to enter the underground economy. London's richly displayed wares and relative anonymity provided occasions for pilfering and fraud, and prostitution throve, fueled by a large population of single, transient men. Most of these were apprentices or servants, described by the maidservant poet Isabella Whitney as:

> handsome men, that must not wed
> except they leave their trade.
> They oft shall seek for proper girls,
> and some perhaps shall find:
> (That need compels, or lucre lures
> to satisfy their mind.)[129]

However, visiting gentlemen, foreign merchants, ambassadors, and young men at the Inns of Court also appeared as clients in the minute books of the Bridewell Court of Governors, as did London citizens.[130] When the reforming governors of the 1570s pressed men and women arrested for lewd living to inform on their erstwhile companions, these harlots, bawds, and clients were often able to provide extensive descriptions of past trysts and notable brothels, embroiling an ever-growing number of people. Humbler streetwalkers and petty thieves also came to Bridewell when they were caught in the act, arrested walking suspiciously late, or captured in raids on houses of bad fame.

For a few London courtesans, prostitution offered rewards far beyond the proceeds of honest labor. Thomasine Breame, who left her husband, the esquire Arthur Breame, around 1574, confessed to the Bridewell governors about two years later that she had been 'kept' by a succession of men who paid her board and gave her fine gifts of money and clothing. Edmund English gave her 'money to discharge things as she needed, and a suit of apparel which cost ten pounds', and one Mr Kingston 'gave her a petticoat of three or four pounds and gave her three or four times two angels at a time to the value of five pounds or more'. Timothy Fielding 'gave her a gown of silk changeable taffeta and other things to the value of twenty marks' and a draper named Rye gave her a morning gown. Since her lovers paid for her living expenses, she was able to afford both a maidservant and a manservant, and to accumulate a splendid wardrobe. Mistress Breame's success only increased her ability to attract wealthy gentlemen and to pick and choose among her suitors: she reported with some pride that 'Mr Bales and Mr Best in Woodstreet resorted to her many times, and asked her the question to have the use of her body, but they never had it'.[131]

Beneath these privileged heights, other women worked in brothels. One of the fullest descriptions of a popular brothel was provided in January 1578 by Elizabeth Kirkeman. She recounted that twelve months before, she 'dwelt at Gilbert East's at

---

[129] 'Wyll and Testament', in *A sweet nosgay, or pleasant posye contayning a hundred and ten phylosophicall flowers* (London, 1573), sig. C5r.
[130] Paul Griffiths, 'The Structure of Prostitution in Elizabethan London', *Continuity and Change* 8.1 (1993), 55.
[131] BRHA, BCB 2, fos. 13r–14v.

Clerkenwell' along with Mary Dornelley 'and divers other harlots whom she knoweth not'. Other women, like one Elizabeth Coop, came there during the day. Mary Dornelley, Elizabeth said, 'had a silk gown and was there abused and kept especially for by gentlemen and wealthy men with velvet gaskins and such apparel and not for the common folk', but this distinction was not absolute, as the pimp William Mekens 'brought many men, most countrymen, drovers, and others unto East to abuse Mary Dornelley and other harlots'. For wealthy clients, the harlots were finely apparelled,[132] as when East's women went to the brothel of his colleague to entertain rich gentlemen: 'Black Luce of Clerkenwell did agree with East and his wife that when Black Luce had any great guests that [Elizabeth Kirkeman] or such other women as East had should go to them to Luce's house and wear Mary Dornelley's gown. And Luce Baynham should have the one half of the money and East the other half of the rest.' When Elizabeth went there, 'a stranger of the ambassador's in Fleet Street had the use of her body' and 'Luce had then half and East's wife had half of the rest'. The prostitutes themselves were left with a mere quarter of the proceeds.[133]

Among the brothel-keepers of London, East appears to have been relatively exploitative: while most prostitutes kept roughly half of their earnings, East demanded an unusually large proportion even when he did not have to share with Black Luce. When two strangers visited Mary Dornelley and Elizabeth Kirkeman, they 'gave either of them to East ten shillings and to Mary and [Elizabeth] five shillings apiece, whereof East had twelvepence a piece besides'. Usually, to make a few shillings a day, the prostitutes entertained several modest clients instead of one great one. Elizabeth noted with awe that 'Mary had sometimes to do twelve times in a day with the knaves'; her own record was four men. The brothel accepted humble men when richer ones were absent: 'when there was not other to serve, many prentices came thither.' Mary Dornelley herself reported that 'the rooms were never empty' and that she 'got some days twenty shillings a day by that means. East and his wife for their parts had commonly fifteen shillings of it.' The women who lived in East's house were kept busy, but their fare was more luxurious than that of women who worked 'honestly', and they certainly had plenty to drink, as Elizabeth and Mary remembered: 'some brought half a sugar loaf and the guests sent for so much wine and good cheer that the wine was so plentiful that they had rather drink beer than wine.'[134]

There is little evidence that East exercised much coercive control over the women in his house, with the notable exception of his wife. Elizabeth Kirkeman reported that 'East would be very angry with his wife when she did weep and was loath to play the harlot and bid her go and earn money with committing whoredom, and thrust her upstairs'.[135] Unlike East's wife, Elizabeth and Mary Dornelley could

---

[132] See Cristine M. Varholy, '"Rich Like a Lady": Cross-Class Dressing in the Brothels and Theaters of Early Modern London', *Journal for Early Modern Cultural Studies* 8.1 (2008), 4–34.
[133] BRHA, BCB 3, fo. 279/pp. 609–10.
[134] Ibid. fos. 279–281r/pp. 609–13.
[135] Ibid. fo. 280r/p. 611.

leave East (as indeed they eventually did) if they thought they could do better elsewhere. Whether their circumstances improved, however, is open to question. When Elizabeth was arrested and brought to Bridewell she was living with the widow Rose Browne, who kept a humbler, more egalitarian brothel: 'divers serving men, blackamores, and other persons resort to her house . . . and such as would not deal with the same Rose she procured them to deal with this Elizabeth.' Both Rose and Elizabeth became infected with a foul disease, and were ultimately arrested in a raid.[136] One of the disadvantages of working in modest brothels was that they lacked the political connections that protected the establishments of Gilbert East and Black Luce.

Keeping a successful brothel seems to have provided Black Luce Baynham with a substantial income. Many women who ran brothels, however, worked like Rose Browne and East's wife alongside their harlots, and suffered from frequent disruptions by the forces of order. Margery Terry, a consistory court witness convincingly identified as a bawd, was by no means prosperous. The evidence provided by other deponents suggests that she had been subjected to constant official harassment, and that she supplemented her income from bawdry with theft and fraud. Margery Terry, 45, described herself as a widow born in Wiltshire who had been living in the parish of St Sepulchre for fifteen years. Others offered a more critical account of her life. According to them, Margery spent several years living in various places in Clerkenwell. John Evans reported that he and others had searched her house in Charterhouse Lane several times within the last seven years and 'there did find wenches that she kept in her house of purpose to give entertainment unto men to be naught with them'. The women were taken to Bridewell and Margery was punished, but she changed her residence rather than her occupation: 'from thence she removed into St John's street where she kept a lewd house for some two years together and there she and her wenches were questioned and punished as before.' More recently, John Snowe reported that she kept a bawdy house in Mr Goodcole's Rent in Clerkenwell. She and some of her 'wenches' were questioned by Justice Houghton and punished in Bridewell, while others 'scaped away'.[137]

Margery's bawdry was not very profitable, perhaps as a result of these constant interruptions. Snowe thought she was 'a very poor and needy woman of no worth'. She was also a thief. William Eagles, a gardener, reported that she had just accosted him and invited him to drink with her when a group of people accused her of stealing a laced ruff band. Margery was taken to the house of a carpenter's wife, where she was further questioned and searched, but 'she very impudently and shamelessly denied it, and that with fearful oaths, and making search about her clothes and pockets it could not be found'. In the end, however, 'they found it about her being tied about her knee and her stockings over it very cunningly'.[138]

---

[136] Ibid. fo. 277/pp. 605–6.
[137] Margery Terry, John Evans, John Snowe, and Edmund Bollifant, *Tobias Awdley c. Anne Elsden*, 1624–1625 (LMA, DL/C/229, fos. 3, 117, 103, 116).
[138] William Eagles and Anne Elsbey, 1624 (LMA, DL/C/229, fos. 117, 119).

These unsavory activities were in keeping with Margery's alleged role in drugging an elderly rich widow to make her acquiesce to an exploitative marriage.[139]

If brothel women's lives were disrupted by exploitative keepers, venereal disease, and legal incursions, still more vulnerable were the independent wanderers hauled to Bridewell as common harlots and nightwalkers. Streetwalkers did whatever they could to piece together a living, combining prostitution with theft, pilfering, cozening, and receiving stolen goods, as well as honest needlework. They were often arrested by the watch in small groups; these loose-knit associations may have helped to protect them from the dangers of the streets. Lone women were at risk, as Margaret Maple discovered when she was found in a churchyard with a man 'having his hose about his heels, of whom she had a groat, and after he had his pleasure of her he would have had the groat again and thereupon threatened to kill her'.[140] Other women specialized in picking, filching, or cozening. Alice Preston was twice punished as a 'cozener of pewter dishes and pots' from alewives, and Isabel Simpson was whipped for 'pilfering a gold ring' and 'filching of buttons'.[141]

Sybil Love, a frequent 'guest' in Bridewell, was labeled a 'common harlot and an idle vagabond' on 21 April 1574 and given 'a passport to go to Ware where she sayeth she was born'. She remained in the city, however, and was arrested again in July. This time she was whipped along with three other women, all 'common runagates, harlots, rogues and idle persons'. Sybil seems to have remained for some time a prisoner in Bridewell, where she and her fellows often rebelled against the matron. On 8 January 1575 they were punished for being 'common spoilers of their work', and by spring, the despairing women threatened to kill themselves. One Dorothy Smith suggested to Alice Sands 'that if she would hang herself she would help her, and that if any of them did so the house should be put down'. Six women, including Sybil, were punished for being 'unruly and swearing and threatening to hang themselves'. At some point Sybil was released, but she found herself back in Bridewell on 19 September 1576 along with a companion, Katherine More, 'for that they broke open a poulter's shop and stole certain conies and eggs'. They confessed that Sybil 'brake open the shop and stole away a basket of eggs' while Katherine guarded the door, and were both 'corrected'. Sybil Love was punished yet again for refusing to work almost a year later, although it is not clear whether she had been imprisoned the whole time.[142]

Elizabeth Graunt, one of the women punished for threatening suicide, also combined prostitution with theft. She was arrested as a harlot and nightwalker in November 1574 and again in December, when she reported that one John Arter

---

[139] For the Star Chamber case and a ballad and play loosely based on the forced marriage, see Charles Sisson, *Lost Plays of Shakespeare's Age* (Cambridge, 1936), 80–124.
[140] BRHA, BCB 2, fo. 251r.
[141] BRHA, BCB 3, fos. 93v (p. 237) and 163r (p. 377) for Alice Preston; BCB 2, fos. 49r and 200r, BCB 3, fo. 13r (p. 77) for Isabel Simpson. See also Garthine Walker, 'Women, Theft and the World of Stolen Goods', in Jenny Kermode and Garthine Walker (eds), *Women, Crime and the Courts in Early Modern England* (Chapel Hill, NC, 1994); Walker, *Crime, Gender and Social Order in Early Modern England* (Cambridge, 2003), 159–209.
[142] BRHA, BCB 2, fos. 31r, 52r, 87r, 135r, 174v; BCB 3, fo. 58r/p.167.

'met her in the street and so willed her to go with him into his chamber where she was from five of the clock unto eleven...a-bed'. The following March she was arrested as a harlot and whipped, and she was found walking the streets at night again in May. This time, Elizabeth confessed 'that she received of one Richard Ward, a little boy, a pair of sheets, two napkins, an apron, and a corner kercher'. She had sold one sheet and half a napkin for 3s. 6d. Despite her long record, Elizabeth Graunt also did honest work: when she came to Bridewell yet again in February 1576, during an initiative to make the prisoners pay for their keep, she told the governors that she could 'knit hose and sleeves'.[143]

These 'common nightwalkers' swept up with depressing regularity by the watch were recognizably not respectable London women. When Margaret Archer, a 'common harlot and a drunkard', walked through Shoe Lane in April 1575, 'she met with Margaret Iveson who railed at her and called her hedgewhore'. Rather than retaliating in kind or defending herself, Margaret Archer 'took of her a hat and carried the same with her and laid it to Joan Seward at the Horseshoe in St John's Street for two pots of beer'.[144] However, some women in the sex trade were primarily honest working women whose experiments with paid sex were occasional or opportunistic. One such woman was Frances Andrews, who had left her husband and lived, she said, by 'starching of ruff bands to shops'.[145] When she lodged with Audrey Burges, one Mistress Booth visited the house. Finding Frances there, Mistress Booth told Audrey Burges that Frances had formerly lodged with her, and 'that in the time she lay at her house she lay with one Dennis an Irishman one night and she had of him for that night's lodging two shillings'. Frances replied: 'By God...thou wast my bawd...It was best for thee to hold thy tongue.'[146]

Bawdry could also be casual or opportunistic. Katherine Parry complained that Philippina Smith sent for her to come to her house under false pretenses: Philippina claimed that her brother was there, but in fact 'there was a Dutchman in her house that desired the company of a handsome gentlewoman and willed her that she would not be squeamish for he was an old man'. In a different case, when a maid was delivering some goods to a Mistress Barnaby, the widow 'led her up into the top of the house to one in the habit of a gentleman, and there whispered in his ear and went away hastily as though she had gone to fetch something in haste, and left her there with the man alone'. Then the stranger 'held her that as she said that she could not get from him sooner, using persuasions to have had her play the whore with him'. She only escaped, the girl said, when 'she offered to cry out'.[147]

Although the sex trade was one area in which women were not accused of competing with men, the opportunities it offered for female profit were constrained by concerns about sexual sin and social disorder. In the 1570s, the attitude of the

---

[143] BRHA, BCB 2, fos. 78r, 86v, 100r, 134v, 135r, 249r.
[144] Ibid. fos. 34v, 109v.
[145] Frances Andrews, 1618 (LMA, DL/C/226, 4th series, fo. 38r).
[146] Audrey Burges, *Thomas Andrews c. Frances Andrews* (GL MS 9189/1, fo. 4r).
[147] William Barret, *Philippina Smith c. Katherine Parry*, 1635 (LMA, DL/C/234, fo. 41v); Edmund Hawes, *Anne Foote c. Lancelot Grimshaw*, 1610 (LMA, DL/C/219, fo. 138v).

godly governors of Bridewell was clear: illicit sex was sinful, and both prostitutes and their clients were to be punished—by whipping and imprisonment for the poor, and by fines for the rich. Harlots were to be reformed if possible, transformed into honest women through marriage or service; if not, they were to be kept in prison, exiled from the city, or intimidated by threats of punishment. However, the Bridewell governors encountered opposition in their attempt to enforce moral order. As Paul Griffiths has demonstrated, wealthy men implicated during the crackdown on London brothels in the 1570s resisted the idea that their private lives should be subject to scrutiny. Although Anthony Bate, goldsmith and brothel connoisseur, lost his case in Star Chamber against Bridewell, subsequent changes in enforcement patterns suggest that the governors abandoned their reforming zeal. After 1600, dwindling numbers of Londoners were accused of specifically sexual offenses, while more men—and especially women—were brought to Bridewell for street disorders. Some of these, especially the almost entirely female population of 'nightwalkers', may still have been prostitutes, but the drive against brothels, courtesans, and their clients faded away.[148]

By shifting their attention from prostitution as fornication to prostitution as a street crime, the Bridewell governors were able to target the aspect of the sex trade that most threatened economic and social order. Like humble alehouses, nightwalking harlots attracted the men who could least afford to waste their money, and for whose disorderly pleasures London authorities had little sympathy. Prostitutes who catered to the wealthy could discreetly find funds—if not fathers—for their illegitimate children, like Alice Newsham, who 'famed herself to be with child' and whose bawd 'procured such gentlemen as resorted to her house to give the said Alice some monies, telling the said gentlemen that the said child wherewith she was great was gotten amongst them'.[149] Streetwalkers' infants, on the other hand, were more likely to fall on public charges. Even as illicit sex ceased to hold the attention of the Bridewell governors, poor women continued to be arrested as disorderly vagrants and thieves. All too often, the survival strategies of the poorest Londoners—and especially the poorest women—looked to the authorities like dishonesty and disorder.[150]

CONTINUITY AND CHANGE

Histories of early modern women's work have long been subordinated to narratives about patriarchy, capitalism, and industrialization. Alice Clark, whose seminal study structured much of the ensuing debate, argued that the locus of production in the household in the early seventeenth century benefited women. Unlike the

---

[148] For Bate and opposition to Bridewell, see Paul Griffiths, 'Contesting London Bridewell, 1576–1580', *Journal of British Studies* 42.3 (2003), 283–315. For changes in the offenses punished in Bridewell, see Archer, *The Pursuit of Stability*, 239; Griffiths, *Lost Londons*, 451.

[149] Thomas Shaxton, *Office prom. Brettingham c. Alice Newsham alias Fawkes*, 1616 (LMA, DL/C/224, fos. 196v–197r).

[150] Griffiths, *Lost Londons*, 204–9.

parasitic middle-class wives of the industrial age or their poorer sisters drudging in factories, Clark claimed, medieval and early modern women worked hand in hand with their husbands and brothers. In consequence, they and their economic contributions were valued.[151] Much of this thesis has since been challenged. Clark's assumption that early modern artisans employed their wives and daughters in their workshops has not been substantiated. The evidence presented here suggests that by the late sixteenth century, artisans' wives were already more likely to pursue different lines of work from their husbands, just as they did a century later.[152] It is also unclear whether working together would have produced the marital harmony and mutual respect that Clark described. London women may well have preferred to work independently rather than to follow orders in their husband's shops. The economic partnership that Clark identified in household workshops may have arisen just as well when husbands and wives worked separately to support their families. A popular ballad held that parallel spheres were best: when husband and wife could not forbear criticizing one another's work, and changed places for a day, both failed miserably.[153]

While later historians have placed less emphasis on the site of work, the descent from a late medieval 'golden age'—or at least from a slightly less leaden one—is still debated. Proponents of a tempered golden age emphasize demography, at least where England is concerned.[154] Caroline Barron has argued that from 1370 to 1470 or so, low population and extensive labor shortages gave women in London unusually broad economic opportunities: 'their range of options and prospects differed only slightly from those of men who shared their level of prosperity.' A rising population in the sixteenth century erased many of these gains, however, steadily forcing women out of protected crafts and trades.[155] Meanwhile, others point out that even in the best of times, women did not enjoy equal access to protected trades and were paid less than their male counterparts. Instead of conceptualizing women's work in terms of change, Judith Bennett suggests, we must realize that this was 'a history, at least for Europe since the twelfth century, of new designs embroidered on a cloth of oppression and deprivation'.[156] Bennett's work on women's declining presence as brewsters after the Black Death challenges the notion of a golden age in the late Middle Ages, emphasizing women's vulnerability to changes in commercial organization and technology: as brewing ceased to

---

[151] Alice Clark, *The Working Life of Women in the Seventeenth Century* (London, 1919).
[152] See Peter Earle, 'The Female Labour Market in London in the Late Seventeenth and Early Eighteenth Centuries', *Economic History Review* 42.3 (1989), 338.
[153] *The woman to the plow and the man to the hen-roost, or, A fine way to cure a cot-quean* (London, 1675). See also Rogers, *Matrimoniall honour*, 198–9.
[154] Demography plays a less central role in the German historiography. See Wiesner, *Working Women*; Martha C. Howell, *Women, Production, and Patriarchy in Late Medieval Cities* (Chicago, 1986).
[155] Caroline M. Barron, 'The "Golden Age" of Women in Medieval London', *Reading Medieval Studies* 15 (1989), 47; and 'Introduction: The Widows' World in Later Medieval London', in Caroline M. Barron and Anne F. Sutton (eds), *Medieval London Widow, 1300–1500* (London, 1994), xiv.
[156] Judith M. Bennett, '"History that Stands Still": Women's Work in the European Past', *Feminist Studies* 14.2 (1988), 280.

be a part-time, domestic trade offering low prestige and low profits, and became characterized by large-scale production requiring large capital, profits increased, and women disappeared from what had previously been a trade they had dominated.[157] Indeed, one cannot ignore the legal and cultural restrictions that prevented women from gaining a sure foothold in the trade and craft world. The medieval London silkwomen, for all their strong occupational identity, did not form into a company that might have kept competition at bay.

It makes sense, then, to think of early modern women's labor in terms of a decline from a not-so-golden age. Even if low wages and restricted opportunities defined the lives of poor women throughout the medieval and early modern periods, their fortunes varied. When population pressure and declining wages eroded the livelihoods of the poor in the sixteenth century, women, always marginal, were especially hard-hit.[158] The hard years of the late sixteenth century may have been a low point, but change was to come very slowly. Earle describes a similar labor market in London for 1660–1750, with most women working in service, nursing, needlework, charring, laundry, or retailing food and drink. Desperate competition meant that women were likely to be underemployed and low-paid, which, he writes, 'is hardly surprising when so many women were chasing so few types of jobs, none of which were organized or protected by guilds or livery companies'.[159] On the other hand, some aspects of the female labor market had improved by the Restoration. If London around 1600 was largely a city of artisans based in the Square Mile, in 1700 it had become a city of consumers, and its center of gravity had shifted towards the West End. One result of this was a burgeoning demand for maidservants, who commanded significantly higher wages. While maidservants in this study made about forty shillings a year, by 1662 Pepys was paying twice that for a cook-maid. The upward trend continued, much to the indignation of employers like Defoe, who in 1725 complained: 'Women servants are now so scarce that from thirty and forty shillings a year, their wages are increased of late to six, seven, and eight pounds per annum, and upwards.'[160] As a result, domestic service, with all its disadvantages, became more attractive to adult women. While fewer than 5 per cent of servants in the 1570–1640 sample were wives or widows, nearly 20 per cent of Earle's later sample of 253 servants fell in these categories.[161]

Other opportunities arose when changing styles introduced new fashions without a history of male professional domination. Elaborate starched ruffs were a thing

---

[157] Judith Bennett, *Ale, Beer, and Brewsters in England: Women's Work in a Changing World, 1300–1600* (Oxford, 1996).
[158] See McIntosh, *Working Women*, 30; Ilana Krausman Ben-Amos, 'Women Apprentices in the Trades and Crafts of Early Modern Bristol', *Continuity and Change* 6.2 (1991), 228.
[159] *A City Full of People*, 121.
[160] Samuel Pepys, *The Diary of Samuel Pepys*, ed. Robert Latham and William Matthews, 11 vols (Berkeley, Calif., 2000), vol. 4, 86; Daniel Defoe, *Every-bodys business, is no-bodys business; or Private abuses, publick grievances* (London, 1725), 3.
[161] Earle, *A City Full of People*, 116. On domestic service after 1600, see Tim Meldrum, *Domestic Service and Gender 1660–1750: Life and Work in the London Household* (New York, 2000).

of the past, but periwigs required extensive care,[162] and beginning in the 1670s and 1680s, women began to wear mantuas, loose-fitting dresses produced by female mantua-makers, not male tailors. Although the tailors' guilds fought the changing tide, their efforts to suppress mantua-makers were ultimately ineffective. Mantua-making was the most prestigious of the needle trades, and attracted many apprentices; a skilled mantua-maker with a reliable clientele could command a considerable income. Similarly, by the mid-eighteenth century, London premiums for apprenticeships in millinery rose as high as £60. However, the lack of protective regulation and the capital required to set up shop prevented skilled female trades like mantua-making and millinery from becoming secure careers; as they became more established, the number of prospective workers surged and journeywomen's wages fell.[163]

Throughout this period, domestic duties, legal regulations, and cultural restrictions effectively prevented women from competing with men for most kinds of work. The restrictions on women's work were not simply derived from the perception that women who 'participated in the cash-based economy in their own right' were 'inappropriately independent, unrestrained by a husband or father and free to indulge in verbal or sexual excess', however.[164] Efforts to keep women out of the paid workforce were unlikely to come from their own households: their husbands benefited from the additional income and neighbors respected wives who kept their households intact and off the poor rates. Instead, opposition was voiced most strongly by male competitors, who successfully argued that scarce jobs should be restricted to the worthy men who bore primary responsibility for the well-being of their households. Women's opportunities waxed and waned as England's population fell and rose, but they were always on uncertain ground, the last to be invited in, and the first to be forced out. Their work—when it ranged beyond a narrow group of largely unregulated occupations—was easily framed as a contributing cause of poverty and social dislocation.

While these restrictions kept male wages—and particularly the remuneration of London citizens—artificially high, female earnings were correspondingly depressed as women battled one another for the few opportunities open to them. Although craftswomen took advantage of the lack of regulation in new manufactures and novel fashions, no amount of skill could compensate for a perpetually overloaded market. Most women were forced to piece together whatever they could find, like the bitter heroine of this pamphlet about a woman who left her uncaring husband:

> . . . then I went to be a nurse,
> my body for to feed.
> Unto a poor woman nurse was I,
> as you may understand:

[162] *Coma berenices, or, The hairy comet* (London, 1676), 24.
[163] Mary Prior, 'Women and the Urban Economy: Oxford 1500–1800', in Prior (ed.), *Women in English Society 1500–1800* (New York, 1985), 111–13; Bridget Hill, *Women, Work, and Sexual Politics in Eighteenth-Century England* (New York, 1989), 95.
[164] McIntosh, *Working Women*, 251.

And always to her work was nigh,
and ready at her command.
Then did I go to housekeeping
which is the best of all:
Three weeks I lay upon a mat
turned up against a wall...
Sometimes I did get sewing work,
and sometimes I got none:
Had not my son Thomas supplied my wants
full hungry had I gone.[165]

[165] With, *Elizabeth Fools warning*, 6–7.

7
Dealing with Death

In 1627, young John Danvers lay dying in the parish of St James Clerkenwell. His wife, Frances, watched by his bedside faithfully: since their marriage seven years before, she had been 'as loving a wife unto him . . . as ever any man had'. However, the comfort Danvers drew from her presence was mixed with sorrow. When a curate visited the dying man and asked him 'whether he was willing to leave the world', he answered: 'with all his heart, for he saw nothing in the world that might make him desire to live, only there was one thing which made him desire to survive this sickness and that was the care he had to provide better for his wife and children.' After his death, Frances Danvers would be left 'in a poor and miserable estate', he feared.[1] Indeed, Frances would soon face a formidable challenge. Left with responsibility for her young children, she would have to decide how to seek a living and whether or not to marry again. If she chose to do so, she would need to find a good second husband. This time, her children's fortunes as well as her own would depend on making a wise decision.

Frances Danvers' dilemma was all too common. Mourning was inevitable in London, where churchyards devoured the young and the old alike, but few could afford to indulge their grief for long. Seeking a tenuous balance, families formed and reformed when disease and accidents struck. For women, the same favorable marriage market that attracted migrant maids helped widows find husbands: they remarried frequently and rapidly, often to bridegrooms younger than themselves. While marriages between relatively young, poor men and older, richer women naturally entailed a certain reversal in the conventional rules of household authority, such matches attracted widows and bachelors alike. London widows were not, however, obliged to remarry for cultural reasons: as household heads, they could remain single, though independence was no guarantee of prosperity. Older widows were more likely to do so, relying on neighborly bonds in the absence of surviving family. For many, the struggle for a fragile subsistence would continue until the end of their lives.

---

[1] William Dugdale and Robert Yates, *Danvers c. Danvers*, 1628 (LMA, DL/C/231, fos. 79r, 77v).

REMARRIAGE IN LONDON

Widows who chose to remarry could claim the support of London's distinctively mercantile and urban culture. Where male lineages are strongly valued, a remarrying widow is easily framed as being disloyal to her adopted family and her children. In contrast, Londoners could appeal to a different kind of loyalty that demanded that money be kept not in the lineage, but in the city, where equitable inheritance and the remarriage of widows supported a dynamic economy.[2]

> [T]his city of London is and hath been happily preserved by the wise and politick consent that all and always the particulars have had to increase the general good estate thereof, thinking it their duty as they got and acquired their substance in this city, so also to spend and defray it in the same: insomuch that whatsoever falleth from the one cometh and groweth unto another.

Some men, the anonymous author of this 1584 treatise wrote, wanted to limit their wives' inheritances, thinking: 'She will marry again, and enrich some other with the fruit of my travail.' But they must learn to 'suffer the goods of this world to have their natural course and condition, which is to be still in exchange, passage, and posting from hand to hand, serving all men'. Any citizen who refused to leave the customary third of his goods to his wife and another third to his children was a virtual traitor to the capital:

> For we often see that one rich man's wealth passeth to the increase of the good estate of another citizen, either by the marriage of the widow, or of the orphan: so that the city though deprived of a member or inhabitant, yet is not destitute of such as may discharge his employment and place. Whereas if this pernicious practice and uncharitable liberty might take root by deeds of gifts and cautelous conveyances to strangers, not only the wife and children may be distressed, but also the state of the city much weakened, and in danger of a great disreputation and decay.[3]

The urban economy demanded that widows be permitted to remarry, and so did religion. 'Marriage is an honourable ordinance of God, fit and necessary for all persons disposed thereunto, to the avoiding of sin and maintenance of a comfortable and sociable Christian life. To restrain or prohibit the same either in maids or widows...is the doctrine of devils.' After all, the author reminded his reader, widowers remarried without pause.

> Make it thine own case, admit thou didst match with a wealthy wife, whose furniture and riches hath increased thy estate, if God should call for her, wouldst thou in a kind memorial of the benefits attained by her means, make thyself a votary to live

---

[2] Barbara A. Hanawalt, *The Wealth of Wives: Women, Law, and Economy in Late Medieval London* (Oxford, 2007), 209.

[3] *A breefe discourse, declaring and aproving the necessarie and inviolable maintenance of the laudable customes of London* (London, 1584), 31, 40, 45.

unmarried? ... why shouldst thou then seem to quarrel with the lawful liberty of thy wife, if she survive thee ... ?[4]

Protestantism, with its rejection of celibacy and the cloister, demanded that marriage be considered as good as perpetual chastity. Gouge insisted that widows and widowers considering remarriage were 'as free as they who were never before married ... We find no restraint from a third, or fourth, or more marriages, if by the divine providence so many wives, or husbands one after another be taken away while there is need for the surviving party to use the benefit of marriage.'[5] A godly conduct book addressed to a widow considering remarriage discussed *whom* to marry, not whether to do so: 'for therein you may best be your own judge, for you know best where your shoe wringeth you.'[6]

Indeed, many London widows found themselves 'inclinable' to new matrimonial ventures. Some young women were already marital veterans, particularly in the seafaring parishes of Whitechapel and Stepney, with their sky-high male mortality rates.[7] Mary Dally, 24 or so, wed Thomas Holder in July 1615, was rapidly widowed, then married the sailor John Brown less than a year later.[8] Anne Philips married Roger Gwin in 1601 around the age of 21, soon lost him, and remarried to Edmund Clifton in 1602 or 1603.[9] Elizabeth Brown was a 28-year-old widow when she married the mariner Jeffrey Dixon of Wapping Wall in 1623. Ten years later, as 'Elizabeth Dixon, widow, of Wapping Wall', she married again, to John Lince.[10]

As London women aged, some acquired formidable marital histories. Rose Downer, 57, was called in 1615 as a witness in a case about mortuary fees in St Andrew in the Wardrobe, and she was indeed an expert, having buried three husbands there, serving as executrix for all three wills: Robert Briggs had died twenty-six years before, Robert Lawson eighteen years before, and Thomas Friend a mere twelve years before. Undiscouraged, she had married for a fourth time, to a wealthy tallow chandler.[11] Indeed, even elderly widows might remarry, although they were less likely to do so.[12] Anne Studds, who deposed in 1627 that she was 60

---

[4] Ibid. 15–16.
[5] William Gouge, *Of domesticall duties* (London, 1622), 187.
[6] Andrew Kingsmill, *A viewe of mans estate wherein the great mercie of God in mans free justification by Christ, is very comfortably declared* (London, 1576), sig. I3v.
[7] The survival rate for East India Company sailors may have been as low as 30% per voyage. Pamela Sharpe, 'Gender at Sea: Women and the East India Company in Seventeenth-Century London', in Penelope Lane, Neil Raven, and K. D. M. Snell (eds), *Women, Work and Wages in England, 1600–1850* (Rochester, NY, 2004), 52.
[8] Mary Brown, 1618 (LMA, DL/C/225, fo. 351v); St Dunstan Stepney register.
[9] Anne Clifton, 1611 (LMA, DL/C/220, fo. 450v); Kings Pyon register.
[10] Elizabeth Dixon, 1627 (GL MS 9189/2, fo. 109r); St Dunstan Stepney register.
[11] Rose Downer, 1615 (LMA, DL/C/223, fos. 251–2).
[12] 17% of widows' marriages by license involved women over the age of 50. Vivien Brodsky, 'Widows in Late Elizabethan London: Remarriage, Economic Opportunity and Family Orientations', in Lloyd Bonfield, Richard Smith, and Keith Wrightson (eds), *The World We Have Gained: Histories of Population and Social Structure* (New York, 1986), 132.

years old, the wife of John Studds, ship carpenter, of Wapping Wall in Stepney, was probably the same Anne Studds, widow of Wapping Wall, who married Edward Ellis, laborer, in 1632. Bridget Mann, who said she was 72 years old when she testified in 1591, had wed her husband, Thomas, a mere eight years before. Joan Webb, 63 in 1588, had married less than a year before her testimony.[13]

While it is only rarely possible to track the marital careers of individual women, quantitative analyses confirm that London widows remarried early and often in the late sixteenth and early seventeenth centuries. To begin with, remarkably few women testifying for the consistory court were widows. As Table 7.1 shows, women had to reach their mid-50s before the proportion of widows exceeded 25 per cent, and even elderly women had a reasonable chance of being married. Many fewer widows testified for the consistory court between 1570 and 1640 than in the early eighteenth century, when the sex ratio had reversed. Fig. 7.1 compares 1,898 married and widowed deponents from 1570 to 1640 with Earle's equivalent sample of 1,054 wives and widows testifying between 1695 and 1720. It shows that women from the earlier period, especially young and middle-aged women, were far less likely to describe themselves as widows. Since mortality rates had, if anything, decreased by 1695 with the disappearance of plague, this suggests that they remarried more often and more quickly. Even the oldest widows had a far better chance of remarrying before 1640 than after 1695.

The absence of widows in London between 1570 and 1640 is best explained by high rates of remarriage. While women's first marriages may have commonly lasted

Table 7.1 Rates of widowhood by age

Age	No. of widows	Total deponents	% widowed
17–18	0	64	0.0
19–21	4	203	2.0
22–24	8	234	3.4
25–26	8	144	5.6
27–28	8	143	5.6
29–31	21	243	8.6
32–33	13	119	10.9
34–35	12	107	11.2
36–38	18	147	12.2
39–42	49	270	18.1
43–47	24	160	15.0
48–52	53	229	23.1
53–57	27	102	26.5
58–65	83	167	46.7
66 and older	36	56	64.3
Total	364	2,388	15.2

[13] Anne Studds, 1627 (GL MS 9189/2, fo. 105r, St Dunstan Stepney register); Bridget Mann, 1591 (LMA, DL/C/214, p. 158); Joan Webb alias Brand, 1588 (LMA, DL/C/213, p. 439).

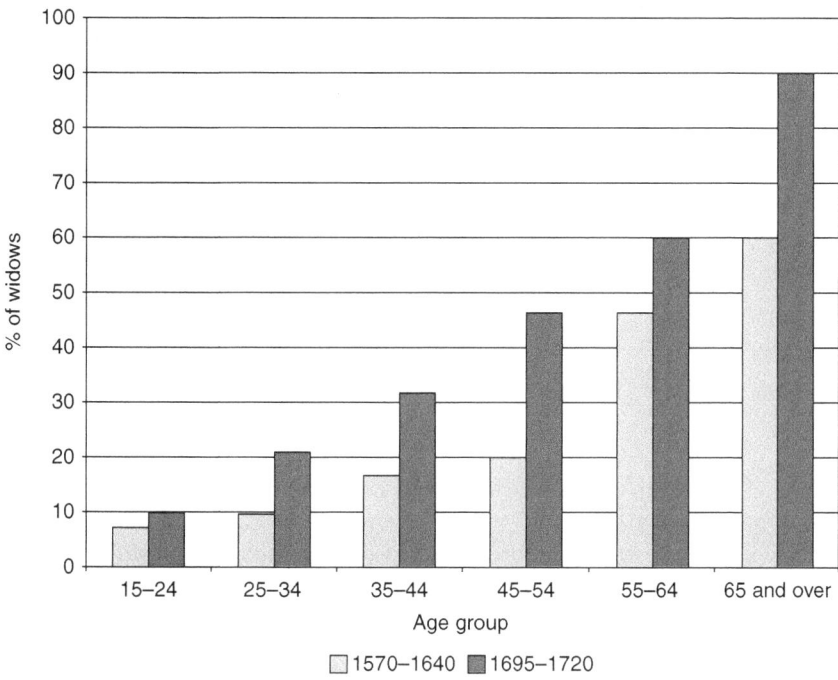

Figure 7.1 The percentage of widows in the ever-married population
Source: For 1695–1725 data, see Earle, *City Full of People*, 163.

as long as twenty years in the country, they were much briefer in unhealthy London. For a sample of 224 middling brides in London between 1660 and 1730, Earle finds that the average duration of marriage was just thirteen years, and the surviving women were widowed at a median age of 35. Similarly, in her analysis of 104 reconstituted London marriages from around 1600, Vivien Brodsky Elliott finds a mean duration of marriage of around twelve years, although this sample includes the marriages of widows and widowers. Even if we optimistically assume that maiden brides (marrying on average around the age of 23 or 24) could expect to be married for fifteen years before their deaths or those of their husbands, then beginning in their late 30s most surviving women would be widowed. Thus many of those in their 30s and older who described themselves as wives must have in fact remarried.[14]

The predominance of remarried widows among older wives can also be demonstrated by an analysis of how long deponents had been married. A little more than 60 per cent of London consistory court wives reported how long they had been married,

---

[14] Peter Earle, *A City Full of People: Men and Women of London, 1650–1750* (London, 1994), 162; Brodsky, 'Widows', 136.

Table 7.2 Estimated percentages of wives previously widowed, by age

Age	Low estimate: wives at least 35 at most recent marriage (%)	High estimate: wives at least 32 at most recent marriage (%)	No. of wives in sample
34–5	1	18	45
36–8	8	24	72
39–42	30	47	117
43–7	35	56	80
48–52	53	60	111
53–7	56	68	41
58–65	57	71	44

making it possible to determine their age at their most recent marriage. Assuming that women who married late were likely to be remarrying widows, one can estimate how many wives had been married before. Table 7.2 provides two such calculations by showing the proportion of women who were at least 35 and at least 32 when they married their current husbands. Since all but about 5 per cent of women were married by those ages (see Table 2.1), these figures are estimates—one surely conservative, the other perhaps generous—of the proportion of remarried widows among wives of different ages. They are by no means perfect, since witnesses' memories of their ages and length of marriage may not have been accurate. Moreover, some women did marry for the first time in their mid-30s, while others were widowed and remarried earlier, so some women have been incorrectly categorized as remarried widows, while others have been mistakenly classified as first-time wives. However, these errors would tend to cancel one another out, and it seems probable that, as the table suggests, most married women from their late forties on had been widowed before.

Yet another way to investigate remarriage rates is to determine the proportion of widows among brides. Here, too, London stands out. The proportion of widows and widowers among marrying English people has been estimated at 30 per cent for 1541, with a slow decline to about 11 per cent for the mid-nineteenth century.[15] In Colyton, Devonshire, about 16 per cent of villagers marrying in 1550–1679 had been previously is widowed, and in Hartland, Yorkshire in 1550–1699 the comparative figure is 12 per cent.[16] In London, on the other hand, as Brodsky and Boulton have found, widows made up 35 per cent of brides marrying by license in

---

[15] E. A. Wrigley and R. S. Schofield, *Population History of England 1541–1871: A Reconstruction* (London, 1981), 258–9.
[16] Charles Carlton, 'The Widow's Tale: Male Myths and Female Reality in 16th and 17th Century England', *Albion* 10.2 (1978), 122.

1598–1619, and about 43 per cent of Stepney brides between 1617 and 1639.[17] Over a third of all women going to the altar had been there before.

These high remarriage rates demand explanation. Why were widows able to remarry, and why did so many of them decide to do so? It is easy to understand why prosperous citizens' widows could remarry: as brides, they had many charms. London law was favorable to the inheritance rights of widows, who through a combination of dower, jointure, freebench, and ecclesiastical thirds were likely to inherit at least a third of their husbands' real and moveable property. By City custom, widows inherited at least a third of their husbands' goods if they had surviving children and half if they did not.[18] If their children were minors they usually controlled that capital as well: since widows did not inherit from their children, the law prudently preferred them to paternal relatives as guardians. While the law was already relatively generous in London, widows were likely to be granted more than the customary minimum. In a study of 315 London husbands' wills, Brodsky finds that in addition to usually being appointed as executrixes, widows generally inherited substantially more than the legal third, usually without restrictions 'beyond a cautionary safeguarding of their children's portions from the possible depredations of a future stepfather'.[19]

While it is difficult to believe that poor widows did not find remarriage a more difficult or at least a less profitable prospect than their richer rivals, they, too, remarried. Consistory court witnesses included many women of humble status, and, as Boulton has shown, widows formed a very large proportion of brides in the impoverished parish of Stepney. Citing the relative scarcity of women in the London population in the early seventeenth century, he concludes that 'in the economy of poorer Londoners, youthful widows possessing even a little property were particularly attractive in the male-dominated marriage market'.[20] Residence patterns confirm the broad possibility of remarriage: although poor and suburban parishes contained more than their share of widows, these made up only a slightly higher proportion of adult women in poor parishes than in rich ones: 17.8 per cent versus 16.9 per cent.[21]

Poor widows attracted suitors who, like many Londoners, were in need of the help and comfort only a wife could provide. The single life had few charms for poor men. The fathers of young children could hardly hope to manage on their own, and

---

[17] Brodsky, 'Widows', 129; Jeremy Boulton, 'London Widowhood Revisited: The Decline of Female Remarriage in the Seventeenth and Early Eighteenth Centuries', *Continuity and Change* 5.3 (1990), 327, 344.
[18] This was no rarity: 42% of 494 wills for 1580–1597 mentioned no surviving children. Brodsky, 'Widows', 136–7.
[19] Hanawalt, *The Wealth of Wives*, 20; Brodsky, 'Widows', 145. For inheritance law, see Amy Louise Erickson, *Women and Property in Early Modern England* (New York, 1993), 156–86.
[20] Boulton, 'London Widowhood Revisited', 327, 344.
[21] Based on the responses of 360 women from 19 poor parishes and 148 women from 34 rich parishes. The classification of parishes is taken from Roger Finlay's analysis of a 1638 listing of households, rents, and tithes: 'poor' parishes were composed of 10% or fewer 'substantial households', while 'rich' parishes included 20% or more households in that category. Finlay, *Population and Metropolis: The Demography of London 1580–1650* (Cambridge, 1981), 168–71.

working wives brought in extra income while usefully diversifying the family economy. Elderly laboring men may have been particularly anxious to wed, since they were often past work and in need of care.[22] This was the case for one of the consistory court's oldest witnesses, an aged gunner who said he was 'neither blind nor deaf although he hath some disease in his eyes in regard of his age being above ninety-one years old'. He reported that he lived 'now upon the means and painstaking of his wife, who taketh extraordinary pains by washing abroad, and some exhibition she hath out of the parish of Aldgate'. A 90-year-old silkweaver also depended on his wife: 'he being so old a man is not able to work but liveth by his wife who being a midwife getteth his living thereby.'[23]

For many poor and middling widows, remarriage—to a good husband, at least—offered many of the same attractions that it did to widowers. Taking over a late husband's trade was by no means easy for a widow who had not practiced it before, and who bore responsibility for running a household and, perhaps, her own business. A hardworking husband could provide a modicum of financial security as well as company and comfort. Richer widows could aim higher, hoping to parlay their capital into social advancement, greater prosperity, or less material forms of gratification. In all cases, however, remarriage involved serious risks.

Careful negotiations and tavern festivities

Courtship looked different the second time around. Among the poor and the middling sort, financial settlements in first marriages were usually limited to ascertaining the portions and prospects of both parties, but in second marriages, a host of other questions arose: children's portions, past debts, and the protection of the widow's estate could all derail a match. Thus when Henry Ashmore, a widower, sued Helen Walker to enforce a matrimonial contract in 1620, she explained that they could not wed because of financial disagreements. Her previous husband had died in 1618, leaving her with a victualling house, two children, and £100 of debt. She had agreed to marry Ashmore on condition that he pay her debts and arrange to be made a citizen so she would not lose her victualling house, and had made some attempts of her own to procure his freedom. However, when she was arrested for a debt of £50, he had refused to help her, 'saying that he had debts enough of his own to pay'. To avoid unpleasantness and 'for the good of her and her children', Helen Walker asked an acquaintance to arbitrate between herself and Ashmore. On his advice, a scrivener's apprentice wrote out a bond binding the two 'never to molest or trouble each other hereafter for any matter'.[24]

---

[22] See Jeremy Boulton, *Neighbourhood and Society: A London Suburb in the Seventeenth Century* (Cambridge, 1987), 128–31; Margaret Pelling, 'Who Most Needs to Marry? Ageing and Inequality among Women and Men in Early Modern Norwich', in Lynn Botelho and Pat Thane (eds), *Women and Ageing in British Society Since 1500* (New York, 2001), 34.

[23] Clatworth Cheney, 1620 (LMA, DL/C/227, fo. 206); James Stockdell, 1608 (LMA, DL/C/218, pp. 74–5).

[24] *Henry Ashmore c. Helen Walker*, 1620: Helen Walker (LMA, DL/C/192, fo. 144v) and Edward Farey (LMA, DL/C/225, fo. 157v).

When widows and widowers had children from their previous marriages, as they often did, conflicts of interest could create marital problems. While godly writers did not forbid second marriages, they were quick to remind their readers of the complications that could result from 'blended' families. Both step-parents (commonly called fathers- and mothers-in-law) and stepchildren were liable to misbehave, causing endless troubles. Gouge instructed his readers that step-parents were 'to account their children-in-law . . . as their own natural children, and according to the age and place of these children to perform the forenamed duties, and every way to seek their good (except in such duties as after a peculiar manner belong to natural parents, as *nursing* to a natural mother, *leaving the inheritance* to a natural parent)'. To do otherwise was a failure both of parental duty and of marital love: 'If the world's proverb hold true (*love me and love my dog*), how much more true is this Christian rule, *love me and love my child.*' Too often, however, step-parents failed in their duties:

> What grievous complaints have in former times been made, and still are made by children against fathers- and mothers-in-law? Whence also direful imprecations have followed. Let widowers and widows that have children seriously think of it beforehand, and be the more circumspect in taking a second or third husband or wife, and after they are married let them take heed of Satan's snares, and let conscience of duty more prevail with them, than corruption of nature.[25]

Just as step-parents failed to love their spouses' children, so stepchildren were often rebellious and impertinent. Stepchildren did not owe step-parents all the obedience they owed to their natural parents; they did not have to obtain their consent to marry, for instance. But they were to do their best to feel, or at least to show, filial respect.

> Very few bear a reverend, dutiful, and childlike respect to stepfathers and stepmothers: but for the most part despise them in heart, grumble at them in speech, and are very undutiful in their behaviour: whence it cometh to pass that they bring much grief to their natural parent, and oft cause much discord and dissension . . . Lamentable experience sheweth that the second, third, or any after-marriages are seldom so comfortable and peaceable as the first: especially if either the one, or other, or both have children. The cause thereof, for the most part, is in children, who brook not fathers- or mothers-in-law.[26]

Blended families had the best chances of living in harmony when provision was made to secure the portions of all children. This was often done through settlements that sidestepped coverture: the prospective husband signed a bond committing him to leave his new wife a set sum to pay her children's portions, or to pay it to a third party on her account. Settlements to safeguard widows' estates and children's portions were extremely common even among people of moderate

---

[25] Gouge, *Of domesticall duties*, 580–82.
[26] Ibid. 488–9.

means.[27] Margery Baines of St James Clerkenwell wanted her prospective husband, Roger Foster, to give her son Owen a portion of £50 or an income of £6 a year. When he refused, though she said she would depend on his courtesy, the parish register shows that she soon thereafter married another man. Anne Breamer, a widow with two children, told a clergyman who wished to marry her that she would never contract herself unless 'she could first have both her own portion of goods and her children's likewise set down and assured unto her'. Ralph Grimes told the court that he was contracted to the widow Joyce Griffin, but she retorted that his weak estate and bad behavior had brought her to dislike his suit. In addition, one neighbor said there was a public fame that Joyce 'should be married to a shoemaker at Islington and that he the same shoemaker had entered bond with surety to pay her daughter £10 soon after'.[28]

While second marriages were financially complicated, courtship could be remarkably free. Unlike maids and bachelors, widows and widowers were both morally and practically able to make their own choices. Even Rogers conceded that a widow was not obliged to seek her parents' consent for a second marriage: 'providence hath settled her upon her own right.'[29] More to the point, widows were often orphaned. Nonetheless, even when courting couples controlled their own estates, widows and widowers still demonstrated a taste for communal involvement. While young people walked out abroad together and met quietly in the houses of friends, the equivalent for older sweethearts was dining with the neighbors in a tavern. Courtship melted seamlessly into neighborly life. For example, Edward Brewer met the widow Margaret Hamlyn through mutual acquaintances. Mistress Hamlyn's middle-aged neighbor Thomas Stevenson spoke to William Frank, an elderly leatherseller, about his desire to help her to a good husband. Brewer, a widower, had previously told Frank 'that he had an intent to marry and desired the said Frank to recommend a woman unto him (if he knew of any) that might be fit for him', so Frank arranged a supper at a tavern where the two met in the company of several neighbors. They liked one another, and thereafter Brewer frequently stopped by Mistress Hamlyn's lodgings, and gave her a pair of gloves and a book for the New Year.[30] As the courtship progressed, Brewer invited Margaret and the neighbors to supper at his house where she met his children and, 'upon commendation of the conveniency of his house', he showed the guests the rooms and furniture. They even discussed what to do with his late wife's satin gown: he

---

[27] See Amy Louise Erickson, 'Common Law versus Common Practice: The Use of Marriage Settlements in Early Modern England', *Economic History Review*, 2nd series, 43.1 (1990), 21–39; *Women and Property*, 130.

[28] John Attell, *Roger Foster c. Margery Baines*, 1615 (LMA, DL/C/223, fos. 174–5); Anne Breamer, *William Paine c. Anne Breamer*, 1597 (LMA, DL/C/215, fo. 17); Ralph Grimes, Joyce Griffin, and William Houghton, *Ralph Grimes c. Joyce Griffin*, 1609 (LMA, DL/C/218, pp. 362, 370–71, 435).

[29] Samuel Rogers, *Matrimoniall honour: or, The mutuall crowne and comfort of godly, loyall, and chaste marriage* (London, 1642), 79.

[30] Brewer later claimed that he had not intended to give her the book: it fell out of his pocket and she asked for it.

gallantly asked 'whether it would not make a petticoat or waistcoat'; she, demurring, said 'she thought it would, but said it would serve to line a cloak'.[31]

Even independent widows and widowers could expect little in the way of privacy for their courtships, as their affairs attracted the opinionated interest of their acquaintances. In 1609, a group of neighbors from St Lawrence in the Old Jewry 'went altogether with others a-walking into the fields, and returning were all invited to supper' at the young widow Bridget Boulton's house, the inn at the sign of the Swan with Two Necks. There, some careless jesting resulted in hurt feelings and an undignified squabble. Trouble began when 'some speeches was moved merrily and in jest about the salt that was upon the table that it was some discredit for the widow to have a pewter salt and that if there were any suitors there unto her they would not think so well of the widow as otherwise they would do'. A silver salt cellar would presumably have better reflected Mistress Boulton's estate, but Margaret Horneby suggested that it hardly mattered because 'there was none there that the widow need to care for'. One of the guests, the hopeful Robert Powell, took offense at this remark and asked Mistress Horneby for quiet. Margaret, annoyed, called him 'beggarly rogue', 'lousy rogue', and 'brokerly rogue', and 'threw a trencher at... Robert Powell and hit him upon the nose', causing it to bleed abundantly. He in turn called her a baggage and a jade.[32] The insult 'brokerly rogue' suggests that Powell was a broker who dealt in used clothes, hardly an enticing match for an innkeeper. His courtship was indeed doomed to failure.

An even more drunken case was that of the widow Perry and Richard Warren, landlord of the Spread Eagle in Wapping. The whirlwind romance, speedily regretted by Warren, only makes sense if one assumes that he was thoroughly inebriated. Margaret Perry, who had already survived two seafaring husbands, one dead in the East Indies and the other hanged as a pirate, went to the Spread Eagle for supper with some lodgers of hers.[33] Warren and Margaret were complete strangers to one another, but having ascertained that she was single, he sat down with them, and 'was very merry and sent for wine and bestowed it on [her]'.[34] Matters progressed swiftly. Warren asked Margaret first whether she would be his wife, and second whether she would wash his clothes, and upon receiving favorable answers, he concluded: 'Why then, Meg, I do frankly give thee this house in token that we are man and wife, and it shall be thine.'[35] After a while, they went home hand in hand to Margaret's house, with Warren pointing out other houses, 'saying to her: "This is thy house," and "That is thy house."' Margaret graciously accepted 'and so they went on lovingly together' to her house, where Warren set the widow on his knees and embraced and kissed her for about an hour, exclaiming: 'that night's work was the happiest night, and happiest work that ever she made in her

---

[31] Edward Brewer, *Margaret Hamlyn c. Edward Brewer*, 1636 (LMA, DL/C/194, fos. 182–4).
[32] Robert Pitts and Elizabeth Bannister, *Margaret Horneby c. Robert Powell*, 1609 (LMA, DL/C/218, pp. 601, 520–21).
[33] Elizabeth Lane, *Margaret Perry alias More c. Richard Warren*, 1610 (LMA, DL/C/219, fo. 87v).
[34] John Johnson (ibid. fo. 81r).
[35] Joan and John Johnson (ibid. fos. 93v, 81r).

246									City Women

life'.[36] He did remember to ask her about her children and her debts; she replied that she had only one of the former and none of the latter. After further protestations, Warren declared that he 'was desirous to lie with her that night', but Margaret 'desired him to pardon her for that, and said she had beds enough, and said she would make him a bed for himself'. Warren indignantly asked: 'Who should let him to lie with his wife?' 'Unless he lay with her he would not lie there at all,' he cried.[37] They resolved the dispute by staying up instead: when the candle burnt out they sallied forth in search of more wine, leaving the rest of the night in an alcoholic haze.

Another mature couple enjoyed an unabashedly public courtship in St Sepulchre in 1625. Joan Neville, the widow of one Richard Neville, kept a cook's shop at Pye Corner. She attracted the interest of at least two local widowers: John Frank, 64, who worked as a 'keeper' for the Royal Exchange, and James Edwards, a clothworker. One evening, Frank came courting to her house, but was told by her daughter that Joan was at a victualling house in Windmill Court nearby. There, he found the object of his affection 'sitting close together' with Edwards in such a way that Frank immediately perceived there to be 'love and goodwill betwixt' the two. Since Edwards was richer than himself, Frank relinquished his suit, saying: 'I thought I had some interest to the same Joan Neville but if I had three times more interest than I perceive I now resign all the same my interest unto you because I know you are a man of ability and able to maintain her far beyond my ability.' Joan's old friend Elizabeth Belcher—they had known one another for twenty-five years—also gave her blessing to the match, joking: 'This woman Joan Neville is my wife, but I give unto you all my rights.' Edwards answered: 'Now you must call her... no more wife for now is she my wife.' He called for beer, saying 'Here, sweetheart, I will drink to you', but Joan insisted that he drink to her only as his wife. He did so, and the shoemaker whose wife ran the alehouse joined their hands, saying 'God give you joy, and God bless you together.' An oysterwoman offered to be a bridesmaid, and Edwards promised everyone gloves, the traditional gifts made to wedding guests.[38] He told Joan 'that his daughter and his maidservant were then shortly to be married, and that he would see them married out of his house, and then he and the said Joan would marry together... he would give over his trade'. The onlookers escorted the newly contracted couple to Joan's house, where more drink was consumed, and the smitten old man announced that 'he should do more than he had done forty years before, viz. to lodge out of his own house': he planned to consummate the liaison that night. Indeed, when Elizabeth Belcher visited her friend the next morning, she found them by the fire, with Joan sitting cozily on Edwards' knee, while he discussed how, as soon as he could get his daughter

[36] John Johnson (ibid. fo. 81v).
[37] Joan Johnson (ibid. fo. 84).
[38] *Joan Neville c. James Edwards*, 1626 (LMA, DL/C/230): John Frank (fo. 125v), Elizabeth Belcher (fos. 128–9), and Robert Briscoe (fo. 127).

married, they would 'go to church together hand in hand' and he would rescue her 'from her drudgery'.[39]

Festive drinking was only one of the options open to courting widows. After the death of George Wickham, his widow Anne became close to William Thomas, who had been her fellow-servant twelve years before and had served as her son's godfather; they had long 'continued as loving friends and acquaintances'. Anne did not need her neighbors to serve as matchmakers or to arrange dinners. Instead, she went with Thomas to the Tower 'to see the Armory and other sights there' and 'to the Red Bull to see dancing upon the ropes'.[40] Thomas tried to buy Anne a new hat, but she, aware of the implications of accepting a token, insisted on paying for it. When he proposed, she prevaricated, answering that 'she had many troubles to undergo concerning her children's portions and other affairs concerning her late husband's will, and that she could not marry without advice of the overseers of her said husband's will'. She also told him, rudely, 'that she would never marry any man that did wear a livery cloak, and that it was a disgrace unto her that any man should come to her so often in a livery cloak'.[41]

As these narratives of drunken carousing and blunt speeches suggest, widows courted differently than maids. This may have been partly because men approached them more aggressively: one such suitor concluded that 'as he that wooeth a maid must be brave in apparel and outward show, so he that wooeth a widow must not carry quick eels in his codpiece, but show some proof that he is stiff before'.[42] However, widows were also able to be more direct than maids: freed of conventional shyness and fortified by the self-assurance and status of adult women, they naturally played a more dominant role. This was particularly true when, as it often happened, they were older and richer than their suitors.

Bachelor bridegrooms

One remarkable difference between first and later marriages is that London widows were likely to marry young men, often bachelors. Brodsky's study of marriage allegations shows that most remarrying widows under 45 did so (see Table 7.3). Indeed, she found that it was much more common for a widow to marry a bachelor than for a widower to marry a maid: the former accounted for 19 per cent of marriages by license, while the latter made up only 10 per cent.[43] The ages reported by husbands and wives serving as witnesses in the consistory court reveal a similar pattern: the older the wife, the more likely she was to be older than her husband. Thus young wives reported being an average of almost six years younger than their

---

[39] John Frank and Elizabeth Belcher (LMA, DL/C/230, fos. 125, 129).
[40] Anne Wickham, *William Thomas c. Anne Wickham*, 1636 (LMA, DL/C/194, fo. 189v, also fos. 205v–206).
[41] Anne Wickham, 1636 (LMA, DL/C/194, fos. 188v–189); Mary Simpson, 1636 (LMA, DL/C/234, fo. [2]84v).
[42] *The Autobiography of Thomas Whythorne*, ed. James M. Osborn (Oxford, 1962), 43. Edition uses modern spelling.
[43] Marriages between widows and widowers accounted for 16%. Brodsky, 'Widows', 126–9.

Table 7.3 Remarrying widows' preference for bachelor bridegrooms

Age of widows	% bachelor bridegrooms	No. of marriages
20–24	82.0	28
25–29	72.0	93
30–34	62.5	192
35–39	57.6	99
40–44	50.3	141
45–49	25.3	51
50–54	29.0	86
55–59	21.0	14
60–64	8.7	23
Total	53.1	727

Source: Vivien Brodsky, 'Widows in Late Elizabethan London', in Bonfield et al. (eds), *The World We Have Gained* (New York, 1986), 131. London license marriages 1598–1619.

spouses, but for married women 40 or older (often remarried widows) this age gap disappeared. For 120 couples in which the wife was at least 40, in 53 cases the wife was the elder, by an average of 8.4 years.[44] As Fig. 7.2 shows, as women aged and the proportion of remarried widows grew, they were increasingly likely to be married to younger men.

While the attractions of prosperous widows for ambitious bachelors are easy to discern,[45] the question of why a remarrying London widow would choose to marry a bachelor deserves consideration. What did she have to gain from the bargain? One explanation is that widowers made relatively unattractive bridegrooms. Conventional wisdom warned that marrying a widower was likely to be unsatisfactory.

> ... Widowers, if they did first abuse
> Wedlock: the sequel you may justly fear
> By instance: if they did directly choose
> And love the first, they will forgetless bear
> That love till death: so precious ointments leave
> An odour, though the substance you bereave.[46]

If a widower had treated his first wife badly, the second could hardly expect better fortune; on the other hand, a well-beloved first wife would make an impossible act to follow. Age was also a setback. Some young widows explicitly rejected aged suitors, like Agnes Bushey, who disdained the elderly Mr Wye, explaining to his go-between, a laundress, 'that she did verily think that Mr Wye loved her and was

---

[44] In 56 cases the husband was an average of 8.1 years older, and the remaining couples were of the same age.
[45] B. A. Holderness, 'Widows in Pre-industrial Society: An Essay upon their Economic Functions', in Richard M. Smith (ed.), *Land, Kinship and Life-Cycle* (Cambridge, 1984), 428.
[46] *The husband A poeme expressed in a compleat man* (London, 1614).

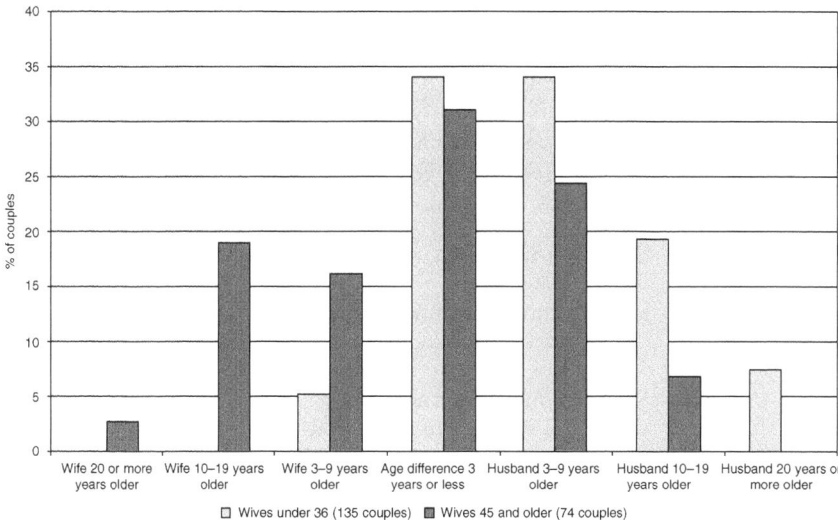

Figure 7.2 Spousal age differences for younger and older wives

an honest gentleman, but he was an old man and going out of the world, and she young, and that his living was at sea, which she could not away with, neither would she ever marry with him, nor have him, but she knew in her heart he was no fit match for her'.[47] Even if Wye's living had not been at sea, his estate might have been encumbered by heirs from a previous marriage, a serious consideration for a young second wife.

Indeed, while old men might be unable to work and could require nursing, even middle-aged men were likely to be burdened with children. Rogers cautioned widowers with children to be realistic about their marriage prospects: he thought that a widower with many children must be willing to accept a significantly poorer bride than he might otherwise be able to attract:

> Again, a man hath by a former venture, a great charge of children, which are like to lay upon the hand of a second wife, both for education and attendance; in such a case, a woman of an hundred or two hundred pounds worth, who is willing to requite that defect with love and painfulness (being otherwise competent for her honest parentage and fashion of life), may be as equal a match, as perhaps one of a thousand pound estate, without that encumbrance.[48]

A Londoner who married the father of young children not only had to care for them, but also saw her potential inheritance diminished: even if her own marriage were childless, her minimum bequest would be reduced by the stepchildren. A prosperous widow's children did not equally disadvantage her second husband;

---

[47] Katherine Freame, *Thomas Wye c. Agnes Bushey*, 1591 (LMA, DL/C/213, p. 829); Gouge, *Of domesticall duties*, 182.
[48] Rogers, *Matrimoniall honour*, 62–3.

instead, they might even increase her attractions, as he could make use of their capital until they came of age.[49]

While age and children dissuaded widows from wedding widowers, young bachelors had their charms. Not only were bachelors personally appealing, early modern writers thought, but widows could expect to wield greater authority within the marriage when they were responsible for most of the household wealth. A ballad called *The complaint of a widow against an old man* illustrates the widow's position:

> Shall I wed an aged man,
> that groaneth of the gout,
> And lead my life in misery,
> within doors and without?
> No! I will have a bachelor,
> of lively blood and bone,
> To cheer me in my latter days,
> or else I will have none.

The widow explained why such a pretty fellow might marry her:

> ... if I take a young man,
> although his wealth be small,
> If that he use me honestly
> he shall be lord of all.

She noted that spaniels 'Will lick, and leap upon, their feet/by whom they find relief', and thought that 'a witty man... Must love the woman faithfully,/that married him of nought'.[50] In a variation on the early modern theme of deference and obligation, this widow expected her money to endow her with loving authority within marriage. This inversion of the usual household order attracted the critical attention of William Gouge, who assumed that 'if a rich woman marry a poor man, she will look to be the master, and to rule him: so as the order which God hath established will be clean perverted: and the honour of marriage laid in the dust'. It was very 'unmeet' when women 'who being aged... marry youths, if not very boys', for they did so 'for this very end, that they may rule over their own husbands', he suspected.[51]

Concern about the inversion of the household hierarchy underlay comic representations of demanding 'merry widows' in popular literature and on the stage. Much of the audience for the theater was composed of just the sort of young men who might have liked to marry a London widow: ambitious hangers-on from the royal court, younger sons studying law, restless apprentices playing hooky. The ambiguous attitude toward remarrying widows in London drama—fascination, contempt, and unease—reflected the preoccupations of these bachelors, for

---

[49] Hanawalt, *The Wealth of Wives*, 108.
[50] *The Shirburn Ballads 1585–1616*, ed. Andrew Clark (Oxford, 1907), 269–71.
[51] Gouge, *Of domesticall duties*, 189–90, 273–4.

whom marriage to a city widow was a very real prospect.[52] As one bachelor worried in a ballad:

> ... if I choice may have
> a maid would be my wife,
> I would not be a widow's slave,
> I'd rather lose my life:
> If I should wed a widow old,
> I had better take a younger,
> For widows will not be controlled.[53]

Others worried that a widow's wealth would lead her to scorn a poor bridegroom once the glow of courtship had faded. This was the moral of a story by Samuel Rowlands:

> His name of *John* is turned into *Jack*,
> She tells him, that her money clothes his back:
> And that he was a needy rascal knave,
> And she hath made a man of such a slave.
> Her words (last week) of love, sweetheart, and joy,
> And turn'd to villain, rogue, and beardless boy,
> And tells him further that it is her shame
> That she hath grac'd him with a husband's name,
> Being unworthy wretch to wipe her shoes.[54]

Nonetheless, many bachelors were willing to swallow their pride for a chance to marry a richer widow. One of these was John Newton, a player of 'the Duke of York's company' and 'one of the company of the players that use to play their parts on the stage at the Curtain and the Boar's Head without Aldgate and in the suburbs of London'. Joan Waters, the object of his affections, had been widowed so recently that she was still with child from her previous marriage. According to testimony, Joan was concerned for the child, and asked Newton if 'he would make much of it if it lived, and he answered he would as willingly as if it were his own'. At a tavern where they celebrated their courtship, Joan affectionately branded her suitor with a mark that did not yet have a name: 'She the said Waters did then with her lips suck his the said Newton's neck in a manner of kindness whereby she made three red spots arise, which the said Newton asking her what she meant by it, she answering said that she had marked him for her own.' When the two lovers spoke the contractual words, both allegedly promised 'to love, cherish and to obey' one another. This may have been a slip of the tongue on the witness's part

---

[52] See Elizabeth Foyster, 'Marrying the Experienced Widow in Early Modern England: The Male Perspective', in Sandra Cavallo and Lyndan Warner (eds), *Widowhood in Medieval and Early Modern Europe* (New York, 1999); Jennifer Panek, *Widows and Suitors in Early Modern English Comedy* (Cambridge, 2004).
[53] *A Batchelers resolution, or, Have among you now, widowes or maydes* (London, 1629).
[54] Samuel Rowlands, *Good newes and bad newes* (London, 1622), sigs. C2v, C3r.

or a scribal error, but given Joan's assertiveness, Newton's vowed obedience seems particularly apt.[55]

The making of a betrothal contract between Marian Crompton, a widow over 60 who kept a victualling house in Shoreditch, and the younger Christopher Dawson in 1606 illustrates many of the concerns that arose when widows contemplated marrying beneath them. Throughout the negotiations, Mistress Crompton set the tone and the pace: she had the most to lose if the match were a bad one. She expected a new husband to work—even to perform a housewife's duties—and not to live off of her, telling Dawson 'that she hoped he would be a good husband and not think scorn to go into the cellar and look that nothing go to wrack there, nor refuse to go to the market to buy such things as was necessary to her use'. With her welfare in the balance, she was slow to consent to a binding contract. When Christopher asked her for a 'resolute answer' to his suit, she told him solemnly 'that she loved and affected him … above all the men that had made suit unto her since her husband's death', and that she would marry no other man. However, when he pressed her for a contract, she put him off.[56]

On a different day at breakfast, Marian Crompton finally agreed to a marital contract, but only after a trusted friend gave her his advice. When he appeared, she said: 'Mr Hawton, you are the man that in heart I wished for, and seeing you are come I will do anything that you shall advise me unto.' She seemed self-conscious about the difference in age between herself and her suitor: '"I wish with all my heart", quoth she, "that I were ten years younger for his sake."' Hawton apparently approved the match, and asked Dawson for a piece of gold to break as a token, but when he was about to do so, the widow's practical instincts intervened: disregarding custom, she 'spake unto him and willed him to stay the breaking of it, "for," quoth she, "the gold is better whole than broken."'[57] She took the coin, saying she would always be 'master of her word'. Hawton asked her a final time whether she was sure about her decision, cautioning her: 'what ye do now can never be undone again.' Finally, Dawson took the gold back, and handed it to her again, saying that he gave her his faith and his troth. Hawton prompted Marian to do the same, so she took a gold ring off her finger and put it on one of Dawson's with similar words, as though he were the bride.

Mistress Crompton pledged Dawson with a glass of wine, kissed him, 'and told him that that day's work must cost him five pounds for that she was to pay five pounds when she should be contracted and made sure to him'. Dawson agreed to pay, but it seems that she had been joking: she replied: 'Nay … thou shalt pay nothing for me, Kit, I have what with to pay all my debts.'[58] Both parties were cognizant of the financial implications of marriage: Dawson would be liable for any

---

[55] William Addison, George Ireland, and William Duke, *John Newton c. Joan Waters*, 1610–11 (LMA, DL/C/219, fos. 410–11, 418v, and DL/C/220, fos. 621). See also Loreen L. Giese, 'Theatrical Citings and Bitings', *Early Theatre* 1.1 (1998), 113–28.

[56] An anonymous soldier (autobiographical section missing), *Christopher Dawson c. Marian Crompton*, 1606 (LMA, DL/C/217, pp. 15, 11).

[57] Ibid. p. 12.

[58] Soldier and William White (ibid. pp. 13, 20).

secret debts that the widow had, while she would lose control over her estate. He tried to reassure her about his intentions, inviting her to safeguard her capital by 'dispos[ing] of what she would either before her marriage or after unto her kindred or friends', saying he hoped for only a modest inheritance: 'If I shall deserve nothing of you by my good usage of you, I will look for nothing otherwise. I hope if I deserve a child's part you will not be unkind to me.' Then the company discussed the wedding: Marian said that she would not be married in her parish, but would rather go away to Waltham. After the expense of hiring horses was raised, Hawton suggested the fair in Southwark as a more convenient destination, and Marian replied that she would think about it that night, asking him to come to her house the next morning with his wife: 'Then I will take order for our wedding and appoint the time and place.'[59] No one seems to have expected Dawson's opinion to be taken into account.

Financial agreements circumventing coverture were key to marriages between rich widows and poor bachelors, and were often mentioned in the courtship suits of widows like Susan Jason, a wealthy woman in middle age. Henry Bowles, her suitor, asked his acquaintance William Durant to approach Mistress Jason on his behalf. He did so, and Susan asked about 'the age of the said Henry, and his ability, parentage, and suchlike matters'. She was interested enough to arrange for Henry himself to visit when her son would not be home, preferring to interview Henry without his knowledge or interference. She told an older gentleman of her acquaintance that she thought Bowles was too young, but 'afterward she confessed that she had made choice of him for her husband', and discussed making alternate arrangements for her younger children so they would not trouble him. Hayes thought she had mentioned Bowles's age to discover whether he thought the match unfitting, not because she disliked his youth. After looking into Bowles' finances, she consented to marry him, saying:

> Sir, you are the only man that I make account of, and I hope you will be an honest man, and be loving and kind to me, and you shall be sure that I will be loving and kind to you, if you will be so to me, for it is all I desire, it hath been my prayer to God to have an honest and loving man to my husband. As for wealth, I desire it not.

However, Susan Jason was not so smitten as to dispense with financial safeguards: she required that Henry Bowles find several substantial London gentlemen to be bound, as she told him, 'that you shall not make away any of my estate during my life. And that if you die before me, you shall leave me your estate except one hundred pounds which you may bestow where you please.'[60]

---

[59] Soldier (ibid. pp. 17, 16).
[60] William Durant and Robert Hayes, *Henry Bowles c. Susan Jason*, 1610 (LMA, DL/C/219, fos. 312v, 315v, 313v–314v).

Dangerous ventures

While marriages between widows and bachelors were common, they were not uncontroversial, especially when large disparities existed in age or estate. Elderly brides were ridiculed at least as much as ancient bridegrooms: one description of a widow intent on wedding an eighth husband dwells cruelly on her toothless gums and stale odor.[61] Even in the absence of marked decrepitude, such marriages contradicted the rule that spouses should be roughly equal in rank, wealth, age, and looks. Daniel Rogers saw little good in mismatched marriages, although he agreed that brides and bridegrooms pretended that a surplus of one good quality could make up for a deficit elsewhere:

> Old women marrying young men justify themselves by this, that they will maintain their husbands, and that shall make up the flaw, and levels that valley. Deformed ones marrying fair or personable, allege, they are penny white: and kitchen-maids marrying gentlemen, may say, they are good nurses, and deny themselves as much another way.

Rogers thought money-driven marriages between young men and old women (or vice versa) were especially risky. He worried that these avaricious young husbands would fail to love their wives and keep their marriage vows:

> What vile affections are bred in secret in many such, desire of the death of their companions being grown decrepit, irksomeness of spirit, in tedious bearing the sickliness, unhelpfulness, and unsociableness of each others' bodies? How many have we known, who being discontent with their lot, seek to other younger ones, and defile them, some within their own dwellings, polluting themselves with their servants? How many murders have unequal matches caused, of infants so begotten and born? Nay, how many have been the cursed attempts of poisoning each other, to be rid of the loathed party, husband or wife?

Often these men, hating their old wives, 'when they have buried them, partly through eager desire of posterity, partly longing after the other extreme, marry a wife forty years younger, and so are lashed with their own whip, and as much loathed by the later, as they loathed the former'. Gouge suggested that those 'who in the prime and strength of their age, for wealth, honour, or suchlike respects, marry those that with age begin to be decrepit, and unfit to be married, hoping that they will not long live' were defying the Lord's sense of poetic justice: 'God oft meeteth with such in their kind, by prolonging the life of those aged persons, and so making the burden to be much more grievous and tedious than was imagined, and by taking away those young ones sooner than they looked for.' Similarly, 'men and women, who being aged, to satisfy their lust, or for some other by-respect, marry such as are but in the flower of their age' were likely to be disappointed if they hoped for cheerful companions. Instead, they would find that 'those young ones finding the society of aged folks to be burdensome, and irksome unto them, soon begin to loathe the same, and thereby cause more grief and vexation, than ever they did give comfort and contentment'.[62]

---

[61] *The olde bride, or the gilded beauty* (London, 1635).
[62] Rogers, *Matrimoniall honour*, 62, 66–7; Gouge, *Of domesticall duties*, 189.

Old men who insisted on marrying young wives were doomed, ballads and stories taught, to be cuckolded despite all their jealous efforts to the contrary: 'he that thus undertakes to manage in his age, what hath shaked the heart of youth, may be commended for his valour, but shall ne'er be crowned for his wisdom'.[63] But if trophy wives could prove troublesome, trophy husbands were positively dangerous.

If all went well, marriage to a young, poorer man could bring a widow all the comforts of marriage without the constraint of subordination. The problem was, of course, that both culture and law made it difficult for widows to maintain their superiority.

Agnes Halloway's experience courting her servant and her eventual decision not to marry him provides an apt illustration of both the attractions and the pitfalls of this kind of match. Agnes's husband, George Halloway, died on New Year's Day in 1615, leaving her mistress of an estate said to be worth £1,000. Shortly thereafter, she showed her servant Henry Rich 'great good will and signs and tokens of love' and cared for him attentively during an illness. Another servant said that in March, Henry began to boast of Agnes's love, claiming that they had slept together, and the neighbors predicted that they would soon wed. Agnes was loath, however, to surrender her authority, and when Henry gave her 'distasteful speeches', she told him 'that he... should no longer stay in her... house' and 'also that she would send for her father'.[64] Subsequent events suggest that Agnes wished to reduce Henry to submission but not necessarily to cut off his suit.

However, with the arrival of her intimidating father, the widow lost control of the situation. A neighboring woman heard Nicholas Ward, Agnes's father, 'find fault with the said Agnes for sitting up late in the night and keeping him the said Rich company at such disorderly times'. He threatened to take legal action against the young man, whereupon the neighbor said she 'could plainly hear the said Agnes weep, and did much commend the said Henry Rich for an honest man, and... told her said father, that the love and good will which the said Henry Rich showed to her... was first sought for by her the said Agnes, and he the said Henry Rich had done nothing but what she had solicited him thereunto'. Agnes 'prayed her father be content, and said that she... had rather spend ten pounds than... Henry should spend forty shillings'. Ward told Agnes that if she persisted in marrying Henry 'she would rue the time that she was ever born, whereunto the said Agnes replied that she had known one in the like case grown mad, and then also wept'.[65] Henry himself hid in the barn, but was eventually persuaded to confess that he could claim no contract.[66] Unmoved by his daughter's tears, Ward had Henry's belongings carried out of the house and deposited in a nearby lane.[67]

---

[63] Alexander Niccholes, *A discourse, of marriage and wiving* (London, 1615), 29.
[64] William Camp, *Henry Rich c. Agnes Halloway*, 1615 (LMA, DL/C/223, fos. 233v–234v).
[65] Anne Cordwell (ibid. fos. 216v–217r).
[66] William Camp (ibid. fo. 234v).
[67] George Cordwell (ibid. fo. 232r).

Rich sued Agnes to enforce the alleged contract, but by the time she testified in June 1615, Agnes seems to have thought better of the match. She told the court that 'she never bare any affection to [Henry] more than was fit for her to perform to a servant', and explained that she had accepted a gift of gloves only to prevent them from being spoiled by lying on the floor. Asked about her physical familiarity with Rich, she explained that he had tried to ravish her.[68] It seems that Agnes had seriously considered marrying her servant, using her wealth to gain a loving and deferential husband. However, his growing arrogance during courtship—a clear warning of what might follow—and her disastrous call upon paternal authority to shore up her own wavering status taught her the difficulty of making that ideal bargain.

Ballads warned widows against hastily committing themselves and their estates to unscrupulous young adventurers. In one of these, an old widow married a young man who made short work of her savings:

> Her house most richly stored
> whereof he made not dainty:
> But in a day
> he consum'd away
> what she had gotten in twenty.

'Old women take good heed,' the poet warned, 'and trust yourselves with no man.'[69] In a 1625 ballad, a remarried wife complained to a widow about her new husband:

> *Married Woman*
> Oh, woe is me, gossip, that e'er I was born,
> I married a boy, that now holds me in scorn,
> He roams among whores both evening and morn,
> While I sit at home, like a creature forlorn.
> *Widow*
> Oh, who would imagine that such a young lad,
> That scarce was worth twelvepence with all that he had,
> Should wed a rich woman, and use her so bad?
> I trust I shall never be so doting mad.[70]

These cautionary tales were echoed in the records of litigation for marital separation. Alice Millington, for example, had an unpleasant awakening on the day after her wedding to Edward Cleter. Her maidservant Mary Cacott was with her when Edward came into her chamber that morning, and reported her mistress's disillusionment. Alice

---

[68] Agnes Halloway (ibid. fos. 201v–202r).
[69] *A merry new song of a rich widdowes wooing that married a young man to her owne undoing* (London, 1625).
[70] John Cart, *The cunning age, or, A re-married woman repenting her marriage* (London, 1625). See also Martin Parker, *A penny-worth of good counsell To widdowes, and to maides, this counsell I send free; and let them looke before they leape, or, that they married bee* (London, 1638).

> coming merrily to him when he came in and spake very kindly and lovingly to him, he willed her stand away from him, saying: 'Think thou that I can love such a musty rusty widow as thou art? Thou hast a face that looketh like the back of a toad. I married thee but to be maintained like a man, so I will be.' And she the same Alice, thinking that he had but jested, said quietly to him, 'Why, so thou shalt be. I hope here is enough to keep us,' and willed him to sit down and be quiet, saying she cared not whether ever he wrought or not, and then he told her he was in debt, and he must have money. 'In debt?' quoth she the same Alice, 'you told me and swore you owed but three pounds.' But he then told her that he owed fifty pounds, and then afterwards a hundred pounds and so vexed her and grieved her continually.[71]

Edward quickly ran through Alice's ready money, then sold off her goods, progressing from foul names and threats to real violence. Mary said that he came in one morning before his wife's hair was dressed, and 'took her by the hair of her head and wound it about his hand and beat her on the face with his other'. He 'told her he must have money and money he would have', but she protested 'that she had no more, she had pawned her rings for money for him'. Edward warned Alice 'that he must pawn the goods in the house' but 'she entreated him to pawn rather her apparel', so he 'filled a trunk with her best apparel and pawned it'. He was also 'very importunate with her for the lease of the house, and she told him it was out of her hands, she had it not, and thereupon he struck her'. When Alice, bloodied, went to a neighbor and explained that her husband had cut her, the two women went to a Lady Crompton for advice, who sent them to Sir Edward Stanhope, chancellor to the Bishop of London. Sir Edward arrested Cleter, and caused him to reconcile himself with his wife, but it did not last. Cleter may have been more careful not to attack his wife thereafter, but the neighbors saw him damage her goods instead with his dagger, destroying her pewter, glass, and featherbeds. Alice bitterly told him that she 'wished and desired of God that she might see him hanged', and the couple eventually separated informally before Alice began proceedings for an official rupture.[72]

A similar case was that of Elizabeth and Henry Carlyle in 1610. Elizabeth had brought a decent estate of £40 to her remarriage to Carlyle, but he was an improvident and violent man. When he went to sea, Elizabeth pretended to be a widow and rented a shop from a leatherdresser in St Botolph Aldgate, where she 'sold sempstry ware and tobacco and thrived very well and had good apparel and ware'. After about half a year, however, Carlyle came home from the sea in a very wretched state. Elizabeth was 'very loath' to admit her marriage to her landlord, but eventually did so, and for three weeks Carlyle lodged with her at the widow Joan Goodwin's house.[73] He exploited her as well as he could: the widow said he 'would take her wares and her ruffs she wore or other things, what he could come by, and sell and pawn it away, and when he had spent the money came home and fetched

---

[71] Mary Cacott, *Alice Millington alias Cleter c. Edward Cleter*, 1609 (LMA, DL/C/218, pp. 327–8).
[72] Mary Cacott, Margery Hewes, and Mary Savage (ibid. pp. 328, 324–6, 333).
[73] Joan Goodwin and Thomas Rogers, *Elizabeth Carlyle c. Henry Carlyle*, 1610 (LMA, DL/C/219, fos. 195r, 193r).

more and when he could not get from her what he would he reviled her'. When he heard that Elizabeth had bought a trunk of wares at Stourbridge Fair to sell in her shop, 'he got it away and pawned and sold thereof until it was all consumed'.[74]

Eventually, 'being weary of his outrages', Mistress Goodwin put them out. Carlyle went to sea again, and Elizabeth took the occasion to decamp to the Minories where she took another shop. However Carlyle, finding it easier to live on his wife at home than to work at sea, soon returned to London and tracked her down again. She finally began divorce proceedings, moving frequently to avoid her husband: 'she dareth not long abide in any one place but fleeth from place to place for fear her husband should take away from her her clothes and such goods as she hath.' Carlyle met with her former landlord to try to discover her new whereabouts, and told him that 'he could not find in his heart to dwell with her, neither would dwell with her, let all the friends she had do what they could. And yet he said he would go to her if he could learn where she was and would take from her what he could get as often as he could get to her so long as he lived until he were divorced from her.'[75]

Unhappily remarried widows relied heavily on their neighbors, with whom they could have strong ties. Margaret Etheridge had been living in Stepney for a long time: one neighbor reported having known her for forty years, and another for seventeen. They had only known her husband, Thomas, for half a year, so the marriage was evidently of recent date. Margaret had the sympathy of her neighbors, who described her as a woman of modest behavior who had brought a good portion to her husband. When Thomas became violent, her daughter ran to the neighbors, and lamented that her stepfather was beating her mother, 'her head being broken and her eye black and blue, and much bruises all over her body'. Katherine Woodcock and Elizabeth White, both middle-aged residents of long standing, rushed to Etheridge's house. They found Margaret in sorry shape, and reproached Thomas, calling him a 'wicked Jew' and asking him if he were not 'ashamed to use a woman so'. He answered: 'Now it is done it cannot be undone', and cast Margaret's dress in the fire, threw her down, and cut her hand. Elizabeth 'demanded the reason' for his actions, and Thomas 'cried out, "The devil shall have me and her too I hope."' 'Though he hath thee, I hope he shall never have her,' Mistress White replied tersely.[76]

Even for dedicated fortune-hunters, widows with legal knowledge and supportive friends could be difficult to subdue. Christopher Percy, a Dorset widower who married a London widow in 1589, found his attempts to 'tame' his bride thwarted by his inability to draw her away from her home turf. According to witnesses, Percy promised Margery Gore, a widow of six years standing, that he could afford to spend £500 a year and would give her a jointure of £100 a year or settle £1,000 with her friends for her use, as well as giving her daughters £100 each in addition to

---

[74] Joan Goodwin and Mary Benson (ibid. fos. 195r, 194).
[75] Joan Goodwin and Thomas Rogers (ibid. fos. 195r, 193v).
[76] Katherine Woodcock and Elizabeth White, *Margaret Etheridge c. Thomas Etheridge*, 1629 (LMA, DL/C/231, fos. 104v–105r, 105r–106v).

the portions left them by their father. However, after they were married, he embarked on a campaign of intimidation and starvation to force Margery to give up what she held from her former husband and to consent to the sale of the lands destined for her jointure.[77]

Percy said in front of witnesses that he 'would tame her and pull down her peacock feathers' and 'that he would make her go a-begging and he did hope to see her go up and down the street a-begging and say "I pray give me some bread for my children."' He frightened Margery with strange and unpredictable behavior, for example when he burst into the dining chamber with 'his naked rapier and his buckler in his hands, and looked very sternly as that he had been mad'. The company was shocked and alarmed, and Margery's son Walter took up a fire shovel to defend them against the intruder.[78] Percy insulted Margery, to her face and behind her back, calling her 'old hag, old dry thing' and telling her 'that he would have as good as she for four or five shillings and therefore what cared he for her'. 'God's wounds,' he swore, 'I will tame you'. At night, Margery ran 'to her maids in her smock only, sometimes her nightgown about her as that she had been frighted', telling them that he 'did so much abuse her that she could not endure it'. One night the maids prayed for her because she looked 'so fearfully and piteously' they were afraid she 'would have lost her wits'. Percy's psychological warfare, designed to weaken Margery's resolve, bothered the whole household: he 'played very bad pranks, rising very early, and put on his boots and made the whole house rise, and then seat him in a chair and sleep there till nine or ten of the clock'. One witness said he behaved so oddly 'as she wondered at him, and would hardly have believed it in him unless she had seen him'.[79]

Percy's London efforts were unsuccessful, so he tried instead to coerce Margery into following him to his country estate: 'he would have her into the country, not for any love that he meant to use her as his wife, but only to hamper her and lock her into a chamber, and then let her see who durst come unto her either to give her bread or drink.' On his own ground, he promised, he would 'make her to do what he would have her'. Unsurprisingly, when he asked his wife to come down to Dorset 'if it were but for a month or a week or two', she and her friends thought his persuasions were 'to no good end'.[80] Meeting resistance, Percy admitted to the court that he '(the rather to induce and provoke her to go with him into the country according to his said request) did forbid the baker, brewer, victualler, woodseller or carter to deliver any provision without ready money to or for the said Margery . . . he would not pay for any such provision.' He would treat her better, he said, when 'the said Margery and her friends deliver[ed] up into [his] hands . . . and to his use all such plate, household stuff, jewels, money, rings, statutes, recognizances, obligations, bills obligatory with other writings and goods' that she had.[81]

---

[77] Isabel Dartnole, *Margery Gore alias Percy c. Christopher Percy*, 1590 (LMA, DL/C/213, p. 712).
[78] Katherine Stokes and Isabel Dartnole (ibid. pp. 722, 713).
[79] Joan Chute (ibid. p. 719), Margaret Smith (p. 716), Isabel Dartnole (p. 713), Katherine Stokes (p. 722).
[80] Isabel Dartnole and Katherine Stokes (ibid. pp. 713–14, 723).
[81] Christopher Percy, 1590 (ibid. pp. 687–8).

However, instead of capitulating, Margery sold some jewels to sustain the household. When Percy sued her for restitution of conjugal rights, she counter-sued for separation on the grounds of cruelty and adultery.

Christopher Percy's explicit attempts to 'tame' his wife by frightening her, keeping her hungry and short of sleep, and isolating her from her friends are strikingly reminiscent of Petruchio's 'taming' of Katharina in Shakespeare's play, thought to have been written at almost exactly the same time. Petruchio starved his bride into submission: 'She eat no meat to-day, nor none shall eat;/Last night she slept not, nor to-night she shall not.' He too forced his wife to follow his senseless vagaries, telling her: 'It shall be what o'clock I say it is.'[82] However, unlike Kate, Margery Percy had her own house and servants and did not go to her husband's country house, where her requests for food might have been met with: 'No, no, forsooth; I dare not for my life.'[83] She was not molded into a loving and submissive wife; her 'peacock feathers', if bedraggled, remained unbowed. Instead, Percy's outrages were presented as evidence of his fraudulent intentions (he was worth much less than he had claimed) and cruelty. In addition to the events described above, Margery's witnesses deposed that Percy was an adulterer who kept company with a cutpurse's wife; and his former maidservant, whom he had seduced, testified against him. Unimpressed by Percy's explanation that his treatment of Margery was designed to reduce her to proper obedience, the judge ordered the would-be fortune hunter to pay the legal fees—and alimony.[84] It was one thing to 'tame' a maiden bride with no wealth of her own or friends to support her, and quite another to take on a seasoned London widow.

This litany of disastrous marriages made by widows who, if not strictly wealthy, were at least 'able to live' in contemporary parlance, prompts the question of why any reasonably prosperous widow would ever remarry. The potential sacrifice, in terms of financial and legal autonomy, was great, and unlike maids, widows had no need to marry to claim adult status and freedom of action. Of course, many widows did not remarry, and the most prosperous may also have been the most averse to matrimony: among the rarified elite of London aldermen's widows, two-thirds chose to remain single.[85] But the fact that so many widows did wed again suggests that they expected marriage to be a source of companionship and mutual care in the harsh regime of the early modern city. In this vein, a sailor lodging with a kinsman of the widow Anne Willett asked her 'what she meant she did not marry and take a husband which should make much of her in her old days'.[86] Although Anne remained single, citing her desire to preserve her estate for her kin, many remarrying widows surely did hope that their husbands would comfort and 'make much' of them. Their optimism seems misguided in light of the experiences of women like

---

[82] William Shakespeare, *The Taming of the Shrew*, ed. Ann Thompson (Cambridge, 2003), IV.i. 168–9, IV.iii.199.
[83] Ibid. IV.iii.1.
[84] LMA, DL/C/13, p. 488 (22 April 1592).
[85] Nancy Lee Adamson, 'Urban Families: The Social Context of the London Elite, 1500–1603', Ph.D. thesis, University of Toronto (1983), 188.
[86] William Gorrell, 1589 (LMA, DL/C/213, p. 521).

Margery Gore and Elizabeth Carlyle, but they were nonetheless more familiar than any historian with the normal course of married life in early modern London.

Legal sources, with their emphasis on marital breakdown, necessarily present a bleak picture. In contrast, an author writing for his widowed sister described a good second husband in glowing terms: 'he shall be to you an husband, to your children a father, to your friends a favourer, to your enemies a terror, he shall willingly bear part of all your blows and burdens, he shall double your prosperity, he shall mourn where you weep, he shall laugh when you are glad . . .'[87] Not all second husbands were of this sort, but while some remarrying widows bitterly regretted their error, many others probably found the comfort of their hopes. Even marriages between old women and young bachelors could prove mutually satisfactory when both parties understood what was expected of them. The astrologer William Lilly, for example, made his fortune by marrying his master's elderly widow:

> My mistress, who had been twice married to old men, was now resolved to be cozened no more; she was of a brown ruddy complexion, corpulent, of but mean stature, plain, no education, yet a very provident person, and of good condition: she had many suitors, old men, whom she declined; some gentlemen of decayed fortunes, whom she liked not, for she was covetous and sparing: by my fellow-servant she was observed frequently to say, she cared not if she married a man that would love her, so that he had never a penny; and would ordinarily talk of me when she was in bed.

Gathering up his courage, young Lilly presented himself as a candidate. '[S]he replied, I was too young; I said nay, what I had not in wealth, I would supply in love; and saluted her frequently, which she accepted lovingly.' From their marriage in 1627 until her death six years later, Lilly reported, 'we lived very lovingly, I frequenting no company at all; my exercises were sometimes angling, in which I ever delighted: my companions, two aged men.' In exchange for his fidelity, Lilly's wife left him almost £1,000.[88]

INDEPENDENT WIDOWS: A PATRIARCHAL DILEMMA?

What of widows who stayed single, either because they did not wish to remarry or because they could not find a suitable spouse? While it has long been understood that early modern widows were relatively free of male authority, some historians have argued that the independence of widows—who, unlike unmarried daughters, maidservants, and wives, were not under male household rule—posed a problem for early modern patriarchy.[89] However, if independent widows challenged

---

[87] Kingsmill, *A viewe of mans estate*, sig. L6r.
[88] William Lilly, *Mr. Lilly's History of his Life and Times* (London, 1721), 19–20.
[89] See Barbara J. Todd, 'The Remarrying Widow: A Stereotype Reconsidered', in Mary Prior (ed.), *Women in English Society 1500–1800* (New York, 1985), 55; 'The Virtuous Widow in Protestant England', in Cavallo and Warner (eds), *Widowhood in Medieval and Early Modern Europe*, 66–7; Bernard Capp, *When Gossips Meet: Women, the Family and Neighbourhood in Early Modern England* (Oxford, 2003), 26; Sara Mendelson and Patricia Crawford, *Women in Early Modern England,*

patriarchal order, that order was remarkably ineffective in forcing them to accept male tutelage. Roughly 80 per cent of English widows lived independently, either alone or as heads of households, and solitary widows headed far more households than solitary men.[90] As this suggests, the importance of female subordination in early modern English patriarchy can be exaggerated. The primary governing rule was that everyone should belong to a household headed by one responsible adult. The subjection of women was a far less important goal than the maintenance of a clear hierarchy. There was no confusion about the place of widows in this schema: they were not troublesome anomalies, but legitimate household governors. Ceasing to be wives, they continued to be mothers and mistresses. Thus Rogers held that although a wife should not usurp her husband's role by leading family prayers, a widow could certainly do so: 'And the wife is as well the mother, as the man, the father of the family: she is a part of the household's head, as the husband is the wife's head. Now if she be free from the dominion of her head, then is she the whole head of the family, and returns to her privileges...'[91]

No household, the moralists repeated, could have more than one head. The specter that terrified them was not the 'headless' widow but the monstrous hydra of the multi-generational family. Married sons and daughters could hardly be expected to revert to adolescent subordination, so an elderly mother moving in with them (or father, as Lear famously discovered) would be obliged to sacrifice her natural authority and become a dependent in her children's house. Such an unnatural reversal of authority could only lead to bitter regret. Rogers wrote direly of how dependent old parents 'must come out of the hall into the kitchen, sit at table's end, or in the chimney corner with a poor pittance sent them, and at last die in discontent, and repenting themselves of their folly'. He thought that even with the best children, cohabitation was doomed to failure: 'Be wise, you parents, yield not yourselves captives and prisoners to your children: no prison can be more irksome to a parent, than a son or daughter's house... Love must descend, not ascend: it's not natural (saith *Paul*) for children to provide for parents, but for parents to provide for them...'[92] Indeed, one widow found to her sorrow that married children made bad hosts. Elizabeth Awsopp moved in with her married stepson, Thomas, and lived 'with him and his wife, and had meat, drink, house-room, washing, wringing and such like necessaries there at [his] costs and charges by the space of four years and three quarters together'. During this time, she reported, she 'for two of the first years was very well used there but for the rest of the time of her abode there she was very evil entreated and used in many points, and much disdained at as she thought for she was constrained for lack of competent meat, drink, and other necessaries that she stood need of to buy herself some

---

1550–1720 (New York, 1998), 175; Marjorie Keniston McIntosh, *Working Women in English Society, 1300–1620* (Cambridge, 2005), 4; Carlton, 'The Widow's Tale', 126.

[90] Erickson, *Women and Property*, 187–8; Peter Laslett, 'Mean Household Size in England since the Sixteenth Century', in Laslett and Richard Wall (eds), *Household and Family in Past Time* (Cambridge, 1972), 147.

[91] Rogers, *Matrimoniall honour*, 269.

[92] Ibid. 92.

meat, drink, and candles to go to bed withal, elsewhere abroad out of the house with her own money'.[93]

It was eminently undesirable, according to early modern patriarchal theory, for a widow to live with her married children. If she were the stronger character, she would tyrannize over them, forcing them into fictitious childhood and threatening the marital bond: 'If they live with their children, they will so pry into everything that their childrens' husband or wife doth, and shew such suspicion and jealousy in everything, as they cannot but cause much discord: and hence it oft cometh to pass, that either parent and child, or husband and wife must be parted: they cannot all in peace live together.'[94] Or, if the children were more forceful, they would domineer over her in a monstrous reversal of natural order. What, then, were widows to do? Remarriage was a popular option in London, but for widows who did not wish to remarry or were unable to do so, independence—either as solitary women or as heads of families—was the solution that accorded best with the dictates of early modern English patriarchy.

In London, widows who could not afford to keep house themselves often lived in lodgings. These were cheaper than maintaining separate households, but could involve conflicts of authority, as one widow discovered. Mary Drane testified in 1620 that she had moved out of John Hopper's house after considerable provocation: 'She for her part cannot report or say that he the said Hopper is a peaceable or quiet man, for she hath put up (being a silly poor woman and a widow) many wrongs and injuries at his hands, and besides he is a man that doth profess religion in outward habit and guise to the world, but she is persuaded in her conscience that he is not the man inwards as men do repute him'. Hopper and his wife, Mary complained, had condemned her for 'keeping out of doors so much' when her sole offense was to have spent one hour in a tavern with a haberdasher who was planning to ride down to her hometown and had asked her if she had anything to send to her mother. What was more, they fed her scantily and even that was 'very ill handled'. On one occasion, Hopper's wife gave her 'some pottage to eat which was taken out of a pan which served him the said Hopper many times instead of a close stool'. Fed up, Mary hired a chamber of one Mr Smith instead, but she was not able to leave before the Hoppers, 'very wroth', pushed her down the stairs and struck her.[95]

Mary Drane's indignation illustrates the conscious independence claimed by widows. Though they might lodge in a man's house, they were not subject to his authority like a daughter or a maidservant, or indeed a wife. In fact, it was considered so important to make independence possible for widows that the rules and regulations preventing maids from living out of service and restricting the economic activity of wives were reversed or moderated in their case. No laws prohibited widows from living independently or from employing servants, and freemen's widows were specifically entitled to take over their husbands' trades and to enroll apprentices. For the poorest widows and those past work, parish pensions

---

[93] Elizabeth Awsopp, 1572 (LMA, DL/C/211/1, fo. 34).
[94] Gouge, *Of domesticall duties*, 583.
[95] Mary Drane, 1620 (LMA, DL/C/227, fos. 195–6).

provided a modicum of support. In a society so resolutely hostile to taxation, the fact that parish rates were largely funneled to poor widows and their children speaks volumes: the independence of widows was not a problematic accident, but the actively subsidized result of early modern English social policy.

Freemen's widows were usually entitled to take over their husbands' trades as freewomen during their widowhoods, with the right to keep current apprentices and enroll new ones. For example, the widow Anne King, 71, reported in 1629 that since her widowhood she had maintained herself by selling books, probably her late husband's trade.[96] It is unclear, however, whether many widows made use of this right for long. While late medieval London has been seen as particularly favorable to entrepreneurial widows,[97] few appear in early modern company records. In the sixteenth century, Rappaport finds that women engaged only 1.6 per cent of apprentices for a sample of seven companies in the sixteenth century.[98] For the early seventeenth century, Brodsky finds that widows appeared only 'sporadically' in the records of enrollment of new apprentices. Seven widow cordwainers enrolled apprentices between 1597 and 1603, she finds, and five widow grocers were mentioned between 1629 and 1633. While some printers' widows remained in business, around 70 per cent closed up shop within a few years of their husbands' deaths.[99] In the eighteenth century, Earle finds widows working as distillers, grocers, butchers, linen drapers, haberdashers, merchants, apothecaries, and more in the policy registers of the Sun Fire Office, an insurance company. However he notes that many widows 'were not likely to stay in business long, just long enough to wind the business up or until their son was old enough to take it over'.[100] Indeed, the pressures of managing a household of servants and apprentices, raising children, and running a business may have been overwhelmingly great. Widowers remarried rapidly to obtain new 'helpmeets', but tradeswomen and craftswomen could not marry wives to take over their domestic duties.

Most widows did the same sort of work as wives. The more fortunate among them ran victualling houses and alehouses, market stalls and shops. Others worked as laundresses or nurses, hawked food abroad, sewed, made lace, or wound silk. The poorest worked for their neighbors as charwomen, clinging to a fragile independence. Nonetheless, some entrepreneurial widows became solid businesswomen in their own right. Joan Bradfield, tripewoman, of the parish of Christchurch, was one of the consistory court's most regular witnesses, deposing in 1609, 1617, 1618, and 1621. In 1609, at the age of 60, she reported: 'she liveth with dressing of souse[101] and keepeth a house with five servants and she keepeth two motherless children besides, and she is worth £10 in goods every man paid.' Her business prospered; in

---

[96] Anne King, 1629 (LMA, DL/C/231, fo. 405).
[97] Caroline M. Barron, 'The "Golden Age" of Women in Medieval London', *Reading Medieval Studies* 15 (1989), 35–58.
[98] Steve Rappaport, *Worlds within Worlds: Structures of Life in Sixteenth-Century London* (Cambridge, 1989), 41.
[99] Brodsky, 'Widows', 142–3.
[100] Earle, *A City Full of People*, 147–8, 150.
[101] Pickled pig ears and feet.

1618 she said: 'she is a tripe woman and by that profession together with her own means formerly gotten she now liveth and is worth £60 her debts paid.' She also rented a tenement containing three furnaces in which to 'seethe tripes' to one Henry Burton, the furnaces being valued at £21. When Joan last testified in 1621, she was a householder of long standing in her parish, having lived there for fifty-six years; she said she was 75 years old. She was still vigorous, however, having recently attended a wedding in Reigate, Surrey, along with her fellow tripeman John Wood of Whitechapel.[102]

Joan Bradfield's prosperity was exceptional. For poor widows supporting children on meager wages, survival was a precarious balancing act. Jane White, 58, explained that she had fallen into debt because of medical expenses for her child. A neighbor had entrusted her with a bag and an apron to sell, which she had done. But when Jane had tried to deliver the money, her neighbor had not been home, and soon after, Jane's 'child fell sick and [she] through poverty laid out the said money'. As a consequence, Jane said, she had 'not yet paid [the neighbor] for the same but she doth intend to pay her when God shall enable her'. Jane owed another small debt of four shillings to a different neighbor, Dorothy Rutherford, and in nine months had still been unable to get the sum together.[103] The hand-to-mouth petty retailing on which Jane White seems to have relied was starkly inadequate for her needs.

Parish pensions and other charity were important components in poor widows' budgets. However, the residents of poor parishes, with many claimants and few ratepayers, were heavily disadvantaged in comparison to small, rich parishes; while the latter did contribute to the expenses of poorer parishes, they tended to take care of their own first, generously. Similarly, widows whose husbands had belonged to one of the great livery companies were much more likely than laborers' widows to have access to company pensions. Residents of the parishes outside the walls were likely to find that local resources were heavily strained. For most poor widows, pensions did not enable them to stop working; instead, they were intended to fill the gap between a widow's own earnings and the basic cost of living. Archer suggests that weekly pensions of five or six pence were standard, and that in the very hard years of the mid-1590s, a widow's pension would have covered only about 35 per cent of her basic needs.[104] Widows who received alms were expected to live humbly, and any luxuries could be grounds for removing their pensions. The widow Kennett reported that she had formerly received a pension from the parish of St Martin in the Vintry, but had lately been denied it because she kept a maidservant, with which the chief men of the parish 'did find fault'.[105] The presence of grown children or lodgers—suspicious 'inmates' who risked becoming

---

[102] Joan Bradfield: 1609 (LMA, DL/C/218, p. 659); 1618 (LMA, DL/C/225, fo. 281r); 1621 (LMA, DL/C/228, fo. 63v).
[103] Jane White, 1634 (LMA, DL/C/234, fos. 8v–9v).
[104] Ian Archer, *The Pursuit of Stability: Social Relations in Elizabethan London* (Cambridge, 1991), 186, 195.
[105] Part of the problem was that the widow could not afford to pay the maid in question, who, according to a witness, was not truly Elizabeth Kennett's servant but merely lodged with her 'and doth

further burdens on parish resources—could disqualify poor people from receiving pensions even as their contributions shored up fragile household economies.[106]

While few consistory court witnesses admitted receiving alms, widows who did so routinely also worked, like Mary Corey, 72, who said 'she is a poor widow and hath a pension in the parish of St Bride where she is a parishioner and is a chorewoman and doth other work such as she is able to do to procure her a living'. Ellen Cuthbert, a widow from Calais living in Whitechapel, said 'she liveth by her labour as spinning and suchlike, a poor widow with the alms of the parish'. Frances Rice, 60, admitted that in addition to being a charwoman, 'she received sometimes alms amongst other poor of the parish'. The recipients of parish charity were expected to do whatever was required of them, like Anne Floud, 60, who attended the labor of an unmarried woman because she was commanded to be there by Deputy Dawson, 'whose pleasure it was that those who had the pension of that parish should help that woman in her travail'.[107] In addition to dispensing alms, parishes regularly hired poor elderly people, often women, to perform a variety of tasks. Some of these, like nursing the sick poor and searching the dead to discover the cause of death, were both unpleasant and, in the case of infectious disease, dangerous. Others were more nominal. Claire Schen writes, for example, that St Botolph Aldersgate hired a number of old women to supervise the maids' gallery in church. Mistress Peirson was the first to be hired, and when she lost her sight ten years later, another woman was engaged to assist her, and then another. By 1594, three women—one blind—were being paid to watch the maids.[108]

A NEVER-ENDING STRUGGLE

Few London women could expect to live to an old age. Death visited the young as well as the old, and indeed, in the case of the plague, victims were predominantly young. For those who did reach an advanced age, earning a living remained a constant of everyday life. Parish pensions did not fully cover the costs of survival, so men and women of the poorer sort simply worked until they could no longer do so: their last years were a desperate struggle not to lose ground. Margery Durham, 50 and no longer in contact with her husband, explained that the hard labor of charring had become too much for her, leaving her with the less reputable occupation of selling ale: 'she hath in her younger time got her living by washing, starching and scouring, but she now doth get her living by selling of drink.' Old women were probably even more likely to continue working than old men. Katherine Currier,

---

take what courses she liketh best to get her own living'. Elizabeth Kennett and Agnes Bartlett, *Emme Logey c. Michael Yardley*, 1614 (LMA, DL/C/222, fos. 196–197r).

[106] Claire S. Schen, 'Strategies of Poor Aged Women and Widows in Sixteenth-Century London', in Botelho and Thane (eds), *Women and Ageing in British Society*, 23.

[107] Mary Corey, 1619 (LMA, DL/C/226, 4th series, fos. 19v–20r); Ellen Cuthbert, 1600/1 (LMA, DL/C/216, sl. 251); Frances Rice, 1639 (LMA, DL/C/235, fo. 197r); Anne Floud, 1621 (LMA, DL/C/228, fo. 87v).

[108] Schen, 'Strategies of Poor Aged Women', 21.

62, made no reference to her husband when asked how she maintained herself, saying only: 'she liveth by her labour in spinning and other business she hath of her own.' Her husband was a carter, but he might well have found the travel too strenuous for one of his age. Similarly, Anne Marten, 65, said 'she maintaineth herself by washing and scouring abroad for other folk' with no reference to her husband, a cordwainer. Joan Helme, a gardener's wife, reported simply: 'she is but a poor woman and liveth of that she earneth which is by winding of long silks to merchants and others.' She had been married to Christopher Helme for twenty-five years and she herself was 56, so Christopher may have been in his 60s and past work.[109]

Aged poor women were subjected to severe stress at a time in life when they were least able to cope with ill fortune. The deposition of Margery Buckley in 1620 illustrates the psychological strain of facing old age and poverty: she had been driven out of her wits, as she recounted, by the loss of some savings. Margery was 80 years old, she said, when she testified in a defamation case involving two of her neighbors in Swan Alley in St Botolph Aldgate. When her credit was called into question because of a rumor that she had been put in the local jail, she told a long and detailed story in explanation. Margery's husband, John Buckley, also about 80 years old, had been a hammerman for the gunmakers, but was no longer able to work, receiving instead a small pension from the parish. Margery herself, though just as old, told the court that she got her living 'by winding of silk', and another witness explained that she wound silk for shops. Like other poor woman, she supplemented her usual income whenever possible with temporary work, and about nine months before her testimony she had kept a poor woman in childbed. For some reason, 'having gathered and put together the sum of nine shillings in money', she left her small hoard with the poor woman in a little box with the intention of collecting it later. Disastrously, when she returned, the box was open, and the purse and the money were gone.

The loss of her savings, Margery Buckley explained, 'grieved [her] not a little, and besides the discontentment which her husband gave her, understanding that the sum was lost, drove [her] into such a perplexity that she was in a manner frantic'. 'Being not contented in her mind', she 'went one evening about the streets and other places discontented, and happened to fall into the constable's hands of the liberty of East Smithfield'. The constable was not unsympathetic to the poor old woman wandering 'in this perplexity', and 'entreated [her] to go home to her own lodging'. At the same time, he 'had apprehended a begging wench and was putting her into the cage, and the same wench was unwilling to go and did beg very earnestly of him to dismiss her and let her go'. Margery explained awkwardly to the court that 'hearing her beg so earnestly to be free from going in, [she] went into the cage her own self, no way constrained to do so either by the constable or any other

---

[109] Margery Durham, 1634 (LMA, DL/C/630, fo. 288r); Katherine Currier, 1616 (LMA, DL/C/224, fo. 119–120r); Anne Marten, 1623 (GL MS 9189/1, fo. 54r); Joan Helme, 1618 (LMA, DL/C/225, fos. 360r, 361r).

but in a foolish humour she had about the loss of the foresaid money'.[110] She herself does not appear to have entirely understood why she went into the cage upon hearing the young beggar's pleas, but we can conjecture that her husband's recriminations and the agony of having lost her money caused her to despair. Her language of 'perplexity' and 'discontentment' hints at an intolerable level of strain for a woman whose good fortune in surviving to be old simply meant that she would work ceaselessly to make ends meet until her own frail life's end.

Dying days

To die surrounded by one's children and grandchildren was, in the harsh demographic regime of early modern London, a luxury that many old women had to forego. Women who lived to be old often outlived their husbands and their children; sometimes neighbors were the only community they had left. In the best cases, neighbors aided, visited, and comforted one another in times of failing health and mortal illness. Philip Brian, a woman of St Martin's in the Fields, was admitted to St Bartholomew's Hospital on 25 September 1615, and was buried the following Monday. According to her neighbors, Philip was not actually a widow, but had been forsaken by her second husband. She had lived in St Martin's since she was a girl, first marrying one Brian, then, after his death, becoming the wife of Thomas Leonard. He proved neglectful: at first he 'did many times go abroad about business and was from her a month or more, and came again to her', but 'at length he ... went into Ireland and lived there'. Philip resumed her first husband's name, and lived like a widow until she fell seriously ill, 'diseased and exceedingly swollen in her body'.[111] In her husband's absence it was her neighbors, such as the widow Joan Cook, 65, and Jane Jones, 63, a bricklayer's wife, who visited her in the hospital. Joan Cook reported that she was 'with her when she lay speechless'. When she stopped by the hospital for a final visit, Joan found Philip dead: 'the women were laying her forth to be buried.' Jane Jones 'and other neighbours were determined to go to the said hospital to see the said Philip Brian', but they canceled their visit when Joan brought them the tidings of her death. Thomas Leonard only returned from Ireland seven years later to assert his claim to his abandoned wife's estate.[112]

The widow Elizabeth Eames lived out her last days more comfortably, not among kin, but with her former apprentice Nicholas Hussey. When Nicholas came out of his apprenticeship, he had 'used himself unto her so gently that she bare him great good will', so the two made arrangements for his advancement and her secure retirement. The agreement, witnessed by middle-aged male neighbors of good standing, was that 'Nicholas Hussey should keep the said Elizabeth Eames during her life giving her house room, meat and drink, fire and washing, and four pounds yearly in monies during her life towards her apparel'. In exchange,

---

[110] Margery Buckley, 1620 (LMA, DL/C/227, fos. 206v–208r).
[111] Thomas Langley and Jane Jones, 1622 (LMA, DL/C/228, fos. 325, 326).
[112] Joan Cook and Jane Jones, 1622 (ibid. fos. 325v, 326).

Elizabeth 'was very well content to give' Nicholas her goods, wares, and chattels, as well as the lease of her house, on condition that he leave them all to her if she outlived him. This careful financial planning paid off, and according to all the neighbors, Elizabeth was so pleased with Nicholas's kind behavior towards her that she left him the remainder of her money when she fell mortally ill seven years later. He for his part buried his former mistress very 'honestly' in the churchyard of St Nicholas Acon, dispensing the respectable sum of £3 10s. on her funeral.[113]

While neighbors might ease one another's dying days, in the face of bodily decay there was little comfort to be had. The cheerless story of Anne Willett's last days was chronicled in the consistory court because she left no will, and had made conflicting assertions as to her intentions regarding her goods. Her closest relative, a daughter, had died in childbed four or five years before Anne's own death. The widow possessed little: her brother had left her five marks and had also left the same sum to her daughter, which she may have inherited. Nonetheless, Anne's kin and neighbors took great interest in how she intended to leave her small estate. John Morton, a young coppersmith who lived next door, said that she had told him 'that she felt herself not half well and that she thought she should not live long, "yet," quoth she, "though my daughter Parnell be gone, I thank God I have an heir alive which shall have all my goods after my death, if it please God to spare her."' He asked her who she meant, but 'she would never confess before witnesses ... who was her heir, for that, as she said, she would not have everyone know what she intended to do with her goods'.[114]

Anne may have employed a strategy of ambiguity to encourage her kin to treat her well. Besides her nephew William White, she had a possible heir in Anne Pearson, the young daughter of Matthew and Katherine Pearson. Katherine appears to have been a kinswoman of Anne's, and Anne dined at their house in East Smithfield every Sunday, giving them the impression that their hospitality would be rewarded after her death. William Gorrell, a sailor who lodged with the Pearsons when not at sea, said he had asked her 'what she meant she did not marry and take a husband which should make much of her in her old days', and that she had replied that she didn't wish to do so because she wanted to leave everything to Anne Pearson. Even Cecily Pearson, Matthew's sister and sometime maidservant, had her claim: she said that the widow Willett had promised her 'one of her gowns not of her worst: which she hopeth to receive'.[115]

On the Sunday before Anne Willett's death, Agnes Kendall, Alice Ward, and Agnes Saunders were sitting outside of widow Kendall's house in the parish of St Alphage, when Anne, 'very weak and feeble', made her way out of Ship Alley where she lived, and sat down next to them on a low stall.[116] All three were widows:

---

[113] Roger Haymor, 1572 (LMA, DL/C/211/1, fo. 17r).
[114] Anne Fretherne and John Morton, *William White c. Matthew Pearson*, 1589 (LMA, DL/C/213, pp. 520, 522).
[115] Cecily Pearson, 1589 (ibid. p. 521).
[116] Alice Ward (ibid. p. 519).

Agnes Kendall, who said she was 60 years old and more, had been living in the parish for thirty years; Alice, 80 years old, had been living in St Alphage for twenty-five years; while Agnes Saunders was a younger newcomer at 46 with a mere sixteen years' residence in the parish.[117] Alice and Agnes asked Anne how she did, and she replied that 'she was sick at her heart'. She must have looked very ill, because Alice said: 'I would wish you to go in and not sit here for you seem to be liker to die than to live, and therefore go in lest you be taken suddenly and so die in the street.' However 'Anne Willett said little to that but sat still'.

The women worried about Anne, who was living alone despite a sickness that would clearly prove fatal. Alice Ward told her that 'her neighbours did judge that she had enough to keep her withal while she lived or else her neighbours would see unto her', and suggested that she contact her heir 'to comfort her'.[118] She answered that he was 'a poor prentice' and had 'nothing to comfort [her] withal'.[119] They asked her where he lived, and suggested that she get him to 'sell somewhat to help you with and die not like a beggar'. Despite their persuasions, Anne was too weak or too discouraged to take action to help herself, so Agnes, 'forasmuch as she saw her very sick and without any company to be with her to comfort her', 'slipped away', telling Alice that 'she would seek forth the young man'.[120] Agnes asked a neighbor, Goodwife Hughes, to tell the boy how his aunt was, then returned to the stall where the old women were gathered. '[B]y and by, the said William White came to his aunt's door, and one brought him to her where she sat, and . . . he asked her how she did.' The widow replied: 'I am sick at my heart, cousin, but how do you?' and 'willed him to come to her as he had occasion . . . and so went into her house with him'. Agnes Kendall thoughtfully brought them 'a stool for the young man to sit down upon' and saw William 'secretly put some money into [his aunt's] hand'.[121]

In her last week of life, Anne Willett ventured out less and less; she did not 'go abroad out of the court, but from one neighbour's house to another within the court'.[122] On Monday, she went to the brewer to buy a gallon of ale and 'the brewer's maid (for that [Anne Willett] was so weak) did bring the said gallon of ale and set it at her . . . door'. Her neighbor Margaret Johnson, a coppersmith's wife, 'used many and sundry times to come and sit at her . . . door and talk oft', and the neighbors 'did lament her the said Anne Willett's sickness, and pity her, and give her good counsel to set such things as she had in a readiness and good order in case God should call her'. On Tuesday she went 'up and down the yard, but not abroad', but after that she 'did not come forth of her doors'. During the night on Wednesday, she 'called very piteously for drink', and one Anthony Widnall 'rose and gave her' some.[123]

---

[117] Agnes Kendall, Alice Ward, and Agnes Saunders (ibid. pp. 517, 519, 529).
[118] Alice Ward (ibid. p. 519).
[119] Agnes Kendall (ibid. p. 518).
[120] Alice Ward and Agnes Kendall (ibid. pp. 517–20).
[121] Agnes Kendall (ibid. p. 518).
[122] Margaret Jones (ibid. p. 614).
[123] Margaret Johnson (ibid. p. 612).

The next morning the neighbors went to see her, and found her 'sitting... on her stairs leaning her head (bowing downward) against a shelf only sitting in her smock, and an old waistcoat, bare-footed and bare-legged'.[124] To die without the help of a nurse to keep things sweet and clean meant that the weakness of the old woman's failing body was horribly exposed. One witness was disgusted to see her

> calling for drink sitting upon her stairs in very bad and indecent manner in her single smock in a most beastly and filthy sort, both the place where she sat on, the ground before her, and her smock and self so beastly berayed that it was not a sight for any creature especially for mankind to see, in that sort that it was enough to make any man loathe her and her sex, nodding up and down... calling for drink, insomuch that some present were urged to keep herbs in their hands and put to their noses for avoidance of the scent and savour that then was.[125]

She had not been left entirely alone, for one neighbor described how they saw 'the smock, arms, head, and all parts of the said Anne Willett filthily used, by reason as it seemed a dog in the house with the said Anne had fawned and licked her about the head, being besmeared with the said Anne Willett's filthiness'.[126] Shocked by the degradation in which they had found their neighbor, the visitors did their best to recall her to a sense of Christian duty. Margaret Johnson and her companions

> did persuade her (for they did see by her face and her countenance and her staring with her eyes and her gazing up and down and going from place to place in her smock like half distraught) that she would call upon God and leave off her bracelets and her rings, and think with herself that God had bought her with his most precious blood... for that they all were persuaded with themselves that she was half mad and distraught of her wits and a woman past womanly modesty or honesty and one without reason or wit.

To the neighbors' dismay, the dying woman 'very unruly bade [them] get them from thence, telling them that they had given her nothing, and that there was nothing for them', so they 'departed leaving her in such beastly sort as they found her'. The following night at one o'clock, Margaret Johnson was called by the neighbors to the widow's deathbed, but by the time she had dressed and gone over, 'she the said Anne was newly dead', and all Margaret could do was to help to lay her out.[127]

This story is a bitter counterpart to the better-known godly deathbed scenes preserved by pious witnesses. The happy deaths of the godly, secure in their salvation, had a rich meaning for early modern observers: there, they learned to despise the pomp and glories of this world and to lay up their treasure in heaven. Anne Willett's slow agony held a different message; it told her neighbors something they could hardly bear to hear. Londoners concealed their mortal flesh in costly

---

[124] Margaret Jones (ibid. p. 614).
[125] Margaret Johnson (ibid. pp. 612–13).
[126] Margaret Jones (ibid. 614) included a 'silver whistle' in the list of worldly goods they advised Anne to take off; perhaps this was for the dog.
[127] Margaret Johnson (ibid. pp. 612–13).

carapaces of stiff cloth that proclaimed their identity and status to the world: when they put on their clothes, they put on their selves. The widow's helpless body, laid all but bare to the horror-stricken eyes of her neighbors, spoke to them of the fragility of the order they strove so fiercely to create and to protect. In her degradation and obstinate refusal to turn her thoughts to the divine, they read a dreadful possibility. If the consolations of religion failed, what was left? Impending death had equally extinguished their neighbor's pride and modesty, dragging her down to a shameless state of animal suffering. So, too, their own cherished dignity, their hard-earned rank, their most carefully laid plans—all were castles built of sand, apt to be swept away by the next inexorable wave.

Conclusion

In 1573, the publisher Richard Jones presented his customers with a remarkable poem. In a mock-testament, the maidservant Isabella Whitney described London in affectionate detail, painting a vivid picture of its 'brave buildings' and busy streets, where butchers, bakers, and chandlers displayed their wares, and mercers, goldsmiths, and tailors tempted finicky customers with fine clothing and jewels. Those with money to spend could meet any material need: linens, silks, French ruffs, caps, knives, combs, plate, swords—all were offered up for sale by eager shopkeepers, if one knew where to go. The poet lauded the infinite variety of life in London: apothecaries and physicians healed the sick, while surgeons treated brawlers. The mint was gorged with coin, and apprentices—barred from wedlock—spent their pocket money on 'proper girls' compelled by need or lured by gain to prostitution. Those who toiled all week could go to bathhouses on Saturdays 'to trim them up/on Sundays to look smug'. Prisons awaited London's debtors, she wrote, while Bedlam—where she had often walked to see the sights—took in those 'that out of turn do talk'. Beadles and matrons oversaw hard labor in Bridewell, while lawyers offered their services to those 'as cannot quiet be,/but strive for house or land'.[1] London's marriage market and the opportunities it offered to the ambitious young warranted a cynical nod:

> For maidens poor I widowers rich,
> do leave, that oft shall dote:
> And by that means shall marry them,
> to set the girls afloat.
> And wealthy widows will I leave,
> to help young gentlemen:
> Which when you have, in any case
> be courteous to them then:
> And see their plate and jewels eke
> may not be marred with rust.
> Nor let their bags too long be full,
> for fear that they do burst.[2]

Isabella Whitney's London was a vibrant, chaotic city where fruitwomen cried their wares, poor poets loitered by the booksellers' shops by St Paul's, and the rich

---

[1] Whitney, 'Wyll and Testament', in *A sweet nosgay, or pleasant posye contayning a hundred and ten phylosophicall flowers* (London, 1573), sigs. C5r, C7r.
[2] Ibid. sig. C6v.

adorned themselves with the latest fashions and sought diversion at playhouses, tennis courts, and dancing schools. But Whitney herself, she wrote, had little reason to love London: 'small cause there is, that I/should grieve from thee to go.' The city where so many young people sought their fortunes had left her poor and friendless: her suitor had forsaken her for another woman, and her mistress thought ill of her unjustly.[3] Her farewell to London could easily have been framed as an invective against the city's sinful ways; instead, it was a bittersweet ode to the mesmerizing attractions of urban life. 'I loved thee best,' she concluded, after cataloguing the city's rich diversity:

> So fare thou well a thousand times,
> God shield thee from thy foe:
> And still make thee victorious,
> of those that seek thy woe.
> And though I am persuade that I
> shall never more thee see:
> Yet to the end I will not cease
> to wish much good to thee.[4]

Whitney's rueful farewell to the metropolis stands out among the spiritual meditations that characterize early modern women's verse. Indeed, she was the first woman to publish a volume of secular poetry in the English language.[5] However, the London she describes is instantly recognizable as the same noisy city inhabited by the urban women of this study. They too were preoccupied by worldly concerns: how were they to navigate the hustle and bustle of the streets, afford the magnificent fineries laid out for sale, stay out of debt, entertain themselves, remain in good health, find suitable husbands, feed their children?

Because of the assumption that women in early modern England were supposed to be chaste, silent, and obedient—that is, passive—women's activity has sometimes been conflated with disorder. Maids who tramped towards the metropolis along England's muddy roads, matrons who haggled in the marketplace and toasted one another in alehouses, widows who embraced their suitors in taverns—these women are difficult to reconcile with the wraith-like feminine ideal, seen little and heard less. However, prescription can be misleading. Women who pursued their preferment, worked for money, and involved themselves in the public life of the neighborhood did not simply threaten the social order. Rather, they abandoned the rigid confines of theoretical gender roles in pursuit of a more pragmatic vision of social and economic stability. Recent work on masculinity has demonstrated the error in restricting analyses of gender to women. Similarly, we ought not to make the mistake of investigating women's lives through a narrow lens that excludes everything but gender. Their economies were often those of the household, and

---

[3] Ibid. sig. C2v. See also Isabella Whitney, *The copy of a letter, lately written in meeter, by a yonge gentilwoman: to her unconstant lover* (London, 1567).
[4] Whitney, 'Wyll and Testament', sigs. C7v, C8.
[5] Betty S. Travitsky, 'Whitney, Isabella (fl. 1566–1573)', *Oxford Dictionary of National Biography* (Oxford, 2004).

their politics those of the neighborhood, but within these worlds, women were assertive and engaged.

Young women traveled to London from near and far—many from neighboring counties, but others from the distant north, or the Welsh hills. They knew, probably, that city dwellers often succumbed to early deaths, but they hoped to dodge those dangers and find their fortunes in the capital. Higher wages and crowds of striving, single young men were a powerful draw. Indeed, after coming to know the city and its ways in years of service, migrant maids could expect to marry and to achieve an independence that might have been denied them in their native towns and villages. Navigating London's active marriage market would require all their ingenuity: in the absence of watchful parents, maidservants would have to locate other 'friends' to provide advice and safe places to court, and the long years of apprenticeship left ample time for misunderstandings, betrayal, and heartbreak. Nor could maids assume that any husband was better than none: an idle, thriftless, heavy-handed spouse would make a wife's days hard and bleak. However, due to the large numbers of young men and anxious widowers in London and the shortage of equivalent women, even poor maids were able to establish themselves as city wives of one sort or another: in stark contrast to the countryside, marriage was near-universal.

As married women and—if they were rich enough—householders, wives took on authority and responsibility. Like their husbands, they governed their children and servants, if they had any, and could expect to be obeyed. They also felt themselves to be responsible for the economic well-being of the household, and played a particularly important role in overseeing expenditures, walking the fine line between subjection and rule. Within the neighborhood, adult women helped mothers in childbed, condemned behavior they considered immoral or threatening to local harmony and order, and reinforced neighborly bonds with charitable gifts and festive consumption. Women also worked, not only cooking and cleaning within the home, but to make ends meet. Widows could choose to live independently or, in London's advantageous marriage market, to marry again, as many women did.

By paying attention to London women's choices and struggles, what they were able to accomplish and what challenges they faced, we not only gain a better understanding of early modern women, but also of the society in which they lived. In particular, it is useful to examine how individuals and communities responded when their priorities collided, when maintaining a rigid sexual order conflicted with the broader need to protect economic and social order. As we have seen, economic priorities tended to take precedence over a strict sexual double standard. Communities were quick to saddle the putative fathers of maidservants' illegitimate children with financial responsibility, so that blame did not simply attach itself to 'fallen' women, and abusing a servant was a risky affair. The wives of thriftless men were expected to do their best to reform their erring spouses rather than to remain silently passive. Cruel and violent husbands may have been the undisputed masters of their households, but their irresponsible actions prompted critical gossip, loss of local status, and neighborhood interventions. Women who entered the public marketplace to support their families drew pride from their achievements, not shame from having left the domestic cloister. When wives were widowed, they became free of male household authority. If they wished to remarry, they might hope to preserve their household superiority by finding a younger, poorer bridegroom who was willing to sacrifice some traditional dominance for hope of future preferment: such matches, while problematic, were a fundamental part of London's economy.

The preference for economic order over sexual order in early modern London should not be confused with liberation or equality. The double standard was tempered by economic imperatives, not eliminated. Men who fathered bastards could expect to pay because they endangered community finances; rape, on the other hand, was nearly impossible to prosecute. Concern about social and economic order did not always work to women's advantage, either. The same theory of household governance that permitted widows to rule their households held that wives were bound to obey their husbands. The moral authority acquired by respectable matrons could be used to repress more marginal women, and female competition could be destructive. As hucksters, nurses, lace-makers and more, women toiled to keep their families fed, but were legally barred from concealing their earnings from their husbands since authorities feared disaster if both spouses shared financial control. Women worked for money, but their exclusion from most crafts and trades ensured that their gains remained meager.

Despite the very real restrictions faced by ordinary women in early modern London, they must be recognized as members of the society in which they lived, with stakes in its survival. In turn, that survival depended on women's efforts. Conflicts between men and women, while important, were overshadowed by the larger struggle for material necessities and a precarious social order. That social order was not a smoothly functioning machine, crushing those who dared defy it. Instead, we might picture a ship sailing on stormy seas, its wooden sides creaking under strain, buffeted by the winds of poverty and plague. Life on board was hard, cramped, deeply hierarchical, frequently drunken, and the crew was denied the rich rewards of trade. The mariners longed for calmer seas and may have dreamed of a better ship, perhaps even of mutiny—yet they labored nonetheless to preserve the fragile vessel. Safe and sound on dry land, we should not despise their toil, nor wonder why they strove to keep the ship afloat.

Bibliography

MANUSCRIPT SOURCES

London, London Metropolitan Archives

Diocese of London Consistory Court deposition books
DL/C/211/1, April 1572–February 1573/4
DL/C/211/2, February 1573/4–June 1574
DL/C/212, June 1574–March 1575/6
DL/C/629, April 1578–November 1580
DL/C/213, December 1586–June 1591
DL/C/214, June 1591–November 1594
DL/C/215, October 1597–June 1600 (Pages are not numbered. Refer to slide numbers (sl.) in microfilm reel X79/119.)
DL/C/216, June 1600–June 1603 (Pages are not numbered usefully. Refer to slide numbers (sl.) in microfilm reel X27/120.)
DL/C/217, February 1606/7–June 1607
DL/C/218, May 1608–November 1609
DL/C/219, November 1609–June 1611
DL/C/220, February 1610/11–December 1611
DL/C/221, January 1612/13–December 1613
DL/C/222, November 1613–February 1614/15
DL/C/223, January 1614/15–February 1615/16
DL/C/224, January 1615/16–July 1617
DL/C/225, June 1617–April 1619
DL/C/226, April 1619–June 1620 (Note that this book consists of eight separate gatherings and series of numbering.)
DL/C/227, June 1620–June 1621
DL/C/228, June 1621–December 1622 (See Guildhall MS 9189/1 for 1622–1624.)
DL/C/229, September 1624–June 1625
DL/C/230, June 1625–June 1627 (See Guildhall MS 9189/2 for 1627.)
DL/C/231, November 1627–December 1630
DL/C/232, December 1630–January 1633/4
DL/C/233, June 1630–November 1634
DL/C/630, November 1632–February 1634/5
DL/C/234, February 1634/5–November 1637
DL/C/235, November 1637–June 1640

Diocese of London Consistory Court personal answers books
DL/C/192, June 1617–February 1620/1
DL/C/193, April 1621–February 1630/1
DL/C/194, April 1631–February 1638/9

Vicar-general's books
'Stanhope Pt.V', DL/C/338, 1601–1605

'Crompton', DL/C/339, 1607–1611
'Edwards', DL/C/340, 1611–1616
'Marten Pt. I', DL/C/341, 1616–1622/3
'Marten Pt. II', DL/C/342, 1623–1627

Repertories of the Court of Aldermen
COL/CA/1/1/25, 7 November 1592–28 October 1596 (Repertory 23)

London, Guildhall Library Manuscripts Section (GL)
MS 4069/1 (Cornhill Wardmote Minutes Vol.1 1571–1651)
MSS 9189/1 (1622–4) and 9189/2 (1627): further consistory court deposition books
MS 9220, 9221 St Botolph Aldgate parish register, 1558–1625

London, Bethlem Hospital Royal Archives (BRHA): Minutes of the Court of Governors
BCB 2, March 1574–May 1576
BCB 3, May 1576–November 1579
BCB 4, February 1598–November 1604
BCB 5, November 1604–July 1610
BCB 6, July 1617–March 1627

PRINTED PRIMARY SOURCES

An acte for the reformation of divers abuses used in the wardmote inquest Together with the articles of the change of the sayd inquest (London, 1617).
ALLEY, HUGH, *Hugh Alley's Caveat: The Markets of London in 1598. Folger Ms V. a. 318*, ed. Ian Archer, Caroline Barron, and Vanessa Harding (London, 1988).
Analytical index, to the series of records known as the Remembrancia. Preserved among the archives of the city of London A. D. 1579–1664 (London, 1878).
A Batchelers resolution, or, Have among you now, widowes or maydes (London, 1629).
The batchelour's guide, and the married man's comfort (London, 1685–8).
A Breefe Discourse, declaring and aproving the necessarie and inviolable maintenance of the laudable Customes of London (London, 1584).
BUSH, RICE, *The poor mans friend, or A narrative of what progresse many worthy citizens of London have made in that godly work of providing for the poor* (London, 1650).
CART, JOHN, *The cunning age, or, A re-married woman repenting her marriage* (London, 1625).
Certain sermons or homilies appointed to be read in churches, in the time of Queen Elizabeth of famous memory (London, 1683).
The city-law, or, The course and practice in all manner of juridicall proceedings in the hustings in Guild-Hall, London (London, 1647).
CLEAVER, ROBERT, and DOD, JOHN, *A godly forme of houshold government for the ordering of private families* (London, 1612).
A compleat journal of the votes, speeches and debates, both of the House of Lords and House of Commons throughout the whole reign of Queen Elizabeth (London, 1708).
CONSETT, HENRY, *The practice of the spiritual or ecclesiastical courts* (London, 1685).
Constitutions and canons ecclesiasticall (London, 1604).
A country new Jigge betweene Simon and Susan (London, 1620).
CROMPTON, WILLIAM, *A wedding-ring, fitted to the finger of every paire that have or shall meete in the feare of God* (London, 1632).

CROUCH, HUMPHREY, *The industrious smith wherin is showne, how plain dealing is overthrown* (London, 1635).
A dainty dialogue between Henry and Elizabeth. Being the good wives vindication, and the bad husbands reformation (London, 1670–77).
DALTON, MICHAEL, *The countrey justice containing the practise of the justices of the peace out of their sessions* (London, 1619).
DEFOE, DANIEL, *Every-bodys business, is no-bodys business; or Private abuses, publick grievances* (London, 1725).
DEKKER, THOMAS, *The batchelars banquet* (London, 1603).
——*English villanies six severall times prest to death by the printers* (London, 1632).
The English Reports, 91 vols (Edinburgh, 1900–1932).
An excellent new ditty q1: or, Which proveth that women the best warriers be, for they made the devill from earth for to flee (London, 1635).
GATAKER, THOMAS, *Marriage duties briefely couched togither out of Colossians, 3.18, 19* (London, 1620).
GODOLPHIN, JOHN, *Repertorium canonicum, or, An abridgment of the ecclesiastical laws of this realm* (London, 1678).
GOUGE, WILLIAM, *Of domesticall duties* (London, 1622).
HAKE, EDWARD, *Newes out of Powles Churchyarde* (London, 1579).
HANNAY, PATRICK, *A happy husband or, Directions for a maide to choose her mate* (London, 1619).
HILDER, THOMAS, *Conjugall counsell, or, Seasonable advice, both to unmarried, and married persons* (London, 1653).
The housholders new-yeeres gift containing a pleasant dialogue betwixt the husband and his wife (London, 1640).
The husband, A poeme expressed in a compleat man (London, 1614).
I tell you John Jarret, you'l breake John Jarrets wives counsell to her husband (London, 1630).
JOHNSON, RICHARD, *The pleasant walkes of Moore-fields* (London, 1607).
KINGSMILL, ANDREW, *A viewe of mans estate wherein the great mercie of God in mans free justification by Christ, is very comfortably declared* (London, 1576).
The lamentation of a new married man briefely declaring the sorrow and grief that comes by marrying a young wanton wife (London, 1629).
A Letter sent by the maydens of London, to the vertuous matrones & mistresses of the same in the defense of their lawfull libertie (London, 1567).
The life of Long Meg of Westminster (London, 1635).
LILLY, WILLIAM, *Mr. Lilly's History of His Life and Times* (London, 1721).
LUPTON, DANIEL, *London and the Country Carbonadoed and Quartered into Several Characters* (London, 1632).
MARTINDALE, ADAM, *The Life of Adam Martindale*, ed. Richard Parkinson (Chetham, 1845).
A merry new song of a rich widdowes wooing that married a young man to her owne undoing (London, 1625).
Middlesex County Records, ed. John Cordy Jeaffreson, 3 vols, Old Series (London, 1974).
N., D., *The Figure of Six* (London, 1652).
NICCHOLES, ALEXANDER, *A discourse, of marriage and wiving* (London, 1615).
The olde bride, or The gilded beauty (London, 1635).
P., L., *The merry conceited lasse, whose hearts desire was set on fire, a husband for to have; in hope that he would certainly, maintaine her fine and brave* (London, 1640).
P., M., *The bonny bryer, or A Lancashire lass her sore lamentation, for the death of her love, and her owne reputation* (London, 1630).

P., M., *The countrey lasse* (London, 1628).
—— *A fayre portion for a fayre mayd: or, The thriftie mayd of Worstersheere* (London, 1633).
P., M., *Merry dialogue betwixt a married man and his wife concerning the affaires of this carefull life* (London, 1628).
PARKER, MARTIN, *The married-womans case, or, Good counsell to mayds, to be carefull of hastie marriage by the example of other married-women* (London, 1627).
—— *The marryed mans lesson: or, A disswasion from jealousie* (London, 1634).
—— *A penny-worth of good counsell To widdowes, and to maides, this counsell I send free; and let them looke before they leape, or, that they married bee* (London, 1638).
—— *Robin and Kate: or, A bad husband converted by a good wife in a dialogue betweene Robin and Kate* (London, 1634).
PARROT, HENRY, *Cures for the itch* (London, 1626).
PEPYS, SAMUEL, *The Diary of Samuel Pepys*, ed. Robert Latham and William Matthews, 11 vols (Berkeley, 2000).
PERKINS, WILLIAM, *Christian oeconomie: or, A short survey of the right manner of erecting and ordering a familie* (London, 1609).
PLATTER, THOMAS, *Thomas Platter's travels in England, 1599*, ed. and trans. Clare Williams (London, 1937).
POWELL, THOMAS, *The art of thriving. Or, The plaine path-way to preferment* (London, 1636).
A pretty new ditty: or, A young lasses resolution, as her mind I truly scan, who shews in conclusion, she loves a handsome young man (London, 1633).
ROGERS, DANIEL, *Matrimoniall honour: or, The mutuall crowne and comfort of godly, loyall, and chaste marriage* (London, 1642).
ROWLANDS, SAMUEL, *The bride* (London, 1617).
—— *A crew of kind gossips, all met to be merrie complayning of their husbands, with their husbands answeres in their owne defence* (London, 1613).
—— *Good newes and bad newes* (London, 1622).
—— *Humors looking glasse* (London, 1608).
—— *The knave of clubbs* (London, 1609).
Seldome comes the better: or, An admonition to all sorts of people as husbands, wives, masters, and servants, &c. to avoid mutability, and to fix their minds on what they possesse (London, 1629).
SHAKESPEARE, WILLIAM, *The Taming of the Shrew*, ed. Ann Thompson (Cambridge, 2003).
The Shirburn Ballads 1585–1616, ed. Andrew Clark (Oxford, 1907).
SNAWSEL, ROBERT, *A looking-glasse for married folkes* (London, 1619).
STOW, JOHN, *Annales, or a generall chronicle of England* (London, 1632).
STUBBES, PHILIP, *The anatomie of abuses* (London, 1583).
TAYLOR, JOHN, *Divers crabtree lectures Expressing the severall languages that shrews read to their husbands, either at morning, noone, or night* (London, 1639).
—— *A juniper lecture, With the description of all sorts of women, good, and bad: from the modest to the maddest, from the most civil, to the scold rampant* (London, 1639).
Tis not otherwise: or: The praise of a married life (London, 1617).
WEST, RICHARD, *The court of conscience or Dick Whippers sessions* (London, 1607).
WHATELY, WILLIAM, *A bride-bush: or, A direction for married persons plainely describing the duties common to both, and peculiar to each of them* (London, 1619).
WHITNEY, ISABELLA, *The copy of a letter, lately written in meeter, by a yonge gentilwoman: to her unconstant lover* (London, 1567).
—— 'Wyll and Testament', in *A sweet nosgay, or pleasant posye contayning a hundred and ten phylosophicall flowers* (London, 1573).

WHYTHORNE, THOMAS, *The Autobiography of Thomas Whythorne*, ed. James M. Osborn (Oxford, 1962).
WITH, ELIZABETH, *Elizabeth Fools warning being a true and most perfect relation of all that has happened to her since her marriage* (London, 1659).
The woman to the plow and the man to the hen-roost, or, A fine way to cure a cot-quean (London, 1675).

SELECTED SECONDARY SOURCES

ADAIR, RICHARD, *Courtship, Illegitimacy and Marriage in Early Modern England* (Manchester, 1996).
ADAMSON, NANCY LEE, 'Urban Families: The Social Context of the London Elite, 1500–1603', Ph.D thesis, University of Toronto (1983).
AGREN, MARIA, and ERICKSON, AMY (eds), *The Marital Economy in Scandinavia and Britain 1400–1900* (Burlington, Vt., 2005).
AMUSSEN, SUSAN DWYER, ' "Being Stirred to Much Unquietness": Violence and Domestic Violence in Early Modern England', *Journal of Women's History* 6.2 (1994), 70–89.
—— *An Ordered Society: Gender and Class in Early Modern England* (New York, 1988).
APPLEBY, ANDREW B., 'Disease or Famine? Mortality in Cumberland and Westmorland 1580–1640', *Economic History Review*, new series, 26.3 (1973), 403–32.
ARCHER, IAN, *The Pursuit of Stability: Social Relations in Elizabethan London* (Cambridge, 1991).
BAER, WILLIAM, 'Housing for the Lesser Sort in Stuart London: Findings from Certificates, and Returns of Divided Houses', *London Journal* 33.1 (2008), 61–88.
BAILEY, JOANNE, *Unquiet Lives: Marriage and Marriage Breakdown in England, 1660–1800* (Cambridge, 2003).
—— 'Voices in Court: Lawyers' or Litigants'?', *Historical Research* 186 (2001), 392–408.
BARRON, CAROLINE M., 'The "Golden Age" of Women in Medieval London', *Reading Medieval Studies* 15 (1989), 35–58.
—— and SUTTON, ANNE F., editors, *Medieval London Widows, 1300–1500* (London, 1994).
BEIER, A. L., *Masterless Men: The Vagrancy Problem in England 1560–1640* (New York, 1985).
—— and FINLAY, ROGER (eds), *London 1500–1700: The Making of the Metropolis* (London, 1986).
BEN-AMOS, ILANA KRAUSMAN, *Adolescence and Youth in Early Modern England* (New Haven, Conn., 1994).
—— 'Women Apprentices in the Trades and Crafts of Early Modern Bristol', *Continuity and Change* 6.2 (1991), 227–52.
BENNETT, JUDITH M., *Ale, Beer, and Brewsters in England: Women's Work in a Changing World, 1300–1600* (Oxford, 1996).
—— ' "History that Stands Still": Women's Work in the European Past', *Feminist Studies* 14.2 (1988), 269–83.
—— and FROIDE, AMY, 'A Singular Past', in Judith M. Bennett and Amy Froide (eds), *Singlewomen in the European Past 1250–1800* (Philadelphia, 1999).
BONFIELD, LLOYD, SMITH, RICHARD, and WRIGHTSON, KEITH (eds), *The World We Have Gained: Histories of Population and Social Structure* (New York, 1986).

BOOSE, LYNDA E., 'Scolding Brides and Bridling Scolds: Taming the Woman's Unruly Member', *Shakespeare Quarterly* 42.2 (1991), 179–213.

BOTELHO, LYNN, and THANE, PAT (eds), *Women and Ageing in British Society since 1500* (London, 2001).

BOULTON, JEREMY, 'Itching After Private Marryings? Marriage Customs in Seventeenth-Century London', *London Journal* 16.1 (1991), 15–34.

—— 'London Widowhood Revisited: The Decline of Female Remarriage in the Seventeenth and Early Eighteenth Centuries', *Continuity and Change* 5.3 (1990), 323–56.

—— *Neighbourhood and Society: A London Suburb in the Seventeenth Century* (Cambridge, 1987).

—— 'Neighbourhood Migration in Early Modern London', in Clark and Souden (eds), *Migration and Society in Early Modern England*.

—— 'The Poor among the Rich: Paupers and the Parish in the West End, 1600–1724', in Griffiths and Jenner (eds), *Londinopolis*.

BRADDICK, MICHAEL J., and WALTER, JOHN (eds), *Negotiating Power in Early Modern Society* (Cambridge, 2001).

BRODSKY, VIVIEN, 'Mobility and Marriage in Pre-industrial England: A Demographic and Social Structural Analysis of Geographic and Social Mobility and Aspects of Marriage, 1570–1690, with Particular Reference to London and General Reference to Middlesex, Kent, Essex and Hertfordshire', Ph. D thesis, Cambridge (1978).

—— 'Widows in Late Elizabethan London: Remarriage, Economic Opportunity and Family Orientations', in Bonfield, Smith, and Wrightson (eds), *The World We Have Gained*.

BRODSKY ELLIOTT, VIVIEN, 'Single Women in the London Marriage Market: Age, Status and Mobility, 1598–1619', in Outhwaite (ed.), *Marriage and Society*.

CAPP, BERNARD, 'The Double Standard Revisited: Plebeian Women and Male Sexual Reputation in Early Modern England', *Past and Present* 162 (1999), 70–100.

—— 'The Poet and the Bawdy Court: Michael Drayton and the Lodging-House World in Early Stuart London', *The Seventeenth Century* 10.1 (1995), 27–37.

—— 'Separate Domains? Women and Authority in Early Modern England', in Griffiths, Fox, and Hindle (eds), *The Experience of Authority in Early Modern England*.

—— *When Gossips Meet: Women, the Family and Neighbourhood in Early Modern England* (Oxford, 2003).

CARLTON, CHARLES, 'The Widow's Tale: Male Myths and Female Reality in 16th and 17th Century England', *Albion* 10.2 (1978), 118–29.

CAVALLO, SANDRA, and WARNER, LYNDAN (eds), *Widowhood in Medieval and Early Modern Europe* (New York, 1999).

CHARLES, LINDSEY, and DUFFIN, LORNA (eds), *Women and Work in Pre-industrial England* (London, 1985).

CLARK, ALICE, *The Working Life of Women in the Seventeenth Century* (London, 1919).

CLARK, PETER, *The English Alehouse: A Social History 1200–1830* (London, 1983).

—— 'Migrants in the City: The Process of Social Adaptation in English Towns, 1500–1800', in Clark and Souden (eds), *Migration and Society in Early Modern England*.

—— and SOUDEN, DAVID (eds), *Migration and Society in Early Modern England* (Totowa, NJ, 1987).

CLARK, SANDRA, 'The Broadside Ballad and the Woman's Voice', in Cristina Malcolmson and Mihoko Suzuki (eds), *Debating Gender in Early Modern England, 1500–1700* (New York, 2002).

CRESSY, DAVID, *Literacy and the Social Order: Reading and Writing in Tudor and Stuart England* (Cambridge, 1980).
DALE, MARIAN K., 'The London Silkwomen of the Fifteenth Century', *Economic History Review* 4.3 (October 1933), 324–35.
DAVIS, NATALIE ZEMON, *Fiction in the Archives: Pardon Tales and their Tellers in Sixteenth-Century France* (Stanford, Calif., 1987).
EARLE, PETER, *A City Full of People: Men and Women of London, 1650–1750* (London, 1994).
—— 'The Female Labour Market in London in the Late Seventeenth and Early Eighteenth Centuries', *Economic History Review* 42.3 (1989), 328–53.
ERICKSON, AMY LOUISE, 'Common Law versus Common Practice: The Use of Marriage Settlements in Early Modern England', *Economic History Review*, 2nd series, 43.1 (1990), 21–39.
—— 'Married Women's Occupations in Eighteenth-Century London', *Continuity and Change* 23.2 (2008), 267–307.
—— *Women and Property in Early Modern England* (New York, 1993).
EVENDEN, DOREEN, *The Midwives of Seventeenth-Century London* (Cambridge, 2000).
FILDES, VALERIE, 'Maternal Feelings Re-assessed: Child Abandonment and Neglect in London and Westminster, 1550–1800', in Fildes (ed.), *Women as Mothers in Pre-Industrial England* (London, 1990).
FINLAY, ROGER, *Population and Metropolis: The Demography of London 1580–1650* (Cambridge, 1981).
—— and SHEARER, BEATRICE, 'Population Growth and Suburban Expansion', in Beier and Finlay (eds), *London 1500–1700*.
FLATHER, AMANDA, *Gender and Space in Early Modern England* (Rochester, NY, 2007).
FLETCHER, ANTHONY, *Gender, Sex and Subordination in England 1500–1800* (New Haven, Conn., 1995).
FOYSTER, ELIZABETH, 'Male Honour, Social Control and Wife Beating in Late Stuart England', *Transactions of the Royal Historical Society* 6 (1996), 215–24.
—— *Manhood in Early Modern England: Honour, Sex and Marriage* (New York, 1999).
—— 'Marrying the Experienced Widow in Early Modern England: The Male Perspective', in Cavallo and Warner (eds), *Widowhood in Medieval and Early Modern Europe*.
FRANCES, CATHERINE, 'Making Marriages in Early Modern England: Rethinking the Role of Family and Friends', in Agren and Erickson (eds), *The Marital Economy in Scandinavia and Britain 1400–1900*.
FROIDE, AMY M., *Never Married: Singlewomen in Early Modern England* (Oxford, 2005).
GOWING, LAURA, *Common Bodies: Women, Touch and Power in Seventeenth-Century England* (New Haven, Conn., 2003).
—— *Domestic Dangers: Women, Words and Sex in Early Modern London* (Oxford, 1996).
—— '"The Freedom of the Streets": Women and Social Space, 1560–1640', in Griffiths and Jenner (eds), *Londinopolis*.
—— 'Giving Birth at the Magistrate's Gate: Single Mothers in the Early Modern City', in Stephanie Tarbin and Susan Broomhall (eds), *Women, Identities and Communities in Early Modern Europe* (Bodmin, 2008).
—— 'Ordering the Body: Illegitimacy and Female Authority in Seventeenth-Century England', in Braddick and Walter (eds), *Negotiating Power in Early Modern Society*.
GRIFFITHS, PAUL, 'Contesting London Bridewell, 1576–1580', *Journal of British Studies* 42.3 (2003), 283–315.

GRIFFITHS, PAUL, *Lost Londons: Change, Crime and Control in the Capital City 1550–1660* (Cambridge, 2008).
—— 'The Structure of Prostitution in Elizabethan London', *Continuity and Change* 8.1 (1993), 39–63.
—— FOX, ADAM, and HINDLE, STEVE (eds), *The Experience of Authority in Early Modern England* (New York, 1996).
—— and JENNER, MARK (eds), *Londinopolis: Essays in the Cultural and Social History of Early Modern London* (Manchester, 2000).
HANAWALT, BARBARA A., *The Wealth of Wives: Women, Law, and Economy in Late Medieval London* (Oxford, 2007).
HENRIQUES, U. R. Q., 'Bastardy and the New Poor Law,' *Past and Present* 37 (1967), 103–29.
HILL, BRIDGET, *Women, Work, and Sexual Politics in Eighteenth-Century England* (New York, 1989).
HITCHCOCK, TIM, ' "Unlawfully Begotten on Her Body": Illegitimacy and the Parish Poor in St Luke's Chelsea', in Hitchcock, King, and Sharpe (eds), *Chronicling Poverty*.
—— KING, PETER, and SHARPE, PAMELA (eds), *Chronicling Poverty: The Voices and Strategies of the London Poor, 1640–1840* (New York, 1997).
HOFFER, PETER C., and HULL, N. E. H., *Murdering Mothers: Infanticide in England and New England 1558–1803* (New York, 1981).
HOLDERNESS, B. A., 'Widows in Pre-industrial Society: An Essay upon their Economic Functions', in Richard M. Smith (ed.), *Land, Kinship and Life-Cycle* (Cambridge, 1984).
HONEYMAN, KATRINA, and GOODMAN, JORDAN, 'Women's Work, Gender Conflict, and Labour Markets in Europe, 1500–1900', *Economic History Review* 44.4 (1991), 608–28.
HOULBROOKE, RALPH, *Church Courts and the People During the English Reformation* (Oxford, 1979).
HOWELL, MARTHA C., *Women, Production, and Patriarchy in Late Medieval Cities* (Chicago, 1986).
HUNT, MARGARET, *The Middling Sort: Commerce, Gender, and the Family in England 1680–1780* (Berkeley, Calif., 1996).
—— 'Wife Beating, Domesticity and Women's Independence in Eighteenth-Century London', *Gender and History* 4.1 (1992), 10–33.
INGRAM, MARTIN, 'Child Sexual Abuse in Early Modern England', in Braddick and Walter (eds), *Negotiating Power in Early Modern Society*.
—— *Church Courts, Sex and Marriage in England, 1570–1640* (Cambridge, 1987).
—— 'Law, Litigants and the Construction of "Honour": Slander Suits in Early Modern England', in Peter Coss (ed.), *The Moral World of the Law* (Cambridge, 2000).
—— 'Ridings, Rough Music and the "Reform of Popular Culture" in Early Modern England', *Past and Present* 105 (1984), 79–113.
—— ' "Scolding Women Cucked or Washed": A Crisis in Gender Relations in Early Modern England?', in Kermode and Walker (eds), *Women, Crime and the Courts in Early Modern England*.
KERMODE, JENNY, and WALKER, GARTHINE (eds), *Women, Crime and the Courts in Early Modern England* (Chapel Hill, NC, 1994).
KING, WALTER J., 'Punishment for Bastardy in Early Seventeenth-Century England', *Albion* 10.2 (Summer 1978), 130–51.
KUSSMAUL, ANN, *Servants in Husbandry in Early Modern England* (Cambridge, 1981).
LANE, PENELOPE, RAVEN, NEIL, and SNELL, K. D. M. (eds), *Women, Work and Wages in England, 1600–1850* (Rochester, NY, 2004).

LASLETT, PETER, 'Mean Household Size in England since the Sixteenth Century', in Peter Laslett and Richard Wall (eds), *Household and Family in Past Time* (Cambridge, 1972).
LEMIRE, BEVERLY, *Dress, Culture and Commerce: The English Clothing Trade before the Factory, 1660–1800* (London, 1997).
MCINTOSH, MARJORIE KENISTON, 'The Benefits and Drawbacks of *Femme Sole* Status in England, 1300–1630', *Journal of British Studies* 44 (2005), 410–38.
—— *Working Women in English Society, 1300–1620* (Cambridge, 2005).
MCSHEFFREY, SHANNON, *Marriage, Sex and Civic Culture in Late Medieval London* (Philadelphia, 2006).
MELDRUM, TIM, *Domestic Service and Gender 1660–1750: Life and Work in the London Household* (New York, 2000).
—— 'A Women's Court in London: Defamation at the Bishop of London's Consistory Court, 1700–1745', *London Journal* 19.1 (1994), 1–20.
MENDELSON, SARA, and CRAWFORD, PATRICIA, *Women in Early Modern England, 1550–1720* (New York, 1998).
MERRY, MARK, and BAKER, PHILIP, ' "For the house her self and one servant": Family and Household in Late Seventeenth-Century London', *London Journal* 34.3 (November 2009), 205–32.
MULDREW, CRAIG, *The Economy of Obligation: The Culture of Credit and Social Relations in Early Modern England* (New York, 1998).
NUTT, THOMAS, 'The Paradox and Problems of Illegitimate Paternity in Old Poor Law Essex', in Alysa Levene, Thomas Nutt, and Samantha Williams (eds), *Illegitimacy in Britain, 1700–1920* (New York, 2005).
O'HARA, DIANA, *Courtship and Constraint: Rethinking the Making of Marriage in Tudor England* (Manchester, 2000).
ORLIN, LENA COWEN, 'Temporary Lives in London Lodgings', *Huntingdon Library Quarterly* 71.1 (2008), 219–42.
OUTHWAITE, R. B. (ed.), *Marriage and Society: Studies in the Social History of Marriage* (London, 1981).
—— *The Rise and Fall of the English Ecclesiastical Courts, 1500–1860* (Cambridge, 2006).
PANEK, JENNIFER, *Widows and Suitors in Early Modern English Comedy* (Cambridge, 2004).
PECK, LINDA LEVY, *Consuming Splendor: Society and Culture in Seventeenth-Century England* (Cambridge, 2005).
PELLING, MARGARET, *The Common Lot: Sickness, Medical Occupations and the Urban Poor in Early Modern England* (London, 1998).
—— *Medical Conflicts in Early Modern London: Patronage, Physicians, and Irregular Practitioners, 1550–1640* (Oxford, 2003).
—— 'Medical Practitioners', in *Health, Medicine and Mortality in the Sixteenth Century* (Cambridge, 1979).
—— 'Who Most Needs to Marry? Ageing and Inequality among Women and Men in Early Modern Norwich', in Botelho and Thane (eds), *Women and Ageing in British Society since 1500*.
POLLOCK, LINDA A., 'Childbearing and Female Bonding in Early Modern England', *Social History* 22.3 (October 1997), 286–306.
POWER, MICHAEL J., 'A "Crisis" Reconsidered: Social and Demographic Dislocation in London in the 1590s', *London Journal* 12 (1986), 134–46.
PRIOR, MARY, 'Women and the Urban Economy: Oxford 1500–1800', in Prior (ed.), *Women in English Society 1500–1800*.
—— (ed.), *Women in English Society 1500–1800* (New York, 1985).

Rappaport, Steve, *Worlds within Worlds: Structures of Life in Sixteenth-Century London* (Cambridge, 1989).

Roberts, Michael, ' "Words They Are Women, and Deeds They Are Men": Images of Work and Gender in Early Modern England', in Charles and Duffin (eds), *Women and Work in Pre-industrial England*.

Rushton, P., 'Property, Power and Family Networks: The Problem of Disputed Marriages in Early Modern England', *Journal of Family History* 11 (1986), 205–19.

Schen, Claire S., 'Strategies of Poor Aged Women and Widows in Sixteenth-Century London', in Botelho and Thane (eds), *Women and Ageing in British Society since 1500*.

Schofield, Roger, 'Did the Mothers Really Die? Three Centuries of Maternal Mortality in "The World We Have Lost" ', in Bonfield, Smith, and Wrightson (eds), *The World We Have Gained*.

Schwarz, Leonard, 'London Apprentices in the Seventeenth Century: Some Problems', *Local Population Studies* 38 (Spring 1987), 18–22.

Sharpe, J. A., 'Plebeian Marriage in Stuart England: Some Evidence from Popular Literature', in *Transactions of the Royal Historical Society*, 5th series, 36 (1986), 69–90.

—— ' "Such Disagreement betwyx Neighbours": Litigation and Human Relations in Early Modern England', in John Bossy (ed.), *Disputes and Settlements: Law and Human Relations in the West* (Cambridge, 1983).

Sharpe, Pamela, 'Gender at Sea: Women and the East India Company in Seventeenth-Century London', in Lane, Raven, and Snell (eds), *Women, Work and Wages in England, 1600–1850*.

Shepard, Alexandra, 'Honesty, Worth and Gender in Early Modern England, 1560–1640', in H. R. French and Jonathan Barry (eds), *Identity and Agency in England, 1500–1800* (New York, 2004).

—— *Meanings of Manhood in Early Modern England* (Oxford, 2003).

—— 'Poverty, Labour and the Language of Social Description in Early Modern England', *Past and Present* 201 (2008), 51–95.

Slack, Paul, 'Mortality Crises and Epidemic Disease in England 1485–1610', in Charles Webster (ed.), *Health, Medicine and Mortality in the Sixteenth Century* (Cambridge, 1979).

Stone, Lawrence, *The Family, Sex and Marriage in England 1500–1800* (New York, 1977).

Stretton, Tim, *Women Waging Law in Elizabethan England* (Cambridge, 1998).

Thirsk, Joan, *Economic Policy and Projects: The Development of a Consumer Society in Early Modern England* (Oxford, 1978).

Thomas, Keith, 'Cleanliness and Godliness in Early Modern England', in Anthony Fletcher and Peter Roberts (eds), *Religion, Culture and Society in Early Modern Britain* (Cambridge, 1994).

Todd, Barbara J., 'The Remarrying Widow: A Stereotype Reconsidered', in Prior (ed.), *Women in English Society 1500–1800*.

—— 'The Virtuous Widow in Protestant England', in Cavallo and Warner (eds), *Widowhood in Medieval and Early Modern Europe*.

Varholy, Cristine M., ' "Rich Like a Lady": Cross-Class Dressing in the Brothels and Theaters of Early Modern London', *Journal for Early Modern Cultural Studies* 8.1 (2008), 4–34.

Walker, Garthine, *Crime, Gender and Social Order in Early Modern England* (Cambridge, 2003).

——'Expanding the Boundaries of Female Honour in Early Modern England', *Transactions of the Royal Historical Society* 6th series, 6 (1996), 235–45.
——'Women, Theft and the World of Stolen Goods', in Kermode and Walker (eds), *Women, Crime and the Courts in Early Modern England*.
WARD, JOSEPH P., *Metropolitan Communities: Trade Guilds, Identity, and Change in Early Modern London* (Stanford, Calif., 1997).
WHITTLE, JANE, 'Servants in Rural England c.1450–1650: Hired Work as a Means of Accumulating Wealth and Skills Before Marriage', in Agren and Erickson (eds), *The Marital Economy in Scandinavia and Britain 1400–1900*.
WIESNER, MERRY E., *Working Women in Renaissance Germany* (New Brunswick, NJ, 1986).
WILLEN, DIANE, 'Women in the Public Sphere in Early Modern England: The Case of the Urban Working Poor', *Sixteenth Century Journal* 19.4 (1988), 559–75.
WILSON, ADRIAN, *The Making of Man-Midwifery: Childbirth in England, 1660–1770* (Cambridge, Mass., 1995).
——'Participant or Patient? Seventeenth Century Childbirth from the Mother's Point of View', in Roy Porter (ed.), *Patients and Practitioners: Lay Perceptions of Medicine in Pre-Industrial Society* (Cambridge, 1985).
WILSON, CHRIS, 'The Proximate Determinants of Marital Fertility in England 1600–1799', in Bonfield, Smith, and Wrightson (eds), *The World We Have Gained*.
WRIGHT, SUE, ' "Churmaids, Huswyfes and Hucksters": The Employment of Women in Tudor and Stuart Salisbury', in Charles and Duffin (eds), *Women and Work in Pre-industrial England*.
WRIGHTSON, KEITH, *Earthly Necessities: Economic Lives in Early Modern Britain* (New Haven, Conn., 2000).
——*English Society, 1580–1680* (New Brunswick, NJ, 1982).
WRIGLEY, E.A., and SCHOFIELD, R. S., *The Population History of England 1541–1871: A Reconstruction* (London, 1981).

Index

abandoned infants 103–4
abortion 102–3
Adair, Richard 87
adultery
  legal aspects 9–10
  servants' knowledge 124–5
  unfaithful wives 124–5, 148n, 156, 170–3
  unfaithful husbands 82–5, 141, 143–4, 167, 174, 178–81, 218–19
age
  of entering service 26
  differences between husbands and wives 61–2, 248–9
  of marriage 23–24, 52–56, 53tab, 56tab, 62tab
  of migrants 20–1, 21tab, 62tab
  old age 266–8
  of witnesses 19, 54tab
Aldeworth, Elizabeth 29–30, 38, 155
alehouses/victualling houses/inns/taverns
  courtship 64–5, 69, 72, 244–6
  excessive drinking 4, 51, 81, 127–35, 143, 156
  female sociability 154–6, 201
  illicit sex 81, 99, 107
  maidservants' employment 41–2, 71
  meetings between neighbors 29, 72, 79, 81–3, 155–6, 187, 245, 246
  neighborhood disputes 177, 210
  proliferation 207
  respectability 209–10
  women's work 207–11, 252
aliens
  underrepresented as witnesses 18n
  work 189
Alley, Hugh (would-be reformer) 200, 203
Amussen, Susan Dwyer 86n, 112n
Andrews, Frances (starcher) 214–15, 229
animals, domestic 183, 271
apprentices
  courtship, case studies 64–76
  female 43–5, 189
  inability to marry 64, 67, 75, 78
  London population 52
  loyalty to mistresses and masters 121–5
  migration to London 16–17
  origins of 18tab
  paternity cases 90–2
  pauper 44
  widows' enrollment of 264
arbitration 79, 167–8, 186–8, 257
Archer, Ian 5n, 205n, 265

babies see children
bachelors
  marrying widows 247–61
  percentage of widows' bridegrooms 248tab
  transition to adulthood 128–9
Bailey, Joanne 12n, 126n
ballads
  on marriage 50–1, 55, 63, 111, 126, 128–35, 201n
  on London life 23, 48–9, 55
  on remarriage 248, 250, 251, 256
  as sources 14–15
  on women's work 206, 209, 233–4
Banning, Sir Paul 167, 217
Barron, Caroline 231, 264n
bastardy see illegitimacy
bawdry see prostitution
Baxter, Thomas (apprentice) 74–6, 78
Baylie, Elizabeth (midwife) 192, 220
Baynham, Luce (Black Luce of Clerkenwell) 226–7
beating see punishment
Bennett, Judith 231–2
Bennett, Sir Thomas (Justice) 102, 186
Berk, Randall (bookseller) and Anne 41, 80–5, 195
Besey, Elizabeth (midwife) 163–4, 221
bigamy 76, 172–3
blended families 243–4
Bonefant, Margaret 139–40, 141
Boulton, Bridget (innkeeper, widow) 208, 245
Boulton, Jeremy 26, 52, 56n, 240–1
Bowling, Rebecca (maidservant) 64–7, 77, 78
Breame, Thomasine (prostitute) 225
Bridewell
  appearance at 85, 102, 179, 186
  fornication and paternity 88, 95–7, 101
  minute books, as sources 14, 88, 225
  punishment 16, 34, 38, 96–8, 101, 109, 227–9
  prostitution 107–9, 227–30
  rape 101
  regulation of fishwives 205
broadside ballads see ballads
Brodsky, Vivien see Elliott, Vivien Brodsky
brothels see prostitution
burial registers 26, 45, 158–9

Cacott, Mary (maidservant) 59, 256–7
Capp, Bernard 34n, 35n, 88, 116, 153, 193
Carter, Elizabeth (maidservant) 87, 201
carting, public 27, 157
cases see court cases

Chare, Elizabeth (sempster) 175, 199
Charing Cross 87, 99, 201
charity
　to abused wives 165, 169
　and credit 192
　to pregnant maidservants 98
　to widows 265–6
Charterhouse 227
charwomen 211–5
childbed nurses 160–1, 196*tab*, 216
childbirth 158–64, 221–2
children *see also* pregnancy; young persons
　abandoned infants 103–4
　child care 40, 81, 82*n*, 183–4
　childlessness 175
　child servants 26, 37–8
　illegitimacy *see* illegitimacy
　infanticide 104
　mortality 163–4, 182–3
　parental anxiety 182–4
　as public nuisances 203–4
　and remarriage 243–4, 249–50
Christ's Hospital 104, 174
Clark, Alice 230–1
Clay, Joan (maidservant) 32, 35
cleaning
　neighborhood disputes 181–2
　charwomen and laundresses 211–15
Cleaver, Robert (clergyman and author) 190
Clingdove, Dorcas (herbwoman, laundress) 201, 217
clothing
　changing fashions 232–3
　and status 23, 51, 111, 175–7, 194
　value 58–61
　women's work 197–200, 212–15
Clypson, Elizabeth (maidservant) 28, 32–3
Cobham, Lord 109
College of Physicians 218
Collett, Jane (marketwoman) 166, 168, 202
conduct books
　as sources 14, 116–17, 146
　writers *see* Cleaver, Robert; Dod, John; Gataker, Thomas; Gouge, William; Hilder, Thomas; Rogers, Daniel; Whately, William
consistory court of London
　geographical jurisdiction 13*n*
　records, as sources 5–15
　types of cases 7–10
Cornhill wardmote 27, 203–5
Court of Aldermen 37–8
court records as sources 5–15
courts
　Bridewell *see* Bridewell
　consistory court *see* consistory court of London
　Court of Aldermen 37–8
　Jury of Annoyances for the Liberty of Westminster 181–2

Middlesex Sessions 104
Star Chamber 230
wardmote *see* wardmote
courtship
　active role of women 78
　case studies 64–78
　constraints on men 78
　prolonged during apprenticeship, case studies 73–6
　money and 77–8
　parental influence 65–7, 77–8
　remarriage 242–7
coverture
　feme sole trader 136, 189
　remarriage 253, 260
　spendthrift husbands 127, 136–8
craftwork 41, 197–200
Cranfield, Sir Lionel 90–1
credit *see also* honor, status, reputation
　age 12
　financial worth 11, 192
Creede, Thomas (printer) and Margery 82–5
crime *see also* prostitution, theft
　by women 224–30
Crouch, Humphrey (balladeer) 209
cruelty as grounds for marital separation 9–10
cuckolds 180–1, 255
cunning-women 219
Curtain (playhouse) 251–2
customary law of London
　feme sole trader 136, 189, 195
　widows' inheritance 236

Dalton, Michael (jurist) 88–9
death
　childbirth 158–9
　children 46, 182–3
　experience 268–72
　maidservants 45–7
　neighborhood involvement 152
　plague 17, 45–6
　and remarriage *see* marriage
defamation
　arbitration 186
　damage to reputation 28–9, 207, 209
　legal aspects 7–8
　social competition 8, 174–5, 178
　trustworthiness of witnesses 14
　women as litigants and witnesses 10–11
Defoe, Daniel 232
Dekker, Thomas (writer) 14, 160–1, 176, 206, 207, 211
depositions, structure and content 6–7
disputes, neighborhood involvement
　within households 164–74
　between neighbors 174–86
divorce and marital separation
　alimony 10, 260

cruelty 122–4, 139–45, 164–70, 256–60
  economic consequences 144, 172
  female infidelity 170–73
  legal aspects 8–10
  male infidelity 174
  reconciliation as alternative 167–72
Dod, John (clergyman and writer) 190
domestic violence 122–4, 139–45,
    164–70, 256–60
doorstep, sitting at 149–51
Drane, Mary (widow) 155, 198, 263–4
dress see clothing
drinking
  in courtship 64–5, 69, 72, 245–6, 252
  excessive 5, 7, 15, 32–3, 42, 50–1, 81, 90,
    111, 127–35, 143, 154, 156, 185
  female sociability 154–6
  in reconciliation 155–6
Driver, Agnes (maidservant) 32 60
ducking of scolds 185–6
Duke of York's company 251–2
Durham, Margery (alehouse keeper) 209, 266

Earle, Peter 18n, 232, 239, 264
East India Company 172
ecclesiastical courts, records as sources 5–15
economic order see social order
education and training of maidservants 39
Elliott, Vivien Brodsky 21n, 36n, 56, 57tab,
    58n, 61, 62n, 63, 237n, 239–41, 247,
    264
engagement see courtship
environment, urban 8, 181–6
Erickson, Amy Louise 60n, 216n, 241n
Exchange see Royal Exchange

fathers see also patriarchal authority
  burden of proof for paternity 97
  consequences of fathering illegitimate
    children 89–90, 110
  illegitimate children see illegitimacy
  influence on courtship 65–7, 77–8,
    118–20, 255–6
Finlay, Roger 17n, 52, 54n, 64n
Fisher, Agnes 163–4, 221
fishwives 205–6
Fletcher, Anthony 153
food, sale of, as women's work 200–11
fornication see sexual relations
foundlings 103–4
free time of maidservants 37
freewomen, citizens' widows' rights as 264
Frier, John and Anne 123–4, 167–8
fruit-sellers 203–4
Fulham, Alice 44, 182

'gadding' 152–4, 193–4
Gataker, Thomas (clergyman, writer) 127–8
Goddin, Joan (poor widow) 11n, 192

gold lace
  manufacture, women's work 43, 196tab, 198
  status symbol 23, 177
Gore, Margery (widow) 258–60
gossip 149–57
gossips' feasts 160–1
Gouge, William (moralist)
  on bad employers 36–7, 39
  on childbirth 160–1
  on immodest dress 176
  on industry and thrift 127
  on law of marriage as to maidservants 24–5
  on marital betrayal 153
  on marriage 113, 113–14, 115–17, 133n,
    135–6, 137, 237
  on masters and paternity allegations 93
  on maternal authority 118
  on remarriage 250, 254
  on servants' behaviour 39–40
  on servants' choices of employer 34
  on servants' loyalty 122, 124
  on step-families 243
  writings 14
Gowing, Laura 4n, 6n, 8, 10, 42n, 78n, 86n,
    90n, 139n, 145n, 193n, 207n
Gracechurch Street 34, 120n
Griffiths, Paul 109n, 205, 230
guilds see livery companies

Hake, Edward (satirist) 176, 195
Hannay, Patrick (poet) 50, 121, 133
Hare, Mary (spurrier's wife) 191, 212
Harrison, James (apprentice) 71–2, 77, 78
Harrison, Susan (maidservant) 69–70, 77, 78
Hart, Elizabeth (silkwinder) 43, 93
hawkers and hucksters 43, 202–7
Hickes, Sir Baptist 186
Hilder, Thomas (clergyman, writer) 136
Hills, Susan (maidservant) 73–4, 78
Hogarth, William 26
Hollinshed, Elizabeth 183, 184, 212
honor see credit, reputation, status
Houndsditch (Street) 28, 41, 66, 73, 84, 104
household hierarchy
  purpose 125–6
  structure 112
household mistresses see mistresses
household welfare
  protection by wives 3, 135–47
Hove, John (baker) and Dorothy 179–80
Howell, Blanche (maidservant) 60, 81
hucksters and hawkers 43, 202–7
husbands see also widowers; wives
  authority over servants, conflict with
    wives' 122–5
  bachelors as potential husbands see bachelors
  choice of husband 49–52
  consent to wives 116–17
  cruel husbands

husbands (*cont.*)
  cases 122–4, 138–46, 164–70, 256–60
  childbirth 161–2
  neighborhood involvement 164–70, 258
  servants' intervention 122–3
  cuckolds 180–1
  destructive 135–47
  inheritance from 236
  irresponsible behaviour 3, 135–47
  love and respect for wives 115–17
  occupational status 57*tab*
  money disputes with 3, 125–35
  patriarchal order 111–12
  power and rights, compared with wives 3, 111–12
  responsibilities 111–17, 190
  spendthrift 125–47, 256–8
  spouses' age differences 62*tab*
  'taming' by wives 128–35
  unfaithful 178–81
  violence 122–3, 138–46, 164–70, 256–60
  wifely domination alleged 177–8
  and wive's pregnancy 159–63
  wives' subordination 112–17

illegitimacy
  abandoned infants 103–4
  abortion 102–3
  evidence for adultery 172
  baptism 97
  case studies 75, 99–102
  consequences of fathering 79–80, 90–3, 110
  infanticide 104
  law as to 88–99
  maintenance of servants' children by masters 94
  mother's recovery of reputation 105–6
  offence of 110
  parishes' response to 86–8, 103
  paternity allegations against masters 93–4
  social attitudes to 79–80, 86, 110
infanticide 104
infants *see* children
Ingram, Martin 6, 101n, 172*n*, 185*n*
inheritance by widows 236
inns *see* alehouses/victualling houses/inns/taverns
Inns of Court, and women's work 224
Ireland 268
Islington (Middlesex) 35, 223, 244

Jacob, Elizabeth 150, 175
Jury of Annoyances for the Liberty of Westminster 181–2

King's Hospital Highgate 46–7, 59
King's Hospital Islington 223

Lambeth (Surrey) 83, 106, 217
Lane, Elizabeth (maidservant) 13–14, 60

laundering, laundresses 211–15
law *see also* courts; social order
  coverture 127, 136–8, 189, 253, 260
  determination of paternity 80*n*, 88–102
  illegitimacy *see* illegitimacy
  London custom 136, 189, 195, 236
  marital contracts 8–9
  marital separation 9–10
  Poor Laws 5, 33, 46, 80, 86–90, 100, 126, 137, 142, 172, 192, 230, 265–6
  as to rape 100–1
  service, servants 24–5, 33
  widows' inheritance 236
Leadenhall Market 201, 202, 204–5
Lilly, William (astrologer) 261
literacy 6, 224
literature *see also* ballads
  as source 14, 20
litigants, consistory court of London, social status of 10–11
litigation *see* court cases
livery companies 17, 148, 189, 198–9, 204–5, 231–3, 264
Loder, William and Elizabeth 124–5, 170–2
lodgings 195, 263
London
  consistory court *see* consistory court of London
  customary law 136, 189, 195, 236
  geographical definition 6, 17*n*
  map (c.1600) 31*fig*
  markets 200
  migration *see* migrants; migration
  mortality 17, 45, 235, 268
  parishes see parishes
  population 16–17
  sex ratio 52
  social cohesion 5
  social order *see* social order
  wages 22
'Long Meg of Westminster' 20
love and marriage 115–7, 146–7
Lowther, Robert (apprentice) 73–4, 78
Luce, Mary (maidservant) 74–6, 78
Lupton, Daniel (writer) 206
lying under oath 13–14

maidservants
  age at entry into service 26
  alehouses/inns/taverns, employment in 41–2
  charwomen's status contrasted 212–3
  child servants 26, 37–8
  choice of employer 34–5
  duration of service 30*tab*
  education and training 39
  finding service 26–36
  free time 37
  illness, effects of 46

law as to 24–5
loyalty to mistresses and masters 121–5
marriage *see* marriage
married 222–3
migration to London *see* migration
mobility 30–2, 35–6
mortality 45–7
possessions 58–61, 59*tab*
pregnancy *see* illegitimacy; pregnancy
procurement by 'woman brokers' 26–8
punishment of 37–9
rape 100–2
references 28–9
replacement, ease of 47
reputation *see* reputation, women's
residence patterns 26*tab*, 27*tab*
responsibilities 39–40
sexual exploitation of *see* sexual relations
shops, employment in 41
social role 23–5
status 36–40
termination of service 32–4
treatment by employers 36–40, 123–4
wages 22, 34–5, 232
as witnesses 9*n*, 12
marketwomen 200–2
marital breakdown *see* marriage
markets 200–3
marriage 186–8 *see also* courtship; mistresses; remarriage; spinsterhood; wives
adultery *see* adultery
as advancement strategy 2–3, 3, 48–9, 54–5
advice 49–50, 112–17, 243, 254
age
   and marital status 53*tab*
   at first marriage 23–4, 52–6, 56*tab*
choice of husband 49–52, 247–60
contracts 8–9
divorce and separation *see* divorce and separation
duration 238–40
engagement *see* courtship
forced 94–6
in London, high rate of 52–63
love 115–17, 146–7
money disputes 3, 125–35, 153–4, 256–60
moral guidance 49–50, 112–17, 243, 254
opportunities 36, 52–63
portions 58–61
pregnancy *see* pregnancy
remarriage *see* remarriage
separation and divorce *see* divorce and separation
in service after 222–3
sex before 64, 75
to widowers 61–3, 76–7, 248–50
and work 222–3

Martindale, Adam (clergyman) 22–23
Martindale, Jane 22–3, 45
manhood, transition to 128–30
masters *see also* mistresses
   maintenance of servants' children 94
   and paternity allegations 93–4
   and servants, law of 24–5
   treatment of servants 37–9, 123–4
maternal authority 65–7, 77–8, 117–20, 262–3
'maydens of London' 22, 28, 36
McIntosh, Marjorie Keniston 190*n*, 195*n*, 216*n*, 233*n*
mediation 186–8
men *see also* apprentices; bachelors; fathers; husbands; masters; menservants; widowers
   advancement strategies, contrast with women's 3
   apprenticeships *see* apprentices
   illegitimate children *see* illegitimacy
   manhood, transition to 128–30
   marriage *see* courtship; marriage
   marriageable age 23–4
   migration to London, experience contrasted with women's 16–17
   sexual relations *see* sexual relations
   sociability 111–12, 153–4
   talk, and women's, contrasts in attitudes to 152–3
   use of prostitutes 225
menservants, loyalty to mistresses and masters of 121–5
   paternity cases 92–5
Middlesex Sessions 104
midwives 162–4, 192, 220–2
migrants to London
   age 20–1
   age at arrival 21*tab*
   husbands' status 57*tab*
   marriage age 56*tab*
   motives 21–3
   origins 17–23, 18*tab*, 19*tab*, 20*tab*
   region of residence 26*tab*, 27*tab*
   spouses' age differences 62*tab*
migration 3, 16–23
miscarriage 143
mistresses *see also* masters; wives
   authority over servants 121
   prostituting of maids 107–9
   protection of household wealth 3, 135–47
   responsibilities and status 111–12
   treatment of servants 37–9
   wives' role as *see* wives
money *see* wealth
Moorfields 213
More, Susan (maidservant) 32, 41, 80–5
Morris, Rose (married servant) 41, 222
mortality *see* death
Mortimer, Christopher 29, 38

mothers *see also* illegitimacy; pregnancy
  anxieties about children 182–4
  social status 175
  illegitimate children 89, 109–10
  maternal authority 65–7, 77–8, 117–20, 262–3
  remarriage 243–4, 249–50
'M P' (balladeer) *see* Parker, Martin
Multhry, John and Mary 122–3, 167

'nagging' wives 133–4
neighborhood and women's public lives
  see public lives of women
Newbury, Thomas and Margery 141–3, 218
Newgate Market 71, 202
Newgate prison 38, 170, 202, 221
Newsham, Alice (prostitute) 109–10, 230
Newton, John (actor) 251–2
Noble, Margery (singlewoman) 55–6, 194
nursing
  childbed nursing 216
  by maidservants 42
  wet-nursing 195–7, 217
  women's work 215–22

old age 266–8
Osborne, Katherine (washerwomen) 192, 211

parents *see also* fathers, mothers
  influence on courtship, marriage 65–7, 77–8, 118–20, 244
parishes
  and abandoned infants 103–4
  City of London 26*tab*
  and illegitimate pregnancy 86–8
  within London boundary 6, 17*n*
  map (c.1600) 31*fig*
  Middlesex 20*tab*
  registers, as sources 26, 45, 97, 158–9
  women's residence 26*tab*
Parker, Martin (balladeer)
  on marriage 51, 131, 133–4, 146
  on migrant maids 15, 23, 48, 48
Parrot, Henry (writer) 112
paternity *see* fathers
patriarchal authority
  of husband 111–12
  widows and 262–3
  of wife 112
Pelling, Margaret 163, 215*n*, 218*n*, 242*n*
Penny, Joan (charwoman) 212, 223
pensions 192, 265–6
Pepys, Samuel 232
Percy, Christopher (gentleman) 99–100, 258–60
perjury 13–14
Pickhatch 81, 83
pimping *see* prostitution

plague 17, 45, 182
Platter, Thomas (German traveler) 154, 175–6
playhouses
  amusements 37, 247
  women's work 223–4
Poor Laws 5, 33, 46, 80, 86–90, 100, 126, 137, 142, 172, 192, 230, 265–6
population
  England 19*tab*
  London 16–17
portions, marriage
  case studies 69–72
  maidservants 58–61
  sizes 60*n*
pregnancy *see also* illegitimacy; nursing; childbirth; midwives
  case studies 80–85
  forced marriage 94–6
  help for pregnant maids 98
  illegitimate *see* illegitimacy
  at marriage 64*n*
  neighborhood involvement 157–64
  sex without 97–8
  social attitudes to 79–80, 85–8
  uncertain proof of 102–3
Pricke, Robert (writer) 117
prostitution 97, 107–10, 224–30
public health 181–6
public lives of women
  acceptable amusements 154–5
  childbirth 158–64, 221–2
  communal harmony, maintenance of 186–8
  difficulties of urban life 181–6
  disputes 174–86
  drunkenness 156
  gossip, moral and popular attitudes to 149–57
  household disputes 164–74
  neighborhood, influence of 149–57
  sociability, moral and popular attitudes to 149–57
  status disputes 175–8
punishment
  parents of illegitimate children 80
  for prostitution 228
  public carting 157
  for rape 101
  scolds 185–6
  servants 37–9
Pye Corner 76, 223, 246

rape 100–2, 210
Rappaport, Steve 264
reconciliation 167–72, 186–8
Red Bull (playhouse) 224, 247
remarriage
  age at 238, 238*tab*
  age difference between spouses 247–61

to bachelors 247–61
courtship 242–7
economic considerations 236–7
elderly widows 237–8
incidence 3, 235, 237–9, 241
inclination for 237, 241–2
moral considerations 237
moralistic literature 244, 249–50, 254
parental consent 244
problems 254–61
reasons 260–1
richer widows 251–2
step-families 243–4
reputation, woman's *see also* defamation, credit
defamation cases *see* defamation
protection 28–9, 209–10
recovery after illegitimate pregnancy 105–6
work and 194
Rice, Frances (widowed charwoman) 211, 266
Richardson, Humphrey 41, 98
Rogers, Daniel (clergyman, writer)
on marriage 49–50, 61, 115, 133, 136
on maternal authority 118
on remarriage 244, 249, 254
on widowhood 262
on wives' duty 193
Rowlands, Samuel (writer) 21–2, 92–3, 111, 128, 134–5, 152–3, 210
Royal Exchange 35, 203–4, 246
ruffs 214–15

sailors 18*n*, 172, 216
Saltonstall, Sir Samuel 215
Samborne, Margaret 32–3, 184–5
satirical literature, as source 14
Saunders, Thomas (apprentice) 69–70, 77
Schen, Claire 266
Schwarz, Leonard 52
scolds 185–6
servants *see* maidservants; menservants
sexual relations
burden of proof for fornication 97
exploitation of maidservants 85–8
forced marriage after 94–6
before marriage 64*n*, 75
rape *see* rape
sexual harassment 101–2
and status 175
without pregnancy 97–8
Shakespeare, William
The Taming of the Shrew 260
Shepard, Alexandra 16*n*, 128
shops
maidservants' employment 41
women shopkeepers 210–11
women's work 199–200, 202
silkwinding 199
Skarlett, Thomasine (surgeon) 141, 218
Smith, Anne (married servant) 40, 223

Snawsel, Robert (writer) 132
Soame, Sir Stephen (Justice) 84–5, 185
sociability, women's 149–57
social order *see also* law
cohesion 5
excessive consumption on apparel 176–7
fluidity 8
and illegitimate pregnancy 79–80, 85–8, 94–8
and irresponsible husbands 136–8
and marital breakdown 164–5
and prostitution 229–30
social constraints, power of 4–5
and women's work 189–90
social status *see* status
Sottiford, Thomas (clergyman) 171
Southwark 20*tab*, 26, 43, 52, 109, 209, 217
spendthrift husbands 125–35, 256–8
spinsterhood, incidence of 53–4, 54*tab*
Star Chamber 230
starching of ruffs 214–15
status
disputes between neighbors 175–8
of husbands, migrants versus London-born women 57*tab*
litigants and witnesses 10–11
maidservants 36–40
marital 27*tab*, 53*tab*
measures of 175
mistresses 111
Statute of Artificers 1563 24
St Bartholomew's Hospital 223, 268
step-families 243–4
Stone, Ellen (maidservant) 46–7, 59–60
Stow, John (chronicler) 214
strangers *see* aliens
street-sellers 202–7
St Thomas's Hospital 49
Stubbes, Philip (writer) 214
subsidy tax 72
surgeons, women as 217–18
Swan with Two Necks (tavern) 41, 208, 245
syphilis 42, 49, 51, 109, 141, 217–18

taverns *see* alehouses/victualling houses/inns/taverns
Taylor, John (writer) 134, 154, 201*n*
teaching 224
textiles *see* clothing
theatres *see* playhouses
theft 34, 35, 227–9
Thomas Savage (apprentice) 64–7, 77
threshold, sitting at 149–51
tobacco 156, 182, 196*tab*, 209, 257
Tower of London 97, 120, 223, 247
training and education of maidservants 39
Turnbull Street 28, 107, 174, 179

unmarried women *see* spinsterhood
urban life, difficulties of 181–6

vagrants, vagrancy 4, 11, 17, 44, 86–8, 230, 107, 110
victualling houses *see* alehouses/inns/taverns
violence
  between women 185–6
  violent husbands 122–3, 138–46, 164–70, 256–60
  violent wives 9*n*
Vulcombe, Richard and Winifred 166, 168

wages
  adult women 198–9
  maidservants 22, 34–5
Walker, Garthine 87, 104*n*, 185*n*
wardmote (court) 27, 203–5
wealth
  courtship and 77–8
  maidservants 58–61, 59*tab*
  marital disputes over money 3, 125–35
  at marriage 58–61 *see also* portions, marriage
  protection of household 3, 135–47
  and status 175
West, Richard (writer) 26–7
wet-nursing 195–7, 217
Whately, William (clergyman, writer) 14, 113, 116*n*, 159
whipping *see* punishment
Whitney, Isabella (maidservant poet) 61, 225, 273–4
widowers
  courtship 76–7
  inclination for remarriage 241–2
  as potential husbands 248–50
  marriage to 61–3
widows
  apprentices enrolled by 264
  businesses 264–5
  freewomen 264
  independent 261–6
  living in lodgings 263
  pensions 265–6
  percentage of ever-married women 239*tab*
  percentage of previously widowed wives 240*tab*
  proportion of brides 240–1
  region of residence 26*tab*, 27*tab*
  remarriage *see* remarriage
  in service 223
  work 192, 196–7*tab*, 198, 209, 216, 223, 264–6
Willett, Anne (widow) 260–1, 269–71
Wilson, Adrian 161, 162–3
Wilson, Elizabeth (maidservant) 71–2, 77, 78
Wincheley, Agnes (maidservant) 32, 65, 66, 217
With, Elizabeth 62–3, 233–4

witnesses
  age 19
  children as 13–14, 26
  demography 12
  demography of female witnesses 13*fig*
  maidservants as 9*n*, 12
  origins of 18*tab*, 19
  perjury 13–14
  region of residence 26*tab*, 27*tab*
  spinsterhood 54*tab*
  status of 10–11
  'Stranger' witnesses 18*n*
  trustworthiness 12–14, 105*n*
  women as 10–14
wives *see also* husbands; mistresses; widows
  adultery 124–5, 148*n*, 156, 170–3
  age at marriage 56*tab*
  age difference between spouses 62*tab*, 249*tab*
  authority over servants 121–5
  domineering, allegations 177–8
  dual role as wife and mistress 3, 112–14
  duty 190, 193
  husbands' occupational status, migrant versus London-born 57*tab*
  inheritance 236
  marital status 27*tab*
  maternal authority 65–7, 77–8, 117–20
  money disputes with husbands 3, 125–35
  nagging 133–4
  pregnancy *see* pregnancy
  protection of family welfare 3, 135–47
  region of residence 26*tab*, 27*tab*
  responsibilities 111–12
  spouses' age differences 62*tab*, 249*tab*
  subordination to husbands 112–17
  'taming' of husbands 128–35
  titles 111
  work *see* women's work
'woman brokers' 26–8
women *see also* maidservants; migrants; mistresses; prostitutes; spinsterhood; widows; wives
  advancement strategies, contrast with men's 3
  apprentices 43–5
  'gadding' 152, 193–4
  London residents
    origins 20*tab*
    region of residence 26*tab*
  marriage *see* marriage
  migration to London *see* migration
  old age 266–8
  pregnancy *see* illegitimacy; pregnancy
  public lives *see* public lives of women
  region of residence 26*tab*
  talk 149–57
women's work
  apprenticeships 43–5, 189
  changing opportunities 230–4

charwomen 211–15
cleaning 181–2, 211–15
clothing 197–200, 232–3
craftwork 197–200
crime 224–30
economic constraints 233
elderly 266–8
feme sole trader, status of 189
foodstuffs 200–11
historiography 230–4
laundering 211–15
lodgings 195
markets 200–2
married women 222–3
multiple occupations 197
nursing 215–22
old age 266–8
prostitution *see* prostitution
and reputation 194
restrictions 189–90
shops 199–200, 202
service 40–2, 222–3
social attitudes to 189
teaching 224
theaters 223–4
types of 194–7, 196–7 *tab*
victualling 207–11
wages 22, 34–5, 198–9, 232
wet–nursing 195–7
widows *see* widows
work *see* women's work

Yardley, Ralph (apprentice) 67–9, 78
young persons
 marriage 52–3
 religious understanding 13–14
 as witnesses 12, 13–14, 26